CW00823542

Psychodynamic Perspectives on Abuse

of related interest

Autobiography of a Theory
Developing the Theory of Living Human Systems
and its Systems-Centered Practice
Yvonne M. Agazarian and Susan P. Gantt
ISBN 1 85302 847 9

Violence
Reflections on a Western Epidemic
James Gilligan
ISBN 1 85302 842 8
Forensic Focus 18

Mutative Metaphors in Psychotherapy
The Aolian Mode
Murray Cox and Alice Thielgaard
ISBN 1 85302 459 7

Forensic Psychotherapy
Edited by Christopher Cordess and Murray Cox
ISBN 1 85302 634 4 paperback
ISBN 1 85302 240 3 two hardback volumes
Forensic Focus 1

Making an Impact – Children and Domestic Violence
A Reader
Marianne Hester, Chris Pearson and Nicola Harwin
ISBN 1 85302 844 4

Children and Domestic Violence
Action towards Prevention
Caroline McGee
ISBN 1 85302 827 4

Psychodynamic Perspectives on Abuse

The Cost of Fear

Edited by Una McCluskey
and Carol-Ann Hooper

Jessica Kingsley Publishers
London and Philadelphia

The extracts from David Mamet's *Oleanna* are reproduced with the kind permission of Random House, Inc.
The extracts from Arthur Miller's *A View from the Bridge* are reproduced with the kind permission of Methuen
Publishing Limited.
The extract from Gabriela Mistral's *The Immigrant Jew* is reproduced with the kind permission of The Permissions
Company and Joan Daves Agency, New York, on behalf of the estate of the author.
The extract from Carolyn Forché's *The Angel of History* is reproduced with the kind permission of Harper Collins
Publishers and Bloodaxe Books.
The extract from Etelvina Astrada's *The Hordes Came* is reproduced with the kind permission of Alice Partnoy.
The extract from Russell Banks' *The Sweet Hereafter* is reproduced with the kind permission of Vintage Books.
The extract from the translation of Otto Rene Castillo's poem *Frente al Balance (Before the Scales)* is reproduced with
the kind permission of Barbara Paschke.

All rights reserved. No paragraph of this publication may be reproduced, copied or transmitted save
with written permission of the Copyright Act 1956 (as amended), or under the terms of any licence
permitting limited copying issued by the Copyright Licensing Agency, 33–34 Alfred Place, London
WC1E 7DP. Any person who does any unauthorised act in relation to this publication may be liable to
prosecution and civil claims for damages.

The right of Una McCluskey and Carol-Ann Hooper to be identified as authors of this work has been
asserted by them in accordance with the Copyright, Designs and Patents Act 1988.

First published in the United Kingdom in 2000 by
Jessica Kingsley Publishers Ltd,
116 Pentonville Road, London
N1 9JB, England
and
325 Chestnut Street,
Philadelphia PA 19106, USA.

www.jkp.com

© Copyright 2000 Jessica Kingsley Publishers

Library of Congress Cataloging in Publication Data
Psychodynamic perspectives on abuse : the cost of fear / edited by Una McCluskey and Carol-Ann
Hooper.
p.   cm
Includes bibliographical references and index.
ISBN 1 85302 686 7 (pbk. : alk. paper). -- ISBN 1 85302 685 9 (hc. : alk paper)
1. Sex crimes --Psychological aspects. 2. Sexual harassment-- Psychological aspects. 3. Family violence--
Psychological aspects. 4. Sexual abuse victims-- Psychology. 5. Sexual abuse victims--Counselling of. I.
McCluskey, Una, 1949– . II. Hooper, Carol-Ann, 1956–
HV6556.P75   1999   99-43181
364.15'3--dc21   CIP

British Library Cataloguing in Publication Data
Psychodynamic perspectives on abuse: the cost of fear
1. Offences against the person – Psychological aspects
2. Offences against the person – Social aspects
3. Victims of crimes – Psychology 4. Victims of crimes – Services for
5. Offences against the person – Prevention
I. McCluskey, Una II. Hooper, Carol-Ann, 1956-
362.8'8

ISBN 1 85302 686 7 paperback
ISBN 1 85302 685 9 hardback

Printed and Bound in Great Britain by
Athenaeum Press, Gateshead, Tyne and Wear

Contents

Section III: Working with Individuals in Clinical Settings

Section IV: Working with Individuals and Groups in Organisational Settings

Section V: Psychodynamic Reflections on Social Policy

Introduction

Abuse, the Individual and the Social

Carol-Ann Hooper and Una McCluskey

Individuals experience abuse, of whatever kind, in the contexts of their own stage in life and past history, of their relationships with the person or persons perpetrating the abuse and with others, and of the social, cultural and political environment in which it occurs. Responses to abuse, societal, political, professional and individual, are shaped by a similar range of influences, including personal experiences, interpersonal dynamics, power relations between social and professional groups, contemporary social anxieties, cultural norms and political priorities. No single theory or academic discipline can claim to offer understanding of these experiences and reactions in all their complexity, and there has been increasing recognition in recent years of the need to move away from theorising only at the individual level (traditionally the domain of the clinical literature) or at the socio-political level (the domain of social science, including the growing feminist literature on abuse). In many ways the intertwining of social and personal history, and the multiple dimensions to abuse and its impacts, are perhaps best conveyed in novels. *Angela's Ashes* (McCourt 1996), *The Smell of Apples* (Behr 1995) and *The God of Small Things* (Roy 1998) are all excellent examples. Professionals and policy-makers, however, need more explicitly theorised accounts to inform their work. This book aims to contribute to the development of the interdisciplinary thinking and dialogue we believe is necessary to the formulation and implementation of effective and com-passionate responses to abuse.

The book brings together writers from analytic psychotherapy, social work and social policy. While most of the contributors know their own fields better than those of others, all have an interest in crossing disciplinary boundaries to develop ways of understanding and responding to abuse which recognise its multiple dimensions, individual, interpersonal and socio-political. Together we hope they will enable readers to integrate insights from psychodynamic thinking and the social sciences and to apply them to interventions whether the intervention is at the clinical, organisational or policy level. The first and second sections of the book offer theoretical building blocks for an understanding of abuse which addresses individual, interpersonal and socio-political contexts. The third, fourth and fifth sections illustrate applications of such an understanding in clinical and organisational settings and, finally, in relation to policy-making and implementation.

The academic literature on abuse is now vast and commonly subdivides into texts on a particular type of violence (e.g. rape, domestic violence, sexual harassment); a particular group against whom it is directed (e.g. child abuse, violence against women, elder abuse); a particular context in which it occurs (e.g. family violence, workplace harassment); and/or a particular aspect of response (e.g. legal issues, clinical treatment). We have deliberately avoided delimiting the scope of this book in any of these ways. Individuals may experience more than one form of abuse and may experience abuse at more than one time and in more than one context. There is growing evidence of such links and increasing recognition of commonalities as well as differences in their impact (see Briere 1992). Responses to abuse (e.g. legal and clinical) develop in interaction with each other as well as with a broader context, whether implicitly or explicitly. It is the impact on individuals – on their development, their emotional lives, and their ability to participate in society – of abuses of many kinds, and in turn the impact of such abuses on society and its collective efforts to protect and enhance the welfare of its citizens, with which we are primarily concerned. Since both policy and practice involve interactions between individuals which occur in the context of their lives, we consider this holistic focus more appropriate to enhancing understanding of individual experience and societal responses than the artificial carving up of the subject by pre-defined categories.

We did not in fact offer contributors any definition of abuse, referring to it simply as a widespread phenomenon with a variety of manifestations occurring in a variety of contexts. Definitions of abuse, as of most social problems, are contested, and the visibility of particular forms of abuse in current definitions and in public awareness are the historical outcome of the interaction between social anxieties, professional interests, pressure groups and political movements within particular cultural contexts. Other manifestations, equally significant in their impact on the individual, are often obscured in this process. Psychotherapists perhaps deal predominantly with the emotional abuse or neglect which accompanies all other forms to varying degrees, yet there has been far less professional and public attention to emotional abuse and neglect than to physical or sexual abuse. It is common too to focus in definition on the harmful actions attributable to specific individuals, yet the effects on the individual of war, extreme poverty, religious, racial and sexual oppression may be very similar and are equally attributable to human agency, albeit in different contexts.

The book has a broad sweep, therefore, to allow for the elaboration and illustration of a multidimensional approach to abuse which is sensitive to the specificity and variability both of individual experience and social context. In this introductory chapter we map out a little more of the theoretical and political context which forms its background, and identify key themes and issues in the chapters to follow.

Psychodynamic thinking and social science – opposing or complementary traditions?

By psychodynamic thinking we mean an approach informed by attachment theory, psychoanalysis and systems theory, which together offer ways of understanding the complexity and variability of the ways in which individuals develop and relate to one another within particular social contexts, via a focus on their past and present relationships. Each of these theoretical perspectives has had a bad press in the social science literature for replicating and reinforcing oppressive cultural norms, and/or for individualising issues which have recently become defined as social problems. Each, however, is being reworked by (some) current thinkers in ways compatible with a recognition of the diversity of cultural contexts, and with anti-oppressive goals.

Attachment theory has been, and sometimes still is, associated with its popularisation in the 1950s in a form which implied the need for mothers to be at home full-time with their children. Bowlby, its key early theorist, is still a *persona non grata* for many feminists, who attribute the guilt many working mothers feel to the influence of his work. The diversity of cultural arrangements for childcare and the evidence that children can experience separations without harm are cited in refutation. Neither of these, however, is incompatible with attachment theory as it stands today. Contemporary theorists have long recognised that children's attachment needs can be met by more than one caregiver, that attachment is an emotional bond which can develop equally with biological parents and others and that the continuity children need can be maintained through separation if separations are handled appropriately. Attachment remains fundamental for children in the development of a secure personality and confidence in relationship with others, and knowledge in this field has implications for their care far more complex than the restricted roles expected of women (to which, filtered through ideologies of motherhood, it has undoubtedly contributed) which we ignore at children's peril. Attachment needs continue throughout life, and since much abuse occurs within the context of attachment relationships, whether in childhood, adulthood or later life, we are unlikely to develop effective responses without an understanding of their dynamics.

The history of psychoanalysis does not immediately inspire confidence in its positive contribution to effective responses to abuse. Freud's role in the suppression and silencing of childhood sexual abuse in the 19th and early 20th centuries has been well documented (Masson 1984; Olafson 1993; Rush 1980), and many adults today have suffered as a direct consequence of professional adherence to his belief that children's accounts of sexual abuse were mostly fantasy. Yet resistance to the reality of abuse is considerably more complex than this and by no means over. Psychoanalysis (among other perspectives) can help us understand it. Some of its core concepts, the unconscious, and defences such as denial, splitting and projection in particular, make an important contribution to understanding the complexity of both the impact of and reactions to abuse. Moreover, psychoanalysis is a diverse field with many differences within it. Object relations theorists in particular, despite their unfortunate habit of referring to people as objects, have actually done much to counter the objectification of people with mental illnesses and restore to them the status of persons whose behaviour is understandable in the context of their experience, which frequently includes abuse.

Systems theory, too, comes in many forms. A particular version which attributed father–daughter sexual abuse to patterns of interaction within families to which all contributed was much criticised by feminists in the 1980s (Macleod and Saraga 1988; Nelson 1987). The problem was not so much the recognition that behaviour occurred within the context of relationships which could maintain or challenge it, but the functionalist model of the family to which this thinking was allied. This resulted in different expectations of behaviour being set for men and women, a lack of recognition of power relations of gender and age within families and society, and the denial or minimisation of men's responsibility for their own actions. There have been significant changes in family systems thinking since, however, and the questioning of normative family structures, the need to address power relations and the responsibility of individual offenders for abuse have all been recognised, at least by some theorists (see Hooper and Humphreys 1998 for an analysis of this debate). The focus of systems thinking on the interactional contexts in which meanings are constructed and behaviour maintained can inform work with individuals, dyads, groups or any range of relationships within families and play an important part in facilitating change which enables people to disengage from abusive relationships and/or overcome the impacts of abuse on other relationships. The work of Agazarian (1997), who has formulated a 'theory of living human systems', has produced a particular method of working with both difference and similarity based on functional rather than stereotypic differences.

While psychodynamic thinking has an important part to play in an understanding of abuse and responses to it, social science, too, plays a vital role, in particular offering ways of thinking about the relationship between abuse and oppression on the one hand and cultural diversity on the other. Abuse may both be an aspect of oppression itself, and always occurs within the context of social oppression. Iris Young (1990) has argued that violence is not just bad behaviour but one of the 'five faces of oppression', along with exploitation, marginalisation, powerlessness and cultural imperialism, for two reasons. First, in a number of contexts violence is directed to members of oppressed groups, e.g. women, children, ethnic minorities, gay men and lesbian women, older people, as a systematic social practice because of their membership of that group. Second, that social context may make the use of violence against these groups possible and acceptable. The most obvious example is that it is still legal for parents to hit their children in the UK, and this entitlement to use violence against the vulnerable is guarded not only by law but by norms of family privacy and parental, especially paternal, authority, although the social acceptability of the practice is more contested than it was.

Options for leaving abusive relationships are also clearly influenced by the broader context of oppression in which they occur. However much the police response to domestic violence improves, while many women remain marginalised in the labour market, at least partly because of their exploitation as unpaid carers of children and others, and while the resulting gender inequalities in income, access to social security benefits and housing remain in place, the cards are stacked against women seeking freedom from abuse for themselves and their children. At a policy level, responses to abuse which fail to address this broader context are only partial, sometimes tokenistic, responses. Practitioners, too, need to recognise the constraints which hold people in abusive relationships if they are to work in genuinely empowering ways.

Those who work with abuse need therefore to be aware of the broader context of oppression, and the individual's relationship to it. They need also to be sensitive to cultural diversity. Individuals develop in cultural contexts which vary in their dominant values, for example, in the emphasis placed on individuality and independence vs. interdependence with family and community, and in their norms for behaviour, for example, regarding the expression of distress. Such differences may affect the way distress is manifested, people's willingness to admit distress and seek help, and the personal and social resources available to them in working through the impact of traumatic experiences. Cultural norms regarding the expression of anger, for example, seem to offer varying degrees of protection against depression which is virtually unknown in some non-Western societies (Schumaker 1996). Measures of personality, well-being and mental health developed in a particular cultural context, and reflecting its values and norms, do not always work well for members of different cultural groups. Critiques of the diagnosis of post-traumatic stress disorder, for example, note that, among other limitations, the medicalising of symptoms may obscure the meaning of them to the person, which is constructed within a particular cultural context (Eisenbruch 1992; Richman 1993). The impact of abusive experiences is always likely to be affected by the cultural filters through which their meaning is constructed.

Disentangling the role of difference from the relations of dominance and subordination within which the meaning of that difference is constructed is not always straightforward. The task, however, is as vital as an understanding of individual developmental history and interpersonal relational context to the goal of developing interventions which adequately address the multi-dimensional nature of abuse.

Personal troubles and public issues: The politics of abuse

Since the 1970s, abuse, initially physical abuse of children followed by many other forms involving children and adults (especially women), has been not only a personal experience but a publicly visible social problem. Despite a high level of public, professional and political interest, social reactions remain complex and divided. Minimisation and overreaction, scapegoating, denial and suppression all coexist, with the particular mix in a given situation reflecting the interests and power of the groups making claims for their own definition of the problem to be accepted, the prevailing cultural values and social anxieties, the priorities in particular institutional contexts, and the identifications (conscious or unconscious) of individuals with different groups (for example, parents vs. children, men vs. women). In a context in which values of family privacy and unity, and of parental, adult and male authority are held by many to be fundamental to the social order and already felt to be under threat, whether from family breakdown, feminism or both, it is perhaps unsurprising that news about abuse is often greeted with less than enthusiasm, and the professionals involved often scapegoated. The false memory debate is (in part at least) just the most recent manifestation of this response (cf. Franklin and Parton 1991; Nava 1988 for discussion of earlier versions). The current high level of public anxiety about 'paedophiles' in the UK might be thought to indicate increased concern for children but for its occurrence alongside numerous ways in which children's needs are not met or acknowledged in society – from the increased numbers living in poverty, through the perception of their care as a barrier to parents' paid work but not a legitimate priority itself, to the increasingly punitive responses to young offenders, despite the evidence of high levels of abuse and neglect among this group (Boswell 1998; FPSC 1998). In this context it is probably better understood as a disowning of much more widespread abusiveness and as diverting attention away from abuse in families.

The increased public visibility of abuse is still partial, therefore, and vulnerable to reversal. In addition, while the suppression of abuse in the past has silenced many who have experienced it, the way the issue is constructed in contemporary discourses also has important effects, offering multiple, often distorting, mirrors. The popular notion of a 'cycle of abuse' – whose language suggests a mechanistic and determined monocausal graduation from victim to perpetrator which is both unsupported by evidence and stigmatising to survivors – has been much critiqued (for example, Herman 1998; Hooper 1995). However, to ignore the part played by experiences of abuse in the development of antisocial and abusive behaviour is equally problematic. Where victims and perpetrators are defined as mutually exclusive groups, the categorisation of a person, even a child, as a perpetrator can become one of the ways in which individual experiences of abuse become invisible.[1] Where survivors of abuse see compassion reserved for victims and hostility for perpetrators, they may be inhibited from owning their own violent impulses (including their retaliatory rage) for fear of losing the sympathy of others, leaving them more vulnerable to depression.

Public visibility is also no guarantee of responsiveness to individual need, partly because of the politics of recognition discussed above, but partly, too, because the old, unproductive debate between psychological and social causation still rumbles on, more because of their different political and policy implications than because they are mutually exclusive explanations. Interventions at the individual level are sometimes seen as depoliticising the issue and where policy ignores the contribution of social conditions or even exacerbates them (e.g. via the increasing numbers of children living in poverty during the 1980s in the UK, while interventions to protect children within marginalised families also increased (Frost 1990)) this can undoubtedly be the overall effect. However, while the problems of ignoring social dimensions and focusing only on the individual are fairly well recognised, at least in the field of social policy where critiques of individualism have a long tradition, the reverse may be equally problematic.

It is sometimes assumed that political activism is necessarily empowering for survivors of abuse, and there may undoubtedly be many beneficial aspects to it. However, activism as the only response or an expected response can also become a repetition of a pattern learnt in childhood whereby the needs of others (e.g. other survivors, children in the future, women) take precedence over the needs of the individual survivor for care. A sociologically reductionist politics which rejects thinking about individual and interpersonal dimensions to abuse altogether can also lead to the pursuit of political goals at the expense of justice for individuals, and hence understandably to backlash (Guy 1996).

There are increasing numbers of clinicians and practitioners who seek to address the emotional needs of individuals in ways which recognise the political as well as the personal context in which they arise. Practice informed by such thinking may increase the individual's capacity to recognise social injustice and act against it alongside managing other aspects of life (Orbach 1998; Phillips 1999). Policy-makers and analysts need also to address the complexity of individuals' relational lives, including their developmental, emotional and unconscious aspects, if effective policy responses to what are predominantly relational issues are to be developed. The distributive paradigm which predominates in social policy is relevant to abuse in many ways, via the effects, for example, of inequalities in income, housing and employment on behaviour. It is not, however, sufficient. To develop non-abusive and anti-oppressive responses to abuse at the levels of clinical practice and organisational or social policy requires us to build bridges between disciplines, to think personally and politically simultaneously and to recognise the complexity of the different dimensions to abuse and their interaction. As Orbach (1998) argues, emotional and political literacy are best seen as complementary and mutually enhancing rather than as alternatives. This book aims to contribute to thinking about what such a vision means in relation to abuse.

Contents of the book

The book is divided into five sections. Section One addresses the individual and interpersonal contexts of abuse. Jeremy Hazell presents an object relations perspective, in which the self is viewed as fundamentally social, possessing an absolute need for relationship with another person for development. The loss or absence of such relationship, which threatens loss of the self too, is at the root of anti-social impulses. Jeremy Holmes presents attachment theory, which places the child's need for security at its centre. The formation of attachment bonds, which result in children seeking the proximity of their caregivers (or 'secure base') when in danger, facilitates both their survival and the experience of intersubjectivity from which a sense of self emerges. The tragedy for children who have been abused by their caregivers is that this instinctive attachment behaviour is aroused by the very people who abuse them, with lasting consequences for their development. Frances Carter introduces a systems-centred perspective in which the person's development is understood not only in the context of their own history but also within the context of the many relational systems – dyads, small groups, larger groups, organisations, society – within which we function day to day. The process of development, involving the discrimination and integration of differences between self and others, continues throughout life and relationship with others continues to be the medium through which it occurs. Phil Mollon begins with the existential reality of the fact of death, and draws attention to the anxiety created by the limits of life. One response to the terror induced by such helplessness can be to identify with what is terrifying. Evil can be understood as inflicting pain and dread on others: annihilating their reality may be an attempt to eradicate one's own vulnerability and dread.

Section Two addresses the social, cultural and political contexts of abuse. Nancy Caro Hollander focuses on the experience of exile of refugees fleeing state terror and political oppression. She examines in depth the complex feelings that leaving one's homeland under such circumstances can provoke. Exile triggers responses and issues related to attachment, loss and mourning from early life, but in the case of political refugees responses to exile may also have origins in the 'persecutory culture of fear designed by state terror'. A similar climate of fear is described by Una McCluskey in her account of the emotional abuse of children by religious personnel. In a country which supported repressive child-rearing practices and where people dared not believe ill of the church, help for those children was not available. One of the consequences for these victims of abuse has been that through economic and academic disadvantage and lack of support in their homeland, many of these people have also found themselves living in exile.

Lennox Thomas addresses the sexual abuse of children within the black community in an historical context. Drawing on the experience of slavery and its effect on family forms, self-esteem, migration and cultural prejudice, he examines the difficulties facing black men and women who have been sexually abused in seeking help from social workers and psychotherapists, who are often located in the dominant white culture.

Stephen Frosh examines the relationship of abuse to masculinity, drawing both on object relations theory and post-structuralist thinking. If identities are seen as fluid, continually reconstructed in relation to contemporary discourses, abuse may be a response to anxieties about masculinity, an attempt to maintain a 'tough' identity to mask vulnerability. While dominant discourses link violence and masculinity in a way which supports such a response, recognising such anxieties and vulnerabilities may create the space for alternative masculinities. Frank Mondimore addresses the ways in which homosexuality has been stigmatised, pathologised, punished and con- demned and the damaging effects of internalised negative cultural images on the development of confident identities among young gay and lesbian adults. He examines the common presumption that homosexuality is often the result of sexual abuse in childhood, finding it to be largely myth. Young people who have been abused in childhood and who also identify as gay or lesbian are clearly a particularly vulnerable group, however, since the impact of abuse may be compounded by negative images of and responses to homosexuality.

Our first chapter in Section Three, the clinical section, is written by Susan Vas Dias. She addresses the phenomenon of 'inner silence', which can develop in response to continuous emotional abuse in early life. She develops, expands and illustrates the view that emotional abuse destroys the capacity to experience affect, without which the development of a sense of self and the capacity to communicate with others may be inhibited. Shirley Truckle traces the enactment of trauma in therapy and considers how it can be understood and integrated, recognising, too, the difficulty for the therapist of maintaining their ability 'to think…in the presence of the unthinkable'. The examples of clinical work she discusses illustrate clearly the need to under- stand all levels of context of traumatic experiences – individual, familial and socio-political – in order to appreciate their meaning to the person and work out how to offer a reparative experience.

Valerie Sinason discusses the experience of abuse of learning disabled people. Learning disability can be a consequence of abuse, and can also increase vulnerability to abuse. She highlights the ways in which others often ignore the meaning of behaviour through which learning disabled people may be expressing distress about abuse, and illustrates the potential for reparative work where emotional meaning is taken seriously. Phil Mollon's chapter on dissociative disorders distinguishes between repression, which involves a split between the conscious and unconscious mind, and dissociative disorders, in which consciousness itself is split. Dissociation is commonly a response to childhood abuse and poses particular challenges to the therapist.

The chapters in Section Four illustrate ways of working with individuals and groups in the roles of supervisor and organisational consultant. The first chapter, by Dick Agass, draws attention to the impact on professionals of working with severe disturbance, where the disturbance may be communicated by projective identification and workers can come to feel contaminated by their clients' experience. Supervision, he argues, is vital in offering a containing space for the worker to maintain and develop their capacity to think about these dynamics, and thereby their ability to contain their clients' experience and reflect it back in manageable form. Judith Brearley discusses abuse in the workplace from the perspective of an analytically trained organisational consultant. From a psychoanalytic perspective a work group may be understood as operating in part unconsciously. The unconscious defensive mechanisms of denial, splitting and projection may be employed to deal with anxieties and conflicts which have a range of origins, for example, in the personal histories of employees, the organisational and policy context or the complex interplay between them. Consequences can include groups divided in entrenched and polarised positions, and distortions of reality which lead to ineffective responses and an increase in levels of stress in individuals. Abuse in the workplace takes many forms, and for the consultant to work effectively in response to it requires an understanding both of all levels of context and of conscious and unconscious processes within the group and between the group and the consultant.

The final section of the book, Section Five, offers psychodynamic reflections on social policy. Andrew Cooper explores the role of child protection work as a cultural intervention operating in 'simultaneous relation to subjective, interpersonal and social being'. He argues that practitioners operate in a world of inherent uncertainty where competing versions of events are common, and that their job is both to bear witness to the experience that 'something happened', and to reinstate the 'reality principle'. The response of the criminal justice system, with its preoccupation with establishing a single truth, is particularly limiting in this context where the 'facts' of events are irretrievably lost. He suggests the need for an 'aesthetic stance', which enables practitioners to hold and work with different versions of the truth, and illustrates the potential of such an approach with discussion of both clinical examples and artistic explorations of abuse. Margaret Bell also addresses child protection work, discussing the professional response to domestic violence in this context. She draws attention both to professional reluctance to face the problem, in the context of the contradictory societal expectations on social workers and a range of other fears and pressures, and to the complexity of the interactions between family members, workers and organisations involved in interventions.

Carol-Ann Hooper and Juliet Koprowska explore the implications of the role of childhood abuse in adult mental health problems for mental health services. They illustrate from their research with survivors of childhood sexual abuse some of the ways in which service providers can, often unwittingly, re-traumatise people rather than offering a reparative experience, especially where mental illness is treated within a medical model and life experience ignored, but also in other ways which reflect the interaction of policy, organisational context and worker experience. Joan Harbison focuses on the issue of abuse of older people, highlighting how both recognition and responses are affected by the predominantly negative constructions of ageing in Western societies, and the way these are both reflected in policy and internalised by older people and others. There is a growing professional and academic interest in this subject, but the goals of practitioners and of older people themselves are often different. A psychodynamic perspective, which recognises the struggle, conscious and unconscious, which may be involved to maintain a positive self-identity during old age, can help to understand this.

As a whole, the book raises a number of issues. With regard to definitions of abuse, it is now increasingly recognised that a focus on particular abusive events may be limiting, and that attention to the broader relational context in which they occur may be equally or more important (DoH 1995). It is also recognised that an element of emotional abuse underlies all forms of abuse. Several of the chapters in this book reinforce the need for greater attention to be paid to the emotional quality and climate of primary relationships (Hazell, Holmes, Carter, Vas Dias). If the need for relationship is fundamental for development, then absence of relatedness, which can occur despite physical presence, is itself a form of abuse or neglect. While this retains the focus on the actions or omissions of primary carers[2] we also need to pay continuing attention to the damage which can be inflicted on individuals' development by accepted childrearing practices, in institutional as well as domestic contexts (McCluskey), by the devaluation of oppressed social groups (Thomas, Mondimore, Truckle, Sinason), by social conditions of disadvantage and deprivation (Sinason), and by cultures of fear, at the political or organisational level, which may undermine the trust on which the achievement of both interdependence and autonomy depend (Hollander, Brearley). Harm is labelled differently in different contexts. Writing at a time when organised state violence is causing massive long-term trauma for many in the former Yugoslavia, it seems particularly important to retain a broad focus in our thinking, as well as an appreciation of the specificity and variability of abuses in different contexts.

The development of multidimensional explanations of abuse is an ongoing task which will need always to be attempted anew in different contexts. Individual propensities may be fuelled by relational failures, which, for example, deprive the person of the experience of empathic relating from which empathy for others develops, or leave the person hating their own vulnerability and weakness and consequently hating others, such as children and older people, who come to represent that vulnerability (Hazell, Mollon, McCluskey, Harbison). We are only just beginning to understand how such propensities may be reinforced by (or alternatively mitigated by) cultural discourses and social, political and economic conditions (McCluskey, Frosh), as well as by later relational experience. There is much room for further work in this area.

The impacts of abuse are the subject of a vast, predominantly clinical, literature, much of which pays scant attention to the social context in which abuse occurs which can intensify or mitigate those impacts (Hollander, McCluskey, Thomas, Mondimore, Sinason, Truckle). At the same time, in the social policy arena there is relatively little awareness of the impacts of abuse on people's experience of themselves and others, their confidence, ability to communicate with and relate to others, and to participate in society (Hazell, Holmes, Hollander, McCluskey, Vas Dias, Truckle, Hooper and Koprowska), which are relevant not only to the ability and willingness to use services, but to broader issues such as social exclusion. Greater interdisciplinary dialogue would be productive for both clinical and policy fields.

We discussed earlier the complexity of social reactions to abuse. Several contributors note both continued resistance to recognition and reluctance to intervene at the societal, community, professional and/or personal level (Hollander, McCluskey, Sinason, Bell, Harbison). The responses of 'by-standers', who know abuse is occurring but are inhibited by a wide range of fears from taking effective action, merit more attention, particularly in the context of the NSPCC's 1999 campaign to encourage the whole community's involvement in 'stopping child abuse'. As with other aspects to abuse, a multidimensional approach to understanding the issue is needed, addressing all levels, from the individual's capacity for empathy through to the role of national and international politics and religious culture. Several contributors also address the 'false memory debate', highlighting the complexity of the issue of memory as well as the irrational character and limiting terms of the debate, which exemplifies the potential for polarised reactions to abuse (Mollon, Cooper).

We return, finally, to the need for interventions at many levels. We believe psychotherapy, which Hazell describes as aimed 'at analysis and repair of the "lost heart of the self" through both transference and the real reciprocal relationship developing between psychotherapist and patients as genuine persons' makes a contribution which is vital, in the literal sense of the word, enabling the person who has been traumatised by abuse to 'come alive' to their emotions (Vas Dias), reconnect with others and regain their capacity for growth and development (Herman 1994). Policies need to allow for the necessarily long-term nature of such reparative work, and to acknowledge its difficulty and the support and supervision needs which accompany it.

Reparative work can be done in many ways – one-to-one or group therapy, for example – and in a range of different service contexts. Several contributors, however, highlight the risk of interventions repeating trauma if insufficient attention is paid to understanding the person's particular exper-ience and its social context, and/or through adherence to inappropriate policy prescriptions, professional frameworks or conventions (Mondimore, Vas Dias, Truckle, Hooper and Koprowska). For example, the current preoccupation in policy with preventing dependency on services is a major impediment to effective reparative work. It needs to be recognised that childhood abuse, which may deny people the experience of safe dependency crucial to early development, may create 'socially necessary dependency' (Fraser and Gordon 1994) in later life. Too much emphasis on brief interventions in the psychotherapeutic field can deflect attention away from the long-term nature of the healing process required in situations where severe emotional damage has been experienced. Policy-makers and psycho-therapists need to consult with each other to strike a humane balance about the costs involved in providing such help. Abuse generates fear. The cost of fear at an individual level is of lives partially lived at a social, intellectual and emotional level. This has consequences for society as a whole.

Therapeutic work is only one of the range of interventions needed, at the political, cultural, organisational and familial as well as individual level, if effective responses to abuse are to be developed. We highlight it because the thinking developed in this context has perhaps gone furthest in addressing the complexity of abuse, its impacts and our reactions to it, and this thinking can therefore usefully inform other forms of intervention. Abuse challenges us all to maintain our capacity to think in the face of the appalling pain human beings can inflict on each other, and in complex and uncertain circumstances. We hope this book encourages a meeting of minds across disciplinary, professional and political boundaries, in the co-operative spirit essential to the development of a more compassionate society.

Notes

1. The story of Mary Bell is an example of this process. The hostile reaction to the publication of Gitta Sereny's book *Cries Unheard* (1998), which makes visible Mary Bell's own abusive childhood suggests that resistance to recognising the overlap between victims and perpetrators continues, despite the increased recognition of child abuse.

2. And as such it carries the risk of intensifying the regulation of women as primary carers. However, while there are potential conflicts of interest between children and their carers, there is also considerable overlap. Work with mothers and children which improves the quality of their relationship, such as the method based on attachment theory devised by Svenberg (1999), can be of benefit to both.

References

Agazarian, Y.M. (1997) *Systems-Centered Therapy for Groups*. New York: Guilford Press.

Behr, M. (1995) *The Smell of Apples*. London: Abacus.

Boswell, G. (1998) 'Criminal justice and violent young offenders'. *The Howard Journal 37*, 2, 148–160.

Briere, J. (1992) *Child Abuse Trauma*. London: Sage.

Department of Health (1995) *Child Protection: Messages from Research*. London: HMSO.

Eisenbruch, M. (1992) 'Toward a culturally sensitive DSM: Cultural bereavement in Cambodian refugees and the traditional healer as taxonomist'. *Journal of Nervous and Mental Disease 180*, 8–10.

Family Policy Studies Centre (FPSC) (1998) *The Crime and Disorder Bill and the Family*. Family Briefing Paper 3.

Franklin, B. and Parton, N. (eds) (1991) *Social Work, the Press and Public Relations*. London: Routledge.

Fraser, N. and Gordon, L. (1994) 'A genealogy of dependency: Locating a keyword of the United States welfare state'. *Signs 19*, 309–336.

Frost, N. (1990) 'Official intervention and child protection: The relationship between state and family in contemporary Britain'. In The Violence against Children Study Group, *Taking Child Abuse Seriously*. London: Unwin Hyman.

Guy, C. (1996) 'Feminism and sexual abuse: Troubled thoughts on some New Zealand issues'. *Feminist Review 52*, 154–168.

Herman, J. (1988) 'Considering sex offenders: A model of addiction'. *Signs 13*, 4, 695–724.

Herman, J. (1994) *Trauma and Recovery: From Domestic Abuse to Political Terror*. London: Pandora.

Hooper, C.A. (1995) 'Women's and their children's experiences of sexual violence: Rethinking the links'. Special Issue on Women in Families and Households, *Women's Studies International Forum 18*, 3, 349–360.

Hooper, C.A. and Humphreys, C. (1998) 'Women whose children have been sexually abused: Reflections on a debate'. *British Journal of Social Work 28*, 565–580.

Macleod, M. and Saraga, E. (1988) 'Challenging the orthodoxy: Towards a feminist theory and practice'. *Feminist Review 28*, 16–55.

Masson, J. (1984) *The Assault on Truth*. Middlesex: Penguin.

McCourt, F. (1996) *Angela's Ashes: A Memoir of a Childhood*. London: HarperCollins.

Nava, M. (1988) 'Cleveland and the press: Outrage and anxiety in the reporting of child sexual abuse'. *Feminist Review 28*, 103–121.

Nelson, S. (1987) *Incest: Fact and Myth*. Edinburgh: Stramullion Press.

Olafson, E., Corwin, D. and Summit, R. (1993) 'Modern history of child sexual abuse awareness: Cycles of discovery and suppression'. *Child Abuse and Neglect 17*, 7–24.

Orbach, S. (1998) 'It's official: The personal will be the political'. *The Guardian*, 12 August 1998.

Phillips, A. (1999) *The Beast in the Nursery*. London: Faber.

Richman, N. (1993) 'Annotation: Children in situations of political violence'. *Journal of Child Psychology and Psychiatry and Allied Disciplines 34*, 1286–1302.

Roy, A. (1998) *The God of Small Things*. London: HarperCollins/Flamingo.

Rush, F. (1980) *The Best Kept Secret: Sexual Abuse of Children*. New York: McGraw-Hill.

Schumaker, J.F. (1996) 'Understanding psychopathology: Lessons from the developing world'. In S.C. Carr and J.F. Schumaker (eds) *Psychology and the Developing World*. Westport: Praeger.

Sereny, G. (1998) *Cries Unheard: The Story of Mary Bell*. London: Macmillan.

Svenberg, P.O. (1999) Paper presented at conference on the attachment dynamic. University of York, March 1999.

Young, I. (1990) *Justice and the Politics of Difference*. Princeton: Princeton University Press.

SECTION 1

The Individual
and Interpersonal Contexts
of Abuse

CHAPTER I

An Object Relations Perspective on the Development of the Person

Jeremy Hazell

No single theory can claim to explain the complex development of the person, hence the use of the indefinite article in the title of this chapter. Indeed, there is considerable variation of opinion among the proponents of object relations themselves, which I shall reflect on later. The object relations theory of the personality emerged in the 1940s as a corrective to the determinism of 19th-century instinct theory, with the work of W.R.D. Fairbairn, of whom Ernest Jones wrote:

> Instead of starting as Freud did from stimulation of the nervous system proceeding from the excitation of various erogenous zones and internal tension arising from gonadic activity, Dr Fairbairn starts at the centre of the personality, the ego, and depicts its strivings and difficulties in its endeavour to reach an object where it may find support. (Fairbairn 1952)

Fairbairn himself predicted that his theory would have far-reaching implications for therapeutic practice, and these are still being explored by contemporary workers, for example, Bollas (1987); Gomez (1997); Scharff (1995); Symington (1986). For the purpose of this chapter I propose to refer mainly to the work of Fairbairn and his contemporaries – Guntrip, Winnicott and Balint, and partly also to the findings of workers in the field of infant research.

According to object relations theory, the personal self is a function of growth in personal relations. It is the psychic centre of the human being, and cannot be reduced to neuronal circuits, biochemical impulses or behavioural patterns. Experience comes to us in two forms: sensory experience and emotional experience. The former is the province of the physical sciences, while the latter can only be known by empathic personal relating, and it is in this medium alone that a human being can come to self-realisation and expression as a person. Psychotherapy has provided much evidence to show that responsive/ible 'use' of our bodies depends substantially upon the extent to which our psychic selves are enabled to achieve a confident sense of personal identity, so that the person at the centre of their behaviour is empathically in touch with other people.

This theory about the way a person develops did not come about in abstract, but through painstaking investigation into the causes of mental disturbance – and particularly into the aetiology of schizoid disorders, in which individuals experience both a profound sense of detachment from others that serves as a defence against an alarmingly intense longing for relationship, and also feelings of weakness at the core of the personality – sometimes even to the extent of feeling non-existent as persons, although often exhibiting highly developed intellectual and other physical capacities.

In their efforts to help such people, the object relations therapists sought to identify with their patients emotionally as well as analysing their problems intellectually, all within the overall frame of psychoanalytic discipline. That is, the object relations therapists sought to promote for their schizoid patients an emotional atmosphere in which their unrealised capacity for experiencing a sense of personal reality and psychic life could be recovered. Often the therapies were very long, but both the therapists and their patients felt that an important new dimension in psychoanalysis had emerged because of the profound emotional significance that developed, giving rise to a new sense of personal meaning, identity and purpose in which both parties shared. Some striking examples of this kind of psychotherapy emerged in the 1960s when object relations theories began to take hold in a big way. I think in particular of Marion Milner's description of the psychoanalytic treatment of a schizo-phrenic patient, in *The Hands of the Living God* (1969), and Hannah Green's autobiographical account of her treatment by Dr Frieda Fromm-Reichmann in *I Never Promised You a Rose Garden* (1964); and a remarkable paper by Yvonne Blake, 'Psychotherapy with the more-disturbed patient' (1969).

There were a number of features common to these psychotherapies:

- the way the apparent indifference of the patient gave way to a frighteningly deep need for personal relations characterised by safe dependency;
- the intense resistance to the above by the patient;
- the need for the psychotherapist to remain at one with the patient while recovery took place.

Because of the similarity of these states with those of early childhood and infancy, the object relations psychotherapists came to associate their therapeutic role with that of the good-enough mother of early life, who nursed the personal potential of the infant into being by empathic relationship. Thus the needs of the patients guided the method of approach. From the 1950s onwards, when this work was being pioneered by Balint (1952, 1968); Fairbairn (1952); Guntrip (1961, 1968); and Winnicott (1958, 1965), a steadily developing body of infant research has supported the view that the earliest relationships have a profound effect, for better or worse, on the way in which the individual develops (see Lanyado 1994). It is indeed significant that findings of object relations psychoanalysis, which inevitably began its search from the standpoint of the mentally ill adult, should accord, at the deepest level of investigation, with the data produced by workers in the field of child psychotherapy, infant research and paediatrics, to attest to the social nature of the infant psyche. When Fairbairn in the 1940s declared that the libido, or primary life-drive, was essentially person-seeking and not pleasure-seeking, he was opening up an entirely new field of inquiry into the cause of psychopathology.

From that standpoint, all problems had to be approached not by reference to predetermined formulae, such as a death instinct, but with the question; 'If human nature is basically social, how do human beings develop antisocial impulses?' If the primary psychological need is not for gratification obtained by the release of instinctual tension, but for personal relationship as the indispensable medium for personal growth, then psychoanalytic investigation, which had been concerned with pathological theories of human nature, should redirect its focus towards the latent natural health of human infants, and how to promote their growth in personal relationships.

Not surprisingly, such a viewpoint aroused much opposition, and even among the core clinicians and theoreticians of object relations there was considerable disagreement, as, for example, between Guntrip and Winnicott over questions of 'innate sadism', and the isolation or otherwise of the core of the self, and between Guntrip and Fairbairn on the one hand and Winnicott on the other as to whether good experience was internalised in the same structured way as bad experience − or simply mentally expressed in ego development. In the wider psychoanalytic world a split arose over the question of whether the hates and lusts of the repressed unconscious were rooted in the primary nature of the human infant, or whether they were always, even the most severe, reactive to failures in early environmental nurture. While classical Freudians and Kleinians held the former view, the object relations workers tended towards the latter. But even then it had to be accepted − as indeed it still does − that even if antisocial impulses were always reactions of an ego to its bad object relations, these reactive states could become so fixed as to be, for all practical purposes, intractable, requiring the strongest containment on the part of those prepared to expose themselves to the dangers of seeking to understand them. To accept the object relations perspective on personal development is not, therefore, to 'excuse' or condone the depths of depravity that humans are capable of, or to suggest some slackening of the social control necessary to protect people from their effects, but rather to respect and work with what seems to be deepest in human nature: an absolute need for an affirming personal relationship in which to realise our deepest personal potential. Thus, whatever their differences over other 'levels' of human development, at the primary level all the object relations workers believed in the inherent value and psychic unity of the infant. All agreed that the quality of object relations determines the patterns of unity or conflict in the ego. Object relations psychoanalysis thus became the study, for psychotherapeutic purposes, of the effects on our personality development of the quality of our personal relations experienced in the earliest formative years of infancy and childhood. These experiences create a deep unconscious deposit of experience, overlaid and repressed as the years go by, by the need for adjustment to the external realities of the immediate present-day outer world.

The question of overriding importance, however, was how to reach and restore, or evoke and sustain, the original unity of the infant psyche, expressed characteristically in an unconscious trust of the good object at the start of life, and an unqualified, wholehearted, energetic outreach towards the object, initially the mother or mothering person (the term 'mother' is used to refer to whoever fulfils this role, whether this is the child's biological mother or another person, male or female, who becomes their primary carer). The object relations theorists believed the answer to lie in the intimate nature of the infant-mother relationship in which a securely related mother's emotional identification with her baby enabled her to know the baby's needs before the baby was aware of them, at the preverbal level of development.

The stage at which the baby begins to emerge from identification with the mother is held to be vital for personal development because the first aware-ness of separateness and incipient selfhood occurs when the infant is still in a state of helplessness and dependence. The infant's ability to accept and enjoy their separateness on a conscious level is dependent upon a persisting emotional experience of relatedness with their mother on an unconscious level. Thus the object relations theorists placed the responsibility for the development of the person upon the human capacity for emotional identifi-cation, as the essential sponsoring quality for confident personhood, with the nursing mother as the main exponent, in view of her long and intimate association with the baby throughout pregnancy. She was the main 'object' with whom the infant sought to experience him or herself as 'satisfactorily in being'. Without her environing warmth the baby would most likely die; but even if the baby lived, the loss of such a primary relationship could mean that the adult would be prey to deep ontological insecurity throughout life, and prone to damage both self and others in desperate attempts to manufacture a sense of personal identity.

All our theorists laid great emphasis upon the infant's need for an experience of 'simple being' in the context of maternal care, undisturbed by impingement, which would cause a reaction, thereby splitting the unity of the ego. The need to provide conditions in which the psychic being could evolve naturally was held to be paramount. It was this almost reverential respect for the infant-being which led Winnicott to state that 'the core of the personality is an isolate'. However, as he revealed to Guntrip in corres- pondence, by referring to the 'incommunicado position' Winnicott was trying to describe 'the state of being alive, with infinite potential for experiencing living': the resting state 'where (non-derivative) creativity comes from' (Hazell 1996, p.250). And, as Guntrip pointed out, such a state could only originate in a relationship of such quality that it supported and nurtured the resting state of the infant, since it was 'only because of the factual existence of a state of "being-at-one-with" that the sense of being and the emergence of a sense of self can come about at all' (1968, p.269). Indeed, this truly object relations view is supported elsewhere by Winnicott in his concept of 'basic ego-relatedness' (1965, p.30) as the essential matrix of the 'true self' (p.148).

It may be that in stressing the 'incommunicado' element Winnicott was overzealous in guarding against the belief, held by many analysts, that the infant's capacity for objectivity and separateness could only be awoken by bad experience, with the implication that the ego could never have any other but an anxious base. Guntrip, however, accepting that 'even the very earliest sensory experience of objects must contain some elementary factor of objectivity, awaiting clarification and development', believed the infant mind to be capable equally of detecting the element of objectivity in both good and bad experience. Insofar as the experience is bad, the infant's only defence against the rapidity of the first fear reactions is the closeness of maternal support, which, in view of their extreme dependence and vulnerability is 'the all-important factor in the way…experience of objectivity develops from being a latent or implicit factor to being an evoked or explicit one' (Guntrip 1968, p.240). It would seem that good experience forms a better basis for objectivity, since it leaves the subject free from the distortion of anxious reaction.

Although it was stressed that the intention was neither to idealise motherhood nor to overload it with moral responsibility but to draw attention to the enormous importance of mothering at the start of life, insufficient consideration was given to the role of the father or to the mother's own need for emotional identification and support from her own human environment in order to remain good-enough. Our needs for personal relations are primary, and not confined to infancy, for as adults we rapidly become incapable of feeling with and for others (and indeed ourselves) if our intimate relationships change or fail. If all goes well, however, the reciprocity of the mother-and-child relation enables each to confirm the value of the other in a steadily unfolding dynamic as the child grows towards separate selfhood.

The extent to which the child is able to acquire a confident sense of differentiated selfhood was held to depend upon the degree to which they could internalise ego-supportive experience. Where all agreed that bad experience remained stuck like a foreign body in the mind, forming an unhappy inner world of sub-ego/object relations, opinion was divided over how *good* experience was retained. As already mentioned, Fairbairn and Guntrip believed that what made good experience good was the fact that it could be mentally digested and, being retained as pleasant memory, used in ego development. Whereas what made bad experience 'bad' was that it could not be used for ego development, and so remained mentally undigested, retained in the inner world of bad object relations in which parts of the ego remained enmeshed. For Winnicott, however, good experience was internalised in a more radical way than memory, forming a secure basis of relatedness to the good object, which remained anchored in the infant's mind as the source of their capacity to be non-anxiously alone. In a sense the argument is semantic, since it would hardly be possible for good experience to be more firmly rooted than by becoming an integral part of the person's psychic metabolism, so to speak. It is necessary to mention these differences of opinion among the theorists because they bear directly upon the development of the person, and they are not, to my knowledge, anything like resolved.

Another argument centred around the nature of the differentiated child. Were children innately ruthless or not? Winnicott was inclined to think so; Fairbairn and Guntrip thought not, although they agreed that children could certainly seem ruthless at times, especially to their mothers! Guntrip, unlike the other theorists, held the view that aggression was not inherently destructive, but was an energetic, striving aspect of the life-force (libido), with the capacity to intensify, potentially destructively when influenced by anxiety, especially separation anxiety (1971, pp.133–139). For Fairbairn, aggression was an ego reaction to frustration of the object-seeking libido, which in object relations terms always implies rejection. Fairbairn asserted that this always resulted when parents, no matter how good in other ways, failed to convey to their children that they mattered for their own sakes and in their own right. Winnicott, however, while stressing the value of the good 'facilitating relationship', suggested that the mother's devotion to her child fosters an illusion in the baby's mind of omnipotence, of which she then disillusions the baby by gradually withdrawing her ego support, albeit at the rate the baby can allow. It begins to sound like a preparation for the school of hard knocks and less like an experience of personal confidence built upon experience of reliable person-to-person identification and communication. This view also fails to ring true with Winnicott's concept of the capacity to be alone – a main indicator of maturity – which he states can only come about when initially someone else (the mother) is present. Thus children developed the capacity to be non-anxiously alone not because they feel omnipotent, but because they are developing confidence through faith in human support – 'the evidence of dependability that is becoming introjected (Winnicott 1971, p.100). Guntrip agreed that, to the degree that they have been able to absorb the reality of their relation to their mother, children feel 'a profound sense of belonging and of being-at-one with their world, which is not intellectually thought out, but is the persisting atmosphere of security in which they exist within themselves' (Guntrip 1968, p.221). In this atmosphere the child is able to discover what Winnicott calls 'separation that is a form of union', (1971, p.98), which children represent to themselves and the world by means of transitional symbols, which mark their emergence from the subjective to the objective world. In Winnicott's view these symbols were the forerunners of cultural and religious symbols in later life, or, more commonly, of a feeling of being at home in the world, of experiencing the environing reality personally. As children grow, the inner experience of personal identity, founded upon recurrently experienced identification with and differentiation from their parents, becomes the basis for confident venturing in the world of relation.

In his original theory Fairbairn described personal development as originating in primary identification of mother and infant, then passing through a transitional stage of gradual differentiation, into a final stage of 'mature dependence, characterised predominantly by an attitude of giving.' (1952, p.39). The implication is that we mature not into independence (a term which suggests fear of dependence rather than genuine confidence), but into a realistic acceptance of our interdependence with others. As Winnicott pointed out 'the individual, seen as an autonomous unit is in fact never independent of the environment, though there are ways by which, in maturity, the individual may feel free and independent, as much as makes for happiness and for a sense of having a personal identity' (1971, p.139).

The confidence of the basically ego-related child is enhanced, not diminished, by the fact that it grew out of an identification with its mother. To the extent to which the child has 'felt with' their mother, the differentiated or individual child is able to 'feel for' their mother spontaneously as development proceeds. It should hardly need pointing out that this spontaneous development of feeling for the mother, proceeding naturally from a primary union, is qualitatively different from reparation for having damaged her, which is a product of anxiety and self-interest; the latter being perhaps an inevitability in an uncertain world as a product of anxiety, not of confidence. Across the widening gap of differentiated being, as mother and child recover and discover self-interest, the sense of their mutual significance provides a bridge, which Guntrip has described as 'separate egos coming together in consciously significant mutuality' (1968, p.222).

Although the early object relations theorists did not regard the father as having the same intrinsic importance for the start of the child's personality as the mother, it was recognised that as the mother developed her capacities for 'doing', so the father's more active role as protector and supporter of the nursing couple should expand to include a capacity for feeling and being with his child as a basis for secure development. As the child continues to differentiate as an individual, his or her developing confidence and experience of a world outside the family will express itself in vigorous competition with the more established values represented by the parents. If relations with the parents are good, earlier dependence is gradually replaced throughout adolescence and early adulthood by a friendship based on equality. This need not involve a dramatic break from the old home, or repudiation of the parents, provided the latter can acknowledge that the young can grow to have real knowledge and wisdom. Complete cleavages between young and old rest upon mutual distrust, insecurity and defensiveness, which arise from inner disturbance.

As in the earlier stages of growth, the basic inner sense of security by which we recognise mental health is closely related to smooth continuity of development. The needs which are so clearly evident in childhood are scarcely less vital in adulthood, despite increased physical growth – rather, maturity in adulthood can be measured by a capacity to own and acknowledge interdependence. Throughout these relationships the element of reciprocity is all important: no one could derive a feeling of personal relatedness, significance and confidence from a technique, but only from a profound sense of reciprocal valuing and cherishing, spontaneously felt and expressed. It is this quality which from the beginning forms the basis of individual development, and which, profoundly rooted in our psychological constitution, object relations theory attempts to conceptualise. As the new person grows into emotional equality, their meaning for their family and the family's meaning for them continually serves to promote a new and original sense of identity and purpose which could not exist without reciprocity. Guntrip writes: 'Each goes on being and becoming aware of what the other is being and becoming in their personal interaction and mutual knowledge...and in such a way that their reality as persons becomes...what neither of them could have become apart from their relationship' (1968, p.389). The need for personal relations experience certainly does not diminish with maturation, for it is not in itself infantile but rather the essential, underlying factor throughout life that enables a person to relate meaningfully to the world, beginning with the mother and extending through the family, neighbourhood, town, country and, ultimately, to humanity.

Just as there can be no one theory of personal development, so there can be no one theory of abuse. If, however, we accept the object relations theory that primary psychic energy is for personal object relating, the greatest abuse a person could therefore suffer would be the absence of relatedness, whether the needed person was present physically or not. Indeed, much physical abuse arises from distorted attempts to extract a response when the parties are emotionally absent from each other.

In the above section, we have traced the development of the related personality, but the means of doing so was through the understanding of those whose incipient personhood remained undeveloped due to paucity or lack of personal relations. Left alone in an indifferent or hostile world, they were unable to experience their reality as persons, to develop a secure sense of identity, purpose or intention. Mostly, when we speak of abuse we are referring to actively bad treatment, but in terms of object relations theory, the most serious distortion of our social nature arises from sheer indifference, a view supported by Lynne Murray's 'perturbation studies' (1985), which demonstrate the dramatically disturbing effect that one-minute of unresponsiveness by a mother can have upon six-week-old babies, who responded initially with intensified efforts at communication, but soon retreated into withdrawal, similar to the separated children in Bowlby's studies (1969, 1973, 1980). At the adult level, Guntrip recorded his own experience of fading away into non-existence because of his mother's inability to relate empathically to him in early life. He offered the suggestion that his problems in later life stemmed from a desperate attempt 'to become a person by manically doing' because of his inability to take his 'ongoing being for granted' (Hazell 1994, p.362). It is relevant that the main feature of his problems was 'feeling apart from others'.

If the primary self, containing the infant's psychic potential for personal development, is not loved and supported it very soon falls prey to detachment and depersonalisation. In the view of the present writer, it is the state of emotional detachment – the schizoid state – that lies at the root of abuse of all kinds, for, whatever active harm may be perpetrated, it ultimately stems from a sheer failure of the basic human capacity of a person to identify emotionally with the other. In some essential sense victim and abuser do not know each other: each is lost in a pattern of reaction to deprivation. Their capacity to identify with each other is unrealised: they cannot relate, but only react.

In the absence of the vital relational link, the object relations theorists believed that the original psychic unity became profoundly divided against itself. At the deepest level, the self's creative core seeks sanctuary in the deep unconscious, motivated partly by sheer fear of the outer world and its own weakness, but also by a secret longing for the safety and unity of the intrauterine state, of which it retains a dim memory. Balint (1968) pointed out that when a person withdraws, they are not simply running away from a hostile or remote outer world, but also running towards a state in which they can recover – the haven of the deep unconscious. This retreat is undertaken not for the sake of gratification (malignant regression), but in search of recognition (benign regression) by the psychotherapist, who is nevertheless feared and resisted, both as an object of painful longing and as a representative of an alien world. Devoid of its essential core, the remainder of the personality functions without feeling in a relationless world. The individual whose development is arrested at a pre-moral level, cannot 'feel for' people at all. Such a person lives in a perfectly rational, but quite impersonal, state of mind, withdrawn from personal relations. Practically, such states may be beyond the reach of psychotherapy. Both the schizoid psychopath and the schizophrenic present us with such strains and risks that the therapist's ability to conceptualise their states of mind is seldom matched by a capacity to reach and resolve them, though there have been some notable exceptions. From an object relations perspective, these are the most alienated states on a continuum of disturbed experience where the dominant emotion is one of pure fear.

At levels nearer the world of personal relations, a less devitalised ego struggles to keep in touch with the human environment, to keep a sense of self alive, exploiting aggressive and sexual energies in the process. However, since a return can only be made in fear of the very environment that prompted the withdrawal, it involves a gross exploitation of the properties of the psyche: the original vigorous, object-seeking aggression intensifies into violent, raging hate; the urge to love becomes a ravenous need to devour the object; original trust becomes a paranoid fear and suspicion of all objects.

The fear arises in the infant that their greatly intensified need-love has become destructive, both to the object upon whom their life depends, and inevitably also to themselves. Moreover, the infant experiences the love of their object as equally threatening. The feeling heart of the personality is thus compromised at a fundamental level. The infant is afraid either to love or be loved, and must function as far as possible in a de-emotionalised world where personal relations are felt to be dangerous, both to the self and to those who may become their 'objects' later in life. This is the schizoid state, in which the individual seeks to eliminate a need for others beneath an appearance of cold detachment, sometimes mistaken for genuine confidence, but which conceals a need of terrifying intensity. The problem here is not primarily one of buried anger, but of enormously exaggerated hunger, which makes all relationships – including the potentially therapeutic relationship – simultaneously craved for and feared.

However, since the avoidance of personal relations if carried to an extreme would threaten the ego with extinction, in another part of themselves the infant carries on a desperate struggle to compel the object to relate to them. This attempt cannot be made constructively, due to the failing relationship, so that the biological appetites and drives are once again experienced in exaggerated distorted ways. For the same reason, the reactions of the object are likely to be retaliative rather than reparative, thereby forcing the infant's disturbed drives back against its needy core, with the additive of parental disapproval. Because of their continuing need for relatedness, the infant, in a further division of their already fractured personality, is driven to identify with these elements of parental persecution and disapproval. They thus come to experience pathological guilt and depression over the same antisocial impulses by which they sought to alleviate the schizoid problem, and thus experience some sense of personal potency. Later in life, such a person is likely to equate personal potency and strength with forbidden 'primitive instincts' that periodically require discharge in personal relationships in order to restore a (spurious) sense of prestige. Potentially loving relations, including therapeutic ones, are always subject to disruption by sudden explosions of hate and/or lust, sometimes followed by depressive guilt, which, unlike a mature capacity for shame, fails to give rise to a true reparative drive. The infant has become a danger to themselves and the object from whom they are nevertheless unable to differentiate, but with whom they remain unconsciously identified. Denied the opportunity to be at one with their object, they cannot become the person they potentially are, but remain a collection of reactions deeply divided against themselves. However, despite the psychic pain, the possession of such active, destructive feelings imparts a spurious feeling of life, which feels infinitely preferable to the fear-ridden, passive, inert state in which the lost creative feeling-heart lies buried.

The insight that antisocial impulses represent a loss of the object and the consequent threatened loss of oneself is a major contribution of object relations theory. The corollary is that antisocial impulse is unlikely to be found in a confident person or in any person when confident. Fairbairn (1952) proposed that when the infant finds that, despite the exertion of all their over-exploited energies they cannot recover and cannot make the object love them, they take the whole unmanageable situation inside and struggle with 'internalised bad objects' in an inner world with parts of their fragmented self. These are representations of the bad, unsatisfying, aspects of the needed parents with whom the infant is partly identified in persecuting and rejecting its needy self. In another division of themselves, they struggle to remain unconscious of this inner turmoil, while they function as best they can in everyday life. However, while the more-or-less devitalised self of everyday struggles to face up to the demands of life and pass as a 'normal' person among peers, the influence of what Fairbairn (1958) called the 'static internal closed' system is a continual threat, assailing the conscious mind with irrational hates, sudden imperious lusts and cravings, and disturbing fantasies which threaten to wreck contemporary relationships, while from deeper down come seemingly inexplicable 'childish fears' and longings to escape to a mythical sanctuary, or into death itself.

When these emotions are 'projected' on to actual, external figures real harm can often result from a failure to understand their origins – and even when they are understood to stem from the desperate strivings of a fundamentally undermined personality, the sheer size of the task confronting the psychotherapist is formidable. Much active abuse perpetrated upon the weak and vulnerable arises from the unconscious projection by the abuser of the unacceptable subselves on to younger individuals, who in some way represent a part of the abuser by their relative immaturity and naivety. For example, a male patient recalled feeling gripped by a powerful, destructive urge when passing his infant daughter's bedroom at night. He was only helped by the insight that he was himself struggling to suppress powerful dependency needs of his own to be protected from a hard external world. The only way he had ever known of dealing with such 'infantile' needs in himself had been ruthless sadomasochistic self-persecution and contempt, an attitude which he was further able to trace to the grandmother who brought him up, and with whom he remained unconsciously identified ever since. As respect developed for his own needs for personal understanding and acceptance in psychotherapy, so the projection on to his daughter was withdrawn. His dependence in the therapeutic relationship gradually gave rise to a new identification, which fostered his genuine development as a person.

Clearly, many other forms and causes of abuse exist, but perhaps a general principle may be proposed that one path to understanding lies in the direction of the abuser's own inner weakness, which is so easily represented by children, a weakness brought about by relational failure. This position is exacerbated when a potential victim's own unmet needs compel them to collude in the abuse. The facts seem to be that our need for personal contact (and consequent self-feeling) is so great that we put up with almost anything to get it.

The situation is complicated by the intense resistance to seeking and accepting help that is felt by sufferers, for when the sub-selves into which the original unity was split are each gripped by intense loathing and fear for one another, they are slow to yield to combined support and analysis – especially when it is remembered that the original stimulus for the divided self was loss, infantile weakness and fear. In these circumstances, the task of maintaining a belief in an original social nature in need of a personal object with whom to experience identity and being is crucial, especially when it is often hardly more than a potentiality locked in a sensation-bound, relationless world. However, I believe that even the analysis of the more developed antisocial personality can only be successfully carried out when this belief is maintained, since it is only in the context of such a belief in the individual that the person can experience sufficient security to tolerate the insights that will set them free to discover their true identity.

In terms of object relations theory, this belief in the unity and integrity of the individual psyche is based not upon sentiment, but upon the facts of clinically validated experience with both adults and children, which continues to demonstrate that even when the need for physical care is fully attended to, and instinctual gratification is experienced, without a positive input of loving, empathic relating from a nurturing parent, the infant's innate developmental potential remains unevoked. Sutherland, in a paper on object-relations theoretical contributions, stated:

> While the future growth of the person, [their] creativity, [their] use of particular talents, etc., entail unpredictable emergents from the experiences and opportunities [they meet], nevertheless the potential for growth is not created without a 'personalised input' from which the infant fashions…an affective field that predisposes [them] to pursue with interest and enthusiasm…exploration of the world. (1980, p.855)

It is this missing sense of self growing in good personal relations that object relations therapists seek to make good for their patients. There are three problems in particular that beset the work: first, the substratum of deep fear and insecurity from which all later psychopathology is thought to arise; second, the extreme weakness of the psychic subject who is experiencing it, which in turn gives rise to the third difficulty, that, as a feeling of trust develops a deep dependency upon the psychotherapist is inevitable. It is useful if this dependency, when it emerges, can be explained to the patient as their original potential for trust and selfhood that became lost in early life.

Ultimately, fear, weakness and dependency can only give way when true reliability and personal consistency are being experienced as a foundation for growth. It is therefore upon the 'emotional health' of the therapist that progress depends, for, like the mother of an infant, any psychotherapist rapidly loses the needed quality when unrelated. In these circumstances, the psychotherapist can no longer identify with the patient in order to know them. From an object relations perspective, our ability to help those involved in abuse, whether assailant or victim, finally depends upon whether we have the maturity to go all the way in identifying with the fear and weakness that lie beneath antisocial impulse, while holding to our own integrity of purpose to stand by and be with the other, in the full acceptance of our own need of those same qualities as the indispensable medium for personal growth.

References

Balint, M. (1952) *Primary Love and the Psychoanalytic Technique.* London: Tavistock.

Balint, M. (1968) *The Basic Fault.* London: Tavistock.

Blake, Y. (1968) 'Psychotherapy with the more disturbed patient'. *British Journal of Medical Psychology 41,* 199.

Bollas, C. (1987) *The Shadow of the Object: Psychoanalysis of the Unthought Known.* London: Free Association Books.

Bowlby, J. (1969) *Attachment and Loss. Vol. 1, Attachment.* London: The Hogarth Press.

Bowlby, J. (1973) *Attachment and Loss. Vol. 2, Separation: Anxiety and Anger.* London: The Hogarth Press.

Bowlby (1980) *Attachment and Loss. Vol. 3, Loss: Sadness and Depression.* London: The Hogarth Press.

Fairbairn, W.R.D. (1952) *Psychoanalytic Studies of the Personality.* London: The Hogarth Press.

Fairbairn, W.R.D. (1958) 'On the nature and aims of psychoanalytical treatment'. *International Journal of Psychoanalysis 39,* 374.

Gomez, L. (1997) *An Introduction to Object Relations.* London: Free Association Books.

Green, H. (1964) *I Never Promised You a Rose Garden.* London: Gollancz.

Guntrip, H. (1961) *Personality Structure and Human Interaction.* London: The Hogarth Press.

Guntrip, H. (1968) *Schizoid Phenomena, Object Relations and the Self.* London: The Hogarth Press.

Guntrip, H. (1971) *Psychoanalytic Theory, Therapy and the Self.* New York: Basic Books.

Guntrip, H. (1975) 'My experience of analysis with Fairbairn and Winnicott'. *International Review of Psychoanalysis 2*, 145–156.

Hazell, J. (1994) *Personal Relations Therapy: The Collected Papers of H.J.S. Guntrip.* New Jersey: Jason Aronson Inc..

Hazell, J. (1996) *H.J.S. Guntrip: A Psychoanalytic Biography.* London: Free Association Books.

Lanyado, M. (1994) 'In the Beginning … Observations of Newborn Babies and their Families'. *Journal of the British Association of Psychotherapists 26*, 3–21.

Milner, M. (1969) *The Hands of the Living God.* New York: International Universities Press, Inc..

Murray, L. and Trevarthen, C. (1985) 'Emotional regulation of interaction between two-month-olds and their mothers'. In Field and Fox (eds) *Social Perception in Infants.* New Jersey: Abex Publishing Corporation.

Scharff, D.E. (1992) *Refinding the Object and Reclaiming the Self.* New Jersey: Jason Aronson, Inc.

Sutherland, J.D. (1980) 'The British object relations theorists: Balint, Winnicott, Fairbairn, Guntrip'. *Journal of the American Psychoanalytical Association 4*, 829.

Symington, N. (1986) *The Analytic Experience; Lectures from the Tavistock.* London: Free Association Books.

Winnicott, D.W. (1958) *Collected Papers: Through Paediatrics to Psychoanalysis.* London: Tavistock Publications.

Winnicott, D.W. (1965) *The Maturational Process and the Facilitating Environment.* London: The Hogarth Press and the Institute of Psychoanalysis.

Winnicott, D.W. (1971) *Playing and Reality.* London: Tavistock Publications.

CHAPTER 2

Attachment Theory and Abuse

A Developmental Perspective

Jeremy Holmes

Attachment theory starts from the power of adults to protect and provide security for children. In abuse, this fundamental biosocial contract between adults and children is ruptured: adults use their power for their own ends rather than those of the child.

The dictionary definition of abuse includes the following synonyms: 'perversion', 'improper use', 'violation', 'adulteration' and 'defilement'. Implicit in these meanings is the notion of a normal or proper use against which ab-use can be measured: violence and the physical or moral rupture of integrity; transgression of sexual propriety; and from 'defilement', the notion of fouling – the introduction of the unclean and excremental into a world of cleanliness and innocence. Any of these meanings, and more, may be triggered off in the listener when abuse is mentioned. To these we can add the Kantian notion of the wrongness of using fellow human beings as means to an end rather than as ends in themselves.

Classifications of abuse usually include four main types: sexual abuse, physical abuse, emotional abuse and neglect. Each of these is a perversion of what a child might rightfully expect from their parents or caregivers. In this chapter I shall outline a model of emotional development based on the principles of attachment theory. The long-term effects of childhood abuse on personality development as they present themselves in psychotherapeutic settings can then be discussed.

Attachment theory was both nurtured by and developed in opposition to psychoanalysis. It can be seen as an empirically based version of object relations theory (Holmes 1996). Some preliminary remarks on similarities and differences between an attachment and a psychoanalytic perspective on abuse are therefore in order. Psychoanalysis puts desire at the centre of its thinking. Parents are their children's first libidinal objects. What is traumatic and confusing for the child about sexual abuse is that the adult world, rather than containing and holding the child's desire, reciprocates. The fruit of the tree of knowledge is eaten before the child can digest it – with resultant shame and loss of innocence, and premature expulsion from the world of play and plenitude. (This use of biblical imagery shows how easily the notion of abuse taps into primal phantasies, and how abuse can become a metaphor for all that is evil and demonic – often one that is uncritically accepted as the cause of all psychic ills.)

From Kleinian psychoanalysis came the idea that parents are not just the object of the child's first love, but also of their hatred. Intrinsic aggression and inevitable frustration of desire leads to murderous hatred in the baby, which, as with libido, is ideally contained and detoxified by the caregiver, so that gradually the child learns to cope with feelings of disappointment and deferments of gratification. In physical abuse this process is perverted: rather than absorbing and buffering the hatred, the adult retaliates, using the child as a container for their own deprivation and pain. In systematic emotional neglect the adult refuses the inevitable intimacy of the parent-child relationship, and the projective processes that implies. In a further perverse twist adults may see the child as deliberately inflicting misery upon them. Following the talion law of the primitive psyche, in the perpetrator's eyes abuse then becomes an act of justified revenge. Perversity can also afflict victims of abuse, which, when unravelled, is a form of protest and retaliation. This flows from identification with a bad or useless self, good only for exploitation and abuse. It is as though the abused person says to the world, 'You have treated me as a worthless object, so that is what I shall *be*.'

Attachment theory starts not with libido, but from the overwhelming need for adults to provide security for their young if development is to proceed. Bowlby observed the extreme vulnerability of young mammals to predation (as many a fox which has dragged off a newborn lamb for their young only to find their own cubs fallen prey to terriers would testify), and hypothesised that behavioural and psychological mechanisms which ensure proximity between adults and their offspring at times of danger were built into our nervous system through natural selection. The perverse paradox of abuse from an attachment perspective arises from the vicious circle in which an adult who is a caregiver can be *both* the attachment figure to whom the child turns for protection, *and* the source of threat which gives rise to the need for that protection. The more frightened or in pain the child becomes, the more the child clings to the perpetrator. We shall return to this vicious spiral in the clinical aspects of this chapter, but let us turn now to the attachment model of psycho-social development.

Secure base

This term, coined by Mary Ainsworth, with John Bowlby, the co-founder of attachment theory, captures the essence of the attachment component of the parent-child relationship. At times of threat, exhaustion, or illness the child turns to the caregiver for protection and security. Under those circumstances the child's attachment needs are activated, and proximity is sought in order to assuage them. A hungry baby yearns for the breast, but may also experience a primitive panic about the breast's absence. The baby's cries say more than, 'I am hungry; feed me.' They also pull the mother or caregiver close, saying, 'Attend to me; come nearer.' The response of the mother comprises not just the arrival of the breast, but the sense of safety that goes with it. The mother is a source of nutrition and sensual satisfaction, but also of the security needed if feeding is to proceed without interruption. The requirement for security is thus a precondition for the satisfaction of other needs, and represents an 'instinct' in its own right.

Unlike nutritional needs, the mechanisms underpinning attachment are from the start personal, or rather interpersonal. The infant can recognise the smell of their own mother's milk within 48 hours of delivery, and the mother picks out her infant's cry from those of other children almost from birth. Attachment depends on *recognition* – on knowing who is, and is not, 'mine' – who, from the adult's point of view it is safe to expend energy in nurturing, and from the infant's (although not until seven months), who can and cannot be trusted. Knowing who one is arises ultimately from the attachment bond.

For Bowlby, 'falling in love' was essentially the formation of this attachment bond. Falling in love with one's baby is a recognisable feeling for most, but not all, mothers – an almost physical sensation of an indissoluble connection, coupled with the desire to hold and cuddle, not to be able to take one's eyes off the baby, an excited delight that comes in any time in the first week after birth. The easier the delivery, the earlier it arises.

Once formed, the attachment bond ensures that the secure base is in place whenever it is needed. The newborn is swaddled in security, and gradually emerges as the early months of life go by, to explore first the breast, the mother's face and body, and gradually more and more of the world. A key feature of secure base is the reciprocal relationship between exploration and security. The secure baby can explore the environment, both interpersonal and material; but at times of threat, attachment behaviours are activated and the child seeks out and clings to the caregiver.

Felt security arises both out of 'knowing who is in charge' – a sense that the boundaries of the relationship are being maintained – and from pleasurable interaction with one's intimates. Abuse generally disrupts both aspects of this, and the balance between what Heard and Lake (1997) call the supportive and companionable (SC) and dominant vs. submissive (D/S) modes of relating. In physical abuse, D/S drives out SC and is used not to maintain boundaries but to inflict pain or gratification; in sexual abuse boundaries are broken, so SC becomes intrusive and threatening. The long-term consequences may well be an individual who construes all relationships as pivoting around dominance and submission, and for whom warmth and companionship are inevitably tinged with fear.

Attunement, intersubjectivity and mirroring

In the early months of life, mother and infant exist in a state of 'primary intersubjectivity' (Trevarthen 1979). Each is acutely aware of the other, and converse in 'motherese', a mutual pattern of gesture, vocalisation, and movement that comprise the 'proto-conversations' that lay the foundations of socialisation. Stern (1985) sees the key to intersubjectivity in his musical metaphor of attunement. Here the caregiver can be observed minutely following the child's behaviours in a 'dance' in which the rhythm, shape, pulse, duration and intensity of activity or vocalisation is matched by the parent in mutually enjoyable bursts of interactive play. New behaviours or sounds are particularly emphasised and praised: 'Aren't you a clever boy/girl!' is, it seems, one of the commonest parental remarks made across cultures (Heard and Lake 1997).

For Stern, this attunement, as well as providing pleasure, is a substrate for the emergence of a sense of self. For example, in 'cross-modal attunement' the parent might tap the child's back rhythmically in time with babbling vocalisations. This responsiveness enables a child to extract from the flux of experience an invariant aspect which will form part of the nascent sense of self. At the same time, the parental response holds up a mirror, so to speak, to the child's feelings, enabling them to begin to say to themselves, 'This is what I am doing, this is what I am like', thus providing the first building blocks for self-reflexive function. Careful observation of these early parent-child mirroring interactions reveals specific characteristics (Gergely and Watson 1996). First, the parent will for the most part follow the child's lead, thereby giving the infant a sense of power and mastery, and precise feedback on the external correlates of the behaviours which otherwise the infant would know only from the 'inside'. Second, the parental response is usually exaggerated, or 'marked', thus enabling the child to distinguish between a mirroring response which provides 'video' feedback on their own behaviour, and a gesture or facial expression that arises spontaneously in the parent. In this way the child begins to differentiate what belongs to the self and what to others in their world.

Thus mirroring and attunement enable the child to begin to know themselves – to see themselves as others see them. Disruptions of this process, especially if violent – perhaps resulting from parental depression or substance abuse – will have long-term effects on an individual's ability to reflect on and understand their own feelings and reactions, which in turn will handicap the formation and maintenance of intimate relationships (Holmes 1996).

Kohut (1977) emphasised another aspect of parental mirroring, central to the long-term effects of abuse on psychological development. For him, the child looks into the parental mirror to find not just him or herself, but a *special* self, a self that is in their parent's eyes uniquely beautiful, valuable and loveable. This narcissistic aspect of mirroring is, in the Kohutian model, essential for good self-esteem, and requires that the parent both confirms the child's specialness and, as development proceeds, helps them to know their own limitations and faults. In abuse this healthy narcissism is almost invariably absent. Abused people see themselves as useless and bad, or good only to service others' needs, however perverse these may be. Such individuals may compensate for deficient primary narcissism by a perverse self-centered-ness or 'secondary narcissism', and often lack the experience of healthy disillusionment which would liberate them from their self- absorption.

Secure and insecure attachment

The special strength of the attachment approach to psychotherapy is that psychological theorising is underpinned by an observational/experimental framework. The 'strange situation' test, devised by Mary Ainsworth (1982), creates a reliable classification of one-year-old children based on their response to brief (three minute) separation from, and reunion with, their caregivers. Ainsworth found that around two-thirds of children from a middle-class Baltimore suburb showed 'secure attachment', in the sense that they were able to protest appropriately about the three minute separation, be pacified on reunion, and to return to normal exploratory play thereafter. The remainder she classified as showing 'insecure attachment', in that they showed rigid and less adaptable variants of this pattern. 'Insecure-avoidant' children protested little on separation, and at reunion were unable to settle, hovering nervously and watchfully near their caregiver. 'Insecure-ambivalent' children, by contrast, often howled inconsolably on reunion and clung to the caregiving parent, also unable to return to exploratory play. A third group were later identified, 'insecure-disorganised', who showed no consistent pattern of response, or one that seemed bizarre and inappropriate, such as slowly collapsing to the floor in an apparently dissociated state on parental reunion. This classification has proved to be a very robust finding: numerous studies in many different countries and with different kinds of parents have confirmed the four basic patterns of response. There is a strong suspicion that insecure attachment patterns may predict vulnerability to later psychological difficulties. The insecure-disorganised pattern in particular, which is commoner in socially stressed families, may be a precursor of the dissociated states which frequently follow abusive experiences, and form part of the clinical picture of borderline personality disorder.

These early findings of attachment research suggested that psychological developmental pathways are laid down early in the first year of life, providing predictable, even if, in the case of insecure patterns, inflexible patterns of interpersonal interaction. Each of the distinct 'strange situation' patterns can be correlated with particular styles of parent-child interaction in the first year of life. Parents of securely attached children tend to be more responsive than their insecure counterparts; they pick their distressed children up more quickly, and engage them in interactive play more often. Parents of avoidant children are brusque and rejecting in their interactions, while those of the ambivalent group tend to be inconsistent, one minute intruding on a happily playing child, the next ignoring them when distressed.

The antecedents of disorganised attachment have been more intensively studied recently (Van Ijzendoorn *et al.* 1995). This pattern is strongly correlated with families under stress: socio-economically deprived, one-parent families, and mothers who have been abused as children.

Long-term follow-up studies suggest that attachment patterns in infancy persist into childhood and adolescence (Grossman and Grossman 1991). Secure infants tend to be confident and outgoing at school-entry, able to ask for help from teachers when they need it, and to interact co-operatively with their peers. Insecure infants, by contrast, tend either to be aggressive loners (avoidant pattern) or clinging, lacking in initiative and liable to be bullied (ambivalent pattern). The long-term effects of the disorganised pattern have not been studied so fully, but there is some evidence that these children are either anxious and watchful compulsive carers (a pattern seen particularly in girls), or aggressive and disruptive (more common in boys).

Different patterns of insecure attachment do not necessarily correlate with particular pathologies in later life, and should be seen as psychological dispositions which represent attempts to adapt to suboptimal rearing environments. They may act as predisposing factors to psychological difficulties – the combination of abuse plus insecure attachment for example can underlie the development of eating disorders in adolescence.

It is tempting to speculate that different forms of abuse may connect with different parental patterns underlying insecure attachment. Avoidance arises in the context of mild parental aggression – child-battering is the extreme example of this, and the frozen watchfulness of the battered child is perhaps a caricature of avoidant wariness. Childhood sexual abuse by parents or step-parents may tap into ambivalent attachments in which, as described at the start of this chapter, the child clings to a caregiver who alternates between being sexually intrusive and threatening or rejecting. Parental neglect, which, taken to the extreme, is a form of abuse, might link with disorganised attachment, in which the child despairs of finding any workable strategy for activating protective behaviour in their caregiver.

This is, of course, over-schematic. In clinical practice the distinction between the different types of insecure attachment is not so sharp, with mixed patterns being common, for example, in eating disorders. This makes psychological sense since avoidance and ambivalence are mirror images of one another: the avoidant person longs more than anything for intimacy, while ambivalent individuals crave autonomy, but both are too fearful to risk reaching for what they really want (Holmes 1996). Thus anxiety lies at the core of insecure attachments (if that statement is not a tautology), and it is the failure of the secure base providing caregiver to alleviate anxiety that inhibits the capacity to develop both intimacy and autonomy.

Aggression and protest

The strange situation test centres around the way in which the infant responds to separation. The 'normal' response involves healthy protest – the parent is 'punished' by the child's cries, and sometimes aggressive clinging for the act of abandonment. The capacity to protest, show appropriate aggression and to 'ask for help' (at the age of one by vocalisation rather than verbalisation) are marks of secure attachment, while insecure children are more likely either to be unable to protest or to be locked into unassuaged aggression. This picture can be linked with the Winnicott-Bion model of a 'breast' (i.e., attachment figure) able to 'metabolise' the rage and hatred of the frustrated infant, and return the feelings to the child in a detoxified form. As Winnicott typically puts it, the child needs to be able to say after an angry outburst: 'Hello object, I just destroyed you', and to find that the object has in fact survived. Security, in other words, arises in part out of the capability of the caregiver to accept and contain protest without retaliation or rejection.

This is relevant to abuse in a number of obvious ways. First, a condition of security is the ability to defend oneself when necessary, either by standing one's ground, or by recruiting a secure-base adult. Secure people are not afraid of their aggression, and can either express it openly or, when necessary, soothe themselves appropriately when faced with the anger so often evoked by pain or fear. Inhibition of protest and appropriate rage is an almost universal accompaniment of abuse: how can one expect an adult who has harmed one to accept and metabolise one's protests? A second, related, point is that potentially abusive parents are in any case unlikely to be able to contain their children's aggression, doubtless because it triggers off their own feelings of uncontainment vis-à-vis *their* parents – the intergenerational pattern of abuse playing itself out here – and so will retaliate against or neglect the protesting child. Abuse can thus in part be both a cause and a consequence of failure to cope with the aggression-containment cycle that is a feature of healthy attachment.

A third point concerns a key feature of sexual abuse: the inability of the child to let their parents know what has happened or, if tentative moves towards disclosure *are* made, to be met with disbelief, rejection or punishment ('How dare you accuse your step-father of such a thing! Go to your bed at once, you filthy-minded child'). Here the child's experience is invalidated or disconfirmed, with consequent distortions in self-understanding. In secure attachment the responsiveness, 'marking' and contingent responses of the parent help the child clearly to distinguish between self-experience and that of the caregiver. In insecure attachment by contrast, especially in ambivalent and disorganised patterns, this differentiation is shaky, such invalidating responses serving to confirm pre-existing confusion and self- doubt.

Developmental pathways

Single episodes of abuse are far less likely to have long-reaching effects on the personality than repeated abuse, suggesting that context is all-important in determining both whether abuse occurs in the first place and, if it does occur, what its consequences are likely to be. Insecure or secure attachment patterns describe developmental pathways representing patterns of repeated parent–child interaction in a particular family constellation. These pathways, if suboptimal, do not 'cause' abuse, but represent one of the many factors which acting in concert can either promote or prevent abuse. Although what we call abuse can be identified as definably inappropriate use of aggression or sexual transgression between adults and children, single or repeated events take place against a background of ingrained patterns of already established behavioural interaction between parents and children. Where isolated episodes of abuse do not have long-term consequences, these are likely to be secure attachment patterns. Where children who are insecurely attached are also abused, however, either by their attachment figures or others, their 'internal working models' of relationship will tend to be maladaptive and hence, in the psychiatric sense, precursors to pathology. An abused child may carry with them into adulthood a set of assumptions such as, 'If anything goes wrong it is my fault'; or, 'Intimate contact with men is frightening and disgusting'; or, 'I must submit to others' demands if I am to gain any safety at all'; 'The way to escape from intolerable situations is to split my mind from my body', which provide a seedbed for disturbed relationships and anxiety/depression in later life.

Thus, the overall context within which the abuse happens is equal in importance to the abuse itself: a depressed, preoccupied or unresponsive parent or step-parent, themselves perhaps abused, at the end of their tether, unemployment, chronic ill-health, low self-esteem, and myriad other psychological and social factors which provide a backdrop to the abusive act.

From a clinical or preventative perspective, this contextual and 'cumulative trauma' must be accorded due weight. Given the dramatic and overwhelming nature of post-traumatic stress disorder (PTSD) symptoms, such as flashbacks and phobic avoidance of the psycho-physiological correlates of the abuse (the smells, sounds, lighting, terror, disgust, unwanted excitement, feelings of being trapped, alone, or preparedness for self-sacrifice in order to protect siblings), it is tempting to focus exclusively on the trauma itself. In practice, both trauma and context need to be addressed. Indeed, in therapy with adult survivors of abuse many months may be needed to build up a picture of the developmental context before the details of the trauma itself can be talked about.

Post-traumatic stress disorder (PTSD), abuse and borderline personality disorder (BPD)

PTSD as a syndrome was originally understood in the context of the Vietnam War and superceded the notions of shell shock and battle fatigue developed by psychiatrists and psychologists in the first and second world wars. The long-term effects of sexual abuse have many features in common with PTSD. Some have even tried to conceptualise BPD as a form of PTSD as 60–70 per cent of BPD sufferers have experienced sexual abuse (Gunderson and Sabo 1993). Herman *et al.* (1989) write of 'complex PTSD' to capture the long-term effects of cumulative trauma and its impact on internal working models. One of the key questions for both PTSD and abuse is to ask what determines whether traumatic events will or will not be 'traumatic', in the sense of producing major psychiatric symptomatology or the distortions of personality development found in BPD. An attachment perspective can help unravel some aspects of this.

A number of apparently perverse features of BPD can be understood in attachment terms. In self-cutting, for example, the body is used as an 'object' which is simultaneously attacked and acts as a source of comfort: self-cutters regularly report a temporary period of peace and calm following self-injury. Abuse interferes with the child's acquisition of the capacity to self-soothe:

the parent, whose soothing actions are normally a template which gradually becomes internalised, instead causes pain and fear. The child then turns to the body as a surrogate secure base for self-soothing. The secondary gain of showing the wound to professional carers further mobilises attachment behaviours. The inappropriate use of alcohol and drugs similarly blots out pain physiologically, and provides a feeling of being held and divested of responsibility, similar to that which is sought when attachment needs are activated and assuaged.

Narrative and attachment

Only a minority of abused children will go on to develop BPD. A number of protective factors have been identified (Belsky 1993), including the existence of at least one good relationship – perhaps with a grandparent or teacher – attractiveness, sporting ability, and the impact of psychotherapy (Styron and Janoff-Bulman 1997). Another aspect of attachment-related impacts concerns the capacity to 'narrativise' painful experience. New neuro-imaging techniques suggest that traumatic memories are processed in the brain in different ways from non-traumatic ones (Van de Kolk and Fisler 1996). When subjects are asked to recall traumatic memories the non-dominant (usually right hemisphere) part of the brain is activated, whereas with non-traumatic memories it is the dominant, speech-generating, part which shows greatest metabolic activity. Most memories are stored in the brain in the form of stories – sequences of events that can be verbally recalled, and in which the sensory and emotional aspects of the memory remain in the background. Traumatic memories seem to exist in a raw sensory form, in which a coherent verbal account is hard to elicit. They are also often near the surface, and easily activated by cues that share features with the traumatic situation, triggering associated emotions such as panic and fear.

All this is relevant to recent work in attachment research that is looking at speech patterns and their relationship to underlying attachment styles. The adult attachment interview (AAI) (Main 1995) was developed as an attachment measure for adults analogous to the strange situation test, based on an in-depth, psychodynamic-type interview which is recorded and the transcript rated for different patterns of narrative style. The key feature of the AAI is that the interviews are rated not so much for content as for the ways in which subjects discuss their histories. As in the strange situation test, four patterns of discourse are delineated: *free-autonomous*, in which the subjects can talk fluently about themselves and their lives, including painful or even abusive aspects; *dismissive*, in which the discourse is restricted and past experience is referred to in stereotyped and unelaborated ways; *preoccupied* where, as the name implies, the sufferer is bogged down in past pain, and tends to produce a rambling dialogue which lacks the appropriate distance found in free-autonomous narratives; and, finally, *incoherent* narratives, which may coexist with the other types and is rated separately, show fractures and fissures in the coherence of the story, and are thought particularly to characterise those who have suffered extreme emotional arousal in the past, including abuse. Another rating scale from the AAI is based on the capacity for *self-reflection* – to see oneself from the outside and think about one's life, with its pleasures and tribulations, in a balanced way.

Exciting research findings using the AAI seem to suggest that there is continuity between infant security or insecurity and narrative patterns in adolescence (Grossman and Grossman 1991), and that AAI status in parents may predict strange situation status of those parents' children (Fonagy *et al.* 1991). Thus the way in which we talk about ourselves appears to be intimately linked with our attachment experience as children. Abuse can inscribe itself in the very way in which we think and speak about ourselves. The incoherent narrative style associated with abuse presumably reflects traumatic memories threatening to break through into consciousness, kept at bay by only partially successful attempts at verbal papering over cracks.

The process by which attachment influences the way in which we think about ourselves and our world can be studied in the self-narratives of three- to five-year-olds, who often talk out loud to themselves while engaging in solitary play (Holmes 1996; Meares 1993). Such self-absorption requires, in Winnicott's paradox (1965), the child to be 'alone in the presence of the mother'. In other words, the parent provides a safe base, which enables the child to focus on themselves and their imagination, and so to play and talk freely in secure solitude. If the base is not secure, the child's capacity to develop self-narrative, and ultimately a self-reliant and positive sense of self, may be compromised. If the child cannot rely on the parent to be there consistently, without interference or neglect, then their play and thoughts will be tinged with anxiety; if 'care' has been abusive, the very coherence of thought patterns and the integration of affect with cognition may be disrupted.

If we accept that the self is ultimately a 'narrative self' (Holmes 1998), then we can begin to see mechanisms by which abuse impacts directly on the core processes which constitute a person's identity, ways of thinking about the world, and of relating to it. Bowlby called these relational dispositions and their representations, internal working models, eschewing the psycho-analytic notion of an inner world. Whatever terminology is used, these concepts assume that adverse experience in childhood can have long-term effects on the way in which we see ourselves, our relationships with others, our capacity to protect ourselves and successfully to pursue our projects in the world.

Theory of mind

Some attachment-inspired authors (Fonagy 1991; Hobson 1993) have linked the above empirical findings with the philosophical question – how do we know that other people have minds? They argue that secure-attachment experiences can only be provided by caregivers who see their charges as sentient beings, centres of their own personal universe. Conversely, in abuse the victim is seen as an object without feelings or memory, and indeed may be coerced into denying their own experience. The title of one of Bowlby's (1988) late papers, 'On knowing what you are not supposed to know, and feeling what you are not supposed to feel', captures this confusion beautifully. We know that other people have minds, the argument goes, because we ourselves have been treated as people with minds. The caregiver's view of us becomes internalised not just as our view of ourselves, but also of others. From this follows concern for others and awareness of others' needs that is so often distorted in abuse-survivors.

Conclusions

Abuse contributes to a huge range of psychiatric symptomatology: feelings of low self-esteem, depression, deliberate self-harm, alcoholism and substance abuse, PTSD symptoms already mentioned, such as flashbacks, and temporary periods of dissociation, regression and psychosis. It is therefore not surprising that more than half of patients admitted to psychiatric wards have a history of childhood abuse (Sullivan et al. 1994). The most significant diagnostic group are those with personality disorders, especially BPD. Despite the experiential suffering implicit in the list above, these patients present primarily with difficulties in their personal relationships which tend to be abrasive, painful, disturbed, dependent, demanding and disruptive.

Attachment theory is relevant to abuse because it is essentially a theory about how people relate to one another, and how those relationships are influenced by the overriding need for a sense of security. An attachment perspective on abuse sees difficult behaviour as an attempt to cope with the paradox of an attachment figure who is also a source of threat and/or seduction. Avoidant patterns of attachment, for example, place the child near enough to the parent to feel safe, while sufficiently far away to escape rejection and punishment (the latter often meted out in response to attachment bids by a parent who feels they cannot cope with any further 'demands'). Dismissive narrative styles similarly enable a sense of self to develop, but one that, by restriction of memory and affect, avoid the pain and rage that might arise if past miseries were encoded in self-awareness and reflected in speech.

The oscillations of mood and turbulent personal relationships which BPD sufferers set up with intimates and carers reflect the simultaneous longing for closeness, and terror of achieving it, that so often characterises the personal relationships of abuse survivors. Ruthless dependency, 'selfishness', refusal to see the other's point of view and defiance, can all be seen as aspects of insecure attachment behaviours in which links with others must be maintained at all costs, even if based on aggression rather than love. In compulsive caregiving, another common post-abuse pattern, especially in females, the object of care is vicariously, and often smotheringly, looked after by a carer who is herself desperate for closeness and security.

The purpose of this book is to look at abuse from a multidimensional perspective. Attachment theory focuses on one of the fundamental building blocks of human relatedness – the need for security. It does not purport to offer a comprehensive theory of abuse and its consequences, but rather emphasises one indispensible strand in any comprehensive account of the scourge by which one generation stunts the development of the next by keeping it trapped in the past.

References

Ainsworth, M. (1982) 'Attachment; retrospect and prospect'. In C.M. Parkes, J. Stevenson-Hinde and P. Marris (eds) *The Place of Attachment in Human Behaviour*. London: Routledge.

Belsky, J. (1993) 'Etiology of child maltreatment: A developmental-ecological analysis'. *Psychological Bulletin 114*, 413–434.

Bowlby, J. (1988) *A Secure Base*. London: Routledge.

Chance, M. (1988) *Social Fabrics of the Mind*. Hove: Erlbaum Associates.

Fonagy, P. (1991) 'Thinking about thinking: Some clinical and theoretical considerations in the treatment of a borderline patient'. *International Journal of Psychoanalysis 72*, 639–656.

Fonagy, P., Steele, M. and Steele, H. (1991) 'The capacity for understanding mental states: The reflective self in parent and child and its significance for security of attachment'. *Infant Mental Health Journal 12*, 201–218.

Gergely, G. and Watson, J. (1996) 'The social biofeedback theory of parental affect-mirroring'. *International Journal of Psychoanalysis 77*, 181–212.

Grossman, K. and Grossman, K. (1991) 'Attachment quality as an organiser of emotional and behavioural responses in a longitudinal perspective'. In C.M. Parkes and J. Stevenson-Hinde (eds) *Attachment Across the Life Cycle*. London: Routledge.

Gunderson, J. and Sabo, A. (1993) 'The phenomenological and conceptual interface between borderline personality disorder and PTSD'. *American Journal of Psychiatry 150*, 19–27.

Heard, D. and Lake, B. (1997) *The Challenge of Attachment for Care-Giving*. London: Routledge.

Herman, J., Perry, C. and Kolk, B. (1989) 'Childhood trauma in borderline personality disorder'. *American Journal of Psychiatry 146*, 490–495.

Hobson, P. (1993) *Autism and the Development of Mind.* New Jersey: Erlbaum Associates.

Holmes, J. (1996) *Attachment, Intimacy, Autonomy: Using Attachment Theory in Adult Psychotherapy.* New Jersey: Jason Aronson Inc..

Holmes, J. (1998) 'Defensive and creative uses of narrative in therapy: An attachment perspective'. In G. Roberts and J. Holmes (eds) *Healing Stories: Narrative in Psychiatry and Psychotherapy.* Oxford: Oxford University Press.

Kohut, H. (1977) *The Restoration of the Self.* New York: International Universities Press Inc..

Main, M. (1995) 'Recent studies in attachment: Overview with selected implications for clinical work'. In S. Goldberg, R. Muir and J. Kerr (eds) *Attachment Theory: Social, Developmental and Clinical Perspectives.* New York: Analytic Press.

Meares, R. (1993) *The Metaphor of Play.* New Jersey: Jason Aronson Inc..

Stern, D. (1985) *The Interpersonal World of the Infant.* New York: Basic Books.

Styron, T. and Janoff-Bulman, R. (1997) 'Childhood attachment and abuse: Long-term effects on adult attachment, depression and conflict resolution'. *Child Abuse and Neglect 21,* 1015–1023.

Sullivan, P., Joyce, P. and Mulder, R. (1994) 'Borderline personality disorder in major depression'. *Journal of Nervous and Mental Disease 182,* 508–516.

Trevarthen, C. (1979) 'Communication and co-operation in early infancy: A description of primary subjectivity'. In M. Bullova (ed) *Before Speech; The Beginnings of Interpersonal Communication.* New York: Cambridge University Press.

Van de Kolk, B. and Fisler, R. (1996) 'Dissociation and the fragmentary nature of traumatic memories: Overview'. *British Journal of Psychotherapy 12,* 352–361.

Van Ijzendoornm, M., Juffer, F. and Duyvesteyn, M. (1995) 'Breaking the intergenerational cycle of insecure attachment: A review of the effects of attachment-based interventions on maternal sensitivity and infant security'. *Journal of Child Psychology and Psychiatry 2,* 225–248.

Winnicott, D. (1965) 'The capacity to be alone'. In *The Maturational Processes and the Facilitating Environment.* London: The Hogarth Press.

CHAPTER 3

Relationships as a Function of Context

Frances B. Carter

From the very beginning, human beings are social beings, developing and living not only in the context of their own experience, but also in complex interrelationships with others, such as friends or partners, nuclear and extended families, professional and social groups, organizations and societies. Just as each individual has their own unique and real set of characteristics, conflicts, level of development and dynamic tensions, so does any social group that may include the individual. How these tensions and conflicts are worked with within the individual, among the individuals in a group and in a group as a whole will effect the potential development of the individuals and the group.

Social groups, including pairings, are in their own right dynamic wholes with their own unique set of characteristics that are different from the sum of their parts (Lewin 1935). An individual's behaviour can be seen as a function of their own dynamics and history as well as that of all the groups of which they are a member. In fact, who one can be at any given moment is as much a function of the dynamics of one's context as it is of one's self. Much of the acute pain human beings experience comes from taking what someone does 'just personally' (Agazarian 1997). When one has the capacity to observe and understand the experience of oneself and others in the larger social context, one becomes able to see the personal as well as the universal human aspects of the experience. When one looks at an individual's behaviour in context, one is able to see how maladaptive and abusive relationships can be maintained over time and how systems-centred[1] therapeutic interventions can facilitate change.

Systems thinking

Systems thinking requires a shift away from the notion that the individual is at the centre of the group world – both the problem and the solution for all that occurs in that world – towards thinking of the individual as an abstraction, a living human system that is merely a part of an interrelated system of systems, or a nesting hierarchy of systems (Agazarian 1997; Whitehead 1952). For example, an individual can be conceptualised as a system, having a level of complexity, structure, energy/information (Miller 1978), goals and dynamic functioning processes. The partnership of two people can be seen as a larger system that contains both individuals. While each person brings their own resources, developmental issues, histories, dynamics, personality, energy and goals to the relationship, at the same time the relationship itself takes on a life of its own, with its own character, defensive structure, communication pattern and developmental process. The couple may also be nested in the larger system of the extended-family system, and then will be influenced by its dynamics. Families exist in communities, and communities exist in societies. Each system level of the individual, the couple, the family and the community can be described similarly in terms of structure, function and energy. However, how each system will appear will differ in different contexts. For example, the defined hierarchy of a couple, family and community in Western Europe will look different from the same hierarchy of systems in Aboriginal society. The norms of behaviour will be different, the relationship patterns will be different, the values will be different and how these values are manifest in the community will be different.

In the hierarchy of systems, living human systems are also isomorphic in that they are similar in structure, as defined by boundaries, and function, dynamic organising principles and processes (von Bertalanffy 1968), and are different in different contexts (Agazarian 1997). What one learns about one system level can add to what one knows about the others. By looking at a cell one can learn something about the condition of the organ; by looking at an organ one can learn something about the individual; by looking at an individual one can learn something about the group within which they are a member; by looking at a subgroup, one can also learn something about the organisation and society within which the subgroup exists.

When one has an understanding of both hierarchy and isomorphy one can begin to identify the most efficient and appropriate interventions for change. For example, if a physician treats only the bruised kidney of a child who has come to hospital, they may miss the fact that the child received the injury from an abusive parent. While treating the child's kidney may solve a problem for the child in the short-term, in the long-term it does not address the problems for that particular child, their siblings and parents, who must all continue to live in a family with physically abusive behaviour patterns.

Human systems are open systems, that is, dynamic not static (von Bertalanffy 1968) with an ongoing inflow and outflow of information up and down the levels of a defined hierarchy, with one level both mirroring and influencing the others. Living human systems engage in an ongoing process of organizing this energy/information (Miller 1978) within boundaries, and directing energy towards the primary goals of survival, development and transformation, and the secondary goals of mastering challenges in the environment (Agazarian 1997).

System boundaries open to information that is similar enough to be integrated, thus potentiating change, and close when differences are too great (Agazarian 1997), and when there is too much ambiguity, contradiction or redundancies (Shannon and Weaver 1964; Simon and Agazarian 1967). This process maintains balance and stability in the system. When boundaries are appropriately permeable and there is clear communication from within the system and between the system and the environment, there is an information exchange at a depth and rate that fuels the discrimination/ integration process and potentiates change. Individuals are able to accept within themselves an increasingly wide range of emotional experience, subgroups are able to integrate differences in the experiences and points of view of others, and societies are able to integrate a broader range of social and cultural beliefs.

Observing the communication pattern in a system hierarchy can provide important information about any system in the hierarchy, and can be a diagnostic tool in assessing the functional flow of communication through-out the hierarchy. For example, if the communication is one of data collection, asking and answering questions, giving opinions and making proposals while building on and reinforcing others' ideas, the system is working in a problem-solving mode. If communication is general, vague and ambiguous, the system is in flight from valid communication. If there is a communication pattern of attacking, blaming and complaining with con-tentious 'yes-but' and interrupting behaviour, the system is in a fight-and-compete mode (Simon and Agazarian 1967).

Groups also maintain equilibrium by requiring one member to carry the too-different difference for the group, thus creating the role of the identified patient who can be 'cured', or the scapegoat who can be attacked or extruded by the group. For example, in the early phases of a group's development (Agazarian 1994; Bennis and Shepard 1957), when underlying issues are primarily related to one's relationship to authority, the creation of the identified patient is often the group solution to managing the conflicts related to dependency, vulnerability, helplessness and the human wish to be looked after by a benevolent authority. In this form the conflicts are denied and acted out rather than explored and used as information for the development of the individuals and the group. With the creation of the scapegoat, any difference, particularly in relationship to authority, will be attacked or excluded. The tensions around complying with the *status quo*, the leader or the rules, and defying or fighting the leader and the rules will be enacted. All the communication will be directed towards the person in that role, and in both cases, the important information carried in the system role, about the system, is encapsulated and unavailable as information for the system development.

In family therapy it is now common to think in terms of treating the family as a system, and intervening in the communication pattern in the family as a whole, rather than simply treating the individual member of the family who has been elected to be the identified patient, required to carry the deviance for the whole group, and presented to the mental health system to be cured. In thinking systems this does not take away from individual responsibility for actions and their consequences, nor does it preclude treatment for individuals. It does, however, offer an additional perspective.

The theory of living human systems and systems-centred thinking provide a comprehensive systemic conceptual framework, a map and language, that can be used to describe all living human systems, the system of one, one and another, the small group, larger subgroups and the group as a whole. With systems centred concepts, methods and techniques, we have the bridge between the world of abstractions and the world of people, as well as a set of interventions and hypotheses that can be tested in the reality of human experience to facilitate change.

Living human systems and systems-centred practice

System-centred thinking provides the operational definition, methods and techniques that put into practice the theory of living human systems. Both have been developed by Dr Yvonne Agazarian over the past 30 years of thought and practice. Dr Agazarian has been influenced by the work of Kurt Lewin (1951) in his field theory, Wilfred Bion's (1961) understanding of group dynamics, von Bertalanffy's (1968) general systems theory, Shannon and Weaver's (1964) information theory, combined with a comprehensive understanding of psychodynamic principles and psychoanalytic thought, to mention a few.

The fundamental, underlying assumption in the theory of living human systems is that all living human systems have an innate and spontaneous drive towards the primary goals of survival, development and transformation, as well as the secondary goals related to environmental mastery (Agazarian 1997). Living human systems function – survive, develop and transform – through the ongoing process of discrimination and integration of differences (Agazarian 1997). How this information is organised and vectored will affect the potential development from simple to more complex, as well as the potential for more complex discriminations and integrations. As a system develops greater complexity, it also develops a greater potential to reach its goals. The state of a system at one level of the hierarchy will affect the state of the other system levels in the hierarchy.

From the first moments of life, living human systems, such as the infant and the mother, engage in a process of ebb and flow, coming together on what is similar, experiencing the frustration of differences, tolerating the frustration, integrating the difference, developing and joining again, thus creating a system that is functional for the survival and development of the system (Heard and Lake 1997). It is through this natural process that all groups of human beings come together, integrate the not-too-different differences in human experience, and create the familiar, stable, comfortable and often stereotypic 'us' with predictable norms of behaviour, rituals and established pecking-order. This can be seen when people come together around age, gender, nationality, religion, profession and ethnic or social background, to mention a few.

Living human systems close their boundaries to differences. All human beings come together on similarities and separate or split on difference. The difference will be denied, split off, projected into the comfortably un-comfortable and stereotypic 'them' when the differences are too different. Boundaries become fixed, stereotypic subgroups become polarised, individuals and groups are blamed, segregated and discriminated against. Battle-lines are formed, people on to whom the differences are projected are displaced, extruded and often attacked. These processes of managing difference may apparently ensure the survival of the system in the short run by maintaining a form of stability, but they can also inhibit or arrest development and transformation over time. When the individual lives only in their stereotypic, defended and adapted self, part of their emotional energy/information is inaccessible for the full development of the self. For the group, part of human experience is unavailable and there is a loss of breadth and depth that potentiates group complexity, flexibility and adaptability.

In as much as human beings require difference in order to continue to develop, this process of discrimination and integration means change, and potential change means conflict. Change requires managing the experience of frustration, turbulence and chaos as the system that 'was' disorganises in order to reorganise and become the system that is 'now'. It is a challenge for any individual to accept an 'unacceptable' or unfamiliar emotional experience within themselves; for a member of a couple to recognise differences in their partner; for the parent when for the first time the child responds with an emphatic 'no'; for a family when a child brings home a 'stranger' to marry; and for the nation willing to open its boundaries and attempt to integrate refugees and immigrant subgroups from cultures with differing norms.

When a difference that is too different does cross the system boundary, it will be encapsulated in an impermeable subsystem in the larger system with many potential behavioural manifestations. It is this process of denial, splitting, projecting and encapsulating differences that fuels the repetition compulsion, nonfunctional pairings or the non-functional locked-in-reciprocal-role relationships fuelled by these projective identifications. It is this process that fosters the creation of the institutionalised containing roles of identified patient; scapegoat, victim and bully, compliant and defiant role relationships to authority, and the one-up-and-one-down relationships to the self and others, sadistic and masochistic role-locks; cult leaders and followers, martyrs, heroes and isolates. These roles maintain the equilibrium of a system by containing the splits, while the system develops the capacity to integrate the differences (Agazarian 1993).

The systems-centred method and technique of functional subgrouping provides an alternative to the common ways in which living human systems manage the conflict, frustration and aggression aroused by differences that inevitably goes hand in hand with any change process. Rather than acting out or 'living in' the underlying individual or group dynamic, conflict aroused by the change process is contained. In the systems-centred approach, conflict is conceptualised as two or more different subgroups each with important information for the system as a whole. For example, any individual may have more than one feeling or experience within themselves at any given moment; excitement and fear, happiness and sadness, wanting to join a group or approach another and not wanting to join or avoid another; wanting to argue and not wanting to argue and so on. A group may have more than one set of experiences, and there may be many subgroups. For example, there may be a subgroup that wants to co-operate with the leader, a subgroup that wants simply to comply with a leader, and a subgroup that wants to defy the leader. By exploring one side of a conflict at a time, in functional subgroups, the differences can be contained in the system until the similarities in the apparently different and the differences in the apparently similar are noticed and integrated at all levels of the systems hierarchy (Agazarian 1997).

Functional role relationships and nonfunctional role-locks

From a systems-centred perspective, roles are seen as boundaried subsystems of a larger system. Each role is activated in the service of a particular goal in a context, and is expressed through recognisable constellations of behaviour. A role, like any subsystem, contains dynamic information, and functions to maintain stability in the system as a whole. Instinctively, these behaviour patterns develop early on to ensure the survival and development of the living human system. For example, the child has instinctive careseeking behaviours that engage the reciprocal caregiving behaviours in the mother, and thus a functional system is created using the resources of the system as a whole in the service of the goal (Heard and Lake 1997). In the parent/child dyadic system the goal is the survival of the child and the preservation of the species (Bowlby 1982).

Information in the family and larger social groups is transmitted through a complex pattern of social interactions. Children learn when and what to eat, how to manage fire, how to stay warm, who to turn to for comfort and protection, how to contain and channel their sexual and aggressive impulses, how to resolve conflict and how to become a responsible member of their larger community. In some cultures, the expression of emotion is encouraged, in others it is discouraged; in some the cognitive analytic aspects of the person are supported, in others they are inhibited; in some cultures anger and aggression is welcomed, and in others it is blocked; in some cultures sexual feelings are accepted, in others they are shamed. All human beings are socialised into role relationships, patterns of response to early experiences, that perpetuate the norms of the family and larger social context, and influence the way in which individuals take up their membership of more complex social groups.

When role relationships are functional, boundaries remain permeable, communication across the boundaries is a fluid give and take, the resources and information in each half of the role relationship can be discriminated and integrated, and the system as a whole can continue to develop from simple to more complex. For example, in the system of learner/teacher, when there is a supportive environment that encourages questions and exploration, both the learner and the teacher become engaged in an interactive and challenging relationship that functions for the benefit of both. The role of the teacher is to teach though giving information, and the goal of the learner is to take in and integrate the new material. With the questions and answers, the flow of information back and forth in the system can be balanced, giving both the learner and teacher the opportunity to clarify and make adjustments in the service of the goal of learning.

However, as human beings are human, we are rarely able to create or live in conditions that are completely optimal for development and transformation. In response to unfavourable environmental conditions, defensive, maladaptive or non-functional locked-in roles are formed. For example, when a teacher takes on a severely dominant, authoritarian and shaming stance in relationship to a learner there is a strong invitation into a submissive, compliant or defiant reciprocation from the learner. While this may be useful to establish order and control in a classroom, it may also inhibit the development of intellectual curiosity, creativity and autonomy in the learner.

When relationships become fixed in a particular pattern, they are described as 'role-locked'. At the heart of the role-lock is projective identification. The shape which early interactive reciprocal role relationships take will lay the foundation for later adaptive or maladaptive patterns of relating to oneself, others and the world. For example, if a child is raised to be 'seen and not heard', then the child may find it difficult to hear their own 'voice', and later become inhibited and unable to bring their 'voice' into a group, along with the valuable information they may have for themselves and the group. In the more extreme situations, where the child/parent system is physically, emotionally or psychologically abusive, the child's entire emotional world view will be coloured by their experience, and the pervasive climate of the family will permeate their perception and expectations of the larger world. The child will also develop patterns of defensive behaviours in response to the abuser that attempt to ensure survival. These will take generally one of two forms: either a submissive, passive or active compliance that can then be galvanised into a victim role fuelled by masochistic character defences, or into defiant identification with the aggressor, the role of the bully fuelled by sadistic character defences. In the case of the abuser, the experiences of helplessness, vulnerability, dependency, terror, horror, compassion and masochistic responses to the retaliatory impulse are split off and projected into another then attacked. With the abused, the murderous rage, the anger, hostility, the retaliatory impulses, sadism and aggression potentially directed out are split off and projected into another. Without intervention, defensive role relationships are repeatedly acted out with predictable and rigid behaviour. There is an ongoing pressure to seek out and re-enact with others, who take up the reciprocal, original role relationships. The identified patient will seek out a caretaker and vice versa; bully will seek out victim, victim will seek out bully; masochist will attract sadist, sadist will attract masochist. All are equally helpless in the face of the dynamics of the role relationship, until the dynamics are made explicit, explored and the similarities in the apparently different are recognised and integrated.

The meaning one gives to a particular role relationship will depend on one's perspective. The role of the identified patient will have one meaning for the individual member who has volunteered for the role, another for the members who have elected the member to contain the projections and another for the group as a whole that uses the role (Agazarian 1997). When one is able to observe and understand behaviour from the perspective of the 'role', the individual, the subgroup and the group as a whole, the members' capacity to see experience in context rather than as personalised is increased. One begins to see a larger picture, place oneself in a broader context and understand experience in a way that is different from the map and explanations from the past. This sets the stage for further data collection, reality testing and choice.

Abuse and the sadomasochistic subsystem

All human beings are born with energy and aggression. Having access to these is what makes it possible for people to set a course and move forwards on the path to a goal; one is able to fight when it is necessary to fight, flee when it is necessary to flee and protect oneself when there is real danger. It is also a fact of human life that when hurt or frustrated, human beings have a natural and primitive impulse both to be angry with and to retaliate towards the hurtful or frustrating object. We see this when a child throws a toy that will not work properly; the child or adult who fights when someone has teased or insulted them. Through the process of containment and socialisation, people learn how to manage anger, aggression and the retaliatory impulse, and channel the emotional energy into functional social behaviour.

From a system-centred perspective, abuse of the self and others can be conceptualised as the ongoing, defensive acting out of the sadomasochistic subsystem, one of many subsystems in all living human systems, which is expressed on a continuum of behaviours that can be both positive and negative, simple and complex. Levels of defensive response vary from the simpler verbal behaviours of complaining and blaming, to the more complex compliant and defiant stances in relationship to authority, one-down-and-one-up relationships to oneself and others, the masochistic and sadistic character defences, stubbornness and resistance to change, the fusion of a cult follower and despair of the isolate. The organisation of these defences can also produce a variety of symptoms ranging from anxiety, somatic symptoms, depression, tantrums, diatribes and the acting out on others or the environment with outrages and righteous indignation, as well as the more serious consequences of acting on one's masochistic and sadistic impulses.

The level of complexity of a system and the capacity of the system to discriminate and integrate at the time of the formation of the subsystem will determine both its shape and its intensity. When a child is faced with real threat before they are sufficiently developed to contain, discriminate and integrate these emotional experiences within themselves, this information will become split off from awareness and organised into either a depressive constellation of behaviours where the anger, hostility, retaliatory impulse and primary aggression is turned back in the self with masochistic defensive behaviour, or discharged and acted out on the others with active sadistic defensive behaviour.

Working with trauma

From a systems-centred perspective, trauma is seen as a system encapsulation of information that threatens to flood the system and override the process of discrimination and integration. For example, when a child instinctively expects nurturing and protection from a parent or trusted adult and instead receives physical pain, neglect or other forms of psychological abuse there is a potential flooding of the system with pain, anger, rage and retaliatory impulses, hatred and terror that must be managed. This experience of potential flooding will stimulate a defensive encapsulation of the life-force energy and the unorganised emotional experience inside a permanent and impermeable boundary within the individual. The boundary becomes a barrier around the encapsulated information, which is then defended with a full array of maladaptive behaviour. The encapsulation will then be defended with stereotypic defensive behaviour, leaving an individual or a group no choice but to act out from the pressure of the unconscious material. When this occurs, the information contained in the encapsulation is unavailable to the consciousness of the system as a whole, communication is at an unconscious level through projective identification, and the discrimination/ integration process is compromised and the potential development is inhibited. For example, when anger, rage, aggression and the retaliatory impulse have been encapsulated early in development, the person will not have access to any form of the information on anger in an adult context without re-stimulating the original flooding responses and terror experienced at the time of the trauma. This creates a particular type of problem for the therapist and patient when there has been severe trauma, for the therapeutic situation itself can be perceived as a threat in and of itself.

In the therapeutic system of the patient/therapist, the therapist must open to the similar experiences in themselves, be aware of their counter-transference, and create a containing subsystem within themselves for the unconscious, raw, primary and unorganised, projected information from the patient. The therapist must contain the experience until it can be discriminated and metabolised, and gradually reabsorbed into the patient subsystem. In this process, the therapist must struggle with the retaliatory and sadistic impulses, the murderous rage, hatred, primary aggression and the helplessness, terror, horror, the masochistic impulses, hostility, pain and grief without acting out on the impulses or taking up the invitation to engage in a repetitive and maladaptive role relationship. There is an ongoing challenge for the therapist to contain his or her own responses, as well as the material from the patient, long enough to make discriminations in the experience and metabolise the information until it takes on a form that is similar enough to be taken back into the patient system.

Treatment of an individual or group of individuals who have been severely traumatised presents some unique challenges for the therapist or mental health professional. All too often a therapist or the mental health system will address and put pressure on the maladaptive defensive behaviour of an individual. In doing so, one runs the risk of the individual experiencing the pressure as a repetition of the original trauma, and the therapist finds they are treating only the defended self of the individual, missing the authentic and primary self completely. There is the temptation to become distracted by the defensive behaviour protecting the encapsulation, as if it were the problem itself, rather than creating the conditions that gradually promote permeability in the barrier that surrounds the energy in the primary self and in the group. When boundary permeability and valid communication are re-established, the important information related to the primary self, and also the human condition, can be integrated into the system as a whole, enabling the system to resume the developmental and transformational processes.

Systems-centred methods and techniques for change

When one works from a systems-centred perspective it is understood that the symptoms, experiences, and feelings people bring in to treatment are all part of the full range of human experience, properties of all living human systems. From this perspective, experiences are legitimised, depathologised, universalised and explored. In a systems-centred treatment context blameful, attacking, complaining, argumentative and interpretive communications are discouraged, and replaced instead with clear, descriptive, building, exploratory communications. The systems-centred method of functional subgrouping creates an environment within which the different sides of a conflict can be contained in the group as a whole. Individual members can learn about themselves and others through the exploration of their experiences and conflicts in the present reality of their group life and in the company of and in attunement with others. By its nature, functional subgrouping restructures the communication in the treatment setting. The 'yes-but' of the contentious relationship is transformed into the exploration of the two subgroups reflected in the 'yes' and in the 'but'.

It is in this shift in communication patterns that individuals also experience the relief from the pressure of conflict, knowing that both sides of a conflict are legitimised and will be explored at one time or another. The communication pattern of all speaking to a leader or a deviant, the beginning of the creation of a containing role, is shifted into a functional pattern where the communication flow is within the context of the work of the member, the subgroup and the group as a whole. For example, in balancing subgroups members can explore the aspect of themselves that wants to depend and be taken care of by the leader and members, as well as the aspect of themselves that does not; they can explore the impulse to attack or scapegoat another, and the impulse to *volunteer* to be scapegoated; to explore the victim side and the victimising aspect; and can explore their masochism and sadism, to name a few.

The systems-centred method of boundarying, reduces the 'noise' in a system and fosters the appropriate permeability of boundaries (Agazarian 1997). People learn to cross boundaries in real and psychological time and space, into the reality of here-and-now experiences and away from the world of fantasy, oft-told tales of 'how hard it was', and interpretations of reality; and into the role that is appropriate to the goal of a given context (Agazarian 1997). Through the technique of defence modification (Agazarian 1997), symptoms are addressed and defensive responses are identified, explored, reduced and the experience defended against is discovered and explored. In systems-centred therapy defences are seen as restraining forces to the natural drive towards the survival, development and transformation. Restraining forces, defences, are modified in a systematic and hierarchical process. The process begins with the easier social behaviours and moves down through cognitive defences, somatic defences, depression and hostile acting out, the role-lock defences and character defences, stubbornness, and the defences against intimacy and work. One level of defence modification builds both a foundation, a floor, for the next level of work as well as a sense of mastery for the members and the group. In this way, regression and acting out is also contained and the experiences can be explored.

It is through the systems-centred method of contextualising that the concept of the observing-self system, the discriminating and integrating function in a system, is operationalised (Agazarian 1997). People begin to develop the capacity to observe themselves and others; learn what it means to contain potential subgrouping energy in their member role; and work in a subgroup to contain and explore differences. Through contextualising, people begin to be able to understand their behaviour and see themselves and others from all the levels of a system hierarchy, while learning to take up functional roles and orient their behaviour to the goals of the context. In doing this, people learn how to shift from taking their experiences 'just personally' to seeing their experience as a part of the experience in a larger environment.

Notes

1   Systems-Centred and SCT are licensed trademarks of Dr Yvonne M. Agazarian.

References

Agazarian, Y.M. (1993) *Roles in the Phases of Group Development.* Unpublished paper.

Agazarian, Y.M. (1994) 'The phases of development and the systems-centred group'. In M. Pines and V. Shermer (eds) *Ring of Fire: Primitive Object Relations and Affect in Group Psychotherapy.* London: Chapman and Hall.

Agazarian, Y.M., (1997) *Systems-Centred Therapy for Groups.* New York: Guilford Press.

Agazarian, Y.M. and Peters, R. (1981) *The Visible and Invisible Group: Two Perspectives on Group Psychotherapy and Group Process.* London: Routledge and Kegan Paul.

Bennis, W.G. and Shepherd, H.A. (1957) 'A theory of group development'. *Human Relations 9,* 4, 415–437.

Bion, W.R. (1961) *Experiences in Groups and Other Papers.* London and New York: Tavistock Publications.

Bowlby, J. (1982) *Attachment and Loss. Vol.1, Attachment.* New York: Basic Books.

Heard, D. and Lake, B. (1997) *The Challenge of Attachment for Caregiving.* London: Routledge.

Lewin, K. (1951) *Field Theory in Social Science.* New York: Harper and Row.

Miller, J.G. (1978) *Living Systems.* New York: McGraw Hill.

Shannon, C.E. and Weaver, W. (1964) *The Mathematical Theory of Communication.* Urbana: University of Illinois Press.

Simon, A. and Agazarian, Y.M. (1967) *SAVI: Sequential Analysis of Verbal Interaction.* Philadelphia: Research for Better Schools.

von Bertalanffy, L. (1968) *General Systems Theory: Foundations, Developments, Applications.* New York: Brazilier.

Whitehead, A.N. (1952) *Science and the Modern World.* New York: Macmillan Publishers.

CHAPTER 4

Is Human Nature Intrinsically Abusive?

Reflections on the Psychodynamics of Evil

Phil Mollon

There are a number of relatively obvious factors which play a part in interpersonal evil. These include: first, a history of abuse in the childhood of the perpetrator of abuse, this having given rise to an identification with the abuser (or predator); second, threats to self-esteem and the sense of self (narcissistic injuries), giving rise to attempts to repair these by bolstering a sense of power by abusing others; third, processes of projective identification, whereby unwanted aspects of the self (feelings of shame, helplessness, vulnerability, etc.) are forcibly evoked in the other. Such processes are commonplace, readily observed and understood. Still, we are left stunned by the vile acts which human beings perpetrate on one another.

George Steiner, professor of literature, comments:

> When I am confronted, via reports, pictures, personal notice, of the infliction of wanton pain on children and on animals, a despairing rage floods me. There are those who tear out the eyes of living children, who shoot children in the eyes, who beat animals across their eyes. These facts overwhelm me with desolate loathing... At the maddening centre of despair is the insistent instinct...of a broken contract. Of an appalling and specific cataclysm. In the futile scream of the child, in the mute agony of the tortured animal, sounds the 'background noise' of a horror after creation, after being torn loose from the logic and repose of nothingness. Something – how helpless language can be – has gone hideously wrong...in the presence of the beaten, raped child, of the horse or mule flogged across its eyes, I am possessed, as if by a midnight clarity, by the intuition of the Fall. Only some such happening, irretrievable to reason, can make intelligible, though always near to

unbearable, the actualities of our history on this wasted earth. (1997, pp.168–169)

Steiner takes us to the heart of the mystery of human vandalism against its own kind, even against its own soul. There appears to be a cruelty, a rage, a latent frenzy in humanity which is not explicable in terms of basic strivings for survival. Steiner writes of horror and dread – and of attacks on the eyes, the windows of vulnerability which allow us to see and be seen by others. The eyes are the most vulnerable part of the body – and here perhaps is the clue. It is an attack on vulnerability, whether perceived in the self or in the other, which drives human beings to defile one another. And if vulnerability can be forced into the other and attacked there, then we can momentarily be relieved of experiencing it ourselves. The most vulnerable human beings are young children. Who better then to serve as containers of our own hated vulnerability – and to be punished for reminding us of it?

Is the word 'evil' justified in psychological discourse? I believe that it is. When I refer to evil I have in mind a degree of malevolence which goes beyond ordinary human anger, selfishness, greed, lust, spite, envy and egocentricity. There can be something beyond these commonplace human attributes which seems to defy understanding because it seems inherently to express a hatred of life, and to involve an idealisation of this hostility to life. Not all of the abuse and exploitation which human beings perpetrate against one another merits a label of 'evil'. Most people possess some inhibitions against their potential to do harm to others, and must engage in cognitive distortions to overcome these inhibitions. Truly evil people appear to embrace and idealise their malevolence and their capacity to deceive and terrorise.

The following discussion is necessarily speculative. I write from the perspective of a psychotherapist immersed in clinical practice.

Death and the law

In our capacity to be conscious and to reflect upon our position we can experience helplessness and dread. The world can appear as if a machine, impersonal and awesome in its utter indifference to our own wishes and needs. Having the ability to discern our fate means that we are haunted, with varying degrees of consciousness, by death anxiety. This gives rise to the wish, the illusion, that death can be evaded. The unbearable quality of death anxiety is, according to the reasoning of Robert Langs (1996), the source of the pervasive attempt to evade boundaries, death being the ultimate boundary: 'There is a universal unconscious delusion in humans that a frame-breaker can defy the existential rule that life is followed by death.' (p.167).

Incest is against the law – not just against the law of certain local cultures, but fundamentally against The Law, the given constraints on our existence, almost as fundamental and unchangeable as the laws of physics which 'govern' our material world. Yet child abuse so often involves forbidden sexual relations between an adult and a child in his or her care. The grotesque and flagrant, almost boastful, abuse of power by those who abuse children in care has been vividly illustrated in many recent high profile cases in Britain. Victims of sexual abuse by their father will often describe a man who appears to assume that his family is his possession, to do as he will with; in the home he is the Law, accountable to no one. The abusive father's will and autonomy eclipse any awareness of a wider law, to which all are accountable. Sometimes the impression is that the father deliberately chose a weak-willed partner, who would not challenge his authority and who would allow him to abuse their children without interference, turning a blind eye to their pleas for her protection. In his own home, the incestuously abusive father can be god. This pattern is illustrated in an extreme form in the case of the mass murderer Fred West (Masters 1996).

The satanic signifier, perversion, psychosis and the subversion of the Law

The biblical figure of Satan epitomises the attitude of refusal to submit to the Law. Satan aspires towards omnipotence and grandiose narcissism. Full of self-deception, he is portrayed as aiming to deceive mankind. The deception is the offer of power and escape from the Law; but what is delivered is further dread. Biblically, he is portrayed as a murderer and a liar.

The 'satanic' may be considered both a state of mind and a particular signifier or rather 'anti-signifier'. Lacan's theorising (1977) draws our attention to the way in which we are constrained by language – the word as law. We cannot choose our own language, but are born into a pre-existing language, to which we must submit unless we are to be psychotic. Our desires must be communicated through words, and these must follow rules (of grammar). The use of language – symbols and signifiers – depends upon an acceptance of separation and difference. This is the tolerance of the Kleinian 'depressive position', in which loss and limitations are recognised. In rejection of the depressive position, there is a resort to defensive illusions of omnipotence; limits and boundaries are denied. As rejection of reality deepens, all limits are denied, such that all becomes equivalent. Coherent linguistic communication is then impossible since all words are homogenised and all meaning is destroyed.

This is also the domain of the psychotic part of the mind (Bion 1962) which hates reality and the pain inherent in development. The psychotic mind will fragment and expel particles of reality which would otherwise form the basis of thought. For the psychotic mind, language no longer has symbolic meaning; words become mere sounds, things to be manipulated. Psychotic hallucinatory voices are usually highly destructive – indeed, 'satanic' in their quality – as if full of hatred of life and reality. They beckon seductively towards the full psychotic break with reality, idealising this alternative realm, and, ultimately, present death as the solution. Suicide is always a potential for schizophrenic patients.

Thus the hatred of reality, boundaries and limits may result in perverse assaults on others or upon the psychotic person's own mind. Perversion, psychosis and the betrayal of children all have roots in hatred of reality and the fantasy that it can be cheated.

Identification with evil

One solution to dread is to identify with the dread; by becoming dread, the experience of dread can be avoided. An example of this process is described very clearly by Barton (1992) in a biography of the satanist Anton LaVey.

Barton offers instructions on lycanthropic metamorphosis, or 'becoming a werewolf'. She advises the satanic adventurer first to enter an area felt to be frightening, such as a lonely path, an abandoned quarry or deserted house, dressed in a manner felt to be vulnerable, with the deliberate intention of becoming as frightened as possible: 'Allow yourself to virtually shake apart with fear and if possible attain an orgasm'. Barton describes how the adventurer will then experience a strange pull back to the frightening area; this will become increasingly compelling. The second visit to the feared area will evoke even more fear. A further stage is then to don an animal mask or skin, to serve as a catalyst for the sense of transformation. Crucially, Barton states:

> When you approach the spots where you would have previously been the most frightened, allow yourself to revel in the thought of how terrifying it would be to another if they were to feel the same fear you had felt, plus the added terror with an actual manifestation of an unfamiliar and grotesque creature. In short, it is now your role to contribute to the fearsomeness of the place. (p.251)

Thus, in place of feeling afraid, one becomes fear and contributes to others' fear. A related process is described by Noyes (1997) in his discussion of masochism. By identifying and orchestrating the means of pain and control, the masochist's sense of helplessness is subverted: '[masochism] draws on stereotypes of violence and the technologies of control in order to convert them into technologies of pleasure' (p.5). He argues that masochism as an elaborated theatre of sexual pleasure was really a nineteenth-century invention, arising out of the Machine Age and its preoccupation with control and the interface of bodies and machines. There arose pressures to create a disciplined, machine-like human being, this requiring quite perverse regimes of training and control. Noyes states his thesis as follows:

> What was intended as a controlling mechanism becomes appropriated as an erotic technique. In all cases, the masochistic move is to seize upon the machinery of domination and pervert its usage, attempting to derive nothing but sexual pleasure from machines that were designed to effect the smooth running of social structures. (Noyes 1997, p.12)

Thus the threat, the inhuman machinery of control, is hijacked and transformed into the very condition of ultimate pleasure. The masochist orchestrates his own humiliation, and thereby paradoxically becomes master of his helplessness.

Are there some individuals who deal with their dread by becoming totally identified with evil, thus making evil itself their good? Here is how occultist William Gray (1990) describes the dedication to evil of serious black magicians:

> Popular ideas of Black Magicians indulging in sex-drug orgies ... are very far-fetched and incorrect indeed. It is true that such events occur in connection with Black Magical activities, but they are indulged in by the victims... Ostensible Black Magicians soaking in Satanism and wallowing in Witchcraft of the worst sort are somewhat inferior imitations of the authentic article. They are far more likely to appear as pillars of the Church whose beliefs they are betraying, staunch supporters of the society they undermine, or the most law-abiding members of the community they corrupt by cleverly converting courses of consciousness into channels likely to have the worst consequences from a cosmic viewpoint. Not a single illegal or even very immoral action in the customary sense of the word can be laid at the door of an efficient Black Magician... He is not recognisable for what he is by any ordinary kind of investigation, and his cover would stand the closest screening by the strictest security checks any human authority might devise. There is just one clue to his nature which he can never completely conceal from even moderately sensitive souls: the most terrible Inner feeling of coldness and isolation when in his presence. It is an

unmistakable feeling of abandonment and 'lostness', as if threatened by a pitiless extinction in some appallingly vast and utterly engulfing Void …an uncanny sense of chill and Inner iciness associated with the aura of intense evil… (pp.18–19)

Gray goes on to describe the attempt to abolish human vulnerability which is inherent in relationships with others: 'From an essentially evil viewpoint, any traces of compassion, affection, mercy or inclinations toward feelings for other humans would be serious defects of character…' (p.20).

Whether or not there are black magicians of the kind Gray describes, his account does illustrate how it is possible to imagine a position in which one steps out of fearing evil and instead embraces evil, becoming evil and intending evil towards others. Part of the essence of this evil would be to conceal it behind a façade of superficial goodness.

A patient who reported a background of severe ritual abuse, by parents apparently involved in some kind of satanic practices, described a family life curiously devoid of human relating. According to her account, her parents were outwardly extremely respectable, quite wealthy, and her father involved in a children's charity. But within the house there was no conversation, no laughter and no trace of affection, either between the parents or from parent to child. She described how all her potential attachments and capacity for trust were systematically attacked. She reported being sexually abused by both parents, and any toy or other object which she valued was always defiled by some perverse sexual activity. Any apparent affection appeared to be always in the service of abuse and betrayal. She was attached to her pet rabbit, but one day found it dead in its hutch, with its abdomen slit and its insides removed. As an adult she described an overwhelming and unyielding longing to die, and a view of life itself as being obscene and abusive. She did form attachments, although she perceived these as superficial and powerfully resented the tie to life inherent in having her own children. She had many fantasies of killing both herself and her family.

Thus, this patient seemed to describe how her parents had eliminated their own humanity, replacing it with an outward facsimile of respectability for public view. They had also succeeded in destroying much, although not all, of her human capacity to seek life, love and attachment.

The following words of Hitler are hung on a wall in the Nazi death camp at Auschwitz: 'I freed Germany from the stupid and degrading fallacies of conscience and morality… We will train young people before whom the world will tremble. I want young people capable of violence – imperious, relentless and cruel' (Zacharias 1994, p.68). By eliminating humanity and idealising cruelty, it is then others who will tremble.

Torture as the projection of dread

The 'solution' to ubiquitous human dread is to make the other feel it instead. This is essentially the theory of psychopathy developed by Meloy (1988), who argues that the psychopath identifies with a primal fantasy of the predator, turning others into prey. In this way, through a particular version of identification with the aggressor, the psychopath avoids feeling like a prey to the predator felt to be always lurking ready to pounce. Experiences of abuse and lack of protection in the early life of the psychopath will have pre-disposed him or her to a powerful imprint of the predator imago, exacerbating unmanageable feelings of dread.

Nietzsche, whose doctrine of the 'Superman' greatly influenced Hitler, apparently was haunted by dread. At the age of 25 he had a hallucinatory experience of a terrifying figure, communicating in 'horrifyingly inarticulate' sounds. Heller (1988) suggests that Nietzsche's vast output of writing was aimed at silencing this terrifying inarticulate personification of dread with his own stream of human words. Nietzsche's doctrine of affirmation, or his *amor fati*, advocated an attitude of transforming fate into desire – 'I wanted it thus!'. A passively experienced trauma is turned into an actively desired outcome, along the lines of a defence mechanism described particularly by George Klein (1976). Nietzsche also idealised cruelty and the exercise of power over 'one who is powerless, the voluptuous pleasure of doing evil for the pleasure of doing it, the enjoyment of violation' (1966).

Alford (1997), basing his conclusions on his systematic study of people's perception of evil, states its essence as follows:

> Evil inflicts pain, abandonment and helplessness on others, so that the evildoer will not have to experience them himself. It is that simple and that complicated. It is why torture is the paradigm of evil, master of all three terrors at once. All evil has the quality of torture, inflicting dread on another so as to escape it oneself. (p.52)

Alford also describes the way that evil is felt to be 'nothing', but a nothing so terrifying in its formless and wordless absence that we are driven to try to give it shape and focus. The threat is not only that our lives are nothing, but that we shall become nothing and that it does not matter, because nothing matters and all our efforts at meaning are futile. There is nothing to hold us and we are left with confusion.

Successful art is both a creation of something, giving shape, texture and rhythm to the formless nothing – a precarious achievement which Alford describes as 'the narrowest of victories over evil' – and at the same time is a submission to reality. Alford sees creativity and evil as terribly close. He points out that torture is frequently spoken of in the imagery and language of drama – thus, the place of torture is called the 'production room' in the Philippines, the 'cinema room' in South Vietnam, and the 'blue-lit stage' in Chile. Alford comments:

> In fact, torture is the reverse of drama. In drama, a transformed larger world is acted out on a small stage. In torture, the world is reduced to the body of the victim ... It reduces the world to the human body. Rather than non-body symbolising body, body comes to symbolise a world reduced to its bare essentials, pain and power...the body becomes the world, it is the world. (1997, pp.103–104)

Some women who have been sexually abused in childhood cut themselves and report considerable pleasure and relief in this activity. What appears to be achieved is the creation of a private chamber of torture in which the abused woman is mistress of her own abuse, an essentially private theatre in which her own omnipotence, to punish her own body, prevails unchallenged. Significantly, the woman who cuts herself will often feel that this is a preferable alternative to cutting others. Thus she overcomes her helplessness temporarily by identifying with the abuser while refraining from becoming an abuser to others – a triumph of feminine altruism!

The wish to torture others reflects the failure of any creative response to dread. The epitome of the inability to be creative is represented by Milton's figure of Satan in *Paradise Lost*. Suffused with narcissism, refusing dependence, his trajectory fuelled by envy and rage, Satan can only create destruction and chaos – Pandemonium – and inflict this on others. Guilt, reparation and sanity is banished from his consciousness.

Projective annihilation of others

This is an interpersonal dynamic which first became clear to me in the context of the debates about recovered memory and false memory. I became aware that quite often therapists and memory researchers whose views were at odds with those of the false memory societies would be repeatedly misrepresented or misquoted in reports in both the professional and popular media. It was as if certain views, beliefs and therapeutic practices were attributed to these people despite the availability of evidence to the contrary. An active process of projective attribution appears to take place in which there is a knowing annihilation of the person's actual identity. A therapist who questions the prevailing rhetoric of 'false memory syndrome' may be forcefully defined as a 'recovered memory therapist' and therefore an abuser. Having noticed this pattern, it then occurred to me that, not uncommonly, with patients who have been sexually abused in childhood, I have the experience of being misheard, misrepresented or misquoted. It seems to me that this dynamic of projective annihilation of identity is something that all sexually abused children experience – they are perceived as other than they are – and this dynamic is then enacted at various levels and in various forms in debates about abuse.

Projective annihilation is wilful. It depends upon knowing, at some level, that projective annihilation is taking place. It is the knowledge that the person's actual identity is being assaulted that provides the sadistic pleasure and triumph. The Nazi projective annihilation of the Jews was the prelude to their physical annihilation. They were to be the scapegoat – but a scapegoat can only function as such if it is actually innocent. Projective annihilation masquerades as mere projection, but is actually much more sinister. The power that is exercised here is that of defining the other – it is as if the perpetrator were saying, 'You will be as I decide you are and as I define you, regardless of what you may have thought you are'. It may be that projective annihilation is a marker of potential abuse.

Cosmic dread

Some questions are legitimate to ask, but we may only be able to grope with imperfect mental tools towards answers. No doubt one dimension of profound apprehension lies in our original, helpless dependence on the mother – and, indeed, this may well be one deep emotional current driving much violence and hatred against women. Could there be an even more fundamental and obscure genesis, an ultimate source of the dread which drives our potential for evil acts towards one another – a ground of disquiet which lies beyond our human lineage? We are not designers, initiators or managers of our own life and death (although some contemporary New Age philosophies may assert that we do 'choose' our moment of conception). Whether we construe our ultimate maker as nature or God, a full encounter with our helpless dependence on the Cosmic Other will evoke either awe or a constellation of dread, terror and overwhelming humiliation.

Often foreclosed from psychoanalytic consideration (Eigen 1998), this dimension of mental life was addressed by Bion (1970) in his concept of the relationship with ultimate reality – 'the terrifying unknown' – to which he gave the notation 'O'. Our apprehension of 'O' is facilitated as we move away from the distraction of sense-based experience. 'O' is the ultimate truth, existing regardless of our perception. It is that which we cannot change. Because 'ultimate reality' is immune to our attempts to manipulate it, we must accept it or flee from it. A patient screamed at her abusive and pervasively dishonest father, 'You can say what you like but you can't change the truth!'. She meant that no matter how he lied and attempted to distort his own perception, the truth of what he had done to her could not be changed;

moreover, he would have to face the reality of his death, which also could not be escaped.

The attempt to escape 'O' is associated with the Kleinian paranoid-schizoid position. In this constellation there is a prevalence of mental defences based around illusions of omnipotence. Disturbing aspects of internal and external reality, including feelings of guilt, are avoided. In this position, the person (whether child or adult) denies their potential awareness of dependence. The person is in flight from reality, including the reality of dependence. When a paranoid-schizoid position prevails, the response to a potential encounter with 'O' will be dread and humiliation. Bion quotes Coleridge's *Rime of the Ancient Mariner* as a representation of this state of mind:

> Like one that on a lonesome road
> Doth walk in fear and dread;
> And having once turned round walks on,
> And turns no more his head;
> Because he knows a frightful fiend
> Doth close behind him tread.

This dread constellation is normally so profoundly intolerable that human beings banish it from awareness much of the time. Nevertheless, it may lurk in the mind – the 'frightful fiend' – prompting continual attempts at defence. This ubiquitous cosmic dread may combine with specific experiences of helplessness and humiliation to create the dynamics of interpersonal evil.

Cosmic dread, when not transmuted into awe and an acceptance of dependence on an ultimately unknowable 'O', may give rise to destructive envy (of creation) and an aggressive atheism. Such atheism asserts that it 'knows' what cannot be known. More extreme developments may result in 'satanic' states of mind. These are characterised by: a search for, and idealisation of, power; an exalting of self; envious attacks on goodness; perversion, involving a reversal of good and bad and a twisting of truth; eroticisation of pain; envious denigration of loving intercourse. The biblical account of Satan depicts a being who, having attempted to exalt himself above his maker, is banished from the source of goodness and life; then like a mad beast caged in darkness, he seeks in rage and envy, to devour the light that is given to others. While I am not here making any metaphysical statement, I consider that the satanic theme does provide a representation of an aspect of the fearsome existential trauma which human beings face in the encounter with the unknowable ultimate reality.

What else may be driving the cycle of abuse, perpetrated by the children of the children of the children of the originally abused? Violence and trauma in one generation begets violence in the next. But where did it start? We do know that early trauma can be represented and re-enacted in behaviour, completely without conscious awareness (Mollon 1998); indeed Freyd (1996) quotes an astonishing Swedish study which found that trauma at birth was associated not only with suicide but also with the means of suicide chosen. Could this principle apply on a vast scale, to some trauma which has saturated humankind? Quite often these days we hear of scientific conjectures that there was at least one catastrophic event in the history of the earth which resulted in the rapid destruction of much of life. I am reminded of Steiner's intuition, with which I started this chapter, of 'an appalling and specific cataclysm ... the "background noise" of a horror after creation'. Given liberty by the stupifying magnitude of the question, I will venture a most speculative hypothesis. Is it possible, I wonder, that there was in the far distant past some unspeakable and utterly shattering apocalyptic experience, the 'background noise' of which is still reverberating through the generations, an implicit memory perpetrated and preserved through repeated interpersonal trauma, never possible to recall, but still causing unbearable misery day after day in every corner of the globe? And might we be compelled, unconsciously and collectively, to bring about actively a devastation that was originally suffered passively, once we have acquired the technology to do so?

References

Alford, C.F. (1997) *What Evil Means To Us.* New York: Cornell University Press.

Barton, B. (1992) *The Secret Life of a Satanist.* London: Mondo.

Bion, W.R. (1962) *Learning from Experience.* In *Seven Servants* (1977). New York: Jason Aronson Inc..

Bion, W.R. (1970) *Attention and Interpretation.* London: Tavistock.

Bion, W.R. (1992) *Cogitations.* London: Karnac Books.

Britton, R., Feldman, M. and O'Shaughnessy, E. (1988) *The Oedipus Complex Today: Clinical Implications.* London: Karnac Books.

Eigen, M. (1998) *The Psychoanalytic Mystic.* London: Free Association Books.

Freyd, J.J. (1996) *Betrayal Trauma: The Logic of Forgetting Childhood Abuse.* Cambridge, Massachusetts: Harvard University Press.

Gray, W.G. (1990) *Attainment Through Magic.* Minnesota: Llewellyn Publications.

Grunberger, B. (1971) *Narcissism.* New York: International Universities Press.

Heller, E. (1988) *The Importance of Nietzsche.* Chicago: University of Chicago Press.

Klein, G. (1976) *Psychoanalytic Theory: An Exploration of Essentials.* New York: International Universities Press, Inc..

Lacan, J. (1977) *Écrits.* London: Tavistock.

Langs, R. (1996) *The Evolution of the Emotion-Processing Mind.* London: Karnac Books.

Langs, R. (1997) *Death Anxiety and Clinical Practice.* London: Karnac Books.

Masters, B. (1996) *She Must Have Known: The Trial of Rosemary West.* London: Doubleday.

McDougall, J. (1980) *Plea for a Measure of Abnormality.* New York: International Universities Press.

Meloy, J.R. (1988) *The Psychopathic Mind: Origins, Dynamics and Treatment.* New York: Jason Aronson, Inc..

Mollon, P. (1993) *The Fragile Self: The Structure of Narcissistic Disturbance.* London: Whurr Publishers.

Mollon, P. (1998) *Remembering Trauma: A Psychotherapist's Guide to Memory and Illusion.* Chichester: John Wiley and Sons.

Nietzsche, F. (1966) *Basic Writings of Nietzsche* (Trans. Kaufmann). New York: Modern Library.

Noyes, J. (1997) *The Mastery of Submission. Inventions of Masochism.* New York: Cornell University Press.

Steiner, G. (1997) *Errata: An Examined Life.* London: Weidenfield and Nicolson.

Zacharias, R. (1995) *Can Man Live Without God?* Milton Keynes: Nelson Word.

SECTION II

The Social, Cultural and Political Contexts of Abuse

CHAPTER 5

Exile

Paradoxes of Loss and Creativity

Nancy Caro Hollander

Since the mid-nineteenth century, millions of people have migrated to Latin America, choosing to endure multiple losses in the anticipation that life in the 'New World' would offer a positive alternative to the limited opportunities in their countries of origin. Chilean poet Gabriela Mistral (1971) captures the complex but essentially optimistic essence of this kind of migration:

> I am two. One looks back
> The other turns to the sea
> The nape of my neck seethes with good-byes
> And my breast with yearning.

However, in the past several decades, another migration has taken place as hundreds of thousands of Latin Americans have been forced from their homelands into exile in a flight from the terrors of political repression.

Exile is a specific kind of migration, without yearning and shorn of hope and aspiration. Refugees are journeying *from*, not *towards*, something, and what they leave behind nags at the psyche, wedding it to the past. My city – Los Angeles – is a city of exiles, where since the late 1970s large numbers of Central Americans have been forced into a continual exodus from civil war and military dictatorship. They bring with them a legacy of social trauma that infuses their experience of arrival in the US with a profound pessimism about the past and about what lies ahead in the uncharted future. Exiled poet Etelvina Astrada describes the conditions that have driven her and other refugees from their countries:

The hordes came,
Created darkness
And terror,
the hunt,
goon squads
kidnappings
walls
interrogations
olive green
transfers
extermination camps
voltages
water torture
saws
gaffs
mutilations...
and thus the dead were created,
the dead
dead
in the streets, on rooftops, in factories
in schools, offices, on doorsteps
in churches, in jungles, in the sea
in barracks, in prisons. (Partnoy 1988, pp.231–332)

For those refugees who had been involved in struggles that challenged the inequitable political and economic structures of their countries, the dead included not only family members, neighbours, and fellow workers, but comrades and the hopes and aspirations of their progressive political projects as well. I met many of them in Los Angeles, where I worked in the solidarity movements with refugees from El Salvador, Nicaragua and Guatemala. These exiles struggled with the dual demands of metabolising a history of suffering and loss and of confronting the painful challenge of assimilating into a new society, one whose human rights movement embraced them but whose government colluded in the perpetration of the political repression that continued to disappear, torture and murder loved ones left behind.

This Central American diaspora of the 1980s was but the most recent chapter of a story begun several decades earlier, when multitudes of refugees fled repressive military regimes throughout South America. One of the most brutal of these dictatorships took power in Argentina in 1976, launching a seven-year-long Dirty War against its own citizens. I had lived in Buenos Aires for four years prior to the coup, and since I could not return, I sought continuity with my life there through contact with refugee colleagues and friends scattered in the far-flung metropolises of Madrid, Paris, Mexico City, Rio and Havana.

By 1983 I began to work with a group of Argentine, Chilean and Uruguayan psychoanalyst and psychologist exiles residing in Mexico City. They represent a tradition within Latin American psychoanalysis that has striven to understand the unconscious roots of mental anguish and the economic roots of social violence. With them I studied the psycho-social vicissitudes of exile and grappled with understanding the paradoxes of loss and creativity that had emerged as a variegated pattern characterising refugees from South and Central American state terror. These Latin American psychoanalysts argued that other disciplines – such as radical political theory, political economy, and sociology – needed to be integrated with psycho-analytic theory in order to explain the human behaviour manifested in inequitable economic structures, political violence and psycho-social trauma.

I have chosen to weave the experiences and insights of several of my Latin American colleagues throughout this narrative because, like clinical case material, they illustrate significant aspects of this psycho-social phen-omenon. (All direct quotes are taken from the author's book, *Love in a Time of Hate: Liberation Psychology in Latin America* (1997).) The first is Marie Langer, an Austrian Jew who emigrated to Argentina following her participation in the Spanish Civil War as a member of an International Medical Brigade. She was one of the six founders of the Argentine Psychoanalytic Association in 1942, and in the next several decades was recognised internationally for her work on female psycho-sexual development. By the late 1960s Langer had become a major figure in the movement to integrate a socially conscious psychoanalysis with the politically progressive mass movements in Argentina during that period. Even before the military coup, the right-wing death squad, the Triple A, was disappearing and murdering people who were active in the struggles for social justice and economic equity. In 1974, when Marie Langer's name appeared on its death list, she was forced to flee her adopted country for Mexico City, where she lived in exile until her death in 1987.

The second colleague whose experiences and insights serve to highlight my analysis of exile is Marcelo Viñar, the son of an immigrant family in Uruguay, who became a prominent psychoanalyst in the mid-1960s, and a participant in that country's mass movement for radical social change. Like hundreds of other mental health professionals, Viñar was imprisoned because of his progressive politics. He was tortured repeatedly before his wife, psychoanalyst Maren Ulriksen de Viñar, could successfully wage an international campaign for his release. Some months later, the military launched a coup, and the Viñars and their two small children were forced to flee Uruguay. They emigrated to Paris, where they lived in exile for over a decade.

Langer and the Viñars, along with many other refugee analysts, observe and study their own psychological responses to exile, as well as those of their refugee patients, in order to analyse the obstacles that often prevent exiled individuals from overcoming this catastrophic crisis. They themselves exemplify the possibility of utilising this profound life disruption in the service of expanding the self and enhancing one's creative and symbolic capacities.

Exile is perhaps the human experience in adulthood that most closely recapitulates the infant's experience of attachment, separation and loss. Certainly it highlights in bold relief the fact that attachment is an invariant that continues throughout the various stages of life. While early patterns of attachment behaviour may alter; attachment, loss and mourning do not cease to be central aspects of human experience during the entire life-cycle. In adults, separation of any kind, but especially caused by exile, may remobilise experiences with attachment and loss from early life, along with the unconscious meanings ascribed to these aspects of interpersonal connection. Often the crisis generated by exile reveals in adulthood the legacy of 'pathological attachments and the pathologies of detachment' (Hamilton 1982, p.5), whose origins lie in childhood. But problematic attachment and separation patterns may also emerge in adulthood in response to the severe impingements of a profoundly disordered social environment, such as the persecutory culture of fear designed by state terror from which Latin American refugees fled into exile (Lira and Castillo 1991).

I find it useful to divide this exploration of exile into its various phases in order to explain the different stressors attendant upon each point in the process (Grinberg and Grinberg 1989). I take note first of the pre-migratory period and then turn to an examination of the subsequent phases of adaptation to the new environment following migration. From my perspective, taking into account the pre-migratory conditions of exile in Latin America allows us to see what is often invisible, namely that refugees come to exile already under extreme duress, having experienced the ongoing and cumulative trauma perpetrated by politically repressive regimes. They have lived in an environment permeated by threat, including political intimidation that was often random in its selection of victims.

In 1981 I interviewed a group of Argentine women who had been living in exile in Madrid. In a kind of testimonial, each described the conditions which led her to flee the country. One woman told of having to abandon her children to relatives as she frantically scrambled to elude the military forces stalking her from house to house. Another revealed how, as she walked along the wide avenues of Buenos Aires, she was kidnapped by hooded men leaping out at her from one of the infamous unmarked Ford Falcons used by the right-wing death squads, only to be left for dead on a remote country road after being tortured and raped in one of the government's clandestine concentration camps. Another spoke of having been sought by military forces who burst into her home without a warrant, found only her younger brother, kidnapped him instead, and then tortured and killed him for no reason in particular. Yet another told of being forced to watch while prison guards tortured her elderly parents in front of her in order to secure information she did not have. And one reported how, when her pregnant daughter suddenly vanished, clearly the victim of a military or death-squad action, her endless searches for her daughter and grandchild had yielded nothing but a gaping hole in her heart. Many told of having narrowly escaped similar fates before they were forced to flee into the uncertainty and dislocation of exile. Such traumategenic experiences were not unique to this group of exiles, but had been the fate of tens of thousands of their compatriots, many not lucky enough to have survived.

Given this kind of assault on the general population, life under state terror exacts a profound psychological price. It collapses the ability of individuals to sustain what Winnicott (1971) suggests is essential to the true-self personality: the successful negotiation of the tension between connection and autonomy, the encounter of one's own unique perspective rather than compliance with the demands of others, and the achievement of a healthy balance between entitlement and an acknowledgment of others and external reality. The culture of fear creates a transitional space whose persecutory political and social symbols – analogous to Winnicott's transitional objects – subvert the true-self personality by demanding unquestioned loyalty and the abolition of independent and critical thought. This is a transitional space whose hegemonic discourse reflects primitive divisions of the world into good and bad, loyalists and 'subversives', and whose central symbols – the disappeared, the tortured and the murdered – represent a threat to the individual's sense of going-on-being. In this context, the 'culture-mother' (Women's Therapy Centre Institute 1994, p.18), like Winnicott's actual mother, fails in its facilitation of the adult individual's capacity to sustain the developmental achievement of a creative tension between autonomy and interdependence. Instead, it induces a regressive pull to primitive states of mind.

The terrorist state's culture of fear and the threat of annihilation it imposes on the psyche make inevitable the development of the false-self as a strategy for survival. Adaptation to authoritarian rule requires extreme personal vigilance, entailing the conscious creation of a false-self and the masking of the true-self that hates and fears the very social order with which the individual citizen appears to identify. This dissociation of significant aspects of the self also takes place at an unconscious level, as many individuals come to disavow their deeply held belief systems and political commitments in the wish to escape the annihilation fantasies induced by the threatening external environment.

Melanie Klein's concept of primitive paranoid-schizoid defensive splitting captures the nature of psychic reality in the culture of fear (Segal 1973). It helps to explain the complex dialectical relationship between the intrusive impingements of the environment and the individual's unconscious manoeuvres to manage the violence and uncontained aggression unleashed by the cultural symbols and rituals of political repression. The terrorist state splits society into victimisers, victims, and bystanders (witnesses/participants), and those who occupy the position of bystander live under constant threat and anticipatory anxiety of suddenly and without warning being thrust into the victim position. The culture's thoroughgoing violence forces individuals back into paranoid-schizoid defences, such as splitting, projective identification, magical omnipotent denial and idealisation. Moreover, the ability to distinguish between internal and external sources of persecutory anxiety is compromised (Hollander 1997b).

Attachment theorists have emphasised that psychological safety and stability depend on the adult's capacity to seek and sustain close reliable ties with other individuals (Bloom 1997, pp.84–85). However, in authoritarian societies it is precisely the social bonds that are the principal target of those in power. State terror assures that people come to trust no one, to confide in no one, to seek self-preservation in isolation. Contact with others endangers. A kind of paranoid character disorder comes to look like a national trait. Individual behaviour in the terrorist state is characterised by silence, inexpressiveness, inhibition and self-censorship, all of which result in depoliticisation. Hannah Arendt (1958) has argued that authoritarian regimes base themselves on loneliness, on the destruction of a sense of community, on the conviction that one is in jeopardy even with one's peers. The children of adults who live in such an environment often manifest fearful attachments that are a reflection of their parents' traumatised states (Main and Hesse 1990).

Attachment, loss and mourning in adults as well as in children are deeply affected by a persecutory environment and become salient issues in all phases of the experience of exile. The first loss suffered by refugees occurs in the premigratory period and entails the loss of life as it once was before it was twisted and reshaped by the repressive state. The persecutory culture of fear exists within the society – the transitional space – whose objects the individual is deeply attached to and identified with. People, things, places, language, culture, climate, occupational and professional identity, and economic or social milieu are all associated with memories and intense affect. As state terror re-configures all aspects of interpersonal and intrapsychic reality, old objects become saturated with new significance. Once familiar and comforting, they have now also become anxiety-laden and terrifying. The experience of loss is inescapable. Chilean psychologist Elizabeth Lira expresses it this way:

> The loss is one of an idea of national identity centered around shared values and beliefs. The past seems lost within all the losses, symbolised by the dead, the disappeared, the tortured bodies, the broken hopes, the elimination of a future, the exiles, the disenchantment with politics. Each individual grapples with all of the losses, employing a variety of defences to mourn less or to completely evade the necessary mourning. (Hollander 1997a, p.112)

Indeed, within the ongoing and repeated trauma of the culture of fear, healthy mourning for the losses suffered is impossible. A kind of 'frozen grief' predominates (Langer 1983–5; Polento and Braun 1985), whose characteristics are, as Bowlby suggests in speaking of disordered mourning, like a festering wound that refuses to heal (1980, p.22). Arrested mourning results in a continuing and nostalgic search for the lost objects, a devaluation of current objects, and a general inhibition of interest in all aspects of life in the present.

The actual migration constitutes the second set of losses experienced by refugees, who often flee into exile so precipitously that they are robbed of the ritual of saying goodbye to loved ones and of the opportunity to take familiar belongings into an unknown future. In such cases, the link to the past and continuity with familiar objects – people, places and things – are abruptly severed, along with the tie to parts of the self that are left behind as well. This forcible uprooting is experienced as a profound rupture that threatens the stable functioning of the psyche. Although the moment of arrival in the new country may be filled with relief, a sense of foreboding and a feeling of abandonment are also present. Poet Carolyn Forché (1994) depicts the lonely moment between past and future when the present does not yet exist:

> ...time slowed, then reversed until memory

> Held her, able to go neither forward nor back

> They were alone where once hundreds of thousands lived. (p.55)

Already in a state of psychic vulnerability, arrival in the new environment of exile is a life crisis for the refugee. It provokes emotional reactions comparable to the helplessness and futility felt by a baby or young child bereft of the containing environment that is needed to help manage frustration, anxiety, loneliness and fears of separation. Suddenly cut off from one's homeland, with its familiar and predictable language, cultural signifiers, and social relations, the exile feels like a defenceless child. Under state terror, to be sure, the familiar containing environment had become a paradoxical one, whose transitional objects terrorised as well as comforted.

But, as Bowlby and others have suggested, the familiar is a fundamentally important parameter determining identification as well as attachment behaviour. Bowlby notes that people often prefer negative environments and objects that are familiar to unfamiliar environments and objects that are positive or potentially positive (Hamilton, pp.162–163). This paradox is often seen in the exile's attitude towards the new environment. Sooner or later the exile must find a way to deal with the fact that while it is relieving to be free from the persecutory environment of home, there is a profound sense of dread in the face of the strange and new features of the host society.

Bowlby's observations of fear-arousing situations for infants and young children is similar to what is observed in refugees. Like the children Bowlby studied who showed fear of strangers, strange objects, strange people or familiar people in strange guise and strange surroundings (1973, pp.100–105), refugees are often fearful of the strangeness of their new environments. While the hypervigilance noted in refugees' reactions has often been interpreted as a symptom of post-traumatic stress syndrome, it is also a sign of the ego's regression in response to the anxiety-provoking features of the unknown. Moreover, like young children who, when separated from their mothers, are anxious because they cannot measure the passage of time and thus determine when their mothers will reappear (Bowlby 1973, p.3) the exile has no idea if or when the return home will be possible. This lack of temporal parameters compromises the refugee's capacity to cope.

Typically, in order to deal with this threatened regression and to defend against extreme anxiety and helplessness, the exile resorts to primitive defences such as splitting of object and self-representations. Splitting affects the ways the homeland and the new society are experienced. The splits oscillate over time, moving back and forth between an idealisation of the country of origin and a devaluation of the new culture and vice versa. Internal representations of the self alternate as well between an idealisation of one's identity in the past and a devaluation of one's status as an exile and then the reverse. For example, manic overcompensation in the form of an exaggerated enthusiasm about the new environment is frequently the first, and fragile, line of defence. Conversely, the exile cannot adapt to his/her new situation and so devalues and then rejects its culture, language and people, and nostalgically idealises the country left behind. The vulnerability that provokes the reliance on splitting characteristic of immigrants in general who have moved from the mother country (symbiotic mother) to a new land (mother of separation) has been interpreted as being like the vulnerability of the rapprochement subphase toddler in the separation-differentiation from mother, and that of the transiently regressed adolescent (Akhtar 1995, pp.1058–1059).

Marie Langer describes her initial reaction to her forced departure from Buenos Aires and her arrival in Mexico City to take up life in exile:

> It's hard to describe. It's a daunting experience, arriving in a country and knowing from the moment you step foot on *tierra firme* that you are not here out of choice. Even more importantly, you have no idea how long your stay will be or if you'll ever return home. You do not know what to feel, and in the beginning, you oscillate from relief and excitement to fear and trepidation. At first you try to deny the gravity of the situation. Many of us plunged into a kind of defensive euphoria, playing at being tourists: 'Did you see how lovely Mexico City is?' 'Did you visit the pyramids – what beauty!' But our startled reactions to the sudden sound of an ambulance's siren or the backfire of a car punctured the fiction that we were here on a planned vacation. We had come from a nightmare, and at night, when we slept, for months that nightmare persecuted us. (Hollander 1997a)

Marie recalls the impact of newspaper reports that detailed ongoing atrocities in Argentina:

> There were the typical scenes… An activist would comment anxiously to a compañero, 'Did you read that Haroldo went crazy under torture?' A distraught mother would tell a friend, 'You know the child my little girl plays with? Her mother just learned that they killed her husband.' And I will never forget the evening when, during a meeting of a Freud study group, one of the female participants answered the phone, listened quietly to the voice on the other end, gasped, and began to scream 'No, no… My god, they've killed my brother'. (Hollander 1997a)

As exiles repeatedly heard about the horrors at home, the denial associated with the first phase of 'happy tourism' shifted to a kind of depersonalisation. Marie recalls that:

> …many friends and patients described 'out-of-body' experiences, observing from outside themselves as they went through the motions of daily life. And then there were the sudden attacks of self-reproach: one would walk the streets, thinking, 'What am I doing here? What is this city?' Or sit on the edge of the bed staring at the cheap ceramics

purchased a day earlier with wild enthusiasm, thinking 'But am I crazy? How did it occur to me to come here? I have to go back right away.' And then there were the slim hopes stimulated by rumors: 'Did you hear about the demonstration in Cordoba?' And, 'What do you think…if the strike in Rosario continues a little more, will it be possible to return?' (Hollander 1997a)

Survivor guilt is prominent in an exile population. Most refugees suffer pangs of guilt for having fled and survived when others could or would not. As an exiled colleague of Langer's describes it, 'You could hear the self-recrimination in the frequently uttered exclamation, "We are all deserters."' Marie's self-reproach was dramatic:

> I remember my worst moment in exile. It was the night I went to a solidarity meeting of the Chileans to hear President Salvador Allende's sister, Laura, speak. She told about how she had been taken prisoner because she hadn't left Chile after the coup. Since she was from such a prominent family, she wasn't tortured, but one night they threw her, naked and blindfolded, on a pile of tortured bodies for the night. When she was released, she continued her activism in the opposition struggle. I went home that evening and collapsed on my bed in tears. I felt a terrible desperation because, unlike Laura, I had abandoned my commitments. I had not continued to struggle, and in Argentina people were suffering and dying. (Hollander 1997a)

In the process of adaptation to the new environment, even refugees who achieve relative professional success may continue to experience disconcerting anxieties and depressive affect. Langer, for example, was almost immediately offered a post at the university, was welcomed to a prominent place among her Mexican and South American psychoanalytic colleagues, and was able to develop a burgeoning private practice. But at times she obsessed about her departure from Argentina: had she left too soon? Could she have withstood torture had she been abducted by the Triple A? Would she have been killed had she stayed? It was hard to escape the doubts and the deep sadness of feeling adrift, cut off from her friends and the movement in Argentina. The only palliative seemed to be her participation in the solidarity movement where she felt she could provide a valuable service to those left behind. 'We all need our self-esteem, and my self-esteem was related to my ego ideal, which I felt I had betrayed by abandoning the struggle and my compañeros in Argentina' (Hollander 1997a).

Besides survivor guilt, a variety of other symptoms appear frequently among an exile population. Latin American mental health professionals suggest that while it is tempting to interpret refugees' symptoms as evidence of post-traumatic stress disorder, it should be noted that exile itself represents an additional and ongoing traumategenic situation. There is, in other words, nothing 'post-' about refugees' traumatised state of mind and the symptoms which manifest it. These include disorientation, confusion, acute self-doubt, nightmares, insomnia, the inability to focus, depression, anxieties, paranoia, and dissociation. Some individuals become accident prone, as if re-enacting the experience of being attacked by a harmful environment. Often psychological conflict is displaced on to the body, and psychosomatic problems emerge (Bloom 1997, p.46). Higher rates of fatal diseases, including cancer, are found among exiles in comparison to the general population.

An important predictor of the exile's capacity to work through the unconscious conflicts represented in these symptoms depends on whether or not the individual has confidence that he/she can rely on the availability of positive attachment objects in the new environment. This capacity in turn depends on the individual's having introjected a good object in infancy and early life (Klein 1932). As Bowlby conceives of it, the individual's 'working models of the world and themselves in it', constructed within the matrix of early attachment figures, frames the way '[they] perceive events, forecast the future, and construct [their] plans' (1973, p.203). The ability of the refugee to work through the vicissitudes of pre-migratory and migratory trauma are, in Bowlby's schema, related to the extent to which their 'working model' is composed of actual and introjected reliable and positive attachment figures as well as a positive sense of their own acceptability in the eyes of the attachment figures.

A particularly interesting somatic (symbolic, yet unsymbolised) disturbance frequently encountered among refugees is related to digestive symptoms. They cannot tolerate the new culture's cuisine, as if its foods – symbolic of the new experience in general – cannot be 'digested' (Grinberg and Grinberg 1984, p.94). Marcelo Viñar recalls how, after living in Paris for a time, he received a letter from a friend whose philosophical advice hinged on eating as a metaphor for 'taking in' the experience of exile: 'I am happy to hear that you are in the process of putting down roots,' he wrote. 'One cannot continue to nibble a little at each thing, as if in passing. It's necessary to sit down at the table and partake of what life offers us.' His friend went on to advise Marcelo to embrace his current situation: 'One must weave a kind of density and thickness around what is provisional in life,' he counselled. 'You and I have lived in a country that will never be the same. Something else will exist in the future. Other youth will make their history, others who will not be us. We must learn to live this grim existence that fate has dealt us. If not, when a new day dawns, we'll be asleep or daydreaming' (Viñar and Viñar 1993, p.87).

His friend wisely suggests that Marcelo recognise and accept the change in his life circumstances. He advises Marcelo to grieve the loss of his country and his own place in it, his own past identity, so as to get on with his life in the present and be able to make a psychological investment in the new situation and in new social relations. However, in contrast to Langer's exile in Mexico, whose physical proximity and cultural similarity with Argentina permitted some sense of continuity, Marcelo's experience of exile was deeply influenced by the fact that he and Maren were refugees on a far-off continent with few links to home. Although they had chosen France as their country of exile because French colleagues had been willing to help them find a professional niche outside Uruguay, they could not foresee the devastating impact of trying to survive in a society whose culture, language and people they knew nothing about. 'Imprisonment and exile were the two most difficult experiences in my life,' Marcelo recalls, continuing:

> There were two especially painful aspects of exile. The first was what I call a narcissistic collapse, like a kind of undoing of the self. And the second was the loss of security, which is related to my origins. I was a child of the middle class, with very protective parents who supported my growth and development. As an adult, I built a successful professional life. I was *somebody* – Dr So-and-so – who was recognised as a specific individual with a specific status in the social group. The disruption of this 'place in the world', which I had taken for granted before it was suddenly ripped away from me in my late 30s, was devastating. We have written about how exile in this sense is a violent and decentering rupture, especially for those who have fulfilled a social role highly valued by themselves and the community. One loses the many-sided mirror by which one has created and nurtured one's own image, one's public persona, one's celebrity, if you will. In exile, what one once was no longer exists. No one knows one, no one recognises one. One finds oneself in a new scene from an unfamiliar play with unknown actors. This is a true identity crisis. (Hollander 1997a)

The anguish of the first years was exacerbated by having to learn to speak and read French, not a word of which either of them had known. Marcelo extrapolates from his own struggles to learn French that one's relationship to language is of key significance in the exile experience. His view echoes what has been noted elsewhere about the psychological impact on immigrants who are obliged as adults to learn an entirely new language. The adult must tolerate re-experiencing the initial helplessness of children as they struggle to acquire language, which is the bridge to becoming an active participant in the social world. One's place in the world is ordered, after all, through the linguistic system of verbal and visual signifiers. Some adult immigrants learn the new language fairly easily, perhaps as a defensive manoeuvre to cope with their feelings of impotence and exclusion from social interaction. Others resist learning the new language, which may reflect their guilt for having abandoned their parents' tongue.

> Each language has a code of customs, laws, relations, and to speak in a language implies the knowledge of more than words, but other things as well about the culture that produces it. One might be able to understand the dictionary and at the same time not know much at all. Alienation comes from not being able to interpret the meaning of words, but even more importantly, the meaning of gestures, references, and social relations. It is an unforgettable experience... (Hollander 1997a)

When, after living in France for almost a year, Marcelo began to treat his first patient – an Argentine – they were able to conduct the analysis in Spanish. This experience represented for him the return to a state of thinking. 'It gave me immense pleasure and joy to once again use my full mental capacities'.

Language can become a wedge between parent and child in the exile family. The fact that children acquire the new language more easily than their parents often leads to mutual bad feelings. Marcelo remembers how in his own childhood the Uruguayans laughed at his immigrant parents and their friends for their '*gringo*' way of speaking Spanish. In France he relived the experience, only this time, as the inept adult who was ostracised. He recalls how his younger son would feel ashamed of him when he spoke French, and that he would pull at his trouser leg and beg him not to speak. Sometimes his children spoke French rapidly together so he and Maren could not understand them, or they spoke French between themselves and Spanish to their parents, as if in doing so, they could establish an authority relation that countermanded the customary one between the generations.

Not only in their facility with language, but in their relative ease in absorbing the codes of the host culture, exiled children often seem like traitors to their parents' ideals. The jealousy and envy of the older generation may turn into an accusatory and condemning attitude towards their children. Marcelo points out that '...there is often lots of conflict between parents and their adolescent kids. The parents have a nostalgic discourse about the *patria*, the ideals, the revolution. The children say, "we were too young, it wasn't our life"'.

Marcelo believes exile taught him something valuable about his children:

> With respect to the theme of political repression, for example, I remember growing up in my small Uruguayan town and being taught about the Holocaust and the oppression of Jews. But we kids would walk

the streets and there was no anti-Semitism, no one pursuing the Jews. I think this discourse about the Jewish people, persecuted and forced to be immigrants, functioned in the children to secure either submission to our parents' discourse or rebellion and family misunderstandings. Now it was my turn to be a foreigner, a minority, and to demand that my children recognise and hold alive the memory of why we were exiles. I realised later that I wanted them to sustain in their minds an identification with my generation's values and struggles, with the revolutionaries who had been repressed. And they, poor things, saw nothing of this in Paris and sought only successful adaptation to their new world. Their parents' nostalgia could only create a powerful familial breach. (Hollander 1997a)

The family in general, the Viñars have argued, suffers many pressures in exile and is forced to play a contradictory role. On the one hand, it provides the context in which its members work through the mourning process, in which the threatened and vulnerable identity of each can be experienced as having survived the crisis. On the other, it is the stage upon which all of the aggression that cannot be expressed elsewhere is dramatically enacted:

The family bears the mark of the social catastrophe. In place of the mutual support that would facilitate cohesion, miscommunication and isolation are often paradoxically unleashed among its members, dissolving the illusion that they might recover from the magnitude of being forcibly uprooted from their country, helpless to defend themselves. Each detail, each small frustration, intensifies the enormity of the loss. It is manifested in the explosions of aggression between husband and wife, parents and children, and within old friendships and even the exile community itself. (Hollander 1997a)

Like any life-crisis, exile represents a transitional period, one that has various potential outcomes. Deprivation and loss may chronically undermine mental health, as the Viñars describe, or else create the possibility for growth. Exile can potentially endanger or empower. Some exiles find it difficult or impossible to overcome internal and external obstacles to adjustment, and they have psychological and physical symptoms that reflect and maintain the vicissitudes of the crisis. Others are able to overcome the initial depressive and anxious responses, which then only temporarily compromise the psychic structure, and work through the mourning process related to lost loved ones and lost aspects of the self. Their resilience represents a positive use of the crisis of exile for the further development of creative and integrative capacities. A kind of psychic rebirth may then take place, leading to the emergence of a new and hybrid identity (Ahktar 1976).

In order for this psychic rebirth to occur, a working through of the splitting between idealisation and devaluation of objects and parts of the self is required. All good and all bad objects related to the past and the present, to the country of origin and the new culture, to the 'old' self and the 'new' self need to be integrated and replaced by whole object and whole self representations. The refugee must also elaborate the traumatic experience of having known firsthand the extent of the human capacity to systematically enact violence towards other human beings, so that faith in love over hate can be rebuilt. The working through of this process enables the refugee to accept reality and to increase the possibility for successful engagement with work and social relations in the present. This achievement is mirrored in the refugee's relationship to language and to the growing ability to accept the different developmental aspects of self that are expressed through one's native (mother) tongue and the language (of separation-individuation) acquired in exile. The ability to mourn that which has been lost or left behind, as Marcelo Viñar's friend advised him, prepares the way for the growth of the refugee's capacity for mutuality: the recognition of, gratitude towards, and concern for the good that characterises aspects of past and present life. The exile's success depends on the ability to use the new environment as a transitional space whose objects are not only increasingly felt as facilitators of the emerging differentiated self, but as sources that potentiate creativity and rejuvenation. Experienced in this way, the transitional objects of the new society – its literature, music, foods, work possibilities, natural environment, customs and mores – can be used psychologically to enhance the capacity for curiosity, pleasure and play. The splitting is then overcome through the evolution of an enlivened integrated personality.

Each exile's journey is unique. For example, Marcelo and Maren Viñar reacted differently from one another to the vicissitudes of exile. Marcelo fell into a depressive nostalgia about the life he had been forced to abandon. 'Five years after we arrived,' he comments ruefully, 'suddenly one spring day, with the tree-lined streets ablaze with colour, I realised that Paris is a beautiful city! I felt so resentful that Maren was enjoying it. For some time already, she had been going to museums and feeding her aesthetic sensibilities, while I still walked around in a grey fog'.

Maren says:

> For me, becoming an exile didn't devalue me. I do not know if this is related to gender roles, but I'm convinced I was helped by my conviction that I had to continue functioning as the wife, the mother, keeping everything and everyone together. I couldn't have a narcissistic crisis with a baby just learning to walk! The children forced me to keep going, they were like a prohibition against having a breakdown! The first year

and a half were really terrible. Things didn't improve. I couldn't get work, and the unpredictability seemed as if it would last forever. Conditions in Uruguay worsened, so there was little hope of an alternative. Finally the moment arrived when I told myself, 'I have to stay here, I have to adapt, this is my life'. And so I began, easier and sooner than Marcelo, to enjoy aspects of being in Europe in the heart of such extraordinary culture. (Hollander 1997a)

For both the Viñars in Paris and Marie Langer in Mexico City, adaptation to exile was facilitated by their ability to sustain a modicum of psychological safety and stability through their participation in the solidarity movement. There they sought and sustained reliable ties with other Latin American compatriots who bore the same wounds. For Marie, work in the solidarity movement had special meaning because it permitted her to maintain continuity with the politics she had been forced to leave behind and thus, as she puts it, with her ego ideal. She and her colleagues organised the Argentine Mental Health Workers in Mexico in order to develop a programme of therapeutic assistance to adult and child refugees from all the dictatorships of the Southern Cone and Central America. 'The solidarity work was extremely important to all of us,' Marie stresses. 'It helped us as much as it did those who received our assistance. Our ability to recuperate, to whatever degree possible, the victims – the enemies – of the military dictatorships gave us back important aspects of our lost political project as well as our self-esteem'.

Postscript: Going home – a new exile

When the military governments in the Southern Cone gave way to popular pressures for a return to democratic rule, exiles were faced with the difficult decision of whether or not to return to their countries. By 1983, following the return of constitutional rule to Argentina, Marie Langer chose to remain in Mexico. She was busily involved in the most exciting project of her life. Reflecting an astounding and youthful vitality at the age of 73, Marie was co-ordinating the efforts of a team of 12 psychoanalysts, psychiatrists and psychologists who resided in Mexico City and travelled on a rotating basis for ten days of each month to Nicaragua. There they aided the new revolutionary government of the Sandinistas to construct that country's first national mental health care system. Marie and her colleagues were now able to transition from the treatment of the victims of state terror to the construction of a mental health care system in a country whose state held values that were consonant with their own.

Marie and her colleagues trained a variety of professionals in Nicaragua who provided direct health and educational services to the citizens of that country. They elaborated strategies for the adaptation of psychoanalytic concepts and treatment models to the social and economic conditions of extreme underdevelopment, which Marie referred to as 'psychoanalysis without the couch' (Hollander 1997a, pp.167–180). To Marie, this work represented the final integration of important aspects of her identity, which she explained in this way: 'I realised on my second trip to Nicaragua what the experience is for me. I realised that there I am not old nor young… I am atemporal…and I live it as if the Spanish Republic…the old republic, had won, and I am collaborating in the reconstruction…it is…a continuity…and finally, and suddenly, I am there' (Hollander 1985, pp.77–78). Marie Langer made exile the ultimate synthesis of her life.

In contrast, with the return of democracy to Uruguay, in spite of the expanded horizons exile had come to represent for the Viñars, after much deliberation they finally opted to return to their country. Commenting on the psychological significance of this decision, Marcelo recalls:

> Very soon after we arrived in Paris, Maren and I wrote about being strangers in a strange land. The sensation of being lost is horrible. Once you've been a stranger, a foreigner, you always carry this somewhere inside. It never goes away. One is irreversibly a stranger. One never returns to the nest, to one's home, one's homeland. Nor to the illusion of completeness. That is lost forever. What remains is a rupture between the individual and his links, and there is always, forever, something lacking. (Hollander 1997a)

The Viñars have written about the significance of returning from exile, of going home again.

> It's complicated [asserts Maren]. In the final analysis, we developed many connections in France and strong ties to the French people. I also had many women friends there. To return home means that you break this link, you destroy the world you've constructed. I still do not know to this day how we could do it. I feel sometimes more intensely the rupture entailed in coming back than the original rupture of forced exile. The exile was obligatory, this return was chosen. Marcelo wanted to be here, but it was a difficult decision for me to make. And it took me five years to feel good about being back in Uruguay. [Marcelo adds:] In reality, it's not a return. It's another departure. [Maren agrees:] Yes, it's going back to begin again. One goes back to Uruguay. But Uruguay is another country. Those who stayed are no longer those you left, and you are no longer

who you were when you went away. In the final analysis, one does not go back, one actually goes away again. (Hollander 1997a)

The Viñars evoke the melancholic aspects of the return from exile. Theirs is a recognition that the achievement of a psychological synthesis is best understood as a lifelong goal. As returning exiles, the Viñars must work through another crisis so that a new integrated identity can be achieved. Their willingness to go home, despite their subjective experience of rupture and the repetitive losses entailed, reflects their ability to tolerate the pain involved in this ongoing process of growth.

How can we explain their courage? Bowlby might suggest that it is the product of early good and positive attachment experience through which they develop a sturdiness to negotiate even the most dramatic challenges of adult experience. We see evidence of this resilience in many of the exiles from Latin America who, in spite of the extraordinary brutalities they have suffered, sustain a profound connection to community and an optimistic belief in the ultimate goodness of human beings. Nowhere is this more poignantly expressed than in Guatemalan poet Rene Castillo's work. Before returning from exile to his country, where he was captured by the military forces, tortured and burned alive, he wrote this about the paradox of loss and creativity:

When the enthusiasm
of our time
is recounted
for those
yet to be born,
but who announce themselves
with a kinder face,
we will come out winners,
we who have suffered most.

To be ahead
of one's time
is to suffer much.
But it is beautiful to love the world
with the eyes
of those still to be born.

And splendid
to know oneself already victorious
when everything around
is still so cold, so dark. (Forché 1993, pp.606–607)

References

Akhtar, S. (1995) 'A third individuation: Immigration, identity, and the psychoanalytic process'. *Journal of the American Psychoanalytic Association 4*, 1051–1083.

Arendt, H. (1958) *The Origins of Totalitarianism.* Cleveland: World Publishing.

Bloom, S. (1997) *Creating Sanctuary: Towards the Evolution of Sane Societies.* New York: Routledge.

Bowlby, J. (1969) *Attachment and Loss. Vol. I. Attachment.* New York: Basic Books.

Bowlby, J. (1973) *Attachment and Loss. Vol. II. Separation.* New York: Basic Books.

Bowlby, J. (1980) *Attachment and Loss. Vol. III. Loss.* New York: Basic Books.

Forché, C. (1993) *Against Forgetting: Twentieth Century Poetry of Witness.* New York: W.W. Norton and Co.

Forché, C. (1993) *The Angel of History.* New York: Harper Perennial/Newcastle: Bloodaxe Books.

Grinberg, L. and Grinberg, R. (1984) *Migration and Exile.* New Haven: Yale University Press.

Hamilton, V. (1982) *Narcissus and Oedipus: The Children of Psychoanalysis.* London: Karnac Books.

Hollander, N. (1985) 'Marie Langer: Psychoanalysis in the service of the people'. *PsychCritique 1*, 1, 67–79.

Hollander, N. (1994) (ed. and trans.) M. Langer, *Motherhood and Sexuality.* New York: Guildford Publications.

Hollander, N. (1997a) *Love in a Time of Hate: Liberation Psychology in Latin America.* New Brunswick: Rutgers University Press.

Hollander, N. (1997b) The experience of internal persecution and its relation to external reality. A paper delivered at the San Francisco Psycho-Analytic Society and Institute, 2 November 1997.

Klein, M. (1932) *The Psycho-Analysis of Children.* London: The Hogarth Press.

Lira, E. and C. (1991) M. Isabel, *Psicologia de la amenaza politica e del miedo.* Santiago, Chile: ILAS.

Mistral, G. (1971) *Selected Poems of Gabriela Mistral.* Translated by Doris Dana. Baltimore: John Hopkins University Press.

Partnoy, A. (ed) (1988) *You Can't Drown the Fire: Latin American Women Writing in Exile.* Pittsburgh: Cleis Press.

Polento, M.L. and Braun, J. (1985) 'La desaparicion: Su repercusion en el indiviuo y en la sociedad'. *Revista de Psicoanálisis 42*, 1391–1397.

Segal, H. (1973) *Introduction to the Work of Melanie Klein.* London: The Hogarth Press.

Viñar, M. and Viñar, M. (1993) *Fracturas de memoria: Crónicas para una memoria por venir.* Montevideo, Uruguay: Ediciones Trilce.

Winnicott, D.W. (1958) *'Transitional objects and transitional phenomena.' Through Paediatrics to Psycho-Analysis.* New York: Basic Books.

CHAPTER 6

Abuse in Religious Institutions

An Exploration of the Psycho-social Dynamics in the Irish Context

Una McCluskey

Some traumas are so horrific that it takes many years, sometimes centuries, to begin to talk about them. The famine is one such event in the history of the Irish people. It is only now, 150 years later, that the events can be discussed and studied, its causes and impact digested. The extermination of millions of Jews, Poles, Gypsies and homosexuals by the German government 50 years ago is one such other. Some episodes in the history of a country are more shameful to reveal than others. This is especially true if the blame has to be located in one's own backyard, one's own territory, or within the inner circle of one's highest ideals. The recent accounts by the victims of abuse by religious personnel in Ireland has created massive turbulence, shame and guilt for many sections of Irish society because they challenge such ideals: the ideal of religious life, unconditional caregiving and spiritual love.

That children were abused by religious personnel is beyond dispute[1] (Parkinson 1977).[2] It is also true that some witnesses to the abuse were more visible and more present than others. Some witnesses did not actually see the abuse taking place, but knew that it was. Others genuinely did not know, but for all the community, whatever their level of participation in the abusive events, their responses are complex and distressing. When eventually the silence around abuse is broken so publicly that a society can no longer maintain that it did not happen, then all sections of that society need to face the reality of the abuse and ask questions about the dynamics that contributed to the development and maintenance of the abusive situation in the first place.

This chapter is mainly about abuse perpetrated by members of religious orders on children delivered into their care by parents or grandparents too poor to care for the children themselves, or who were not in a position for physical, emotional and psychological reasons to provide adequate parenting. The context of the abuse raises issues to do with power and gender, as well as issues to do with group dynamics – both in the larger culture of Irish society at that time, as well as the smaller culture of the religious community that facilitated and allowed the abuse of others too vulnerable to retaliate or defend themselves in a meaningful way. It also raises issues about the way a society perceives and responds to the emotional, intellectual and physical needs of children, and whether attuning to children's feelings and responding empathically is seen as something that is to be cultivated in adults who are in a parenting role or not. Critical to this is whether the society as a whole has a shared belief that children are not seriously affected by their experiences of care during their early years.

The purpose of this chapter is first, to locate the social context in which the abuse took place, addressing briefly the economic conditions, the relationship between church and state in matters concerning family form and functioning, and consequently the role of the church in making welfare provision; second, to place the abuse of children by religious personnel in Ireland alongside the abuse of children in secular residential care in the UK and draw attention to some of the structural issues in society that allow children to be abused and adults to condone such abuse; and, third, to discuss the nature of cultural values which support abuse.

Ireland in the 1940s and 1950s

Until the 1970s, in Ireland the clergy had power and control over the main institutions of health, education and social welfare.[3] Most of the schools, hospitals, children's homes, orphanages and adoption agencies were under the control of the diocese or the control of religious orders, and under the management of individual priests and nuns and the religious communities to which they belonged. The church had access to every aspect of people's lives, and was in a position to rule its congregation by fear and shame. Members of the congregation who were known to the local priest to be 'in sin' could be and were (contrary to the guidance of the church hierarchy) refused Communion in full view of their friends, neighbours and townspeople. In some parishes, the amount of money handed over by each member of the congregation for the upkeep of priest and church was read out from the pulpit during all Sunday masses twice a year, thus locating everyone in terms of their position in the class hierarchy, and in terms of their support (or otherwise) for the church. The church had an expert knowledge of the power of shame and humiliation as controlling and motivational forces.

The constitution of the Republic of Ireland (1937) upheld

> ...the family as the natural primary and fundamental unit group of Society, and as a moral institution possessing inalienable and impre-scriptible rights, antecedent and superior to all positive law. In particular, the State recognises that by her life within the home, woman gives to the state a support without which the common good cannot be achieved. The state shall therefore, endeavour to ensure that mothers shall not be obliged by economic necessity to engage in labour to the neglect of their duties in the home. No law shall be enacted providing for the grant of a dissolution of marriage (Article 41).[4]

In addition, abortion in Ireland was prohibited by ss 58 and 59 of the Offences Against the Person Act 1861. A referendum was held in the Republic of Ireland in 1983 which confirmed the right to life of the unborn child [article 40.3.3 Irish Constitution]. It was an offence for a pregnant woman to attempt to procure a miscarriage, or to help a woman to do so. Social attitudes in Ireland towards pregnancy outside marriage right up until the 1970s were very harsh and unforgiving. There was no organised social provision designed to support a woman who wished to keep and rear her child on her own. Women who found themselves pregnant outside marriage had three choices: first, to go to England, have the baby and put it up for adoption or fostering; second, to go to England and have a termination; or third, to have the baby at home in Ireland, keep it or have it adopted. Unless the woman came from fairly wealthy circumstances and had the support of her family, the third option was the worst of all: to be a pregnant woman, without money, without the support of family and friends in Ireland any time until the late 1970s. The consequences of being pregnant in this situation are almost unimaginable. Frank McCourt's (1996) autobiography *Angela's Ashes* vividly depicts the lot of poor people in Ireland in the 1940s, living without any state provision. The picture he paints is not an exaggerated one, and continued much as described into the 1970s, when social policy legislation was updated in the form of various acts in relation to marriage, children and employment.

In the 1940s and 1950s, pregnant women were forced through destitution to apply to be taken in by the nearest religious institution which catered for unmarried mothers. There they were expected to take part in the work of the institution prior to the birth of the baby, and to give two years' work in lieu of services received after the child was born. They were therefore essentially imprisoned in the convent for two years following the birth of the baby. In fact they were free to leave, they had committed no crime punishable by the law of the land, but this would rarely have occurred to any other than the supremely confident and self-assured. In the eyes of the church, they were guilty of very serious wrong doing, and they found themselves in the paradoxical situation of requiring help and assistance from the very dispensers of such canonical views.

Relationship between church and state in health and social care

Health care in Ireland until 1972 was available under the provisions of the old British Poor Law national health insurance scheme. It is incredible to think that the role of the church in matters of health and social care was so great that there was no independent ministry for health until the mid-1940s. Responsibility for health provision was under the control of the Catholic hierarchy, and in Dublin, the capital of Ireland, that meant under the control of the archbishop. When in 1947 the government brought forward a Health Bill, proposing among other things that children be required to submit themselves for school medical examinations, and to curb the right of parents not to send their children to primary school, this was attacked by the opposition and by the Catholic hierarchy as unnecessary interference by the state in matters concerning the family. When, one year later, the minister for health, Dr Noel Browne, tried to extend the no-means-test principle (established under the Health Act 1947, primarily to deal with the treatment and spread of tuberculosis) to the health care of mothers and children, he was bitterly opposed by the Irish Medical Association – which considered the scheme to represent the 'socialisation of medicine' (Browne 1986, p.151) – and by the archbishop of Dublin. The church's role according to the archbishop at that time was 'to determine and to control the social attitudes of the family in the Republic, especially in the delicate matters of maternity and sexuality' (Browne 1986, p.151). On 6 September 1947 the Catholic hierarchy sent a letter privately to the Taoiseach's (prime minister's) office in which they expressed their disapproval of the new Health Act 1947 and its free, no-means-test, proposals. The letter stated:

> ...that for the State, under the Act, to empower the public authority to provide for the health of all children, and to treat their ailments, and to educate women in regard to health, and to provide them with gynaecological services, was directly and entirely contrary to Catholic social teaching, the rights of the family, the rights of the church in education, and the rights of the medical profession, and of voluntary institutions. (1986, p.153)

The 'mother-and-child-scheme' proposed by Browne aimed to provide full free medical care before, during and after childbirth. There was to be an entirely free family doctor/medical-consultant service, and if need be free GP and hospital care for all children up to the age of 16. Visits to the home by the midwife were also to be free. On 10 October 1950 Browne was summoned to attend the Bishop's Palace in Dublin to discuss his mother-and-child scheme. He was then read out a letter outlining the Catholic hierarchy's opposition to his health scheme for women and children (Browne 1986, p.159). A couple of quotes suffice to convey the attitude of church to state at that time: 'If adopted in law they would constitute a ready made instrument for future totalitarian aggression'; and, 'It may help indigent or neglectful parents; it may not deprive 90 per cent of parents of their rights because of 10 per cent necessitous or negligent parents.' Following the reading of the letter, the Archbishop of Dublin, Dr McQuaid apparently asked the minister why it was necessary to go to so much trouble and expense simply to provide a free health service for the ten per cent necessitous poor. Browne pointed out it was not ten per cent who were in such a position in Ireland at that time, but 30 per cent. The church's attitude to the vulnerable and to those in poverty is clearly visible from the whole interchange.

The scheme was never implemented; the cabinet supported the views of the hierarchy, the minister for health was forced to resign six months later in April 1951. The government was dissolved a short time later and a general election was called for 30 May 1951. This incident is critical for under-standing the situation that poor, ill, vulnerable, pregnant unmarried women found themselves in Ireland at that time, with only the church to care for them.[5] It must be understood that the 'primary purpose of social provision for the Catholic church was to disseminate and safeguard the faith, not to combat social inequality or reform society' (Fahey 1998, p.415).

The secular context

Just as the children were placed sometimes in a hostile environment, the religious institutions themselves existed within the environment of the country as a whole which at that time had no child-care service, no system of state-run social services departments, and no state help whatsoever in the provision of alternative care for children who could no longer live with their parents. The state's attitude to such children was to some extent to sweep the problem under the carpet and leave it to the religious orders to sort out.[6] What could not be expelled to Britain, in the form of unwanted pregnant mothers, could be cared for out of sight by the nuns and brothers.

Ireland was not unique in its desire to export social problems. Barnados and other major child-care agencies exported children from Britain to Canada and Australia as late as the 1960s. What is particular to Ireland is the fact that to be pregnant out of wedlock was not only a social disgrace reflecting badly on the woman's family of origin, but sinful. To a lesser extent this was the social attitude in Britain as well, though flourishing a decade or so earlier. It was compounded in Ireland by the fact that these children were then cared for by religious men and women.

To be abused mentally, emotionally, physically and, as we know, sometimes sexually by people of 'high moral standards' places a unique strain on the emotional defences of the children in question. Felicity de Zulueta, in her book *From Pain to Violence* (1993), describes the physiological as well as the psychological effect of abuse on children. The effects are particularly severe when the physical, emotional or sexual abuse takes place in the context of caregiving relationships on which the child must rely for their survival. Bowlby (1988) describes the psychological mechanism of defensive exclusion which is involved in keeping knowledge of the trauma at bay, including full knowledge of the perpetrators of the trauma. This has severe consequences for the child in terms of their cognitive and emotional development and their capacity to make and sustain supportive companionable relationships in later life. Research by Crittenden (1995) on traumatised children, writing within the field of attachment theory, would support the idea that these children are very likely to become disorganised in relation to attachment figures. To be abused by one's attachment figure, the person one needs to support one's very physical survival, is not merely frightening, it is terrifying.

Abuse in religious and secular institutions

Evidence that the Catholic church is not unique in its attitude and behaviour towards the care of vulnerable children is to be seen from the many inquiries into abuse in children's homes in the UK which have taken place over the past couple of decades.[7] One of the most important inquiries was the Leicestershire inquiry (1992) following the conviction of Frank Beck, officer in charge of three children's homes between 1973 and 1986, 'on 17 counts involving both sexual abuse and physical assault' (p.235).

From his review of the literature and his own research into the child-care system, particularly his interviews with children who have been through the care system (1986, 1990, 1992), Stein (1993) identifies four different and distinctive types of abuse. First, *sanctioned abuse*, which Stein implies are known practices, not secret, that are likely to have the support of the employing authority, of senior professionals in disciplines other than social work, (such as psychiatry and psychology), of referring authorities and of persons consulting to the residential institutions. The practices are likely to be based on notions of human growth and development and possibly inspired by reading or experiences of applied psychoanalytic theory (Stein refers to the 'regression therapy' used by Frank Beck). Second, *institutional abuse*, defined as 'the chronic failure of much of residential care (as well as some forms of substitute care) despite the commitment and caring of most of its largely untrained and poorly paid workforce. Third, *systematic abuse*, defined as 'the organised emotional, physical or sexual abuse (or some combination of these) of numbers of children in care by members of staff or adults over a period of time. Fourth, *individual abuse*, defined as generally involving one member of staff abusing one or more young persons physically or sexually, or both. Stein's work is salutary because not only does he locate abuse in the context of gender, power, social class, ethnicity and hierarchy; but in identifying the different types of abuse, he locates the practice of abusing children in the formalised 'care system', within the social structures and practices which support these institutions explicitly or implicitly.

Personal accounts of the abuse suffered

It would be both wrong and inaccurate to suggest that it was or is only members of religious orders who abuse children, or that a substantial number of priests have paedophilic tendencies or are active paedophiles. Because of Ireland's unique cultural, historical and political position, attitudes to children that were dominant in the society as a whole when acted out in relation to children who were in substitute care were acted on by members of Irish society who commanded high status and social respect. The fact that the child-rearing practices were likely to be little different to those pertaining in the society as a whole (though there were aspects to providing child care in religious communities discussed in the next section which would have influenced the level of warmth, companionship and delight that children being reared in a religious community would have experienced and enjoyed) have made it doubly difficult for those who experienced abuse or who observed the abuse to speak out against it.

Our increased willingness as a society to accept that some adults, if not a substantial number, do inflict pain on children (see Chapter 12) has made it possible for more and more people to come forward and describe their experiences. For the last ten years or more we have been hearing about the atrocious abuse of children by priests and nuns, the providers of non-statutory and voluntary care. The Catholic church in Australia, the US and Canada has paid millions of pounds in settling compensation claims.

Images of the nuns involved in cruel and sadistic behaviour towards children in their care have been dominant in the *Irish Times*, as have images of priests proven to be involved in the sexual abuse of children. What has got to be of immense interest and concern to all of us is the silence which surrounded these actions and behaviours, which took place in children's homes in the 1950s. It took place in full view of children who were not themselves resident in the orphanages and 'industrial schools' (a name emanating from the Poor Law 1865) run by these nuns, but who attended the day schools run by these same nuns and attended by these same 'orphans' or 'industrial children', as they were called by the nuns. It also took place in full view of the parents of these day pupils, and the residents of the local towns who could hear what was going on in summer time through the open windows of the schoolrooms. This was not secret abuse.

The nature of the abuse revealed by residents in these convents and orphanages is set out in a television programme written by Christine Buckely called 'Dear Daughter', shown on Irish television in 1997, which described the regime in Goldenbridge orphanage in Dublin in the 1950s and 60s. The abuse took the form of starvation, isolation, being locked in cupboards for hours, beatings, scaldings with boiling water, shaming by asking children to display their soiled underwear, and humiliations in connection with bed-wetting. A similar documentary programme was screened on Australian television in 1998, describing the abuse carried out in orphanages run by the Sisters of Mercy nuns. An article in the *Irish Times* (30 April 1998) described the spokeswoman (a nun) who was responding on behalf of the Sisters of Mercy orphanages, likening the practice of locking a child in a cupboard for the afternoon as equivalent to sending a naughty child to its room. What is extraordinary is her complete lack of empathy for the child. Apparently, by the time the programme was screened the order had issued a general apology.

In 1998, Channel 4 screened the documentary 'Witness: Sex in a Cold Climate', about physical and sexual abuse in the Magdalene asylums in Ireland in the 1940s. The programme's helpline was inundated with calls from women who had either experienced similar situations to the four women described in the programme, or were ringing to see how they might trace lost relatives.[8] An article in the *Irish Times* the day following the television programme quoted a Ms Paula Snyder, support services organiser for viewers of Channel 4, as saying:

> ...many of the callers said they had been beaten and abused when they were in Magdalene institutions and Catholic boarding-schools in Britain and Ireland. There was a lot of bitterness and a lot of the callers were very angry. Even the most experienced advisers who have worked on

helplines after programmes on child abuse said that it was the most
upsetting thing they had done. (*Irish Times*, 19 March 1998)

Patrick Parkinson (1997), in a remarkable book written from a Christian
point of view and directed to practising Christians and members of religious
orders, gives a chilling account of the multinatured layers of complicity that
supported the abuse of children by adult religious men and women in
Australia. The account of 'Robert' (pp. 140–143), placed in an orphanage in
the charge of nuns at birth illustrates this. 'Robert' was sodomised by a priest
from the age of 11. He told one older boy, who was sympathetic, and he told
the nuns. He was beaten severely; they did not confront the priest. When the
priest went overseas for a few months the nuns would not let 'Robert' go to
Confession to another priest. Parkinson describes 'Robert' soiling himself
having been subjected to sodomy, and then being punished for this by the
nuns by having to stand naked in front of the other boys with his dirty sheets
around his head. On one occasion a nun rubbed his faeces in his face and in to
his mouth.

Evidence that abusive practices were ill thought of by some in authority in
religious life is provided by research carried out by Fintan O'Toole. Writing
in the *Irish Times* (3 April 1998), O'Toole describes how as long ago as 1861
the then superior general of the Christian Brothers, Brother Michael Riordan
sent a circular to all his members on a subject of so painful a nature 'we prefer
to throw a veil over its naked deformity…the resort by those unable to win
the trust of their pupils to the humiliating alternative of enforcing submission
by coercive measures'. In the 1930s the superior general, Brother J. P.
Noonan, decided that corporal punishment ought to be entirely outlawed,
and suggested that as long as it was allowed it could and would lead to abuse.
O'Toole quotes another superior of the order in the 1920s, a Brother Patrick
Hennessy, writing: 'the fondling of boys, the laying of hands upon them, in
any way, is contrary to the rules of modesty and decidedly dangerous… Such
things should not occur'.[9]

Dynamics of authority and responsibility
in closed religious communities

The victimisation of children took place within closed religious communities
that had changed very little since they had been established in the last
century for the relief of the poor. These institutions were on the whole
established by Irish Catholic women or their counterparts in France. They
were formed between 1860 and 1880 and had houses in Canada, the US and
Australia. They tended on the whole not to be self-governing but accountable

to local bishops. They differed from their colleagues in the monastic life who tended to be self-governing.[10]

The structural nature of accountability and the relationship with authority that these orders fostered is an important consideration in trying to understand how such notorious sadism could go unchecked by members of the community themselves. What we know is that some nuns were responsible for vicious acts against the children. We are also told by survivor children that 'some of the nuns were nice'. So, some nuns, witness to the events under discussion, did not themselves participate and we may assume from the accounts quoted earlier referring to the writing of the three principals of the Christian Brothers, did not condone what was going on. Why did these religious women remain silent and do nothing? Why did specific individuals not seek each other out as allies in their condemnation of these actions and try to change the system they lived within?

Superiors in religious life worked hard at engendering high levels of personal responsibility and guilt in the members of their order. Intellectual differences or differences of any sort expressed by a member of one of these religious orders could be perceived as the expression of personal pride, a quality in the individual that was not appreciated by the community as a whole or by religious training and formation. In this, religious orders had the support of the host culture, which also supported obedience to authority at the expense of understanding or responding with attunement and empathy towards children's feelings, intentions and actions.

Alice Miller (1983) provides a cogent analysis of the roots of violence towards children in the views and attitudes conveyed down the generations. These attitudes consist in seeing children as basically evil and in need of correction and discipline; potential monsters who will rule one's life unless controlled and made to do one's will. Miller's research revealed that it was commonly held in the seventeenth and eighteenth centuries that a child's will should be broken by the age of two, and she quotes from an essay on the 'Education and Instruction of Children,' written in 1748, to make her point. I will quote briefly from that source to illustrate:

> One of the advantages of these early years is that then force and compulsion can be used. Over the years children forget everything that happened to them in early childhood. If their wills can be broken at this time, they will never remember afterwards that they had a will, and for this very reason the severity that is required will not have any serious consequences. (Sulzer 1748)

We now know that this is totally untrue. What happens to children in the first two years of life and how they are responded to by their caregiver has enormous implications for their future health and wellbeing, including social and intellectual competence and their capacity to make and sustain emotional bonds (Ainsworth 1978, 1991; Bowlby 1969, 1973, 1979, 1980, 1988; Bretherton 1995; Crittenden 1995; Fonagy 1999; Grossmann et al. 1988; Heard and Lake 1997; Main 1995; Stern 1985). But as Miller points out, and as Bowlby (1988) and Vas Dias (Chapter 10, above) confirm, what happens preverbally is much more difficult to retrieve later on, especially if one has been terrified by the person on whom one has depended for survival and if one's experiences have been subject to distortion by one's caregiver and witness. One develops not only an inner silence, as described by Vas Dias, but an inability to get at the experiences that lie at the core of one's being because the words given to them at the time and subsequently repeated by one's caregivers bear no resemblance to the actual facts of one's experience.

Adults who were brought up in this system of child-rearing and who subsequently entered convents where the ethos was uniformity and conformity to a higher authority would be unlikely to have the strength of character to stand out against an abusive system even if they could have recognised it as such. Individual nuns were encouraged to see faults in themselves and others as faults to do with the self. Shame and humiliation were encouraged as necessary correctives to an independent, assertive and confident spirit. The natural expression of anger as a result of misunderstanding or injustice was suppressed. In such a system the relationship between parts of the self and the relationship between self and other would be dominated by the need to manage anger in ways that did not disrupt the functioning of the system as a whole. In terms of managing the self, this requires suppressing both the experience of anger and its expression. Where it could be expressed by those nuns, priests and brothers unable to manage this level of containment was in relation to the children in their care. One can see how for some religious personnel, managing the wilfulness of the children and breaking their spirit for the good of their soul by inflicting on them all the shameful and humiliating practices they themselves submitted to could be an unprocessed and unrecognised response to the many layers of abuse they had experienced themselves.

The members of the religious orders who took on the care of the children had renounced family life, sexuality and intimacy. The attachment needs of children for affection, intimacy, love and acceptance must have presented these adults with particular challenges and activated unconscious and dissociated parts of themselves. These willing or unwilling caregivers would have found themselves struggling not only with their responses to the children's need for affection and intimacy, but also with the children's previous experience of attachment relationships which may have been abusive or neglectful. In addition, the children symbolised the product of illegitimate sexual intercourse, which is and was thoroughly disapproved of by the Catholic church. To like these children may have required an attitude that did not hold them accountable for the sin of their parent – we do not know how easy or otherwise this was for those concerned. We do know that it is easier to abuse someone whom one sees as different from oneself in some unacceptable way or who represents subversion or threat to one's valued order of being.

If one lives in a group where challenging accepted practices is not encouraged, and differences of perception and affect are not treated seriously by the person in authority, this disconfirmation of one's reality has the potential to disorientate, particularly, if one's experiences of reality have been disconfirmed as a child. If a group such as a religious community is maintained at the first stage of group development by a structure which promotes uniformity, attacks difference, encourages dependency and reliance on the leader; then members of such a group are not supported by the group as a whole to deal with their frustration, hatred, their impulse to retaliate, their sadism or their aggression in ways other than to seek targets for their aggression or to turn the aggression inward and become depressed. This is also the culture that promotes paranoia, anxiety, tension and psychosomatic disorders (Agazarian 1997).

This is the climate that allows the abuse of children to take place by adults in full view of other adults. To challenge such behaviour would be to draw attention to a difference of opinion, value or moral view, and to risk being scapegoated, with all the consequences of that. Leaving the convent or brotherhood was not an option many considered in the 1940s and 1950s. Remaining in the convent and in good standing with members of one's community was for some at least seen as necessary for economic and social survival.

The attachment dynamic: Supportive and companionable caregiving in contrast to dominant vs. submissive caregiving

Abuse of children or vulnerable people is not particular to Irish society or to the Catholic church. The abuse, torture and killing of others occurs across the world. Social structures can promote or make it difficult for abuse to flourish, but at its heart, abuse of others starts with the original experiences we had as children with our own caregivers. Infants are sentient beings, communicating from the start of life (see Bowlby, Emde and Stern, all who have written extensively on this subject). Ian Suttie (1935) called attention to our need for sociability, companionship, to love and be loved, and that when this primary social love or tenderness fails to find the response it seeks, the frustration produces a kind of anxiety which is the starting point for neurotic maladjustment. Behind that anxiety lies the dread of separation, the dread of being cut off from human sympathy and contact.

Heard and Lake (1997, 1999), building on the work of Suttie, Bowlby, Balint, Guntrip, Maclean and others, put forward the view that attachment theory (which only addresses the complementary relationship of careseeking and caregiving) cannot account for the complexity of human motivational forces. They have extended the theory to encompass other instinctive goal-corrected systems, which include sexuality, interest sharing and self-defence. Together these systems comprise what they term the 'attachment dynamic'. These systems are kept in dynamic equilibrium by a supraordinate organising principle of self-care and care for others with whom there is an affectional bond. Each of these systems will be activated under specific environmental conditions and will shut down when the goals of the particular system have been met. Of particular interest to the subject of abuse by caregivers of careseekers under discussion in this chapter is that the model of the attachment dynamic proposed by Heard and Lake has within it an explanation of how relationships get repeated over time, and also how the dynamic functions to enable minimal survival as well as maximum well-being and social competence. Individuals develop and retain working models of the experience they have had of relationships from the moment of birth, which they use to guide, predict and interpret subsequent relationships. Heard and Lake describe these as internal working models of the experience of relationships. Each person retains an internal working model of all the relationships they have experienced. If the majority of the relationships experienced are of a dominant-submissive nature, abusive in form or in their effect, then there is little in the way of an internal supportive structure which the person can draw on from within themselves which will help them to experience the world of relationships and contribute to the relationships they have in a supportive, companionable fashion.

The theory of the attachment dynamic predicts that if the person seeking care from a particular other fails to have their careseeking needs met, the behavioural patterns which accompany careseeking cannot shut down and the system for careseeking is infiltrated by the activation of the personal defence system. In this way careseeking is then expressed by whatever behaviours have been found to evoke in the caregiver responses that assuage the pain of not reaching careseeking goals. When the caregiver is activated to provide caregiving, frustration of this goal to give care is also likely to cause distress. When the needs of the caregiver and the careseeker are met, there is satisfaction and relief in both parties. If both parties, the careseeker and the caregiver fail to reach the goals of their respective systems this will arouse pain and distress in both which will be defended against, thereby activating the system for personal defence. McCluskey (1999) has tracked this process by a frame-by-frame video analysis of interaction in the context of adult psychotherapy between careseeker and caregiver under experimentally designed conditions. The research supports the theory of the attachment dynamic that affect attunement and empathy are part of supportive and effective caregiving. People operating from the system of self-defence respond to others without empathy and this provides the culture and supportive climate for the abuse of others. To speak of the self as a system might seem unnecessarily clinical, but is a helpful way to catch the complexity of the person and the infinite variety of methods people adopt to keep themselves going in the face of adversity. It makes sense of the best and the worst type of behaviour and practices to which human beings can resort.

The attachment dynamic describes an interpersonal process which takes place through two different kinds of social exchange, which present usually in mixed form. These two kinds of social interactions are supportive and companionable or dominant vs. submissive. A supportive-companionable interactive stance will generally support exploratory behaviour in whichever system is activated within the attachment dynamic; a dominant-vs.-submissive type of social interaction will generally lead to intermittent, incomplete and unsatisfactory exploratory processes at the individual and interpersonal level. A supportive-and-companionable interactive stance towards caregiving puts attunement to feeling and empathy for others at the core of responsive interaction between caregiver and careseeker (McCluskey *et al.,* 1999; McCluskey 1999). Cultures based on values that require unquestioning obedience to authority contribute to an interpersonal behavioural pattern of dominance and submission as the basis for social order. This can create a climate of fear which fosters abuse and which is antithetical to the meeting of attachment needs of children, adolescents, adults and elderly people.

Conclusion

I have sketched the social context in Ireland prevailing this century which fostered the prominence of Catholic institutions as leaders in the field of health education and social care. Poverty, ignorance and no doubt seven centuries of domination by a foreign power contributed to the dynamics of dominance and submission that I suggest were part of the prevailing child-raising strategies. The Irish people themselves were regarded by the British as inferior, they were kept in a position of poverty and ignorance and were not allowed to speak their own language or to practise their religion. The dominance of the Catholic church as a force within the state that could topple a democratically elected government over a piece of child-care legislation must be seen within the larger historical context of the role of the church in maintaining a separate and national identity in the face of colonisation by a foreign state.

A society which promotes and condones a dominant vs. submissive form of relating will foster the suppression of a wholehearted response in caregivers to careseeking; will suppress signals of distress in self and others; will affect the perception of distress in self and others; and will promote the needs of the adult above those of the child. In such a society attunement to feeling and empathy is something that adults will seek from children rather than adults will offer children. Abuse of children is not particular to Irish society or to those who have taken religious vows; our tolerance of the abuse of children and vulnerable others is based on a lack of connection with our own feelings, and an inadequately formed capacity for empathy.

Notes

1   The Christian Brothers issued a public apology in March 1998 to victims of cruelty and sex abuse at its schools and orphanages: 'We say to you who have experienced physical or sexual abuse by a Christian Brother, and to you who complained of abuse and were not listened to, we are deeply sorry.' The publication was made after consultation with the entire order, and with the agreement of nearly all of them (*Irish Times* 31 March 1998). The order was founded in 1820 to educate poor Catholics, and has schools in 26 countries. Fintan O'Toole, writing in the *Irish Times* 30 April 1998 described the Christian Brothers as 'The Irish Catholic Institution, through the role they played in the destruction of the embryonic non-sectarian state education system in the nineteenth century, they shaped the denominational nature of our schools.'

2   Between 1983 and April 1998, 23 priests and religious men and women were convicted on child sex abuse charges in Ireland, North and South (*Irish Times* 30 April 1998).

3   In relation to education, the church is still the dominant provider (see Lynch 1998).

4   The Irish people voted to introduce divorce in a referendum held in 1996.

5   For an account of the role of the church in social policy during this period and since see Fahey (1998).

6   See Burke (1987) for an account of the welfare system in the last century, much of which remained unchanged into the 1970s.

7   The Staffordshire 'Pindown' inquiry, set up to explore the practice of depriving children of their liberty (Levy and Kahan 1991); Ty Mawr Community Home in

Wales was investigated following incidents of suicide and self-harm (Utting 1997; Williams and Macreadie 1992).

8   *The Guardian* (12 February 1998) gave an account of two sisters reunited after 74 years. When young they and another sibling had been placed by their father in an orphanage when their mother had died of a heart attack. The orphanage was in the charge of nuns who apparently would cane the children for wetting themselves, wake them up several times a night to check on bedwetting, and force them to scrub long corridors with cold water. When one of them was 15 and sent out to work as a domestic servant, the sisters were separated with no regard to their relationship with each other or their need to have information about each other's whereabouts.

9   The document referred to is in the National Library in Dublin.

10 Caitriona Clear (1988) places religious life in the social and economic context of Ireland at the time. The author takes account of the position of women, their access to education, financial independence and the influence thereof on 'vocations'. It is interesting to read this book now as it clearly avoids the present concern with the abuse of power that went on in these institutions by members of religious orders.

References

Agazarian, Y.M. (1997) *Systems Centered Group Psychotherapy*. New York and London: Guilford.

Ainsworth, M.D.S. (1991) 'Attachments and other affectional bonds across the life cycle'. In C.M. Parkes, J. Stevenson-Hinde and P. Marris (eds) *Attachment Across the Life Cycle*. London: Tavistock: Routledge.

Ainsworth, M.D.S., Blehar, M.C., Waters, E. and Wall, S. (1978) *Patterns of Attachment: A Psychological Study of the Strange Situation*. New Jersey: Erlbaum Associates.

Bowlby, J. (1969) *Attachment and Loss. Vol. I. Attachment*. London: The Hogarth Press.

Bowlby, J. (1973) *Attachment and Loss. Vol. II. Separation*. New York and London: Basic Books.

Bowlby, J. (1979) *The Making and Breaking of Affectional Bonds*. London: Tavistock Publications.

Bowlby, J. (1980) *Attachment and Loss. Vol. III. Loss*. New York and London: Basic Books.

Bowlby, J. (1988) *A Secure Base: Clinical Implications of Attachment Theory*. London: Routledge.

Bretherton, I. (1995) 'The origins of attachment theory'. In S. Goldberg, R. Muir and J. Kerr (eds) *Attachment Theory: Social, Developmental and Clinical Perspectives*. London: The Analytic Press.

Brown, N. (1986) *Against the Tide*. Dublin: Gill and Macmillan Ltd.

Burke, H. (1987) *The People and the Poor Law in 19th-Century Ireland*. West Sussex: The Women's Education Bureau.

Clear, C. (1988) *Nuns in Nineteenth-Century Ireland*. Dublin: Gill and Macmillan.

Caudill, W. (1958) *The Psychiatric Hospital as a Small Society*. Cambridge, Massachusetts: Harvard University Press.

Channel 4 (1998) 'Witness: Sex in a Cold Climate.'

Crittenden McKinsey, P. (1995) 'Attachment and psychopathology'. In S. Goldberg, R. Muir and J. Kerr (eds) *Attachment Theory; Social, Developmental and Clinical Perspectives*. London: The Analytic Press.

de Zulueta, F. (1993) *From Pain to Violence: The Traumatic Roots of Destructiveness.* London: Whurr Publishers.

Emde, R.N. (1983) 'The prerepresentational self and its affective core'. *Psychoanalytic Study of the Child 38,* 165–192.

Emde, R.N. (1985) 'An adaptive view of infants emotions: Functions for self and knowing'. *Social Sciences Information 24,* 237–341.

Emde, R.N. (1990) 'Mobilising fundamental modes of development: Empathic availability and therapeutic action'. *International Journal of Psycho-Analysis 69,* 881–913.

Emde, R.N., Biringen, Z., Clyman, R., B. and Oppenheim, D. (1991) 'The moral self of infancy: Affective core and procedural knowledge'. *Developmental Review 11,* 251–270.

Fahey, T. (1998) 'The Catholic church and social policy'. In S. Healy and B. Reynolds (eds) *Social Policy in Ireland: Principles, Practice and Problems.* Dublin: Oak Tree Press.

Fonagy, P. (1999) The male perpetrator: The role of trauma and failures of mentalization in aggression against women – an attachment theory perspective. The 6th John Bowlby Memorial Lecture, Centre for Attachment-Based Psychoanalytic Psychotherapy, 20 February 1999, London.

Grossmann, K., Fremmer-Bombik, E., Rudolph, J. and Grossmann, K.E. (1988) 'Maternal attachment representations as related to child-mother attachment patterns and maternal sensitivity and acceptance of her infant'. In R.A. Hinde and J. Stevenson-Hinde (eds) *Relations within Families.* Oxford: Oxford University Press.

Heard, D. and Lake, B. (1997) *The Challenge of Attachment for Caregiving.* London: Routledge.

Heard, D. and Lake, B. (1999) The attachment dynamic. Paper presented at day conference, 'The attachment dynamic from childhood to old age.' 26 March 1999, York.

The Leicestershire Enquiry (1992) Leicester: Leicester County Council.

Lynch, K. (1998) 'The status of children and young persons'. In S. Healy and B. Reynolds (eds) *Social Policy in Ireland: Principles, Practice and Problems.* Dublin: Oak Tree Press.

Main, M. (1995) 'Recent studies in attachment: Overview, with selected implications for clinical work'. In S. Goldberg, R. Muir and J. Kerr (eds) *Attachment Theory; Social, Developmental and Clinical Perspectives.* London: The Analytic Press.

McCluskey, U. (1999) The attachment dynamic in adult psychotherapy: Evidence from research. Paper presented at day conference, 'The attachment dynamic from childhood to old age.' 26 March 1999, York.

McCluskey, U., Hooper, C.A. and Bingley Miller, L. (1999) 'Goal-corrected empathic attunement: Developing and rating the concept within an attachment perspective'. *Psychotherapy Theory Research Practice and Training 36,* 80–90.

McCluskey, U., Roger, D. and Nash, P. (1997) 'A preliminary study of the role of attunement in adult psychotherapy'. *Human Relations 50,* 1261–1273.

McCourt, F. (1996) *Angela's Ashes: A Memoir of a Childhood.* London: HarperCollins.

Miller, A. (1986) *The Drama of Being a Child.* London: Virago Press.

Miller, A. (1987) *For Your Own Good: the Roots of Violence in Child-Rearing.* London: Virago Press.

O'Toole, F. (1998) Article in *The Irish Times,* 30 April.

Parkinson, P. (1997) *Child Sexual Abuse and the Churches.* London: Hodder and Stoughton.

Report of the Constitutional Review Group (1996) Dublin: Government Publications Office.

Report of the Kilkenny Incest Investigation (1993) Dublin: Government Publications Office.

Stein, M. (1993) 'The abuses and uses of residential child care'. In H. Ferguson *et al.* (eds) *Surviving Childhood Adversity.* Dublin Social Studies Press: Trinity College.

Stern, D.M. (1985) *The Interpersonal World of the Infant. A View from Psychoanalysis and Developmental Psychology.* New York: Basic Books.

Suttie, I.D. (1935) *The Origins of Love and Hate.* London: Kegan Paul.

Trubner and Co. (1988) *The Origins of Love and Hate.* London: Free Association Books.

Utting, Sir W. (1997) *People like us: The report of the review of the safeguards of children living away from home.* London: Stationary Office.

CHAPTER 7

What Cost Assimilation and Integration? Working with Transcultural Issues

Lennox K. Thomas

It would be folly to talk about the assimilation and integration of African-descended people in this country and not speak about the earlier experiences of large numbers of African people being moved to the Caribbean and the Americas. To some extent it could be said that the history of African-descended people is one that is punctuated by abuse and betrayal. Writers such as Hooks (1982), Sutherland (1997) and Wilson (1993) have been interested in how formerly colonised people have repeated abuses learned from their period of colonisation. Some writers have argued that the evidence of dysfunctional family structures within some African-Caribbean and African-American families are directly related to their experience during slavery and post-slavery society. During enslavement, family groupings were forbidden. When bonds developed, there was always fear of being found out and sold to another plantation. It is not surprising that post-emancipation family structure reflected that which was known to them. Forms which were emulated and adapted from the period of slavery became the norm and bore little relation to the pre-slavery African family life. Domestic relationships and the raising of children is thought therefore to reflect the abusive, violent, exploitative relationships that slaves endured at the hands of white masters and others with some hierarchical power. After 400 years of assimilation into a way of life in which the Africans had no choice, they came to claim as their own the degraded and violent relationships that they had known with their masters. This history of enslavement was a catalogue of sexual abuse, rape, betrayal and sacrifice of children. It is a saying in the Caribbean that, 'if you want to know about the sexual proclivities of the former masters, the people to talk to would be the children and the women'. Indeed, many anecdotes survive about the ways that people fared under certain estate masters.

Among the many damaging things that happened during the period of enslavement and colonisation was that black African-descended people were valued for their physical attributes, their sexual availability and their reproductive capacities. Reproduction was encouraged in order to increase the stock of saleable labour and therefore the wealth of the slave masters. One hundred or so years after emancipation, the former slaves began to move from this position to one of valuing themselves for who they were: human beings with a capacity for love and affection, a need for warmth and family relationships. The damaging experiences nevertheless left some residue of psychological damage, resulting not only in a complex set of emotions in relation to white people, but also to themselves.

People of African descent carry at some level a sense of guilt, shame and responsibility for the lives that they had lived. Hooks (1982) describes the psychodynamics of relationships between black people as well as between black and white people in mixed relationships as a result of slavery. How people behave towards each other reflects their histories of how relationships have been, and the value that their particular social group places on them. After generations of the dehumanisation of intimacy and trust in relationships, the result is at worst a muddle of forms and at best the recognition of fresh opportunities for evolving better ways of relating. The mistrust that has existed between black communities as a result of forced separation now seems ready for discussion. Some attempts have been made in the literature by Frantz Fanon (1986), Audre Lorde (1978) and Langston Hughes (1954) among others.

The social implications of the relationship between master and slave: The disregard for attachment bonds between family members

The practices that were used during the period of enslavement, of men being moved from island to island or from estate to estate as an easily accessible source of labour, carried on after emancipation. Newly freed slaves – particularly those who had not become tenants on small plots of land rented from the estates – would travel to other islands selling their labour. There was always a need for cheap labour in North America, Cuba and Haiti and during the construction of the Panama Canal. Labour was informal or, on occasions, organised by the colonial office (for example, for the building of roads or other infrastructure in colonial territory). While this had a damaging effect on families, it was, alas, what they had grown accustomed to, and some families were able to enjoy the better standards of living this sacrifice provided.

This established practice of fluid labour in turn provided servicemen and women for the First and Second World Wars. The moves for independence and the disbanding of colonial rule, as well as the failure of the plantocracy classes to provide employment for the landless poor, contributed to the need for people to seek work further abroad. People from the Caribbean had travelled to the US in search of work or new lives since the dawn of the century. During the 1950s, colonial citizens from the Caribbean began emigration to the UK, the mother country, to answer the call for post-war reconstruction. There was a shortage of labour, and Britain needed to get back on its feet.

Two World Wars had strengthened the relationship that Caribbean subjects felt between themselves and Great Britain. Many civil servants in the Caribbean as well as other privately employed people had contributed a portion of their time at work voluntarily to the war effort. Many had purchased war bonds, and others, through their church and youth organisations, had contributed financially to their English cousins who were experiencing hardship and adversity as a result of the war with Germany. Arriving here on the Empire Windrush in 1948 as the first large group of émigrés from the Caribbean, they failed to experience that familial relationship that they once thought they shared with the people of the UK.

Social policy was unaffected by the arrival of black citizens from the Caribbean. They largely made their own way through the maze of housing and employment, experiencing on the way the rejection of racism and discrimination. It was not until 1958 after the death of Kelso Cochrane and the so-called riots in some British cities, that policy-makers began to think about the process of assimilating these migrants into British society and barring the way for others who wished to join them through policies which curbed Commonwealth immigration. The 1960s were considered to be the period of assimilation and integration of people from the Caribbean, Africa and India. During that time social caseworkers and social policy makers became interested in the issues of migration and the effect that it was having on family life. A few articles appeared in the professional journals (Ellis 1978; Fitzherbert 1967; Patterson 1963) and there was debate around working with those who had arrived from the Caribbean and Africa.

Working with unfamiliar cultural patterns

While many immigrants from the Caribbean spoke English as well as Creole based on English or French, and were raised and educated within the framework of the British colonial system, they had their own particular forms of family structure. Fitzherbert (1967), who had some experience of colonial life in the Caribbean implied in her writing that people from the

Caribbean shared the same cultural and family norms as white English people. It would be fair to say that many people from the Caribbean would pay homage to this particular family form, though they would have inherited other forms that were indigenous to their African cultural heritage or acquired as a result of slavery. Given this lack of recognition among white British professionals for what were essentially many variations on a theme, helping to find solutions for family difficulties that were presented to social workers and others was problematic.

During the 1960s research (Daniel 1968) was carried out to discover the extent of racial prejudice in Britain; the findings presented a grim picture. Discrimination was endemic, and post-holders in local and central government as well as trade unionists saw no impediment to expressing their prejudiced views or discriminating on the basis of their own particular racial beliefs. Legislation was introduced in order to preserve the civil rights of those who came to the UK from the Commonwealth. Caribbean immigrants themselves had come to accept racism and discrimination as part and parcel of living in a land in which they were not born. They did, however, hold out hope that their children would not endure this situation, and believed that in time prejudice would die with familiarisation with and acceptance into UK society.

Issues of race and difference provoke a range of personal views. Some of these, it was found, were due to ignorance, and others were informed by political or organised thinking about race and immigration. It took some time for civil servants and government officials to begin to think about tackling prejudice as an unwelcome aspect of their professional duty. New family forms presented new challenges for housing and social services departments. Practices such as the fostering of West African children (Ellis 1978); the large numbers of children from the Caribbean who were assessed as educationally subnormal (Coard 1971); physical chastisements in families and the reunification of previously separated families (Robertson 1977) were themes pursued at this time. The bonds of family attachment became an important issue for children who had been left behind in the Caribbean.

Social workers and others were at one with large numbers of immigrant families who believed that assimilation and integration was the right and proper policy to pursue. These ideas were, however, challenged by the end of that decade when it seemed that racial discrimination would always be a barrier to assimilation (Husband 1980). The diversity that existed in childcare among the people of Caribbean backgrounds led to tension between that community and social workers. Social workers began to take up the challenge to move away from the Eurocentric standard which was used in child assessment. It would be hard to say that this has been entirely achieved, but the notion of social and ethnic diversity would now be acceptable to most professionals in social care, even if practice and theory is slow to demonstrate this.

Child abuse in the context of societal race abuse

The expectations of those coming from the Caribbean that they would assimilate seamlessly into British society did not happen. Most people from Africa and the Caribbean occupied what would now be termed a subclass in society. The differences that exist between those immigrants and their children and grandchildren, is that the younger generations have claimed Britain as their own. In many respects they have few illusions, they are aware of the existence of racism and do not expect that it will disappear like their parents and grandparents did. Given their realism about this situation however, they have come to terms with the fact that living and surviving in the country of their birth is not easy, but they nevertheless hold it as their country.

Paradoxically, the people who arrived in Britain in the 1950s and 1960s feel less British now after 50 or more years in this country than they did when they arrived. Their disillusionment is palpable. The process of the mental colonisation of these people is in a gradual state of reversal. When the colonisation of thinking has been broken, the endeavour of colonisation is broken. Many had mimicked the British, seeing little difference between themselves and their masters. For them, living in the UK and dealing with the daily betrayals of racism has enabled this generation of immigrants to see themselves differently. The promise of serving the mother country in reality changed the way that they saw their lives. Living as a black minority within the context of a white majority society brought home to many Caribbean immigrants the reality of being second-class citizens. What had remained constant in the southern states of the US, where black people possessed few civil rights, had become apparent in the UK. While of course there is no real comparison with the US, being the recipient of second-class civil protection or being of little consequence in UK society changed the thinking of black immigrants. Bell Hooks considered that the reason why black women and children were raped and abused in the US was because there was little interest from the authorities when it was a black-on-black offence. When it was white males abusing black women and children it would not be believed, and such a case would never get to court. Historically, black people were property and could be raped and abused with impunity. More often than not the victims would not even dream of bringing a prosecution because they had adjusted to their situation. Hooks (1982) discussed this in terms of black people believing that they were inferior, believing the many projections that were put on to them as bestial, over-sexed and immoral. Although no longer slaves, the prevalent beliefs held about African-descended people continue to affect the way that abuse and child protection issues are assessed and judgements are made. While Hooks argues that slavery and the sexualisation of the enslaved individual has affected all of their relationships in contemporary society, she expresses concern about how family unity can be achieved in the light of this.

As the topic of childhood abuse is more debated in the media, people who had not talked about their abuse are now coming into contact with counsellors and therapists. This trend is similar in both majority and minority ethnic communities. Some of the reasons given for people's failure to disclose earlier or at the time of their abuse are complex and sometimes influenced by their status as minorities. Those who had been abused by members of their family felt betrayed because the trust in the family as a supportive place which protected them from the prejudice of racism outside the family was broken and rendered'home no longer safe.

African- and Asian-descended men and women are increasingly referring themselves for help after recalling incidents in their childhood which they had not thought of before as sexual abuse, although they were suffering from the associated effects of having been abused. Many said that it was not until adulthood that they had put together the words for what had occured and realised that it was not right. Being the first step for many people, this led them to think about the effects that abuse might have had on their lives. The abuse had various effects on them during their childhood, including suppressing intellect, freezing emotion, exacerbating acting out or difficult behaviour in adolescence. More often than not, they did not talk about these abusive incidents. Some had picked up the taboo about sexual matters or anything to do with their bodies; others, who were unaware of the significance of the abuse, had no real need to talk about it, not having grasped what had taken place. While some survivors talked about feeling a sense of shame as a result of what had happened to them, others stated that this served to top up the shame they were already made to feel on account of being black in British society.

Feeling a sense of unacceptance for being black at the time when they were growing up was a large part of their experience. Being a black child and feeling excluded was further exacerbated by the experience of abuse, which eroded self-confidence and self-worth. In retrospect, many clients were angry about having to keep it quiet. While this happens in many communities, it serves to further isolate ethnic minority children. The sense of needing to preserve ethnic minority communities as free of abuse or other negative aspects can only exist because of racism. If minority communities did not already receive projected messages from white society that they were second rate, over-sexed and immoral, then there would be no need to feel a sense of fear for laying oneself open to criticism by acknowledging the existence of abuse.

Comments from white child protection professionals like, 'Well, what do you expect from these people?' have been heard at professional meetings. Racial prejudice exists around the issues of abuse as it does among other aspects of people's lives, and decisions will of course be affected by such racism. The sense of exposing one's community becomes an additional burden to young people, who feel that they are letting down their family by talking about their present or past abuse. It is particularly distressing to witness young people of African and Asian descent trying hard to deny the abuse, keeping it to themselves, and in part feeling that they should not be talking to professionals whose job it is to understand and help them. The dilemma for young people in freeing themselves from abuse can also mean that they are freed from their family and community against their will. Making a disclosure is always going to be making a disclosure to white people, who have their white power in their white institutions and in turn will bring their white value judgements to bear on black and other minority communities. A 24-year-old Sikh woman said that she kept quiet about childhood abuse by her father because she could not bear to lose her mother and go into a white children's home only to get the racial abuse that she got enough of at school anyway. What had seemed very complex ideas about why black children disclose or not had been explained to me quite simply.

It is important to remember that the Asian or Caribbean family home has to serve as a protective environment for its members, particularly children and the vulnerable, and that protection is as much against virulent racism like faeces through the letterbox or death threats, or racism encountered on a day-to-day basis. The minority family serves to value its members and to detoxify the daily accumulation of racism in society at large. Abuse in the family robs children of this facility. As long as racism exists, young black people will be under-protected from sexual and other abuse through their own reluctance to disclose, as well as being over-protected or under-protected depending on the stereotype that is used to assess Asian, African and Caribbean families.[1]

Young people who do seek help may confront the racial bias in institutions which can result in abuse against blacks being under reported to and under-investigated by the police (Hooks 1982). The case of Geoffrey Dharmer, who was able to kill 16 black Hispanics and other minority boys and young men in the US before he was arrested, exemplifies this bias. One young man who escaped and reported the matter to the police was ignored, his testimony not taken seriously. His ethnic minority status worked against him – presumably his life, safety and well-being would have been of greater value if he were white. Racial bias in institutions can only be fed by what exists in society at large. It would be difficult to consider that the values of police and social workers and other law enforcers are very different from others in society.

Vera

'Vera', a 45-year-old Caribbean woman, was referred by her psychiatrist as needing supportive therapy to cope with a diagnosis of longterm schizophrenia, and how this had affected her life and that of her two children.[2] She had been diagnosed 18 years earlier after the birth of her second child, a son. Vera told a story of coming to the UK at 15 to join her father. Her mother and siblings followed some years later. She found her father dominating and violent, hitting her for the slightest reason, one of these being the sexual relationships he imagined that she was having with men in the neighbourhood. She left home and married at 21 and was happy until her husband began having a series of affairs; she left him after the second child was born, around the time she was hospitalised. Since then, Vera has thrown herself from a moving train and has taken two major overdoses, surviving them with little physical damage. Her doctor believed that medication alone would not help her to develop the confidence and belief in herself to help her to survive.

Vera seemed fragile and self-effacing, smiling at all times and ever-grateful for the time she spent with her therapist. She was able to talk about her isolation and her reluctance to go out. She said that her heart would race and she wished that she were invisible. After four months, she was able to tell the therapist about her experiences of sexual abuse in her rural Caribbean village. She talked about being touched inside her underwear on two occasions by older boys, first when she was three years old and then when she was seven. She was very upset and frightened by the abuse, and was not able to tell anyone about it. What distressed her, she added, was the fact that she was too frightened to tell her mother. She said that even at that age she knew that she would have been smacked for being a dirty girl for letting boys do this to her. Vera described her village as having an undercurrent of abuse which was not spoken about in mixed company or by women. She said that a couple of girls, aged 14 or so, were being abused by adult men, and this seemed to be common knowledge. She said that the mother of one girl would send her weekly to collect school lunch money from the man who abused her. Vera was not able to make sense of this. The abuser, a construction worker, commented to workmates about what he got for the money and it seemed a source of amusement. She said that there were some good things for her in the village and that she was under the protective care of girls who were older than herself. At age seven she would tag along with them at play and at school and they looked after her. She said that the girls warned her about who to keep away from. She described herself as having been a very frightened child and indeed grew up to be a frightened adult.

During her period of therapy, Vera told her therapist of a memory she had of buying a 'farthing bun' at the local bakery. She was so pleased with her little treat that she walked home savouring the thought of eating it in comfort. As she approached the gate she saw two older children coming towards her and she handed them her farthing bun. She said that it felt like instinct to do this in order to prevent them from teasing or bullying her. She wanted to stop being frightened and to stop appeasing people.

Vera went on to say that talking about her abuse had helped her to understand her relationship with her father when she left the Caribbean to join him in the UK. She always feared him and never understood why he accused her of having sex with various men in the neighbourhood. She said that she was attending night school and working in a factory by day and was not at all interested in boys at 15. Her first boyfriend was the man she later married at 21. She had always thought her father cruel to think this way, as well as for undermining her efforts to learn typing and shorthand in the evenings. It finally came together years later when she remembered whispers about her father, who had, without success, propositioned one of the teenage village girls. She said that she now understood why she feared and despised her father, who was a 'dirty old man', no different to the others in the village.

Vera's early attempts in the UK to get help to escape her father's violence failed with her first visit to a social worker. She said that she was given a little 'pep talk' and warned about getting into trouble with boys. She said that the woman she saw did not seem to think differently from her father, so she stuck it out at home and things improved when her mother and other siblings joined them. Her father's image of her as promiscuous was obviously formed by his own ideas about young women. The social worker might well have been influenced by social stereotypes often reflected in popular culture and songs like 'Brown Sugar' and 'Island Girl' describing what black girls like to do all night. As long as racist stereotyping exists, abuse in black families will be a double betrayal for black children, who are at risk of being exposed to damaging aspects of a racist society, where their blackness and identity will be yet another casualty. As they see it, those who choose to remain in abusive families have no choice at all but to minimise risk.

Peter

'Peter' was born to African-Caribbean parents in Britain. Not long after he had started to walk his mother and father separated and she left home. With the help of childminders, Peter and his older brother 'Mark' remained at home until being put into care at aged four and six. Two years later, when Peter was six, their father remarried and the boys came home. Peter has little recollection of this period in care apart from it being a bit like the army. He and Mark did not settle at home, and he talked about being beaten by both parents, locked in cellars and deprived of food. A white neighbour who was kind to them offered to take the boys on day trips to the seaside or to the park with his own children. The boys were abused by this man for three-and-a-half years; they did not tell their parents.

The brothers are now in their early 30s and for the first time are able to talk to each other about the abuse. Peter said that for many years, having been returned to care at the age of ten, they thought that this neighbour was the kindest person to them during their childhood. Peter was able to forget the abuse for many years until some months earlier when he was propositioned by a black male colleague. This approach by his colleague appeared to unleash recurring nightmares of being followed by a man who he knows will catch him, bugger him and kill him. Peter was not able to work, and was signed off sick with a nervous disability. He said that the memories of his abuse had become vivid, and that he is kept awake at night unable to stop thinking about it. As well as being preoccupied with the abuse memories, he was worrying about protecting his newborn son from the life that he had. He believed that his present life was a disaster and could not value his business success. Mark does not like Peter to talk about the past, and tells him that it was a long time ago and that he must put it out of his mind. Peter was mistrustful of men, and said that he really wanted to see a black female therapist because he felt that he would not be able to talk openly to a white person about his experiences, and that a black male therapist would only make him feel inferior and stupid.

Peter expressed no anger towards the man who sexually abused him, but both he and his brother at the time thought it a bit odd that he wanted to do what he did. His colleague's sexual interest in him triggered anxieties of the abuse and left him fearing that the abuse was somehow visible, and that this led to him being propositioned. Although he had not forgotten about his early sexual abuse, this was only one component of his early life. He seemed less forgiving of his father and stepmother, who he has no contact with.

RACIAL SEXUAL STEREOTYPING AND ABUSE

While an evaluation of this case would lend itself to the classic ideas of the paedophile targeting and grooming children already physically abused, one aspect might be missing. That any child is targetable is a fact, but given societal racism and how this has permeated sexual contact between black and white people, there is an extra cachet from contact with black boys and girls. This is a little-mentioned social pathology which can find expression in the sexual abuse of the black child. Some black children have talked about the fetishistic interest that their abusers have had with their skin, hair texture, lips or other physical features. This, with the racial sexual stereotype of black as more sexy, black as more kinky, renders black children vulnerable. Because of the unequal histories of black and white people, black sexuality and black skin has long been both a lure and revulsion. Social and historical divisions make it possible for black people to remain a fetishistic interest. While social power and dominance play a part in this, there is also a part played by the perversion of sexual attraction, and hatred for yielding to it.

A teacher in a boarding school was convicted of abusing two girls in his care. He was suspected of having abused many others because he had the opportunity to do so over ten years at the school. It was a school favoured by expatriates and diplomats. Both girls were the daughters of wealthy Pacific Asian business people. The teacher had an interest in Asia and was popular with the few children in the school from this background. The probation officer who was preparing the pre-sentence report asked him why he had singled out these Asian children. He replied that they 'seemed so isolated and lacking in affection in the school'.

Another child of African-Caribbean background, now adult, thought that he was abused by a staff member in care because he was the only black child in his children's institution some 20 years earlier. While it seems unlikely that he was the only child who was abused, he seemed to have attributed this to his being different. Seeing this at the time as the 'reason' for the abuse could be related to how his ethnic difference was regarded or what was said to him by the abuser. He had no recollection of what was said.

These cases might imply a degree of racial stereotyping. Sometimes the connection between sexual and racial abuse is more explicit. 'Susie', an eight-year-old African-Caribbean girl, was made to touch a 13-year-old white boy who lived a few doors from her foster parents. During the course of the abuse he called her 'black shit'. She asked her white foster mother at bath time if she was 'black shit'. Children have talked about abusers who admired their lovely, velvety black skin, curly hair, or in the case of others, beautiful blond tresses. This can at times lead the child to hate these aspects of themselves, to cut off their hair or to self-mutilate. The eroticisation and abuse of children because of their skin colour or other physical attributes is also an aspect of race and sexual abuse, hard though it may be for some to believe.

There is an interesting interplay between those in minority cultures and those in the majority. Racial stereotypes and projection on to minorities has seen people belonging to minority groups as containers of the bad, dirty and sexual. Black people and gypsies have endured this for many years, but it has from time to time been levelled at other minorities who have settled in the UK. In turn, many minority communities have retaliated by accusing the majority British society of being immoral, of offering little guidance to their young on matters of decency, and of putting their elderly in institutions. From this morally superior position, many from minority ethnic communities have claimed that sexual abuse does not take place in their own community. This no longer being a position that can be maintained in the face of prosecutions in the courts, others have said that sexual abuse began in their community after settling in the UK. Some people will disavow that sexual abuse takes place in their community, feeling the need to protect themselves from what seems negative. A social worker from East Africa said that sexual abuse was something that came about with the advent of television in her country.

Somehow there is a denial that it can and does happen in all cultures and all communities. Childhood abuse can be projected on to the decadence of white Western society as easily as it is projected on to natural uninhibited people. Some from minority communities who seek to protect their community from accusations of abuse are at risk of leaving its children and young people vulnerable and isolated, and at the same time allowing abuse to proliferate unchecked. Sexual abuse can be dealt with in different ways in some communities where the protection of family honour and the marriage-ability of children is a very important matter. These cases usually escape the attention of the police and the authorities. It might be the case that a community has its own way of protecting its children from abuse. This would only be effective in the long term, however, if the child's interests are not ignored or subordinated to those of others in the solution.

Conclusion

Assimilation would not now be considered to be the best future for minority ethnic communities in modern British society. There is, it seems, a greater tolerance of difference and diversity. Inevitably, younger generations of people from visible ethnic-minority backgrounds will become more British and therefore assimilated incrementally. Earlier moves for assimilation of African-Caribbean and Asian people has borne a cost. The process of cultural absorption began long before colonial immigrants arrived on the British shores. The building of the Empire and the colonies elevated whiteness and Britishness as an ideal. The privileging of British and European ideas above those held in their own culture undermined new arrivals. Immigration to the UK therefore asked many to make an adjustment to a new identity.

Abuse can harm or traumatise individuals, families and groups; it can also get into systems and remain unrecognised and uncorrected. When this happens there will always be a greater risk of abuse being repeated. The brutalisation and abuse of communities and peoples under slavery and colonisation had a lasting effect which has never been fully recognised. Few academics or social commentators have drawn together the links between domestic violence and abuse in its many forms and the violent experiences from history. The importance of bearing this history in mind is to be witness to the experience of how this moves through the generations. When the experience of brutality is in childhood and is not ameliorated, the individual can justify meting it out to another person usually smaller than themselves and stating that the violence has done them no harm. Until this is understood in its historical context, family violence in African-Caribbean communities will remain an area of tension. In addition, if we are concerned about the abuse of black children, this concern must include racism as a form of abuse itself, the effects of racism on children's ability to seek or accept help from others when abused within their families, and the role that racial sexual stereotyping may play in fostering child sexual abuse.

Notes

1   Confusion about race and culture issues can leave children of African and Asian descent on the one hand under-protected in their families or, on the other hand, grossly over-protected. In a 1989 paper, Bandana Ahmad cites examples of professionals accepting incest as a norm in ethnic minority families. Playing it safe and not wanting to get involved, having stereotyped views, and perceiving the standard of care in ethnic minority families as substandard were seen as contributing factors in this lack of professional effectiveness in the protection of black children. On the other hand, the hard-pressed worker can sometimes find themselves protecting black children from their parents who are seen as harsh and outdated. Many children from African-Caribbean backgrounds were taken into care against the background of their families being seen as disciplinarians who hold their children back from fully participating in modern British society. Research into black children in the care system has indicated that black children found themselves in care sooner than their white counterparts, against a background of housing and other social indicators of deprivation (Barn 1993). Kutek (1987) has emphasised that if white social-work agencies are to engage effectively with those from minority-ethnic backgrounds, race and culture needs to be recognised as an integral element of good practice.

2   Where individual cases from clinical work or research are discussed, in this and other chapters, names have been changed to preserve confidentiality.

References

Ahmad, B.C. (1989) *Protecting Black Children From Abuse.* Social Work Today.

Barn, R. (1993) *Black Children in the Public Care System.* London: Batsford.

Coard, B. (1971) *How the West Indian Child is made Educationally Sub-Normal in the British School System.* London: New Beacon Books.

Daniel, W.W. (1968) *Racial Discrimination in England.* London: Penguin.

Ellis, J. (ed) (1978) *West African Families in Britain.* London: Routledge and Kegan Paul.

Fanon, F. (1986) *Black Skin White Mask.* London: Pluto Publishing Ltd.

Fitzherbert, K. (1967) *West Indian Children in London.* London: Bell and Sons.

Hooks, B. (1982) *Ain't I a Woman, Black Women and Feminism.*London: Pluto Publishing Ltd.

Hughes, L. (1954) 'Dream Variations'. Poem in *Selected Poems.* USA: Alfred A. Knopf Inc.

Husband, C. (1980) *Notes on Racism in Social Work Practice.* London: Multi Racial Social Work, No. 1.

Kutek, A. (1987) 'The Race Dimension in Child Protection. Some Prompts for Practice'. *Journal of Social Work Practice 3*, 1, London.

Larde, A. (1978) 'Between Ourselves'. Poem in *The Black Unicorn: Poems by Audre Larde.* USA: W.W. Norton and Co.

Patterson, S. (1963) *Dark Strangers.* London: Tavistock.

Robertson, E.E. (1977) *Out of Sight - Not Out of Mind, Studies in Intercultural Social Work.* Birmingham: British Association of Social Work.

Sutherland, M. (1997) *Black Authenticity. A Psychology for Liberating People of African Descent.* Chicago: Third World Press.

Wilson, M. (1993) *Crossing the Boundary, Black Women Survivor of Incest.* London: Virago Press.

CHAPTER 8

Intimacy, Gender and Abuse

The Construction of Masculinities

Stephen Frosh

> Traditional 'masculinity' focuses on dominance and independence, an orientation to the world which is active and assertive, which valorises competitiveness and turns its face from intimacy, achieving esteem in the glorification of force. The fear at the heart of this image is of emotion – that which makes us vulnerable and 'womanly'; emotion is dangerous not only because it implies dependence, but also because it is alien, a representative of all that masculinity rejects. This fear of emotion in turn makes sex both over- and under-invested in by men… The link between such a form of masculinity and sexual abuse is apparent: it is not just present, but inherent in a mode of personality organisation that rejects intimacy. Sex as triumph and achievement slides naturally into sex as rejection and degradation of the other. (Glaser and Frosh 1993, p.32)

This passage was written during the traumatic phase of reassessing masculine sexuality in response to the dramatic increase in disclosures of child sexual abuse during the 1980s. It reflects a wish to make sense of what might be thought of as a systematic, perhaps structural, relationship between masculinity and abusiveness. Influenced by feminist and anti-sexist thinking, this perspective emphasised the effect that traditional patterns of socialisation of boys has on their capacity to forge nurturing, dependent, intimate relationships rather than those characterised by competitiveness and violent domination of others. Bolstered particularly by feminist readings of object relations theory, which portrayed boys' development as characterised by flight from dependent absorption in the mother and towards identification with an emotionally absent father, a coherent theoretical scheme emerged in which male violence could be understood to be the predictable consequence of patriarchal social relations organised around the disavowal of emotion and dependent feelings. 'Masculinity' as a construct was used to refer to a particular pattern of psychological states, traditionally occupying the 'hard' end of a series of bipolar oppositions: independent-dependent, instrumental-expressive, intellectual-emotional, active-passive, rational-irrational and hard-soft itself (see Frosh 1992). Socially, this form of masculinity had economic and political determinants; psychologically, it emerged from the nexus of gendered family relationships.

This mode of theorising has had many beneficial consequences. It has, for example, demonstrated how issues of abuse and issues of masculine identity run together in ways which are profoundly connected with the so-called 'masculine crisis' in contemporary culture. This is signposted by men's uncertainty over their social role and identity, sexuality, work and personal relationships, and the way in which these are often manifested in violence or abusive behaviours towards self and others (see Frosh 1994, 1997; Jukes 1993; Seidler 1989).

What is not so clear from this way of looking at things, however, is how thoroughly the conventional notion of identity itself has been deconstructed in recent times. Traditionally conceptualised as the relatively stable and enduring sense that a person has of himself or herself in relation to gender and ethnicity, as well as less tangible aspects of selfhood, the notion of 'identity' has been radically rethought by contemporary sociological and psychological theory. This has stressed that a person's 'identity' is in fact something quite fluid, constructed through experience and linguistically coded. In developing their identities, people draw on culturally available resources in their immediate social networks and in society as a whole. The process of identity-construction is therefore one upon which the contra-dictions and dispositions of the surrounding socio-cultural environment have a powerful impact, making it difficult for an individual to describe the sources and nature of her or his identity positions. Add to this the 'post-modern flux' in which contemporary human subjects are immersed and we have a sense of identity as contingent, variable (for example, developmentally or situationally) and, most of all, multiple. The notion of a person having a 'true identity' which it is their life task to find has become problematic and unstable; rather, what we are faced with is the emergence and occlusion of various 'identities', sometimes sequentially but often (confusingly) together (see Elliott and Spezzano 1996; Rattansi and Phoenix 1997).

Applied to questions of masculinity, this deconstructive process has displaced the idea of a homogeneous masculine identity (either biologically essentialist or produced through regular socialisation practices) and challenged the assumption that gendered identity is ever fully attained. Instead, gender has come to be seen as the unstable product of a process of constant construction, using markers of sameness and difference to establish itself, but also always open to disruption and disturbance. Maintaining a gendered identity is thus a certain kind of work; as such, it is a social process, embedded in power relations and underpinned by a socially induced fantasy structure.

Developing this theme of the deconstruction of notions of 'masculinity', it is apparent that this is not just a matter of recognising different masculine styles or variations on an essential core masculine state, but of dealing with genuinely distinct masculinities, with their own dynamics and specific content. Some of these will be hegemonic or dominant with respect to others (see, for instance, Connell's [1995] analysis of how performances of strength and toughness function to establish particular kinds of masculine identity as superior to others); others will be marginalised or subordinate. This latter kind might even represent examples of resistance to hegemonic masculinities, offering alternative visions to, for instance, the one presented in this chapter's opening quotation. However, not all subordinate masculinities are anti-oppressive; they may be marginalised yet still draw on aspects of hegemonic masculinity, such as misogyny, for their survival.

The point here is that the lived experience of actual people in society seems no longer one in which 'natural' explanations of male or female behaviour carry conviction; rather, what is up front is the multifariousness of gendered experience, its richness, excitement and flamboyant uncertainty. Under these conditions, multiple identities – masculinities and femininities in the plural – have to be acknowledged; some of these might be radically at variance with others. Speaking psychologically, this is felt as problematic from the point of view of the individual subject: each person's version of masculinity can only be partial, always lacking in sureness and secure content.

Within psychoanalytic theory, the influence of this kind of thinking can be seen in the increasing attention paid to describing the problematic nature of masculine development. Much of this work has been extremely productive and provocative. Examples here include uses of object relations theory to examine the way boys and men struggle with dependence and intimacy; work by Jessica Benjamin (1998) and other 'intersubjectivists' on multiple identifications in the context of post-Oedipal development, allowing greater diversity of gendered positions than is usually accommodated within psychoanalytic thinking; and Lacanian and post-Lacanian explorations of the 'fixing' of gender through fantasies of phallic mastery and power.

From the perspective of social constructionism, recent work on 'performativity' is also particularly helpful in thinking about the production and maintenance of gendered identities. This approach argues that identities, and meaning more generally, are created as effects of language and symbolic action. Judith Butler (1990) has been the most persuasive and creative elaborator of this position. If gender is performative, she claims, then gender identities are effects, not causes; they are retroactively claimed as sources of action, but they are more like rhetorical solutions to the problem of what produces gendered activity – in the terms of contemporary social psychology, they are called into existence by accounting procedures. In more recent work, Butler has clarified her view of the limits to which gendered performance is free and determinant of gender identity; specifically, psychoanalysis is called upon to show that there are always unconscious elements of gender which are kept out of expression. Gender identities are produced through the enacting of certain images and the barring of others, which themselves act as a kind of unmournable loss – that which we cannot avow or be. Butler (1995) comments: 'Gender itself might be understood in part as the "acting out" of unresolved grief' (p.32); it is performance in the sense that it is something we act out on a stage, always problematic and contradictory, premised on the subjugation of alternative gender positions.

These various theoretical positions have different foci and claims, but they also link together in arguing that masculinities may be constructed around anxieties of loss and engulfment, and that the performance of masculinity reflects these anxieties in its suppression of alternatives to certain hegemonic masculine ideals. An unsettled edge is thereby given to gender performance, so that masculine identities have to be constantly proclaimed for fear that they will fall away. The abusiveness associated with men is thus to be seen not as intrinsic to some stable entity, masculinity, but as performed in the construction and maintenance of certain hegemonic masculinities. These, as has been established many times, particularly by ethnographic studies of young men as well as by more direct investigations of rape and other forms of male violence (see Pattman, Frosh and Phoenix [1998] for the former; Segal [1990] for the latter), are indeed built around displays of hardness, aggression and refusal of intimacy and dependence. However, they are also based on the subjugation of alternative masculinities, some of which are organised differently. Hegemonic masculinities of the abusive kind exist in tension with subjugated gender identities, creating more complexity than our earlier theories of abusiveness might have acknowledged.

Racist accounting and emergent masculinities

As an example of the interweaving of abusive and subjugated masculinities, I will present some material from a study[1] Ann Phoenix, Rob Pattman and I are conducting of 11 to 14-year-old boys in London schools. The issue here is a consideration of how racist activity in one particular boy arises as part of a cross-cutting set of identity struggles in which he presents himself both as hegemonically hard, and as searching for a way of accounting for his actions which also recognises his need for emotional contact (particularly with men), and the feelings of loss and anxiety that constantly threaten to undermine his surface assurance. It should be noted as the outset that it is not a necessary part of my argument to claim that racism always has such underpinnings though there has been some intelligent psychoanalytic theorising on the issue which suggests that it might commonly be based on the projection of inner anxieties into the external 'other' (see Frosh 1997; Rustin 1991). Rather, what I am interested in examining here is the complex way in which abusiveness (here, racism) and masculine identity-construction intertwine.

The example worked on below concerns one particular white, working-class, 13-year-old boy ('John'), who presents himself as a violent person caught up in a rough and dangerous male culture. He enjoys violence on TV, and sees his own violence as something inherent to him, not within his control: 'It's like smoking or drinking coffee – you want to stop but you can't'. He is not interested in academic work, and hints that he finds it difficult to understand complex things, even including more sophisticated TV soaps. John's description of his relationship with other boys is in terms of hardness and aggression; reputation is important, and tenderness with boys is automatically connected with homosexuality. There is, however, quite a lot of thoughtful material about the difficulties of making emotional contact with boys, and John describes how he has a male best friend in whom he can confide, reasonably safe in the knowledge that he will not be made fun of. He generalises out of this experience about how relationships between best friends should just be accepted as all right, but he also shows a lot of sensitivity to the danger of being labelled 'gay' because of this. Given the strength of his own explicit homophobia ('I mean, that's just grown on me and I just can't stand gay people'.) this is a particular worry for him, fuelling his dislike of too-close contact with other boys.

The general need to demonstrate hardness is frequently reiterated in John's interview, but there is also a recognition of the price that he is paying for this: 'So people try to help me and then I just push them aside and then they don't come back. So I feel sorry for them and I feel sorry for myself.' Significantly, he also uses the early part of the conversation with our white, male interviewer to muse on the absence of his father, who has left the family home, expressing anger but evoking a strong sense of loss:

John: But then now, he's, he's like stopped ringing an' he's, he's got his other family now. I think he's just... I don't think he just wants to see me any more.

Interviewer: Right. How d'you feel about that?

John: I feel upset an' angry.

Overall, John portrays his emotions – particularly and explicitly his temper but also implicitly his angry sadness – as outside his control. It sounds as though he needs a 'container' for all this, and seeks one in his idealisation of girls, who can take him seriously and manage his distress. In many ways he seems very clearly to embody a conventional split between masculine hardness and feminine receptivity; he partly recognises but then represses the 'soft' aspects of himself, including his need for some tenderness, and then projects it into a split off, feminised object. This suggests that he can probably switch quickly between idealising girls and denigrating them when he feels let down.

A fair amount of the interview material with John concerns his ethnic identity and his attitude to racism. At one point in the first of the two interviews, he has been trying to build up a picture of himself as unproblematically white, comfortable in his ethnicity and able to mix with others on his own terms. However, there are reasons to think that he is struggling with a more complex view of himself than he can acknowledge. For example, when asked about his ethnicity he does not simply state that it is white and/or English; instead, he works his way into his 'Englishness' through a mounting yet hesitant series of clauses about his parentage, which seem to have the function of drawing up the evidence, or perhaps naming something for himself:

John: [I dunno] I'm just English... Um ... My ancestors could be German for all I know, but I am English... I'm all English. My mum, my dad's English. My nan an' granddad are English. And so basically I'm English.

The impact of this is to raise a question about the security of this identity judgement, especially as it is followed immediately by a 'but', which has a defensive rather than a logical function:

Interviewer: Do you think of yourself as white? Is that...?

John: Yeah, but, um, I don't try and mix in with the Blacks. I don't start listening to the, like, swing. I like a bit of swing, yeah, but

I don't try and fit in with the, like, the backwards hat, the baggy trousers an' stuff like that. I just wear what I wanna wear. [*Int.* Right] Rather than trying to fit in. I just wanna wear what I think looks good on me.

The construction of himself as white English seems immediately to raise for John the question of the 'other', of whether somewhere lurking inside him is the wish to be Black. It is as if John has an awareness, perhaps not quite unconscious, that identity is built on the basis of an occluded otherness; in his case, the energy which he puts into defending himself against the imagined accusation that he might be what he calls a 'Black wannabe' is very striking, suggesting that an important piece of emotional work is taking place here, keeping something troublesome at bay. What this interview raises for John is an uncertainty over the security of his 'hard, white, English' identity, so the interviewer comes to represent ('in the transference', one might say) a slightly persecutory, questioning voice. Along with this uncertainty comes the question of racism.

John: Yeah. But it's racism I really hate. [*Int.* Do you, yeah?] Yeah, I hate racism. Think it's just out of order. It's wrong.

Interviewer: Do you ever come across racism?

John: Not as much as I thought in this world would be. No. Not at all. Um ... But there are quite racial things, like, say, if we go to a shop an' it's run by Asians [*Int.* Mmm] and, um, they can't speak very good English, and, um, so people go in there and they get, and they get cussed because of their race, an' then they said stuff like, 'You shouldn't be over here. You should go back to your own country'. And stuff like this.

Interviewer: Who says that?

John: Some boys round my area. I didn't like... I didn't wanna say that but I mean round my area if you go into a shop, the ... um, they want somethink an' they can't afford it an' then they say 'Put it back. You can't afford it.' An' then they start cussing 'em because of what their race are. [*Int.* Mmm] I've never really taken part in that. [*Int.* Yeah] Yeah. I've just always stepped away from racism. I hate racism. It's not, it's not a good thing to do really.

John is concerned to position himself as antagonistic to racism, but his description of his actions is to a considerable degree at variance with this: he goes around with boys involved in racist abuse, even though he claims not to take part in their activities. What is not clear from this is why he is at such pains to present himself as so fervently anti-racist in the first place. The dynamics of the interview almost certainly come into play here, in that John has elicited a positive response from the interviewer and might be eager to hold onto this, particularly as his relationships with other males are starved of emotional content. Although the interviewer is careful not to adopt any particular position around racism, it would be surprising if John did not assume that he would have a non- or anti-racist position, given the professed values of most adults working with boys in schools. However, earlier in the interview John has dwelt on his enjoyment of violence and has not seemed to be trying particularly to cast himself in a socially conventional good light; rather, he appears more intent on showing how hard and independent he is. On this evidence, therefore, it is likely that his conscious intention is to show that he cannot be stereotyped and that he is confident in himself and his own opinions. He is truly 'hard' if he does not have to show how hard he is by getting involved in racist abuse; he does not have to be a 'troublemaker' in the way some of this group do. At an unconscious level, it might also be that John's construction of his anti-racist identity, even in the face of evidence of his racist activity, is a way of appeasing his own internal trouble, in which fragments of otherness crop up as repressed desires and have to be violently beaten away, and of reaching out for a supportive or containing contact with a sympathetic man.

In the follow-up interview, two weeks later, the issue of racism emerges in a context in which John positions himself as a victim.

Interviewer: 'Cos you said at the first interview that…you didn't like the policeman because you felt you got picked upon by the police and, er, one of the occasions was when you'd been cussing Asian people and they phoned up the police to come along.

John: What really bugs me is they can pull me over when it wasn't even me. And that really bugs me then I go around to the shop or wherever it was and then I can have a go at them.

Interviewer: The Asian people? I see, yeah.

John: And say why, why you saying, giving my description and stuff and start cussing them.

Interviewer: But presumably it's because you hang around with other boys who were doing it.

John: Yeah and that, looking up and then I get pulled over while I was walking down the street. I can get searched as well most the time and get asked questions. I just don't like it. I really hate it, I hate getting pulled over 'cos it just really pees me off and they just accuse you of doing it when you hardly, didn't even do anything…

Interviewer: Are there other occasions apart from cases of racism that they pick you up for?

John: Yeah, mm.

Interviewer: Like what?

John: Well cause they can … They can see me with a short haircut like this and they can, 'cos they're like racial groups, they can be a racial group with that and they can call me over and say was you cussing so-and-so and if I say no, sometimes they don't believe me and sometimes they do. And that can really bug me as well.

Interviewer: Are there people that, I mean the boys that you go around with, is there, when they're cussing people of other races, is it always Asian people, or is it Black people?

John: It can be any sort of people, white people, Black people, Asian people, half-caste people, anybody they wanna pick on.

Interviewer: But when they're picking on Asian people or Black people they're referring to their race when they cuss them?

John: Most of the time they [inaudible] their features, what they're wearing, anything like that.

Interviewer: How do you actually feel when that happens?

John: Sad, I feel sorry for the person. I mean they don't really need that, say if they're walking home from work they don't need to be stopped and cussed when they haven't done anything wrong.

Interviewer: Do you join in the cussing?

John: No, not really, no. I just sort of stand back and let them do what they wanna do. I think it's quite wrong.

Interviewer: Do you find it kind of quite difficult going around with these boys then?

John: Mm, prob, now I sit at my mate's house really and talk to him.

What John works on in this section is a discourse of unfairness – how he is picked on just because he hangs around with a group of boys who are involved in racism and because he fits the racist stereotype in terms of his appearance, even though he is, by his own account, actually the one who defuses or at least limits the group's racist activity. To some degree, this espousal of the agentic position of the 'victim' might be understood as a way in which John creates a justificatory account of his morality. However, it is still worth noting the agitation John seems to feel around the issue of how unfair it is that he should be picked on by police, and the way in his account this legitimises his own racist aggression, now seen as a response to the mistreatment he receives from those Asians who report on him. He is really 'bugged' by the whole thing, as if his attempt to keep himself separate from the aggression surrounding him is being systematically undermined by people who will not let him be.

Even in the midst of this self-serving narrative, something more vulnerable in John is communicated. He seems to switch back and forth between a defensive need to persuade himself (here, through the interviewer) that he is secure in his identity and moral standing, and the expression of a wish that things would be different – that there would be less dissatisfaction and more understanding. The 'sorrow' John feels for people who are picked on might then be fuelled in part by his sorrow for himself: what his group do to those they pick on is a replica of what John complains happens to him – that he is blamed and attacked when he has done nothing to deserve it. By the end of this narrative, John is claiming that he is beginning to opt out of the gang activity, spending more time just talking to his mate at his house, where he feels more comfortable and safe. To the extent that one can judge the emotional tone of this, it seems to be that for all his apparent hardness, John is depressed by the constant abrasiveness of his life; he wants something much more secure.

Conclusion

In the light of the theoretical arguments presented earlier, this material exemplifies the sheer complexity and labour of the task facing boys as they strive to construct a viable gendered identity. It is quite apparent that John draws upon culturally dominant discourses of hegemonic masculinity in creating his own narrative of identity – 'hard', self-sufficient, instrumental, heterosexual, nobody's fool. This is reproduced in its racialised manifestation, in which John constructs a version of himself as inhabiting a masculinity securely grounded in its ethnic identity of 'white Englishness', and demonstrates an involvement in gendered race politics. The construction of his masculinity is shot through with racialised imperatives, manifested in the energy he puts into extracting himself from the position of 'Black wannabe'. Neither his ethnic nor his masculine identities can be fully understood in isolation from each other. However, what is also clear from the way these identities are constructed and enacted in the interview is that John's habitation of the hegemonic white male position is achieved only at considerable cost and with a great expenditure of emotional energy. In the very moment of constructing himself in this way, he reveals ambivalence, uncertainty and anxiety, articulating in only a loosely disguised form the loss involved in repudiating otherness, and projecting his vulnerability and 'softness' into the interviewer.

The contention here is that this process is endemic to the construction of masculine identities. Just as psychoanalytic theory draws attention to the way masculinity exists only in tension with its denied and denigrated other, so John's narratives of ethnicity and 'race' reveal a struggle to remain separate from the other more than they communicate any clear notion of what it means to be white and male. Moreover, John's sadness and the way a sense of loss seeps in around the edges of his conscious articulation of his identity is highly reminiscent of the material on identity construction as involving what Butler (1995, p.34) terms the 'never loved and never grieved', the un-conscious and hence unrecognised repudiation of alternatives, leaving the psyche depleted and ill-at-ease. Psychoanalysis routinely claims that when people are faced with loss and deprivation, they are likely to search for ways of establishing themselves as 'hard' and self-sufficient. As with John, one would expect men to gender this activity and link it with rampant and anxious homophobia. Their performance, to the degree that it fulfils the demands of hegemonic masculinity (tough, cool, unswayable), generates their gender identities and with it the conventional abusiveness associated with masculinity; yet even among those who present themselves as successful in this regard, there is a pervasive sense that something important is missing.

As ever, none of this is meant to push the responsibility for male violence, either racist or sexual, away from those who perpetrate it. Rather, it is intended to make more complete our understanding of the roots of this abusive complex. Hidden among the narratives of anger and hurt which men, young and old, burst out with when given a chance, there is a story of missed masculinities, of possibilities unrealised and often even unrecognised. These possibilities are excluded through the iterative processes of masculine socialisation, but this does not mean that they disappear completely. Abusive masculinities abound, without a doubt; in that sense, nothing has changed since the time of writing of the passage with which this chapter began. However, if we are to do more than simply repeat eternally that men are abusive, it is important also to unravel other masculinities, subjugated at present and through much of history, but still, thankfully, alive.

Notes

1 The study, 'Emergent identities: Masculinities and 11 to 14-year-old-boys', is funded by the Economic and Social Research Council as part of their 'Children 5 to 16' research programme.

References

Benjamin, J. (1998) *Shadow of the Other.* New York: Routledge.

Butler, J. (1990) *Gender Trouble.* London: Routledge.

Butler, J. (1995) 'Melancholy gender/refused identification'. In M. Berger, B. Wallis and S. Watson (eds) *Constructing Masculinity.* London: Routledge.

Connell, R. (1995) *Masculinities.* Cambridge: Polity.

Elliott, A. and Spezzano, C. (1996) 'Psychoanalysis at its limits'. *Psychoanalytic Quarterly 65,* 52–83.

Frosh, S. (1992) 'Masculine ideology and psychological therapy'. In J. Ussher and P. Nicholson (eds) *Gender Issues in Clinical Psychology.* London: Routledge.

Frosh, S. (1994) *Sexual Difference.* London: Routledge.

Frosh, S. (1997) *For and Against Psychoanalysis.* London: Routledge.

Glaser, D. and Frosh, S. (1993) *Child Sexual Abuse* (2nd edn). London: Macmillan.

Jukes, A. (1993) *Why Men Hate Women.* London: Free Association Books.

Pattman, R., Frosh, S. and Phoenix, A. (1998) 'Lads, machos and others: Developing "boy-centred" research'. *Journal of Youth Studies 1,* 125–142.

Rattansi, A. and Phoenix, A. (1997) 'Rethinking youth identities: Modernist and postmodernist frameworks'. In J. Bynner, L. Chisholm and A. Furlong (eds) *Youth, Citizenship and Social Change in a European Context.* Aldershot: Avebury.

Rustin, M. (1991) *The Good Society and the Inner World.* London: Verso Ltd.

Segal, L. (1990) *Slow Motion: Changing Masculinities, Changing Men.* London: Virago Press.

Seidler, V. (1989) *Rediscovering Masculinity.* London: Routledge.

CHAPTER 9

Sexual Orientation and Abuse

Francis Mark Mondimore

Consideration of the psychological consequences of abuse when the abuse victim is homosexual or bisexual requires a special appreciation of the developmental experiences of these individuals. Several decades of psychological and sociological research have yielded models of sexual orientation development that have proven extremely useful in understanding better the psychological, social and cultural experiences of homosexual and bisexual persons. These models provide valuable theoretical underpinning for the development of successful clinical perspectives and techniques for the treatment of psychological problems in these groups. It is also clear that sexual orientation issues are often raised in victims who do not identify themselves as homosexual or bisexual.

Historical perspectives on sexual orientation

Although only about three per cent of the general adult population consider themselves homosexual (Lauman *et al.* 1994), there has been enormous interest in homosexuality in Western cultures since the late Middle Ages, when religious condemnation and criminalisation of homosexuality replaced the relative indifference towards and tolerance of same-sex eroticism that existed in ancient Greek, Roman and Persian cultures. Early church fathers warned that 'famines, earthquakes and pestilences' would be sent by God to punish 'sodomites', and that 'because of [homosexuality], cities have indeed perished, together with the men in them' (McNeil 1988, p.78). Homosexuality came to be regarded as a particularly heinous 'crime against nature' in secular law, punished by severe, sometimes gruesome penalties, as in a thirteenth-century English law calling for persons who had sexual intercourse with members of their own sex to be buried alive (Boswell 1980, p.277).

In the nineteenth century, physicians and psychologists formulating explanations of various aspects of human behaviour incorporated by then culturally pervasive anti-homosexual attitudes into their theory, adding 'pathological' to 'immoral' and 'illegal' as the acceptable attitudes towards same-sex eroticism. Mid-nineteenth century medical explanations emphasised neuropsychiatric degeneration as an aetiologic factor for homosexuality, as discussed, for example, in Krafft-Ebbing's encyclopaedia of abnormal sexualities, *Psychopathia Sexualis*. Although this idea faded into obscurity as the disease model replaced degeneracy theory in modern psychiatry, the word 'degenerate' remains as a common term used to refer to a person with 'abnormal' sexual practices.

Several decades later, Freud sought to explain mental life as a dynamic interplay between conscious and subconscious processes and proposed a number of different explanations for homosexuality. Although he was unusually compassionate towards homosexual individuals for a physician of his time, Freud nevertheless considered them deviant, and explained the development of persistent same-sex erotic orientation as resulting from various arrests in psychosexual development, particularly unresolved Oedipal conflicts (see Freud 1920; Lewes 1988). Many psychoanalytical theorists later expanded on, but usually distorted, Freud's ideas about homosexuality, insisting that homosexuals were invariably psychological defectives, incapable of mature intimacy or normal social functioning.

During most of the twentieth century homosexuals have been condemned as immoral sinners, punished as criminal sexual predators and described in professional journals as psychological degenerates by religious, legal and medical authorities. Not surprisingly, anti-homosexual bias continues to be firmly entrenched in Western culture, and homosexuality is highly stigmatised through most of the world.

Modern theories of sexual orientation

Perhaps the first psychologist to seriously question the prevailing views of homosexuality as always and completely pathological was the English physician Havelock Ellis, who in 1897 set out the case histories of 31 'inverts' in his book *Sexual Inversion*, the first of his landmark five-volume series on human sexuality, *Studies in the Psychology of Sex*. Ellis noted that the mental experiences and non-sexual behaviours of the homosexual men and women that he had studied were not characterised by aberration, but rather that these individuals 'usually pass[ed] through life as ordinary, sometimes honoured members of society' (Ellis and Symonds 1897, p.68).

In the 1940s and 1950s, the American biologist Alfred Kinsey published the results of sexual behaviour surveys of thousands of individuals showing that homosexual behaviours were quite common; for example, about 37 per cent of the men surveyed reported at least one homosexual experience to the point of orgasm at some point in their lives. American psychologist Evelyn Hooker demonstrated in 1957 that homosexual men did not differ from heterosexual men on measures of psychological health such as the Rorschach test, and further, psychologists could not identify the sexual orientation of test subjects by looking for evidence of 'psychological disturbance' in psychological test results (Hooker 1957).

In 1973 the American Psychiatric Association deleted homosexuality from the *Diagnostic and Statistical Manual of Mental Disorders*. In 1978 social psychologists Alan Bell and Martin Weinberg published the results of a landmark study of the psychological functioning of homosexual men and women, and concluded that, 'Homosexual adults who have come to terms with their homosexuality…are no more distressed psychologically than are heterosexual men and women' (Bell and Weinberg 1978, p.216).

In the 1990s researchers for the first time discovered biological correlates of sexual orientation, suggesting that sexual orientation is at least partly a result of biological factors. Groups of homosexuals have been found to differ from heterosexual peers in the size of several brain structures, and on several measures of cerebral dominance such as visuo-spatial abilities and language processing. Several studies have found a significant genetic component to homosexual orientation. One study of homosexual brothers and their families located a region on the 'X' chromosome strongly linked to male homosexuality (Hamer *et al.* 1993).

Despite intense research interest, there are still no comprehensive medical or psychological theories that adequately explain homosexuality. Psycho-analytic theories that have postulated aberrations in psychosexual develop-ment have not been supported by psychological and sociological research. Although behavioural psychologists have attempted to explain homosexual orientation as resulting from stimulus-reward mechanisms operating on early sexual experiences, aversive conditioning techniques developed to reorient homosexuals (and bisexuals) have not been successful in doing so. Comprehensive explanations for homosexuality based on sexual biology have proven inadequate as well. Genetic factors, for example, although clearly important in the development of homosexuality, have been found to explain only about 50 per cent of variance in sexual orientation.

An individual's sexual orientation appears the result of a poorly under-stood interaction of biological and psychological factors, and social and cultural factors as well, that begin to operate prenatally in the form of genetic and hormonal influences on the developing brain. These factors interact with as yet unidentified experiential influences during early childhood development. Sexual orientation towards members of the same or opposite sex – or, more rarely, towards both sexes – appears largely to be determined by the time of puberty, especially in men. During puberty and young adulthood, the erotic life of most individuals comes to centre on the same or opposite gender, largely as the playing out of a sexual script written many years previously.

Sexual orientation identity development

The process by which people in modern Western cultures come to identify themselves as homosexual individuals is surprisingly consistent from one person to the next. Behavioural scientists have described developmental milestones unique to homosexual identity development that illustrate this process and provide for better understanding of psychodynamic processes in gay men and lesbians.

At a very young age, children, including those who will later develop homosexual and bisexual orientations, internalise the pervasive societal stigmatisation of homosexuality that surrounds them. Young children assume that they will grow up to be 'just like everyone else', to be 'mummies' and 'daddies', that is, heterosexual. Exquisitely sensitive to gender roles at a very young age, children taunt and ridicule those who do not conform to expectations of gender-differentiated behaviour, often using the epithets applied to homosexuals to do so. An association begins to develop between words like 'queer' and gender-nonconforming behaviours such as rough-and-tumble play in girls and playing with dolls in boys. Children learn to associate these words with being different and unwanted. When adult homosexuals are interviewed, many report that they felt 'different' from other children when they were young. Frequently, this sense of 'differentness' centres on the fact that they had different play interests from their peers.

Differences in temperament may be noted as well. Psychoanalyst Richard Isay (1990) has written that 'every gay man that I have seen reports that beginning at age three or four he experienced that he was 'different' from his peers... More sensitive, crying more easily, having his feelings hurt more readily...and being less aggressive than others of his age' (p.15). Surveys of lesbians report similar findings, adult lesbians often recalling more interest in athletics and other active forms of play than their peers, and having a more independent and self-reliant temperament.

Pre-homosexual children often experience psychological marginalisation from peers. Feelings of being different from same-sex peers cause these children to feel a sense of separateness from them and often within their own family as well. If gender-nonconforming behaviours cause them to be identified as the class 'sissy' or 'tomboy', these children can be singled out for ongoing verbal or even physical abuse. But even children whose gender-nonconforming behaviours are not significant enough to make them the targets of this level of abuse are sensitised to gender issues and to the highly stigmatised nature of nonconformity along gender lines during childhood.

In adolescence, the feeling of being different from same-sex peers begins to include a feeling of being sexually different, as these children come to recognise an incongruity between their own sexual feelings and those reported by peers. This may take the form of a lack of the intense interest in the opposite sex reported by peers, an awareness of sexual feelings for members of the same sex or both. By now having acquired at least some knowledge of the meaning of homosexuality, the adolescent develops the awareness that this phenomenon may have personal relevance. A stage of identity confusion is reached where the adolescent is unsure about who he or she is sexually and what sort of person he or she may become. The adolescent is confronted with the possibility that a previously held self-image as a 'normal' person may be incorrect, and that he or she may in fact be terribly 'abnormal', 'perverted', 'sinful' or any number of other characterisations that spring from internalised stigmatisation of homosexuality. Some adolescents experience clinically significant anxiety, depression or substance abuse problems related to these conflicts.

Other individuals, however, experience a great sense of relief when they first come to recognise that they might be gay or lesbian. Years of vague uneasiness about an undefinable differentness from peers can crystallise into the realisation that he or she is gay or lesbian in a sudden flash of insight. Isay (1990) refers to this as the 'Aha!' experience that many gay men and lesbians have as adolescents: 'like the pieces of an old puzzle falling into place' (p.295).

For other adolescents, however, there may be a tremendous struggle, perhaps largely unconscious, to avoid self-labelling as homosexual. They may throw themselves into activities and interests they have come to associate with heterosexuality, and avoid those they associate with homo-sexuality. Individuals who remain conflicted about homosexual feelings may postpone dealing with sexual orientation issues indefinitely through various degrees of denial, redefining, and compartmentalisation of feelings and even behaviours, a developmental shutdown that Australian psychologist Vivian Cass has called 'identity foreclosure' (Cass 1979).

Fortunately, the increasing availability of accurate information about homosexuality, the disappearance of 'crimes against nature' laws throughout most of the industrialised world (with the notable exception of about half of the US) and the visibility of more and more successful and happy gay men and lesbians in their communities makes it easier for individuals to work through their internalised anti-homosexual biases and accept and success-fully incorporate their sexual orientation into their fuller identity.

Sexual abuse and sexual orientation

Surveys of sexual behaviour in adults have suggested that there is a positive correlation between childhood sexual abuse and homosexuality. A 1990 survey of 412 American university students found that students who reported their sexual orientation as gay, lesbian or bisexual reported a two-fold higher lifetime incidence of sexual abuse than heterosexual students (Duncan 1990). Findings such as these have often been interpreted as indicating that childhood sexual abuse is an aetiological factor in the development of homosexuality in both males and females.

An increased incidence of lesbian orientation in abused females has been explained as the victim simply turning away from sexual activity with all males as a post-traumatic response to sexual abuse by a male perpetrator. An intriguing psychoanalytic elaboration of this idea in the case of father-daughter incest is that of the 'Persephone complex' (Starzepyzel 1987), which suggests that little girls are 'stolen' emotionally from their mother by the incestuous perpetrator (as the mythical Persephone was abducted from her mother, the goddess Demeter) disrupting an intense pre-Oedipal bond with mother. The girl victim experiences a subconscious sense of abandon-ment by and an intense longing for mother that is later transformed into sexual orientation towards female partners.

Psychodynamic understandings of childhood sexual abuse as influencing the development of female homosexuality are appealing in light of research suggesting that sexual orientation appears to be more fluid and changeable in at least some women than it is in men. Erotic attraction and sexual behaviour seem less important, and affection and emotional bonding more important in women's erotic relationships compared with those of men. Numerous studies have shown that women have more 'cross-preference' sexual fantasy than men (Bell and Weinberg 1978; Masters and Johnson 1979), and more women than men rate themselves towards the middle of the Kinsey homo-sexual–heterosexual scale (that is, within a bisexual range) and report more significant shifts along the homosexual–heterosexual continuum during their lifetime (Pillard 1978).

A study of 94 women in long-term sexual relationships found that women with a history of childhood sexual abuse who were in lesbian relationships expressed greater overall satisfaction and greater sexual satisfaction with their relationships than women with a history of abuse who were in heterosexual relationships (Weingourt 1998). This would argue against understanding homosexuality as a pathological outcome of a traumatic event in women with a history of abuse. Development of a lesbian orientation, perhaps facilitated by predisposing biological factors, may be an adaptive and positive response in some women following childhood sexual abuse.

Male homosexuality has also been explained as a reaction to childhood sexual abuse. Finkelhor, who found a four-fold greater incidence of abuse among homosexual males compared to heterosexual males, theorised that boys who have been sexually victimised by older males assume that they have been selected for abuse because the perpetrator 'knew' they were gay. Worry that sexual activity with a male necessarily indicates homosexuality is thought to somehow lead these boys to identify themselves as homosexuals as adults (Finkelhor 1984). Sexual abuse of boys perpetrated by older females has been linked to male homosexuality as well, with the explanation that boys who are frightened by sexual contact with an older woman, or who merely find the experience unpleasant, generalise their feelings to all heterosexual experiences, assuming that they must be homosexual because they did not enjoy the abusive heterosexual experience.

These theories are at odds with data showing a strong biological component to male sexual orientation. Also, sexual orientation development data show that male sexual orientation appears to be fairly well set by early latency, whereas sexual abuse of boys typically occurs at a later age (Mendel 1995). In a study of 137 homosexual and bisexual males aged 14 to 21, those who had a history of sexual abuse usually reported that the abuse had occurred after their self-identification as gay or bisexual (Ramefedi, Farrow and Deisher 1991).

These data suggest that rather than sexual abuse putting males 'at risk' for the development of homosexual orientation, the reverse is probably true. Pre-homosexual boys may be vulnerable to sexual abuse because of the psychological marginalisation they experience. The self-stigmatisation of the young gay male may cause problems with boundaries and assertiveness – in Finkelhor's (1984) words, cause the child to be 'emotionally insecure or deprived' (p.57) – making him more vulnerable to exploitation. The same may be true of female victims of sexual abuse who self-identify as lesbians during latency.

There is some evidence that a history of physical or sexual abuse makes the process of homosexual identity formation more difficult. Gay, lesbian and bisexual youth have been identified as being at increased risk for a variety of self-endangering behaviours, including suicide, HIV-risk sexual behaviours and multiple substance abuse (Garofalo *et al* 1998). These studies also indicate that the sexual minority youth who engage in self-destructive behaviours frequently have a history of abuse (Ramefedi, Farrow and Deisher 1991), indicating an interplay and probable additive effect of these two factors in the development of psychological problems. Abuse during childhood and adolescence and a developing homosexual orientation both raise identity questions that may pose severe threats to an adolescent's feelings of self-worth. Just as abuse victims often blame themselves for having been abused, sexual minority adolescents frequently blame themselves for the negative consequences of being homosexual. Both groups struggle with feelings that they are 'defective' in some way, and therefore deserving of mistreatment by others and not worthy of being loved. Both groups may experience depression and anxiety that arise from confusion about sexual roles, the meaning of sexuality, and the relationship between sexuality and love.

Victims of abuse and sexual minority youth both must navigate troubled waters of shame, secrecy, isolation from peers and mistrust of adults on the way to healthy identity development. Homosexual identity development, essentially replacing a negative self-image with a positive one, will be more difficult when there is a history of abuse.

The non-gay male victim of abuse

Although there is evidence that earlier studies under-estimated the proportion of female perpetrators of sexual abuse of young males, many, perhaps most, male sexual abuse victims have been abused by other males. Since the majority of male victims of abuse are or will later identify themselves as heterosexual, a common abused-male scenario will be that of a pre-heterosexual or young heterosexual male abused by another male.

Sexual abuse by a male perpetrator seems to be more disturbing to the victim and leads to more severe symptoms and clinical problems than does abuse by a female perpetrator. A 1997 UK study of 115 men who consulted a counselling service for male victims of sexual abuse found that 87 per cent of the men had been abused by a male perpetrator. In this clinically selected population, only seven per cent reported abuse by a female perpetrator, a number significantly lower than most survey studies that have measured the incidence of male sexual abuse by female versus male perpetrators (King and Woolett 1997). Although other selection factors may be at work in this study, its findings suggest that abuse of a male by a male perpetrator is more likely to lead to problems significant enough for the victim to seek treatment. Another study of 124 men sexually abused as boys found that abuse by a male perpetrator was one of the strongest predictors of significant scores on a scale that measured trauma symptoms, poor self-worth and sexual maladjustment (Mendel 1995).

Abuse by a male perpetrator appears to cause male victims to question their masculinity and their sexual orientation identity in profound ways.

Abused boys worry that having been selected for abuse indicates that their masculinity is defective in some way, that they are weak, unmanly and helpless. The possibility that the nature of this 'defect' might be homosexuality causes them to experience profound fear and anxiety and to question their sexual orientation. Their internalised stigmatisation of homosexuality causes feelings of intense shame and worthlessness.

Older adolescents, and even adult heterosexual men, presumably more settled in their self-identity as heterosexual, also typically report strongly negative psychological reactions to unwanted sexual advances initiated by other males. These reactions also usually revolve around sexual orientation issues, mostly fear and anger arising from worries that they would not have been approached if they did not look or act 'homosexual' in some way (Struckman-Johnson and Struckman-Johnson 1994).

Changing attitudes towards homosexuality and the greater availability of accurate information about homosexual persons will presumably lessen societal stigmatisation of homosexuality. Consequently, the virulence of the internalised anti-homosexual bias that men develop may lessen as well. It will be interesting to see if these developments change the pattern of psychological reactions of males to sexual abuse by other males in the future.

Clinical implications

Sexual orientation issues are frequently raised by sexual abuse, and therapists treating victims of sexual abuse should acquire a solid grounding in the understanding of sexual orientation issues. Since clients will not always volunteer a homosexual or bisexual identity, the therapist should not automatically assume that his or her client is heterosexual when inquiring about relationships or sexual partners. Clients are even less likely to spontaneously discuss sexual orientation issues during counselling and therapy if they are unsettled about their sexual orientation – unless the therapist has in some way given them permission to do so. This may be as direct as questioning about same-sex sexual interests in all clients, or as subtle as having AIDS awareness or diversity-themed educational posters picturing same-sex couples hanging on the office wall.

Therapists will not infrequently be asked by their clients, or by the parents of their adolescent clients, to offer an opinion as to whether particular feelings or behaviours indicate homosexuality. Popular attitudes reinforce the idea that clear boundaries exist between 'gay' or 'straight', and quick identification of individuals as falling into one category or another is often expected, an expectation at odds with clinical realities. Instead, therapists should help educate clients and family members as to how complex developmental processes lead, over time, to sexual orientation identity.

All therapists should be comfortable helping clients explore the personal meaning of their same-sex erotic feelings, fantasies or behaviours and their attitudes towards gay and non-gay individuals, whether the client identifies himself or herself as gay, lesbian, bisexual, heterosexual or simply 'unsure'. It is clear from a broad-based body of research that these skills are especially necessary for the successful treatment of victims of sexual abuse.

Conclusions

There is a complex and dynamic interplay between the psychological issues raised by homosexuality and by all forms of personal abuse. Indeed, it has been proposed that all gay, lesbian and bisexual persons are, without exception, victims of pervasive, culturally condoned forms of abuse such as housing and employment discrimination, 'crimes against nature' laws, and differential treatment of homosexual relationships, and that they frequently suffer adverse psychological sequelae as a result (Neisen 1993). Just as victims of physical, psychological and sexual abuse frequently blame themselves for having been abused, most homosexual persons struggle at some point in their identity development with a negative self-concept, internalised while growing up in a heterosexist culture, that is, a culture strongly biased against same-sex eroticism. In addition to such 'cultural' victimisation, homosexuals are frequently victims of more easily visible forms of emotional and physical abuse, ranging from name-calling and taunts in the schoolyard to 'gay-bashing' beatings and even murder – abuse where the victim has not been selected at random, but is singled out because they are homosexual.

All of the complex psychological and social problems that arise when an individual internalises a 'defective' self-concept or a 'victim' role are seen in some homosexual and bisexual persons simply because of the problems encountered during their sexual orientation identity development. When actual physical, psychological or sexual abuse experiences are inflicted upon often already psychologically beleaguered sexual minority youth, the potential for more serious problems grows. This may, in fact, be the group of adolescents at the highest risk for self-destructive behaviours yet identified by research.

Sexual abuse frequently activates internalised anti-homosexual stigma in heterosexual males abused by older males as well. Thus sexual orientation issues are frequently raised by sexual abuse even when the victim does not self-identify as homosexual or bisexual.

An understanding of the psychological responses of individuals to various forms of abuse, victimisation and stigmatisation has greatly enhanced our understanding of the process of sexual orientation identity development. Thorough understanding of the process of homosexual identity development will likewise enhance the understanding of the psychological and social consequences of abuse.

References

Bell, A. and Weinberg, S. (1978) *Homosexualities: A Study of Diversity among Men and Women.* New York: Simon and Schuster.

Boswell, J. (1980) *Christianity, Social Tolerance and Homosexuality: Gay People in Western Europe from the Beginning of the Christian Era to the Fourteenth Century.* Chicago: University of Chicago Press.

Cass, V. (1979) 'Homosexual identity formation: A theoretical model'. *Journal of Homosexuality 4*, 3, 219–235.

Duncan, D. (1990) 'Prevalence of sexual assault victimization among heterosexual and gay/lesbian university students'. *Psychological Reports 66*, 65–66.

Ellis, H. and Symonds, J. (1897) *Sexual Inversion.* New York: Arno Press, 1975.

Finkelhor, D. (1984) *Childhood Sexual Abuse: New Theory and Research.* New York: Free Press.

Freud, S. (1920) 'The psychogenesis of a case of homosexuality in a woman'. In *The Standard Edition of the Complete Psychological Works of Sigmund Freud, Vol. XVIII*, pp.155–172. James Strachey (trans. and ed.). London: Hogarth, 1957.

Garofalo, R., Wolf, R.C., Kessel, S., Palfrey, J. and DuRant, R. (1998) 'The association between health risk behaviours and sexual orientation among a school-based sample of adolescents'. *Pediatrics 101*, 895–902.

Hamer, D., Hu, S., Magnuson, V., Ho, N. and Pattatucci, A. (1993) 'A linkage between DNA markers on the X chromosome and male homosexuality'. *Science 261*, 321–327.

Hooker, E. (1957) 'The adjustment of the male overt homosexual'. *Journal of Projective Techniques 21*, 18–31.

Isay, R. 'Psychoanalytic theory and the therapy of gay men'. In D. McWhirter, S. Sanders and J. Reinisch (eds) *Homosexuality/Heterosexuality: Concepts of Sexual Orientation.* New York: Oxford University Press.

King, M. and Woollett, E. (1997) 'Sexually assaulted males: 115 men consulting a counselling service'. *Archives of Sexual Behaviour 26*, 5, 579–558.

Krafft-Ebbing, R. von (1965) *Psychopathia Sexualis.* Trans. Franklin Klaf. New York: Bell.

Lauman, E., Gagnon, J., Michael, R. and Michiels, S. (1994) *The Social Organization of Sexuality: Sexual Practices in the United States.* Chicago: University of Chicago Press.

Lewes, K. (1988) *The Psychoanalytic Theory of Male Homosexuality.* New York: Simon and Schuster.

Masters, W. and Johnson, V. (1979) *Homosexuality in Perspective.* Boston: Little Brown.

Mendel. M. (1995) *The Male Survivor: The Impact of Sexual Abuse.* California: Sage Publications.

McNeil, J. (1988) *The Church and the Homosexual* (3rd edn). Boston: Beacon Press.

Neisen, J. (1993) 'Healing from cultural victimization: Recovery from shame due to heterosexism'. *Journal of Gay and Lesbian Psychotherapy 2*, 1, 49–63.

Pillard, R. (1990) 'The Kinsey scale: Is it familial?' In D. McWhirter, S. Sanders, and J. Reinisch (eds) *Homosexuality/Heterosexuality: Concepts of Sexual Orientation.* New York: Oxford University Press.

Remafedi, G., Farrow, J. and Deisher, R. (1991) 'Risk factors for attempted suicide in gay and bisexual youth'. *Pediatrics 87*, 6, 869 875.

Starzecpyzel, E. (1987) 'The Persephone complex: Incest dynamics and the lesbian preference'. In The Boston Lesbian Psychologies Collective (eds) *Lesbian Psychologies: Explorations and Challenges.* Urbana and Chicago: University of Illinois Press.

Struckman-Johnson, C. and Struckman-Johnson, D. (1994) 'Men pressured and forced into sexual experience'. *Archives of Sexual Behaviour 23, 1,* 93–114.

Weingourt, R. (1998) 'A comparison of heterosexual and homosexual long-term relationships'. *Archives of Psychiatric Nursing 12, 2,* 114–118.

Working with Individuals in Clinical Settings

CHAPTER 10

Inner Silence

One of the Impacts of Emotional Abuse Upon the Developing Self

Susan Vas Dias

Proust (quoted in Maurois 1950) may not have intended to describe the profound nature of the effects of emotional abuse upon the developing human being when he wrote 'a great silence rings me round', but his phrase evokes its impact. Emotional abuse to date does not have a legal definition, but is probably the most common form of abuse. It is likely that it is also the bedrock from which other forms of abuse, such as physical and sexual abuse, stem.

Felicity de Zulueta (1993) defines emotional abuse as 'a form of child maltreatment which can take the form of consistent negative attention such as repeated criticisms or belittlements, or a lack of attention such as withdrawal or rejection.' It also occurs when there is over-stimulation of the child by insensitive, forcing and intrusive interactions, which compel the child to take care of themselves by avoiding relationships and withdrawing (Heard and Lake 1997).

The manifestations of emotional abuse are many and varied, but can range from an inability to form satisfying relationships, anxiety states, sleep problems, conduct disorders, precocious ego development, difficulties in learning and eating disorders, to the more extreme problems of disturbances of the self. The nature of the emotionally abused person's difficulties will depend to some extent on the level of intensity and cumulative nature of the abuse.

The study of the extreme in human conditions can lead to greater understanding of the norm. This chapter will explore the impact of severe, cumulative emotional abuse, drawing on my work with ten people treated in attachment-based psychoanalytic psychotherapy during the past 20 years. Each person was referred for different reasons, but each had in common an inability to communicate verbally: they were all predominantly silent. The clinical work in each instance was on average three times a week over a mean period of four years.

Exploring the different aspects of silence as a form of communication eventually led to each individual speaking in their own way about what one person termed their 'inner silence'. Characteristic of the inner silence was the fact that 'there is no sound inside…just silence', an inability to experience affect, and what seemed to be an unintegrated use of cognitive ability. Each individual was unable to work satisfactorily or form relationships, and each was at times actively suicidal.

The capacity to experience affect is vital to our perception of ourselves as unique individuals. Everyday happenings as well as the major life decisions and events which change the direction of our lives are normally accompanied by associated affective experience. This helps us build the cumulative picture of our own individual story, our self-narrative. Although speculative, it is likely that without accompanying affect, an experience cannot become part of our internal story. A difficulty in experiencing oneself as unique and as someone with a self-narrative can then arise, which might then affect the individual's capacity for healthy functioning in the external world.

Why the experience of affect is so central in human development is an area which demands further scrutiny. There are several ways of approaching it. It is clear that emotional experience is always accompanied by visceral arousal, i.e., physical sensations caused by organs in the chest and/or abdomen, as a necessary pre-condition. This means that our affective world is intricately intertwined with our physical being, the very foundation of the experience of ourselves.

But the quality of emotion is dependent on the cognitive and perceptual evaluations we make of the external world and our internal world (Schachter 1971). Events in our lives become especially significant if they are experienced in an 'emotional' visceral context: those ideas, events, relationships, and so on, which evoke emotional arousal are the ones which occupy a special place in our memories. These then contribute to the 'files' in our 'internal reference library', which we use to consult as we go about experiencing ourselves in daily life.

The developing infant comes into the world endowed with his or her own physical, cognitive and perceptual capacities, which continually interact with the external world. In the first months of life the growing awareness of one's self emerges to a large extent through physical and perceptual sensation, the experience of one's visceral being. Our cognitive capacities facilitate the process of defining ourselves, but our visceral nature remains one of the fundamental building-blocks of our perception of 'that which is me'. This gradually also incorporates the emotional visceral experience of the infant and child as they interact with the environment in which they develop.

To be unable to experience affect might be akin to not being a fully living self. The psyche is often defined as the soul, but is also thought of as 'a principle of individuality for living things' (Banner 1987). Psychotherapeutic work, especially with people whose affective world has been silenced by emotional abuse or other trauma, is the slow, careful fostering of the coming alive of a person. The demands of such work require a shift from a 'talking cure' to a listening-centred provision of help. It does wonders for the therapist's preconceived idea of therapy to have to listen to silence week in week out!

What this type of therapeutic interaction provides is 'developmental help' (Freud 1965): therapeutic work which is focused on the various levels of early development in each individual which had, for whatever reason, not been allowed to proceed, either at all or adequately enough for age-appropriate development. These subsequently could lead to difficulties in development, such as problems of autonomy, separation-individuation, in processing the intersubjective world, depleated ability to experience affect, difficulty in development of a solid sense of self, and poor attachment relationships.

Central to the whole of the work was the gradual evolution of the therapeutic relationship. This was based on providing each person with someone who could listen and attune in such a way that eventually they were able to allow themselves to experience affect, know it for what it was and be able to integrate it. In the process the person became aware of the existence of their inner world, and developed the ability for inner dialogue. Only after this had occurred were they in any way able to use verbal language as a means of communicating themselves.

The development of the capacities for the representation, subsequent perception and internalisation of ourselves and others as individuals who have ideas, thoughts, wishes, fantasies and feelings is dependent upon the availability of attachment figures who can provide a solid and consistent secure base from which they can evolve. A child comes into the world programmed to interact with his or her environment (Bowlby 1979; Fairbairn 1952; Parkes 1991). The most important aspect of the infant's world is the quality of interaction between themselves and their caretakers, their attachment figures, usually the parents. It is the nature of these relationships which impacts upon a child's genetic endowment and facilitates the development of the capacity to experience oneself as 'welcome in the world', of value to oneself and to the world at large. From this basic secure sense of self the ability to form satisfying adult relationships and the ability to work and play develops.

What constitutes being of value to oneself, having a solid, secure sense of one's own individuality and capacity to deal with the stresses and strains of living? Filtered through the central role of relationship with primary caretakers, extended family, siblings and peers, other factors which contribute to the development of a healthy sense of self are reasonable nutrition, physical care and appropriate cognitive stimulation.

But it is the experience of our emotional, feeling world which helps us to build up a sense of our unique 'going-on-being' (Winnicott 1958), our understanding of our self as an individual with a unique past and present: 'Our affective core guarantees our continuity of experience across development in spite of the many ways we change' (Emde 1983).

Our ability to develop a self-narrative which combines our affective and cognitive understanding of what has happened to us is a crucial part of our ability to have a dialogue in our internal world. This ongoing, usually preconscious, 'conversation-with-ourselves', or inner dialogue, allows us to remain comfortably rooted in our own identity, which then in turn helps us to interact with the external world in ways which enable us to work, form relationships, play and experience the range of feelings evoked.

From observation in clinical practice it would seem that those people who have little or no self-narrative and/or no awareness of the existence of an internal world are also those for whom the experience of affect is alien. They do not have any understanding of the word 'feeling' beyond a dictionary definition. It would seem that when the capacity to experience affect is curtailed or demolished by severe and/or cumulative emotional abuse early in infancy or childhood, the development of that which Stern (1985) describes as the core and intersubjective self are adversely affected.

Stern suggests that the infant has four self-experiences which combine to make up the core self from two to six months. These are *self-agency, self-coherence, self-affectivity,* and *self-history.* Each of these describe different aspects of the core self, such as the infant's developing experience of his or her actions as being their own, separate from others; having intention; and the control to be self-generated (self-agency). Self-coherence is the experience of being a whole, non-fragmented being with their own boundaries who has the capacity for integrated action both in behaviour and while being still. The experience of emotional – affective – response as being part of oneself (self-affectivity) contributes to that part of the core self which has a sense that it will endure, maintain continuity with its own past and go-on-being, remaining the same while still capable of change (self-history).

The intersubjective self is built on the foundation of the core self, and is characterised by the infant's discovery that he or she has a mind and that other people also have minds (Stern 1985). Gradually, between seven to nine months, the baby becomes aware that inner subjective experience, that which goes on in one's inner world, is potentially able to be shared with another.

This normal development presupposes that the infant has been able to develop in an environment which is nurturing and not abusive. As Wolf (1980) says, 'one may compare the need for the continuous presence of a psychologically nourishing self-object milieu with the continuing need for an environment containing oxygen. It is a relatively silent need of which one becomes aware only when it is not being met, when a harsh world compels one to draw breath in pain' (p.128).

In treatment, it emerged that all ten of the people who came with their silence had developed from birth in environments which were grossly emotionally abusive. None had primary caretakers who seemed able to interact with their infants or were available to pick up on their cues. All were cared for physically but without appropriate interaction. Four had mothers whose level of depression prohibited them from being able to respond to their infants at all. Three had mothers who were so narcissistically needy and disturbed that the babies were either extremely over-stimulated, or used to fulfil their mother's own emotional needs. The last three people had mothers who were psychotic and unable to respond appropriately, either to their children's attachment behaviours, such as crying, smiling, eye contact and physical actions, or to their affect vitality. None of the ten primary caretakers seemed able to experience and value their baby as an individual who was welcome in the world, just for themselves. They did not have any capacity for empathy, or ability to reflect back either in affective tones or by 'labelling' the baby's feeling state.

Most mothers quite naturally attune well enough to what their child might be feeling. They will scan the child and comment in one form or other, which will usually include a mirroring of the child's feeling as well as labelling it. For example, the mother might greet their baby with, 'Hello! How are you today? Oh! You're feeling happy (sad, angry, bored, worried, and so on).' Their tone will mirror the baby's affective state, the baby will feel attuned with and emotionally held, and their inner state/self validated. The labelling of the feeling state will facilitate the infant's ability to be familiar with, know, and scan how he or she is feeling. The affective reciprocity of these interactions gradually becomes part of the baby's memory bank, upon which he or she can draw as they begin to make sense of themselves in relation to their environment. Through this interactive process the child internalises the caretaker's acceptance and valuing of his or her feeling world. This then facilitates the child's sense that their core being is intrinsically of value, and will be able to build upon this to develop their own self-narrative and internal dialogue.

When a baby's or child's internal, emotional world is repeatedly invalidated – not recognised, misattuned with, rejected, mocked, humiliated or totally ignored – the end result is the cumulative trauma of severe emotional abuse. The consequences of this can lead to stunted, stymied, and distorted emotional development, especially in the child's sense of him or herself as a viable, valued, integrated human being capable of functioning well in the world.

My observation is that many of the children and adults who have experienced this type of cumulative emotional abuse early in their development seem to protect their core self by doing the equivalent of putting it in a bubble. It is as if they had taken a good look around the environment in which they found themselves, realised that it was not going to respond in a way conducive to healthy development, and surrounded the Lego-brick structure of their core self which had developed so far with clear perspex. From then on their core self could sit and look out, safe from harm, unable to be reached, until such time as it might be rescued. The result of this encapsulation was that they would begin to perceive the world only through their cognitive abilities. Their capacity to feel, and to enhance their lives with the world of affect was stopped. They could have an ongoing internal list of activities by which they tried to live life, but were always just one step ahead of their inner silence.

Each of the ten severely emotionally abused people had been left very much alone as infants, if not always physically, certainly psychologically. There were no other consistent, responsive caretakers to offset this situation. 'Solitude, psychological solitude, is the mother of anxiety' (Wolf 1980).

The dialectical theory of self-development 'assumes that the psychological self develops through perception of oneself, in another person's mind, as thinking and feeling' (Davidson 1983). When describing someone who was emotionally abused, Fonagy and Target (1995) say, 'where in [the] mother's mind there should have been a child with thoughts and feelings, there was too often emptiness, a space, nothing on which [the child] could build a viable sense of [themselves] as thinking, believing or desiring'.

An understanding of emotional and psychological infant and child development is crucial when working clinically with people who have been emotionally abused. The difficulties with which a person is struggling often give an indication at which developmental level their problems arose. Once this becomes clear, appropriate developmental help can be provided.

Clinical applications

Each of the ten individuals treated presented different therapeutic challenges. Two people will be used to illustrate some aspects of working at different developmental levels. The therapeutic work revealed that one person had particular difficulties in experiencing affect, the other in maintaining autonomy. Both presented with extreme forms of withdrawal into silence.

'Elizabeth' was a 27-year-old woman who was referred for therapy by her psychiatrist in order to see if it could help with her catatonic-like silence. Over a period of six years what happened to her was painstakingly pieced together. She had been born into a well-off professional family. Her mother was hospitalised just after Elizabeth's birth with severe postpartum depression. She then developed a psychotic illness, which waxed and waned throughout Elizabeth's development. She was an ever-present but psychologically absent mother, who terrified her daughter by her total inability to interact with or respond to her. As Elizabeth eventually said, 'She made me feel I wasn't there'.

In therapy, through years of attempting to attune with and then labelling what Elizabeth might be feeling behind her wall of silence, she began to trust the therapeutic relationship enough to allow herself to begin to experience affect. She was utterly terrified when this began to happen, as if she were an infant without words or ability to conceptualise, one who was suddenly overwhelmed by some sort of physical rush which threatened to destroy her. The panic and blind state of confusion were palpable in the consulting room.

Haltingly, over many months, Elizabeth began to be able to label and identify her own feelings. It was during this period that she spoke of what most terrified her, the place inside her she called 'my inner silence'. In this place it transpired nothing existed; it was 'just silent ... nothing'.

Throughout the therapy Elizabeth had not been able to make much eye contact. During the phase when we were exploring the inner silence, at times she became like the young infant who uses their every sense, especially their eyes, to study the world with enormous intent and concentration, such as Mahler's differentiating infant's 'customs inspection' (Mahler and McDevitt 1968). Elizabeth would solemnly stare at me as if everything about me was startlingly new and needed serious study.

She became able to put into words her terror of her mother's emotional absence. Although it is not really possible to know the small child's, or preverbal infant's, psychic reality, it could be conjectured that his or her inner experience is equivalent to and therefore is external reality. Elizabeth's mother's 'silence' (emotional absence) in relation to her infant seemed to equate in Elizabeth's mind with silent nonexistence: 'If I don't exist in my mother's [caretaker's] eyes, I don't exist.'

Through the gradual process of providing Elizabeth with a caretaker who was not emotionally absent, and who could provide a space in which the attuned reciprocity of early caregiving could begin to be received and then internalised, Elizabeth was able to come out of her bubble. She spent years in therapy going through the agony of coming alive to feeling, to her 'self-affectivity'. Through this process she became much stronger, surer of her right to be alive, to exist, and to value herself as a separate unique individual. She had regained her core self and been able to consolidate her self-agency, and self-coherence. But most important of all to her she became able to 'talk with myself... I know where I come from and now it isn't silent any more!'

Elizabeth left therapy after six years. She was no longer silent. However, she was not able to work very well and continued to need hospitalisation from time to time. Years after she had finished she wrote to say that no matter how bad things might seem at times she felt grateful that she could make sense of her life in a way which gave her strength.

Developmental help

The fine-tuning of one's capacity to listen and attune as a therapist, which working with profound silence requires, raises many questions about the nature of therapy being provided. It would seem that a lengthy period of developmental help is necessary with people who have been so emotionally abused that they are silenced both internally and externally.

Listening to silent communication demands scrupulous scanning by the therapist of their own experience of the therapeutic work so that there is little chance of superimposing their own thoughts, feelings and wishes upon the person with whom they are working. At the same time, it also demands that they constantly scan and attune with the non-verbal messages being conveyed in the silence. The two years of infant observation required by some psychotherapy trainings are invaluable preparation.

The infant's active communication and attachment behaviours are primarily through body language, facial expression, affect vitality, eye contact and vocalising. Words are not necessary for understanding the infant's needs, just as they can often get in the way of the therapist attuning to that which is behind the words in clinical work. The work with the extremely silent person requires lengthy periods of picking up cues and clues from body language, slight shifts in expression, tone when speech does occur and sifting these through one's own subjective experience, and suspending that in the service of attunement, mirroring, validation and labelling of what they might be experiencing.

Developmental help is therapeutic help which is based on an under-standing of the stresses and strains of infant and childhood emotional dev-elopment and the problems which can arise at various times during that development. Anna Freud's (1965) concept of developmental lines provides a useful tool for assessment of 'emotional maturity, immaturity, normality or abnormality'. They also help to further our understanding of the dynamic and intricate processes involved in a child's journey to maturation.

Anna Freud proposed that there were many different lines of development along which a child needed to proceed, such as from dependency to emotional self-reliance and adult relationships. Along these lines there were various levels which the child reached by accomplishing the developmental tasks associated with each line. The lines and the levels reached along them could give someone assessing a child's development 'historical realities which when assembled, convey a convincing picture of an individual child's personal achievements or, on the other hand of [their] failures in personality development' (Freud 1965). She concentrated to a large extent on post-verbal development.

Today's clinician might reformulate developmental lines as develop-mental modalities and overlaps in the light of current understanding of infant and child development. The emphasis would perhaps be on pre-verbal development and the centrality of the infant's biological programming for attachment and interpersonal interaction, from the moment of birth throughout the whole lifecycle, and the different aspects of the self which are brought to and develop within this interaction.

The discipline of studying and understanding the intricacies of early development are particularly relevant for work with people who have suffered emotional abuse. People whose development has been severely curtailed by abuse often manifest their difficulties in such a way that without this knowledge the risk of repetition of the emotional abuse in the thera-peutic situation is quite high.

Working with people who are extremely silent can lead the therapist into repeating past emotional abuse by not listening carefully enough to the quality of the silence. As therapists we sometimes find that our own discomfort with the silence pushes us into understanding it as commun-ication, either of reflection, anger, resistance to anxiety-producing uncon-scious thoughts and wishes or a state of contentment. We can tend to view it predominantly as arising from defensive manoeuvres, which, when the underlying anxiety is understood, are modified and replaced by verbal communication.

This would presuppose a level of development in which the inner world was at least known to exist, and to a considerable extent was an integration of affective, symbolic, cognitive and somatic experience. The assumption that silence was the result of defensive manoeuvres might cause the therapist to miss completely what was happening, and be in danger of repeating emotional abuse.

A useful indication that the silence is of a more profound nature than that which is defensive is the utter helplessness experienced by the therapist when in its presence. Resistive or contemplative silence usually evokes tension or a peaceful sense of being together. The anxiety and awe which this powerless helplessness evokes in the therapist are crucial clues to the experience of inner silence in the other person. They can help the therapist explore at a developmental place which will not repeat abuse.

'David' was a young man of 23 who was referred because he had great difficulty in speaking, which was felt to be a manifestation of extreme anxiety. David could not make eye contact, sat slouched over with his chin in his anorak, and spoke in broken syllables. Each syllable was punctuated by very long silences of five to ten minutes. Initially, it seemed as if he was learning disabled until a pattern appeared which let it be known that he was cleverly separating the words as a means of communication. Approximately nine months into our work together, it became evident that David was trying to tell me about the secret world in which he had been raised. His story gradually emerged over a period of three years.

His parents were both psychotic: one believed the outside world would electrocute those who went out into it, and the other believed David was their little girl who had been lost a few years prior to his own birth. David was required to remain indoors most of his childhood, with the exception of being allowed to go to school and do the daily shopping. Once back home he was made to put on girl's clothing and remain totally silent, in case his forays into the outside world had infiltrated him with dangerous electric rays which might then come out of his mouth.

David's spacing out of syllables eventually shortened as he began to feel that he was not going to be controlled by the therapy and that his autonomy was respected. The work with David was highly complex, but one aspect was central to all of it: the fact that the acceptance, understanding and valuing of his style of communication gave him the experience of someone who validated his right to be autonomous. It was as if part of himself was stuck at the point before which language can be used to express one's own thoughts and wishes. Clearly, David's verbal means of communication was an indication of his struggle for belief in his autonomy. He used it to hide the fact that he was a separate individual who wanted to go out in the world as the man he was.

The danger in working with David was that it would have been all too easy to fall into the trap of emphasising the defensive nature of his language pattern, and try to interpret this as a means of getting to underlying anxieties. Without the underpinning of the experience of repeated validation of his need for control of himself and his right to his own identity David would have felt intruded upon and told yet again who he was and how he was to be. The cumulative emotional abuse would have only been repeated and the trauma re-enacted. As it happened, David became able to explore his own mind and feelings, to develop his self-narrative, and eventually became able to be employed and to speak in a more normal way.

Discussion

Both David and Elizabeth required developmental therapeutic help at several levels. The work with each of them was fraught with pitfalls and the danger of repeating emotional abuse. By painstakingly establishing a secure therapeutic space, it gradually became clear which developmental levels were the ones creating the most difficulty. Elizabeth's inability to experience affect stemmed primarily from the pre-verbal period of her development. Using Stern's understanding of early-infant development, her completely emotionally unavailable attachment world was experienced as truly traumatic, and quite likely prohibited a safe journey into the intersubjective world. Instead, she needed to shut down and encapsulate her experience of herself and others.

Despite the emotionally abusive nature of David's attachment world, he had received enough adequate care that he had been able to achieve some idea of himself as an autonomous being with the nascent capacity to use words to express his experience of himself. He then had to defend himself by using numerous verbal disguises from the dangers of his attachment world, almost hiding from himself the development of his autonomy.

In each of the ten people there was a failure to develop a self-narrative. Each had needed to put a ring of silence around themselves, and none of them had access to the experience of affect. They all in their different ways had encapsulated different aspects of their selves in order to survive the impact of the cumulative emotional abuse that each had suffered in different ways.

Working with such extreme difficulties is a very humbling experience. But it has also required thinking about therapeutic technique and how to adapt and develop it in ways which will give the best chance of an outcome which is right for each individual. It has continued to challenge at every turn and constantly evoked the question, 'What is it that therapy does, if anything, which brings about change?'

Working with those whose early life histories have required them to suspend aspects of their development due to extreme emotional abuse has reinforced the belief in the fundamental need for primary relationships which provide the basic listening, attunement, validation and reciprocity necessary for a child to develop with a solid sense of being valued and able to contribute to the world in which they live.

The relationship which develops in the therapeutic environment cannot fully undo the original damage done by emotional abuse at an early stage of development. But it can provide a developmental space which, over time, can pave the way within the abused person for internalisation of the therapeutic relationship. This usually involves years of careful work that gives the person being treated a chance to carry with them the experience of someone who validates their existence. Paving the way for internalisation of the therapy takes different forms depending upon the nature of the difficulty; with those severely damaged by emotional abuse it will initially need to be in the form of developmental help.

The lengthy experience of the therapist identifying and understanding the gaps in early experience, and the provision of facilitative attunement and validation can provide a healthy scar tissue over the developmental wounds. This acts as a foundation from which a more solid sense of self can emerge and no longer need to remain in a bubble. Only after the encapsulation has been undone and an affective self-narrative established can any kind of psychotherapeutic work involving the capacity for symbolisation, imagination and understanding of defensive manoeuvres against underlying anxiety be undertaken. However, sometimes helping someone out of their inner silence has to be good enough.

References

Banner, J. (1997) 'Psyche'. In R.L. Gregory (ed) *Oxford Companion to the Mind.* Oxford: Oxford University Press.

Bowlby, J. (1979) *The Making and Breaking of Affectional Bonds.* London: Tavistock Publications.

Davidson, D. (1983) *Inquiries into Truth and Interpretations.* Oxford: Oxford University Press.

Emde, R.N. (1983) The affective core. Paper presented at the Second World Congress of Infant Psychiatry, March 1983, Cannes, France.

Fairbairn, W.R.D. (1952) *Psychoanalytic Studies of the Personality.* London: Tavistock Publications and Routledge Kegan-Paul.

Fonagy, P. and Target, M. (1995) 'Understanding the role of the violent patient: The use and the role of the father'. *International Journal of Psycho-Analysis 76,* 493–494.

Freud, A. (1965) *Normality and Pathology in Childhood: Assessments of Development.* New York: International Universities Press.

Heard, D. and Lake, B. (1997) *The Challenge of Attachment for Caregiving.* London: Routledge.

Mahler, M.S. and McDevitt, J.B. (1968) 'Observations on adaptation and defense in statu nascendi: Developmental precursors in the first two years of life'. *Psychoanalytic Quarterly 37*, 1–21.

Mahler, M.S., Pine, F. and Bergman, A. (1975) *The Psychological Birth of The Human Infant.* London: Hutchinson and Co. Ltd..

Maurois, A. (1950) *The Quest for Proust.* London: Penguin Books in association with Jonathon Cape.

Parkes, C.M., Stevenson-Hinde, J. and Marris, P. (eds) (1991) *Attachment Across The Life-Cycle.* London: Routledge.

Schacter, S. (1971) 'Emotion, obesity, and crime'. New York. In R.L. Gregory (ed) G. Mandler (1987) Emotion. *Oxford Companion to the Mind.* Oxford: Oxford University Press.

Winnicott, D.W. (1958) *Collected Papers.* London: Tavistock Publications Ltd..

Wolf, E.S. (1980) 'Developmental line of self-object relations'. In A. Goldberg (ed) *Advances in Self-Psychology.* New York: International Universities Press.

de Zulueta, F. (1993) *From Pain to Violence: The Traumatic Roots of Destructiveness.* London: Whurr Publishers.

CHAPTER II

Treatment or Torture

Working with Issues of Abuse and Torture in the Transference

Shirley Truckle

Sadly, I have worked with a great many children and adults who have been the victims of sexual, emotional and physical abuse, sometimes at the hands of individuals, and sometimes at the hands of organised gangs, such as the South African secret police and the Nazis, and sometimes just by ourselves in our prejudice and laziness and lack of caring. This has raised many questions about what, if anything, I could offer as a therapist. It has also led to a great many sleepless nights and chocolate feasts; and while at first I saw these as signs of my personal weakness and inability to split between work and the rest of my life, I now think that what I was looking at and suffering from was an essential side-effect of the treatment process.

I suspect that when faced with the cruelty with which human beings can treat each other, both the patient and the therapist are working at the cutting edge of their ability to stay in touch and think in the presence of the untouchable and unthinkable. This struggle is, I am sure, reflected in my inability to formulate some of the ideas in this paper as anything other than questions; as well as in the urgency with which I need to ask them, even when I suspect them to be unanswerable.

What I want to explore are patients who ask the therapist to do different tasks for them, directly or indirectly, and my attempts, first, to recognise and take seriously their experiences of trauma or pain, and later, to conceptualise what has happened.

What I mean by trauma is something which happens or is done to the ego which totally overwhelms it. At this point I would like to introduce a concept from Hanna Segal's work (1957), which we need to proceed further in our thinking: that of symbolic equation. This is a very concrete form of thinking

172

in which A equals B with no as if about it. For example, if we are tracking the transference in someone in this state of mind, if he sees you, the therapist, as a Nazi dentist, he will be too afraid to open his mouth, in case you hurt him. This will be impossible to interpret, because even raising the idea of a Nazi dentist will immediately confirm to the patient the therapist's identity as said Nazi, creating a nightmare situation. Thus thought is impossible, and nonsense prevails. The first two cases I will discuss give a flavour of this experience.

I should like to tell you about a young Jewish woman of 30 called 'Mrs Goldstein'. I was taking over as her therapist, supporting her six-year-old son's therapy, from a young Welsh social worker, who had completed her year's course at the Tavistock Clinic in London. As we went into the therapy room, I was aware of feeling enormous, as though I loomed over Mrs Goldstein, who in reality was probably an inch shorter than me. She sat down, hands clasped between her knees, looking at her feet, with tears streaming down her face. Taken aback, I spoke gently about the difficulty of having a new therapist, and so on. After a minute, I said that it felt as though I was the confirmation of her worst fears of who she might be passed on to – or who she might be thrown away to. Mrs Goldstein looked up, glaring at me venomously, suddenly dry-eyed, and almost spat at me. 'Yes. I've always hated tall, thin, Teutonic types!'

It was with great difficulty that I could find enough presence of mind and thinking space to talk to her about her perception of being handed over to the Gestapo. I did not feel it appropriate to challenge this view of me in any way (in reality I am short and fat) because at that moment there was no symbolism. Mrs Goldstein was *actually seeing me* as elongated and terrifying. I talked about my being a figure from her nightmare. 'How did you know I dreamt about you last night?' she said, and produced a long Holocaust dream with elements which were obviously received memories from her grand-mother, Bobba, a concentration-camp survivor with whom she had shared a bedroom throughout her childhood. It was only after weeks of listening, and doing little more than tackling how terrifying I was to her as this perceived Nazi, and how inhuman the behaviour she attributed to me in her dreams was, that Mrs Goldstein gave me the crucial bit of information. As a child of nine, she had almost broken down when her grandmother woke her nightly in order to pour out the terrifying horrors of the camps to her granddaughter. Mrs Goldstein had been taken by her mother to her GP who had put her on tranquillisers.

To Mrs Goldstein, I was someone who did not think. I was mindlessly cruel and robotic. I saw her as the Jewish problem, and had a solution. At no time could I see her in her own right, with dreams, hopes, or terrors. Her abuse was two-fold. Bobba had filled her head with terrifying images of a ghastly reality, but the nine-year-old girl had been abused in her own right, in that she had been expected to contain, detoxify and digest for herself and the old woman the most unthinkable atrocities, the acting out in reality of our most perverse, anti-life phantasies. When Mrs Goldstein finally got the courage to feel enough to scream, she was offered anaesthetic, as if the problem was her oversensitivity. Her mother, father, GP and Bobba all ducked the issue and sent her back to hell with happy pills. They attacked her sanity. This was who I was felt to be in the transference.

It was only after weeks of painstakingly slow, gentle work, reflecting back to her how she perceived me and how awful it was for her, and how ghastly it must have been for little Sadie Goldstein, to have been asked to do the impossible that Mrs Goldstein began to have the experience of being seen and heard: 'It's as if this Bobba-me is asking you to take responsibility for all the evil in the world and to make it better... It's as if this Nazi-parent me is saying, you can leave Sadie alone and tortured in the middle of the night. After all, she is only a Jew, not human. Besides, she has got her pills...' I was treating her as a human being, therefore I was not the Gestapo at that moment. Only after this shift had happened and she experienced my capacity to think in the face of terror, without negating or minimising it, could she start to internalise an expectation of what a parent might be; to have an internal parent who allowed her to know that she had been in an intolerable situation, which was illegitimate; a parent who was devastated, and enraged on her behalf. This enabled her to start to work towards withdrawing her projections from her own son, and to start relating to him more appropriately.

Michael was my second training case, a three-year-old with an IQ of 60, who lived with his father and sister. I had heard that his mother was depressed, and that the social worker and father felt that the parents' divorce had scarred the children. Michael's first session was dominated by his fear of being in the room with me. I left the door ajar, and asked the lady who brought him to me to sit, out of earshot but easily visible in the corridor.

Michael ran in and out quite a lot, and then spent a long time painting the (washable) walls brown with streaks of red. When I interpreted this as showing me what a 'poohey' world he felt we lived in, and what a 'poohey' place this is, and how things hurt and bled inside him, he nodded very seriously and redoubled his efforts at covering even more space. Later, while I cleaned the room, he sat on the windowsill with his pillow and blanket, drinking water from the little plastic teacup I had put in his box for him. One could almost hear him purr.

The next day, Michael put his arms up for me to carry him, looking limp and deathly pale. I didn't want to interpret in a crowded waiting-room, so gathered him up and carried him to our room. As we got to the room, his head lolled back, and I started to feel panicky. Was this child ill? Was he having a fit? I wanted to scream for help, but I took him into the room, and sat down on the floor with him. He struggled, and I let him go. Then he sat scrunched up like a rag doll, and cried and cried, the most despairing, hopeless, desolate crying I have ever heard, completely oblivious of my presence. We were both alone, together in that room.

I talked, but it did not touch either of us. I started to feel giddy, and then, like the crystallisation of a nightmare, a clear image came into my mind from a book about the Holocaust that I had been misguided enough to read. The Nazi doctors put Jewish babies in glass boxes and watched to see how long they could survive without liquids. I was there with Michael, seeing and hearing his unbearable distress, and yet he had no expectation from me; neither of help, nor of a sadistic interest in his agony; each of us, behind our side of the glass, was alone. Michael was there with his despair; I was there with my bloodless, passionless, sphinx-like watching. It had taken about 10 minutes to get to this point. I could not, would not, accept this transference. I knew in my gut I must not abide by the rules. 'I'm making you a nest, and getting you a drink,' I said to Michael, picking him up, and placing him on the windowsill with a blanket, and pillow and his teacup of water. The sobbing subsided, and he drank deeply.

Michael needed me to taste, feel, hear, see, shiver with the quality of his helplessness. He needed me to act. Nothing less could reach him, or convince him I was there as a therapist, rather than a concrete repeat of his past experience of mothering. It was only three weeks later that Michael's notes were forwarded from the paediatric doctor who had referred him. Michael's father was a long-distance lorry driver, and while he had been away for two weeks, the mother had gone off and left Michael, aged 18 months, and his sister, age two-and-a-half, locked in their home. His sister had kept them alive by feeding Michael dry cornflakes through the bars of his cot, and water from the toilet.

If we return to the idea of Segal's symbolic equation, and think of Mrs Goldstein and Michael, we will see how the 'as-if' link is totally missing. For Mrs Goldstein I was the Gestapo; for Michael the absent, deserting, mother. With Mrs Goldstein, I had to listen, comment, be quiet and alert until slowly the experience of me made her pause to think and re-evaluate. I had to accept the projection without losing my sense of who I was, without pushing the distorted feelings and projections back at her or by acting them out: 'Don't be silly. This Gestapo violence is yours, not mine'. With Michael I had to be a different type of mother before he could begin to explore anything with me.

I had to be very firmly there before he could start to need, berate and hate me in the transference.

Michael's need was more fundamental, and so preverbal and prethought that it is hard to conceptualise. He had never had a container object, like a mother-type-person, who *felt* him, and thought him. The trauma had been woven into his very being, from conception onwards. Michael was never a live baby but rather a living doll, picked up, put down, cuddled and then dangerously ignored, on a schedule that bore no relationship to his behaviour or needs.

It is worth knowing more of his history, not because it explains Michael in a causal way, but because it activates our nightmares and incredulity in a way that helps us understand. Before he was born, his mother and father went out one night leaving four children, aged seven, five, four, and three months old alone in their home. One of the children played with matches, and only the baby survived. Michael was a replacement baby, conceived immediately. His mother was on strong tranquillisers throughout the pregnancy. Michael spent his first few months in and out of hospital with respiratory infections. The father of the children said proudly of his wife – his only favourable comment – 'She was very good with babies. She put Calpol in their bottles, so that they were ever so calm and never cried. In fact, you would hardly have known that there was a baby in the house'. Who could be angry on Michael's behalf? Certainly not Michael. His father tried, but a children's-home child himself, he could not see beyond his wife's leaving the children to die to the more insidious starvation Michael had experienced.

If Michael represents an invisible doll-child, my next patient, Donald, represents the damage done by chronic distortion on an individual's capacity to experience themselves – to see, feel, and think of themselves – as fully human. 'Donald' was a 22-year-old man with moderate learning difficulties. At first glance he is striking looking, having short, black cropped curls, and Paul-Newman-grey-blue eyes. The minute you focus on Donald you see someone who absolutely reeks of handicap. His clothes are immaculate, but have a 1950s style about them, and he walks with a shuffle reminiscent of Dustin Hoffman in 'The Rainman'. This combination of animal magnetism, and 'kick-me' helplessness is profoundly unsettling.

Donald was brought to me from a considerable distance by his social worker, who had persuaded his local health authority that the astronomic fees which the NHS charged at that time were worth paying. Because of this, we worked with an initial contract of four sessions; renewed to six sessions, then four, and finally to a ten sessions contract, until we finished. Again this peculiar dichotomy: a young man for whom quite extraordinary stops were being pulled out, but in a way that was also tantalisingly abusive. On two occasions I woke up drenched in sweat with nightmares that our contract would not be renewed. The effect that it had on Donald can only be imagined.

Donald was brought to me because he had sexually abused his three-year-old niece; as he put it later, 'First I did her front, and then I turned her over and did her back. She did cry and she did bleed, but I just went on'. Donald himself had been anally raped three times while at a residential college, by the same young man (called Henry) each time. After Donald had told his father, his father removed him back home. So Henry got to stay on at college and have a chance at preparing for independent living, and Donald got to stay at home, be bathed by dad and help mum clean the house. He was spoken to twice about this experience by a counsellor. I decided when I saw Donald to start with the abuse he had suffered, and to wait and see what, if anything, he told me about his attack on his niece.

I introduced myself to Donald and his mother in the waiting-room, and asked Donald to come through with me to the therapy room. He chatted brightly all the way down the corridor, in a perfect parody of someone at a cocktail party. When we got in the room, he sat down and smiled brightly at me. His eyes looked vacant and blank. I told him that his mother, father and social worker were very concerned about all the unhappy things that had happened to him in the last year, and had asked me to talk to him to try to help him to understand some of the confusing things that he had experienced.

Donald smiled benignly and blankly at me. I found my palms going all sweaty with the horrid conviction that he wasn't going to understand a word of what I said, and therefore that he would be totally inaccessible. Rather desperately, I prodded Donald into starting his story, rather than waiting in the way that I would have with anyone else, for him to formulate his response. 'What happened in Wales?' I asked him. I think at this point I had exemplified the kind of abuse that people with learning difficulties suffer at the hands of professionals. My panic and my feeling of incompetence – which I'm sure were exacerbated by Donald's terror, that he wouldn't understand me and give me what I required, 'get it right' – totally destroyed my capacity to allow him to work at his own speed, and find his own way of communicating.

'Oh, with Henry', he said, smiling his learning-difficulty smile. With a few more prompts from me, the story unfolded:

> I was sleeping in bed, and Henry came in and he jumped on my back, and he poked me, and he did what I don't like and I screamed and Susan and James came in, and they said, this ought not to happen, and they told

Henry to go back to his bed. And they said we *are* sorry Donald, this ought not to happen! And I went back to sleep. And the next night I was asleep in bed…and the night after that I was asleep in bed, and Henry…

All this was told brightly, with a social smile, and a lot of dead eye contact. I decided to allow my anger to show, and said to Donald, 'How on earth did you manage to lie down, and go to sleep? It was obvious what was going to happen?' 'What do you mean?' he said, looking at me, oozing stupidity. 'Well', I said, 'couldn't they give you a bedroom with a lock, so that you could sleep safely?' Donald looked at me, his eyes alive and sparkling, and said slowly and thoughtfully, 'I would really have liked that.'

I would like to jump to another conversation about six months later, after the summer holiday. I asked Donald what he had done during his holiday, and he said, looking stupid, 'I helped my mummy clean the house each day'. I commented that that sounded terribly boring. 'Oh, no', he said, 'You don't understand, Mrs Truckle. I've got learning difficulties'. I said that I did not understand. I knew that he had learning difficulties, and that meant that he could probably not read or write very well. Donald added, 'or do maths'. But I could not for the life of me see what that had to do with a 22-year-old not being bored out of his mind by six weeks spent dusting and hoovering. 'I don't get bored', said Donald. 'I have learning difficulties'. I said that he must think that I, as someone without learning difficulties, was just plain stupid if I believed that he could never be bored. Stupid and cruel. Donald looked at me for a moment in amazement, then his eyes came alive. He threw his head back, and roared with laughter like a normal adolescent, and looked at me very shyly, and said very quietly, 'Yes, I do sometimes'.

Michael was invisible; his emotional needs were not even perceived, let alone met. Donald had a different experience: he saw in his mother's eyes a reflection of puzzlement and hurt at this baby's difference. Donald had LEARNING DIFFICULTIES, spelt with capitals. Being a disqualified sub-human, the ordinary rules did not apply to him. He was told that he was a happy, sweet-natured creature who would enrich others' lives by enhancing their capacity for charity. He was schooled not to see, hear, want or think. He was groomed to be defenceless and stupid.

Donald was a normal adolescent, full of rampaging hormones and sexual feelings, heavily into pop music. Yet I discovered that he did not have the most rudimentary sexual knowledge. No one had ever used the words 'erection', 'ejaculation', 'masturbation', or 'contraception' with him. It was as though he was perceived as asexual. During the time that I worked with him he was suspended from college for inviting a fellow female student, also with learning difficulties, to come to bed with him; and following it up by asking a normal male engineering student to come to the toilets and do exciting things with him, that he did not like. In this context, I tried to explain to Donald that the female student's parents might be afraid that she would get pregnant. 'How?' he said, looking bright-eyed and alert. I explained to him in much the same way that I would to a five-year-old, but Donald's reaction was totally different from a child's. It was adult. 'Wow', he said, with his eyes glistening with what I thought might be tears. 'I could make something as perfect as a baby'.

I was also aware that Donald might be gay, so I decided to tackle both the female and male students in one fell swoop. I said to Donald that he had the same problem that any young man had: he wanted to be held and touched and made love to. He nodded. I asked him if he knew the word 'tactful'. Donald shook his head. I explained it, and that he had to manage to get whoever to have sex with him in a tactful way that didn't scare them, and allow them to say 'No'. We had by this stage talked extensively about Henry, and how frightened and confused he must have been when he leaped on Donald's back and got shouted at, and not helped to understand his feelings.

I reminded Donald of how confused and frightened he had been, and said that this is what is meant by abuse, and if you really force yourself on someone, that is rape. And that it is cruel and selfish. Donald looked at me very sadly and said, 'Like what I did with Geraldine?' We could then think about the abuse he had perpetrated on Geraldine, his niece, in the context of confusion and pain and overwhelming urges that he had felt, but at the same time he could still identify with Geraldine in her pain, terror and horror at the way he had betrayed her trust. At times like these, Donald would be as white as a sheet, his arms clasped round his body, rocking, whispering 'It's hard, it's hard'. I would have to take up both his horror and his pain, and his feeling that the hardness in his penis, his erection, was caused by my words, and that he could not decide whether I was trying to help him, in trying to enable him to think about his hurting Geraldine so he never ever did anything like that again; or was I wanting to torture him, punish him for his deeds and his feelings?

I spoke to him directly about the enormous difficulty in the outside world, that he had in meeting potential partners, particularly as we, the so-called intelligent people, could not understand that his learning difficulty made no difference to his wanting exactly the same things out of life that we did; that he wanted to love and be loved, even if he could not live alone and look after himself, and so could not look after a baby.

One of the things that it is very difficult to convey is how Donald and I communicated. There were times when he seemed incapable of saying anything, but would lean forward, gazing penetratingly into my eyes, willing me to try and put his feelings into words for him. We spoke about his difficulty and how he envied my capacity to talk and think and make sense of things. We experimented, first with drawing. Donald produced a picture of a clown with a vacant smile painted on, and eyes without pupils. When I spoke to this blind, smiling, clown-picture of himself, and his despair at seeing and understanding and being seen and taken seriously, he rocked and whimpered, 'It's hard. It's hard', and the pain in the room was almost unbearable.

I wondered whether the box of toys which I use with young children would be of help, and explained to him that I was not being daft in offering him toys as such, but that they were things which could be used instead of words to show me how he felt. He said 'Let's try'. Initially this was very successful. Donald used two dinosaurs, one of which has a hole in its tummy, to show me how violent his picture of intercourse was, and how unsafe all the baby animals were from the marauding dinosaurs, which I felt both represented himself in relation to Geraldine, and a child part of himself in relation to his own sexual and aggressive feelings.

Towards the second summer break, the work with Donald changed drastically. On once-a-month therapy, this young man was finding the courage to explore his own destructiveness. It took me almost a year to ask him if he had any dreams, something I would normally introduce early in therapy, as a source of help in understanding his feelings. 'Yes,' he said, 'nightmare.' I asked him what of? 'Hands coming out of the wall, and touching me. And him in the cupboard.' 'Who?' I asked. 'Peter Cushing', said Donald. I then got the information that although his world was severely truncated, he was allowed to watch horror movies with his parents, and these had fuelled his nightmares both about Henry and Geraldine, and his aggressive feelings towards his parents; and towards me and my husband, when we were coupling and excluding him. Donald felt like the vampire shut out of daytime living in a world where he had accepted that people with learning difficulties don't get bored, don't have ambitions and fears, and certainly don't want to marry and have children.

But alone in his room at night, he experienced a different picture of yearning, of the impossibility of fulfilment, and of a feeling that even his masturbation was some uniquely awful part of him. Something peculiar that no one else ever did. He was excluded by day by virtue of his stupidity. He was excluded at night, the life vampired out of him by our misperceptions, and then longed and feared for revenge on us, and our exclusive coupling. His horrific abuse of Geraldine which denied her cries and her blood, showed an internalised cruelty, a dehumanising viciousness, which made him the vampire. I felt Donald had been culpable and responsible for his actions, but also that we, the intelligent ones, had groomed him for it. Trying to articulate some of this meant Donald came to rely on me to feel his feelings and think his thoughts for him. I became his self-respect. He saw himself through my eyes and liked what he saw. He also learnt to disagree with me, saying 'no' firmly if he felt I was off-beam.

The summer break turned out to be longer than expected, lasting for two months because of Donald's and my holidays not coinciding. When he returned, I was shocked at the change in him. He was emaciated and grey; even his curls seemed to droop. He shuffled down the corridor after me, wheezing like an old man. 'Donald,' I said, 'What has happened to you?' He just sat mutely, climbing into me with his eyes, and rocking slightly. Helping me by nodding, and shaking his head to indicate whether I was on target or not, I was able to gather partly from his coughing and pointing to his chest that he had been very ill, and feeling that he had been drowning in horrid stuff inside his chest; and felt that he would never see me again. I felt overwhelmingly guilty at seeing this man monthly, when he needed five-times-weekly psychotherapy, and knowing how hard I had fought, and how many letters I had written to get even this amount of help for him. We only had two more sessions left, and I wondered out loud how Donald felt about coming, and my fighting for ten more sessions when the cost of the therapy was so horrendous for him. As if to confirm this, Donald said, 'Don't want to', and went into a paroxysm of coughing, which left me dizzy with anxiety that he was about to collapse. When he could draw breath, he said, 'It's hard. It's very hard. I need to come. I must come'.

We got ten more sessions, and I telephoned Donald at home to tell him immediately after I heard. He was very excited as no one had ever phoned him before. When I saw him again, three weeks later, his cough had gone, and he looked well. I cannot explain what happened in the next ten months, but Donald seemed to bloom before my very eyes. Over the Christmas holiday, he confided to me: 'I'm going to Torquay. But it doesn't matter, because you say things in my head, so I'm not lonely. It would be nice if I could write, because then I could send you a postcard'. I told him he had just sent me a more important message; that he knew he was my Donald, who had learning difficulties, and sometimes could not think, but was also a warm, loving, intelligent, thinking person, even when I wasn't there to help him know who he was. 'How many more times have we got?' he asked. 'Four more', I said. 'That's enough', he said. And we started working towards an ending.

Interestingly enough in the third from last session, Donald told me very straightforwardly that a student from college had been touching his bottom and penis when they were gardening together, and that he didn't like this, and he was afraid that he, Donald, would get so excited that he would do something that he didn't want to do. I asked him whether he felt that he could tell his tutor. Donald said, 'No, Steve is a nice man, but no, I can't.' I asked him if he wanted me to do it either directly or through his social worker. Donald said, 'You phone please.' It was nearly time to end, and I promised to phone that day, although I could not promise that I would be able to speak to the tutor immediately, but when I did, I would ask him to speak to Donald as soon as possible about what he would do. I also wrote out the clinic number for Donald, in case he needed to phone me. In fact, the tutor was very charming, and supportive of Donald, and had wondered what was happening between the two lads. He spoke very sensitively to the two of them, and started discussing sex with them in a very helpful way. Donald seemed quite cheerful when I said goodbye to him for the last time; though I must admit that I went away and had a private cry at the thought of him trying to reach maturity in a world that offered him so little help, recognition or respect.

Finally, I should like to talk about a family from Soweto who, like Donald, were shaped by a society which was deeply prejudiced and which marginalised them and could not treat them as human beings. With Donald, I think we were all to a certain extent culpable in our inability to identify with him as one of us. With my Sowetan family, the White South Africa which they grew up in inflicted deep wounds on them by forcing them to stay separate, and each in their own shells to protect each other from over-whelming torture. They, as Donald, took me into a new area of experience, which taught me a great deal.

In 1992 I received a letter asking me if I would take on an African National Congress (ANC) family from Soweto for therapy privately. The father had been in and out of jail for his beliefs, and the mother had had to manage alone with three children: Ken (17), Fred (12) and Greta (9) (I have given them English names). The father's last stint in jail was five years on Robbin Island. The father, whom I shall call Tim, was felt to be suffering from post-traumatic shock, and the referrers felt he needed help.

I suggested that the family be referred to me at an NHS clinic where I also worked, as it seemed gross for people who had been damaged by a society to be treated by an individual for money. It felt right that they received help from an institution such as the NHS. I saw Tim and his wife Brenda weekly for three years. Obviously, I can only give an impression of our work, and only certain aspects are relevant to this chapter, but they underline much of what has been said before.

We started at a point where sharing feelings, particularly of being overwhelmed by newness in the minutiae of everyday life – new money and very little of it to cope with; Greta being asked home by a white English family, being a student at last. It puzzled me that sharing their reactions to all this seemed a new experience in itself and quite alien at first. One day, I said as a passing comment to Tim, that I wondered if he had ever shared any of his prison experiences with Brenda, or if she had shared her struggles to bring up three children and be the breadwinner, with him? They both shook their heads vigorously. Tim's eyes rolled back a bit as they always do at moments of great emotional tension: 'I've never dared. If I told her and it happened again, she would have to live with a clear idea of what was happening to me. That would be too much for both of us'.

The most crucial link between the experience of abuse or torture is who you are. Tim was a freedom fighter. The humiliation of pain and terror and being let down by your body's reactions were separate from any feelings of self-worth. He knew his torturers were doing evil. He told us movingly of being rushed to casualty when they thought that they had gone too far and had permanently crippled him. As he was rushed on a stretcher through the Blacks-only hospital, he was recognised. Black staff and patients stood to attention, and broke into the ANC anthem 'Sekeli Afrika'.

It was the small-scale, human things which broke the camel's back. Solitary confinement with the light on; being watched; waiting for another session on interrogation was holdable. Until a gecko got into his room. He was terrified of geckos.

Tim cannot sleep beyond 4.15 am, and cannot bear mess and disorder. This is hard on Brenda who gets very irritated with him. This could be thought about when he told us how 40 of them were in a small room in triple bunks, with only a few toilets and showers. In order not to be controlled by the guards or lapse into their expectations of being 'filthy Kaffirs', some senior prisoners got up very early so that they had time to wash properly every day. Obsessionalism equalled pride, self-control and dignity.

In the transference I felt I, as a White South African, and as the parent, had to see what I had done. I had to look and be sickened. I had to try not to cry. Weeping copiously in that context would be too easy; it is really a way of taking on the emotionality and pushing the pain straight back: 'Look how soft-hearted and sensitive I am' is what it says. I had to have the experience of not being sure if I could cope with the next session, and knowing, as a fighter for his freedom from solitary confinement, that I could not duck. I was enormously helped by Brenda, and felt that she held my hand in her awareness of my pain every bit as much as I held hers.

In the middle of this work, with the whole family's defences crashing down in disarray and trauma crowding in, Tim and Brenda's year of funding was coming to an end in only four months. Tim reminded me of this in one session. I thought if he went back at this stage (when Inkatha and ANC were still being murderous and the police highly dubious) he would not be able to stand the uncertainty, and that he would either go mad and be locked up, or get himself killed in a political, but provoked, confrontation. Tim nodded sombrely and Brenda hugged herself, rocking slightly in her chair. In a breathtaking bit of acting out, which I still feel was absolutely right, I said, 'It's cruel and mad for you to go back now. Will you allow me to talk to people and get the money for you to stay?'

I am not sure if this was acting in or acting out in the transference, but it could certainly be considered a major break in technique! But how can one witter on about feelings and stand by, giving a sensitive, running, commentary while your analytic child is horribly and predictably abused? That, too, is an acting out, this time of the role of the collusive, nonabusing parent, for whom honesty costs so much that it cannot be bought with the child's pain and scars. The discarding of truth to protect the status quo (the analytic work, the integrity of the family) is in my opinion the most poisonous and abusive cut of all. If I colluded, every word, every harrowing experience shared becomes a cynical nonsense. Hypocrisy reigns supreme. So we come full circle: what can I, as a therapist, offer?

All these clients are broken or scared in their capacity to trust, and for good reasons. This has complicated effects. The task is either to heal, or to give a primary experience, that is, of Bion's mother capable of reverie and detoxification of the poisonous experience. Ann Syz (1997) who works with child victims of sexual abuse, puts it, 'With these children, the task is not mending, but constructing a self in therapy'. Unpacking the lies and distortions of reality and the impact on their concepts of their selves is a major task.

The task is made more difficult by the extensive armour of omnipotence and invulnerability, or non-thinking, non-perception which any survivor has had to construct. Sometimes mindless stupidity, or madness, seem safer options than knowing and feeling and reality. Dismantling these barriers can often be experienced by the patient as profoundly dangerous and cruel behaviour on the part of the therapist, and can constitute re-abuse if we protect ourselves by going out of touch with this pain in a simplistic, cathartic, tin-opener-therapist mode.

Bringing the indigestible, insane experiences into the transference may be impossible, and ultimately they may have to be encapsulated. Syz feels that we can help patients sort, launder and repack their suitcases, but in one a snake might have to be accommodated. I would add that therapy should make it a known snake of acknowledged precedents, packed in a particular marked case; for snake, read radioactive waste capsules, and I think the image approximates the truth.

I should like to end by telling you a story about one of my home children. When he was three, he became, for some reason best known to himself, a believing Christian. He asked me, 'Mummy, how do I know Jesus is true?' I answered, 'Well, a religious person might say it it is the same as you know that I love you. You feel it inside you'. 'Oh, thank you, mummy,' he answered, 'now I know he is real'. Four years later he watched the news and saw the Shatila massacres; his first brush with the trauma of organised cruelty. That night he told us, 'I don't believe in God anymore. How could he let that happen?' We acknowledged that it was incomprehensible. A week later my son announced at bedtime, 'I think I understand it. Hate is stronger than love in this world, and evil is stronger than good. The devil is stronger than God. So we all have to hold hands with God against the devil!' I cannot get any further than that in my thinking, and it seems like a usable stab at facing reality to me.

References

Segal, H. (1957) 'Notes on symbol formation'. *The International Journal of Psycho-Analysis 38*, 391–397.

Syz, A. (1997) Personal communication with the author.

CHAPTER 12

The Abuse of Learning Disabled People

Living and Working with the Consequences

Valerie Sinason

We have always lived with the consequences of abuse: frozen children, hypervigilant children, over-sexualised children, children living with nightmares; children hurting and hurting others, children growing up into hurting adults have all grown up with us. We have always known at some profound level why they were suffering; however, we have only recently dared to consciously realise what a traumatised society we are. Those of us born in the post-Second World War baby-boom were brought up learning to read from colour picture books like *Janet and John*, which provided images of loving, affluent two-parent families living in the leafy suburbs. Perhaps it took nearly half a century since then to properly understand the scale of catastrophe – both internal and external – that such books provided delusional escape from.

Bowlby (1979) highlighted for us the way illegitimate knowledge, which we are not supposed to know, leads to cognitive distortions. I consider this is as relevant to society in a group response as to an individual. When respected and loved attachment figures offer danger, the dependent child (and society) needs delusionally to see them as loving and safe. Indeed, Orr (1999) has pointed out that the biggest false memory is of a happy childhood. The loved-enough child can remember both positive and negative aspects of childhood, but the child with the insecure attachment is more likely to cosmetically edit. The cosmetic editing that went into the creation of post-war images of the family was enormous, and we are only beginning to dismantle them now.

If knowing what you are not supposed to know creates distortions in the mentally able population, what happens to those who are born with, or acquire, a learning disability? As Ferenczi commented (1928):

...in the early states of embryonic development a slight wound, the mere prick of a pen can not only cause severe alterations in, but may completely prevent, the development of whole limbs of the body. Just as, if you have only one candle in a room and put your hand near the candle, half the room may become darkened, so if, near the beginning of life, you do only a little harm to a child, it may cast a shadow over its whole life. (p.65)

First, we need to consider who 'learning disabled' people are. The language for describing this group tends to change every few years in keeping with psycho-linguistic understanding of the meaning of euphemism. Where a word has to contain feelings that are not societally bearable it becomes contaminated and has to be changed. While the change is hailed as a liberation and a step forward in human relating, the new word all too often becomes infected by the same process because the underlying fear has not been dealt with.

When psychoanalyst Neville Symington staged a workshop at the Tavistock Clinic in 1979 for working with this population, he used the correct term at the time: 'subnormality'. Within a few years this word became contaminated, and I brought in the new word 'mental handicap'. Just a few years after this the term changed to 'learning difficulty', and is currently 'learning disability'. In the past it has been 'backward', 'retarded', 'special needs'. All the terms are struggling with how to name a difference, a difference that has not been chosen and is not wished for by the parents, the child or society.

Basically, a learning disability means that a child or adult is not able to do what someone else their age would normally be expected to be able to. It covers the emotional and social consequences of such mental impairment too. Rather importantly, such a disability, while open to some amelioration, does not fundamentally alter. In the UK, over one million adults and children are in the mildly learning disabled range. Rather painfully (Rutter *et al.* 1970) there is a political aspect to mild disability. Maternal deprivation, paternal unemployment, large numbers of siblings and foster care significantly increase the risk of mild learning disability. World malnutrition, violence to the pregnant mother, homelessness, torture, accident and pollution may contribute to this category.

The political nature of the majority of mild learning disability can also be seen in the fact that the majority of such children and adults in the UK come from Social Class Five (i.e. the poorest social class). In a way, the existence of mild learning disability can, in many cases, be seen as a consequence of societal abuse. With regard to organic and severe or profound learning disability, which usually is accompanied by physical disability too, there are over 300,000 (Ricks 1990, p.518) children and adults in the UK. This group is more evenly spread across all social groups.

What is the emotional experience of being different in a way that is not chosen? Before we can begin to consider the extra impact of sexual abuse, we need to consider the multiple experiences of stigmatisation that come from being different. Learning disabled children can often experience a dislocation of affect and cognition right from the start when the fact of their disability is not worked through and causes bonding problems. The mirror of mother's eyes can lose its nurturing, approving look, and the disabled baby can face an active mirror of hurt, depression, guilt and revulsion. Family and health services often rally round on the practical side, but rarely offer help with the emotional impact. Communication links that would aid the disclosing of abuse are therefore often pre-damaged.

What then happens when, in addition to cognitive problems and the impact of societal and familial responses, we add on the trauma of abuse? Physical and sexual abuse (which automatically includes emotional abuse) affects the body and mind of non-disabled children. Trust in adults is often broken and the ability to move from a secure base into the wider world of learning and social interaction and attachment can be damaged, especially where there is not a believing, loving parent.

While many abused children have their capacity to learn inhibited, delayed or damaged, some children actually become learning disabled as a result of such treatment (Sinason 1986). Buchanan and Oliver (1979), in researching causes of learning disability found that three to eleven per cent of their sample had become learning disabled through violence, and they coined the term 'violence-induced mental handicap'.

If it is possible for the act of abuse and its consequences to cause disability in some cases and to increase learning problems in many, what happens when there is pre-existing disability? Cognitive and sexual learning are closely linked in childhood. In the oedipal period a normal child plays with the fantasy of marrying a parent and grows emotionally by learning that this wish cannot be fulfilled in reality. However, the child abused within the family has become mother or father's partner: symbolic functioning has been destroyed and there can be, unsurprisingly, a further reduction of intellectual development (Sinason 1990).

Abused children with a pre-existing organic or environmental learning disability are damaged even further by lack of cognitive ability, which can make it harder to process the complex interplay of internal and external factors that are stirred up by such trauma.

Against this, of course, it is important to remember the resilience of the constitutionally resilient child, especially the child whose disclosure is met with belief by their mother and others. When 'Jennifer', aged 24, was sexually abused by a respite home worker, her mother immediately believed her. This confirmation of psychic validity empowered Jennifer to maintain her limited cognitive ability. Her resilience in turn encouraged the police to consider that she would manage to be a viable witness, and the Crown Prosecution agreed. Having had to face hostile adversarial questioning, including, 'You are lying aren't you, Jennifer?' from the barrister for the worker, she was able to reply spiritedly, 'I am not lying. He is lying. He hurt me and he should be in prison'. The worker was imprisoned.

It is important, always, for us to remember the resilient group who have the emotional capacity to cope with trauma regardless of their level of disability. However, in the biased clinic sample, we see the creative, although depleting, ways in which the pain of abuse is defended against.

Without the cognitive ability to read books that would help them work through the experience of abuse at a profound imaginative level, and, often, without the economic and social freedom to go to adult films which deal with such topics, the consequences of abuse can take a severe toll. Indeed, at St Georges' Hospital Medical School, Psychiatry of Disability Department, we have developed a series of colour picture books for learning disabled adolescents and adults who have been abused to try and alter this process.

However, for the majority of those referred for assessment and treatment there has been significant behaviour change. The most common reasons for referral of children and adults who were abused (Sinason 1994) are excessive masturbatory activity and self-mutilation. Unfortunately, such behaviour is all too often dismissed as a component part of the handicap rather than a sign of trauma or despair. Masturbation is reframed as an infantile source of satisfaction that has been turned to because there is a lack of inhibition. This is a dangerous pathway; it destroys the emotional meaning.

'Maureen', aged 23, was referred by her parents for compulsive masturbating. Before she had been able to disclose abuse, her inappropriate sexual behaviour was of concern to her parents. When they tried to point it out to the agencies involved in Maureen's life-plan they were told it was just her way of relaxing. They added a social skills session to try and teach her not to undress in public.

When Maureen entered my consulting room she faced her father, sat down and compulsively masturbated. Her father, naturally, was extremely distressed at seeing his adult daughter behave this way. 'I am sorry, Dad. Don't be cross with me. I am sorry, Dad. Don't be cross with me!' she shouted imploringly, while continuing to masturbate. 'I am not cross with you', said her father wearily. 'But no father likes to see his daughter behave like this'.

I spoke to Maureen, who did not turn to look at me. 'Maureen, I wonder what you are thinking in your head while you touch yourself. Is there a picture in your head or words in your head?' Still looking at her father and still masturbating, she answered, 'Well, it is like this, Dad. When I think of what that man did to me I touch myself and then I put your face on his head, Dad, and I am sorry, Dad'.

It was an extremely moving moment. I said, 'Well, you really worked that out well, Maureen. That man touched you without permission and when you touch yourself you are being that man instead of him. But that man did not love you and you want to make his picture safer by having someone you love. So you put your Dad's face on the man's head. But then you say "Sorry" to your Dad because you know your Dad would not do that to you. It is not what good Dads do with their daughters'. Maureen stopped masturbating in public and has made a good recovery. However, it needed her parents to insist on emotional meaning and finding a therapist.

The same misinterpretation applies to self-injury that is a consequence of abuse. Indeed, the new form 'challenging behaviour' all too frequently masks emotional meaning. 'John Brown', aged 32, cut his penis with a pair of scissors and pulled his hair out. He compulsively washed his hands and equally compulsively smeared faeces and pulled up floorboards and cut wires. Such behaviour poses enormous burdens on staff and family, and it is not surprising that without support there can be little space to consider the emotional meaning.

In a first assessment meeting John picked up the young male anatomical doll and pulled the anus apart. Then he yowled with pain, jumped off the seat and threw himself on to the floor trying to pull the floorboards up. It became painfully clear to both of us that his body house had been ripped open underneath and, lacking the ability to communicate this directly, he had resorted to symbolic equations (Segal 1957) whereby symbolisation has been attempted but fails, and the object that could stand for an experience becomes equated with it. In this way, John's pain was too great to contain and express symbolically through a toy house. He had to rip the structure of a real house to make it the same as his body.

Some can defend themselves from the trauma of their experience by creating a secondary handicap (Sinason 1986; 1992). This means that they exaggerate aspects of the real organic handicap to such an extent that the secondary handicap might even be more severe than the primary one. The tragedy of this defence is that it depletes their emotional and cognitive resources. As part of such secondary defensive handicap, many such children develop a falsely smiling face or manner under which they hide their pain and despair. Unfortunately, because so many carers and professionals cannot bear to deal with the emotional experience of learning disability, the 'happy' expression is often responded to as if it were real. It remains disturbingly common still to hear workers comment that handicapped children are 'so friendly'.

Indeed, at the extreme end of this range are the schools where no formal sign is provided for the crucial autonomous statement 'hate' (Sinason 1993a), or 'I don't like'. The 'stupidity' of the network (Sinason 1992) is exacerbated by failing to provide sign language that offers negatives, and by failing to offer and encourage choice and autonomy. Failure to offer formal terms for sexual areas of the body or indeed sex education also adds to the vulnerability of this client group.

Other kinds of secondary handicap developed to avoid psychic pain include the exaggeration of speech defects, motor impairments, and way of dressing or carrying out tasks. These defensive ways of exaggerating handicap are not the primary reason for referral, nor is the abuse itself, which may not have been uncovered. However, I consider these subsidiary consequences of abuse to be extremely serious and corrosive.

Children with disabilities have added emotional vulnerability, which exacerbates the impact of abuse. Their sense of being unwanted and their shame at their disability makes it harder for them to speak out. Additionally, many have a fantasy that they are the products of a bad intercourse, which made them turn out wrong (Sinason 1988, 1993b). This makes psychosexual development even harder. In these cases there is a need for regular supervision and support. The sense of loss and despair hidden under the handicapped smiles is enormous. I also consider it helpful always to keep in mind Suzanne Sgroi's comment (1982) '...recognition of sexual molestation in a child is entirely dependent on the individual's inherent willingness to entertain the possibility that the condition may exist'.

In running groups for learning disabled sexual offenders with Professor Sheila Hollins, we have become aware of a tragic further consequence of abuse: the possibility of a small minority identifying with the aggressor, the abuser, and repeating the abuse on another. All too often the learning disabled offender has his/her offence laundered and transformed into 'inappropriate sexual behaviour due to a severe disability'; 'he plays with six-year-olds because mentally he is the same age'. This is extremely dangerous as, in common with all paedophiles, offences only increase. We have found it essential to work on the original traumatising experience of being abused so that there is compassion for the hurt child in the abusing adult before we consider the abusing behaviour. It is not possible to have empathy for victims when the self as a victim has not been acknowledged.

After several years of group work, one man commented, 'I hate my secure unit. I have been here so long. I cannot go anywhere on my own in case I hurt children. I would hurt a child if I was on my own and so I can't be on my own. But I hate being locked up. Will I ever be safe to come out and not hurt children?' This authentic *cri de coeur* echoed round the room as all acknowledged the painful predicament. It is worth noting that all the men had either been sexually or physically abused in childhood, many sadistically and chronically. Indeed, we consider that many are still suffering from post-traumatic stress disorder.

There is one last issue I would like to raise. In long-term psychoanalytic psychotherapy the deepest issue that gets raised is the fear of the learning disabled client/patient that the therapist would like to kill them, abort them. Whereas the abused non-disabled child is scared of disclosing abuse for fear of being punished, the learning disabled child is often *sure* they will be killed. It is that terrible, primitive fear that leads to the handicapped false smile. 'When people see my face,' said 13-year-old 'Ella' with Down's syndrome, 'they see my Mum and Dad did something dirty, and then they want to kill me. So who can I tell?'

It is an achievement of the field of learning disability that we have been able to put this subject on the map in the last decade. Parliamentary pressure groups such as Voice have sprung up to aid the learning disabled victim's rights. However, the consequences are long-term.

Abuse is accepted as reality. However, this hard-won acceptance is met with projection, splitting, denial and blame. The increase in accusations of 'false memory' is just one of the societal counter-responses. Of course, there can be distorted memories but learning disabled people are no more prone to this than others.

I would like to end where I began. The biggest false memory is of a happy childhood. As we slowly manage to confront the true nature of childhood in the UK today, a culture in which the majority of babies under one year are hit by their mothers (DoH 1995; Newsom and Newsom 1978), we will become a stronger less delusional society. That will aid the safety of our most vulnerable citizens.

References

Bowlby, J. (1979) 'On knowing what you are not supposed to know and feeling what you are not supposed to feel'. *The Canadian Journal of Psychiatry 24*, 403–408.

Buchanan, A. and Oliver, J.E. (1979) 'Abuse and neglect as a cause of mental retardation'. *Child Abuse and Neglect 3*, 467–475.

Department of Health (1995) *Child Protection: Messages from Research*. London: HMSO.

Ferenczi, S. (1928) *Final Contributions to the Problems and Methods of Psychoanalysis*. In M. Balint (ed). (1955) London: Hogarth Press.

Mrazek, P.B., Lynch, M. and Bentovim, A. (1981) 'Recognition of child sexual abuse in the United Kingdom'. In P.B. Mrazek and C.H. Kemp (eds) *Sexually Abused Children and Their Families*. Oxford: Pergamon.

Newsom, J. and Newsom, E. (1978) *Seven Years Old in the Home Environment*. London: Penguin.

Ricks, D. (1990) 'Mental handicap'. In H. Wolff *et al.* (eds) *University College Hospital Textbook of Psychiatry*. London: Duckworth.

Rutter, M., Tizard, J. and Whitmore, K. (1970) *Education, Health and Behaviour*. London: Longman.

Segal, H. (1957) *Notes on Symbol Formation. The Work of Hanna Segal*. New York: Aronson.

Sgroi, S. (1982) *Handbook of Clinical Intervention in CSA*. Massachusetts: Lexington Books.

Sinason, V. (1986) 'Secondary mental handicap and its relationship to trauma'. *Psychoanalytic Psychotherapy 2*, 2, 131–154.

Sinason, V. (1988) 'Richard Ill, Echo and Hephaestus: Sexuality and mental/multiple handicap'. *Journal of Child Psychotherapy 14*, 2.

Sinason, V. (1990) 'Child sexual abuse'. In H. Wolff *et al. (eds) University College Hospital Textbook of Psychiatry*. London: Duckworth.

Sinason, V. (1992) *Mental Handicap and the Human Condition*. London: Free Association Books.

Sinason, V. (1993a) 'Hatred towards and in clients with a mental handicap'. In V. Varma (ed) *How and Why Children Hate: A Study of Conscious and Unconscious Sources*. London: Jessica Kingsley Publishers.

Sinason, V. (1993b) 'The special vulnerability of the handicapped child and adult: With special reference to mental handicap'. In C.J. Hobbs and J.M. Wynne (eds) *Baillieres Clinical Paediatrics Child Abuse*.

Sinason, V. (1994) 'The treatment of people with learning disabilities who have been abused'. In J. Harris and A. Craft (eds) *People with Learning Disabilities at Risk of Physical or Sexual Abuse*. London: British Institute of Learning Disability.

CHAPTER 13

Dissociative Identity Disorder and Memories of Childhood Abuse

Phil Mollon

For most of the twentieth century, neither psychological trauma and abuse, nor dissociation were well recognised and understood. Although 100 years ago Pierre Janet developed a sophisticated theory of trauma and dissociation (Van der Hart and Horst 1989) which was highly congruent with modern perspectives, his approach was eclipsed first by the psychoanalytic theories of Freud, which emphasised repression rather than dissociation, and second by the concept of schizophrenia developed by Bleuler (1950). Multiple personality disorder, or as it has more recently been renamed, dissociative identity disorder (DID), has never been an accepted theoretical or diagnostic concept within mainstream psychoanalysis in any part of the world. Occasional accounts which did appear (for example, Schreiber 1973) were until recently regarded as oddities, having popular appeal but not worthy of serious clinical or scientific interest.

There have been some exceptions to this general position. The psycho-analyst Ronald Fairbairn wrote extensively about splitting of the ego (1952) and undertook his Master's thesis on multiple personality disorder. Another psychoanalyst, Herbert Rosenfeld, described internal 'mafia' and 'gangs', which certainly have some resemblance to phenomena found in DID; Rosenfeld, however, saw these as manifestations of a biological 'death instinct', following Melanie Klein's development of this Freudian concept. Freud's own contribution to an understanding of dissociation was his paper on splitting of the ego (1940), where he describes how a person may simultaneously hold two incompatible beliefs. In an early work, Freud and Breuer (1893) distinguished repression and dissociation: in repression, the mind is split into areas of consciousness and unconsciousness; in dissociation, consciousness itself is split, so that what is known in one state of consciousness is not known in another state of consciousness.

The current understanding of dissociative states arose from the appreciation of post-traumatic stress disorder (PTSD) that emerged in the 1980s, particularly from studies of Vietnam War veterans, combined also with the recognition of the prevalence and nature of child sexual abuse, which also surfaced in general awareness during that decade. Some clinicians and theorists began to consider the possibility that PTSD might provide some clues about the long-term effects of child abuse and the relevance of these to certain psychiatric conditions, especially personality disorders (Herman 1992; Herman and Van der Kolk 1987).

The shock of encountering severe dissociation

There can be no doubt that patients with DID have presented for treatment by psychotherapists and psychoanalysts, but the nature of their disturbance may have often been construed differently. For example, Rosenfeld (1987) wrote about a patient, Caroline, a medical doctor, who he had treated (unsuccessfully) in the mid-1960s. He described her as having

> ...a destructive, murderous and criminal part in her personality which was both so completely split off and, eventually, so powerful and so serious that I came to know about it (along with her husband and indeed, in some ways, Caroline herself) only through a newspaper story and the intervention of the police. (p.134)

None of this was apparent when he took Caroline on; she appeared to be happily married and to have a good relationship with her parents. She asked for analysis because she wanted to understand herself better. However, after about a year and a half of analysis, she reported that she had been abruptly dismissed from her job in a psychiatric clinic, but appeared both outraged and mystified by this. Later, Caroline became director of a clinic for treating drug addicts. While working in this capacity, seemingly very successfully, Caroline one day reported to Rosenfeld that she had been questioned by police in connection with allegations of criminal drug prescribing. Caroline again appeared bewildered and extremely upset about this. She speculated that some envious person was trying to defame her. After she was subsequently arrested and taken into custody, Rosenfeld was visited by Caroline's solicitor, who told him that the allegations against Caroline were true – she had been selling prescriptions for large amounts of money. He asked Rosenfeld to tell the court that he was treating Caroline for schizophrenia.

At the same time Caroline was writing to Rosenfeld protesting her innocence and insisting he should tell the solicitor and the courts that she was both sane and innocent. She was sent for observation to a major London psychiatric hospital, but the professor there diagnosed only a hypomanic state, and could find no sign of a severe psychotic illness. Rosenfeld comments:

> The split in Caroline's personality was so severe that neither her husband, her friends, nor I had the slightest notion about her criminal activities. Yet these were so extreme that while she was in prison awaiting her court case she tried with a large amount of money to hire someone to murder her assistant.

He adds:

> The outcome of Caroline's treatment was a severe shock for me, although I could not see that there was anything I could have done to prevent it. What seems so incredible even now is the extent of the split between the destructive criminal part of the patient and the part with which she related to me. The first represented the complete opposite to the second. (p.136)

It is clear that Rosenfeld was completely at a loss in trying to understand the nature, function or origin of Caroline's disturbance. His references to narcissism and a split off, destructive part of her personality are merely descriptive and explain nothing. He gives no history nor any hint as to what might have led to the development of this severe bifurcation of her personality.

The shock that Rosenfeld clearly felt in encountering severe dissociation is typical. Having thought he knew his patient reasonably well, he is suddenly faced with evidence of a personality state quite incongruous with his perception. Moreover, it is a dissociated state, which is also incongruous with the knowledge and beliefs of the patient's usual state of mind when she comes to her sessions. When faced with the evidence of the incongruent behaviour, the patient, in her other state of mind, resorts to confabulation in an effort to make sense of what has been happening. This does not appear to involve conscious lying. Both patient and analyst are severely shaken by the revelation of incongruent information.

In another example, a psychotherapist approached me for supervision because a patient she had been seeing for some time suddenly, with no prior warning, and in a manner which was extremely disconcerting, presented evidence of marked dissociation. The patient turned up one day wearing quite different clothes from usual, speaking in a different voice, and using different mannerisms. She announced, 'Hello – I'm "Shirley" – and I would like to come too!' Shirley, and subsequently a number of other dissociated personality states, gradually became participants in the therapy.

A case of my own was similarly startling. I had been seeing a patient for some months. She had given hints of severe abuse in childhood, but had not talked about this explicitly. There had been no prior indication of DID. One day she came to her session and did not speak to me at all. She appeared frightened, curled up in a chair, and seemed to be trying to escape from some terrible torture. She then hid under the chair, where she remained until the end of the session. When I indicated it was time to stop, she got up and left without a word.

Later that morning I received a telephone call from her, speaking quite normally, but apologising for not having come to her session. She 'explained' that she had driven to the hospital where I see her but had felt upset and so had not been able to bring herself to enter the building; instead she had sat in her car for the duration of her session. When I tried to tell her that she had in fact come to her session, albeit in an unusual state of mind, she assumed first that I misunderstood her explanation, and then concluded that I must be lying, although she could not see any reason why I would want to lie. Over the next few months she revealed dissociative phenomena which were both complex and very extensive indeed, involving multiple personality states. She also presented narratives of very severe childhood abuse. Eventually she broke off treatment. This was not surprising since parts of her mind, as well as (according to her account) actual persons involved in child abuse, were fiercely opposed to her participation in psychotherapy.

Although doubts are often expressed about the validity of the diagnosis of DID (see Fahy 1988; Merskey 1992; Piper 1994), examples such as those just described illustrate that there are complex and confusing phenomena which require thoughtful consideration.

Confabulation

In two of the above cases, Rosenfeld's and my own, there were clear indications that in one state of mind the patient confabulated an explanation of incongruous information reflecting the activities of another dissociated state of mind. Thus, Rosenfeld's patient speculated that someone was trying to defame her by making untrue allegations, while my own patient presented an account of having sat in her car for the duration of her session as an explanation to herself of her dissociated state. It will immediately be apparent from these examples that there can be problems with the reliability of explanations and memory narratives presented by patients suffering from DID.

A further vivid example of this is described by Stone (1994). In 1978, Ruth, a 48-year-old married woman, approached the police complaining of receiving threatening anonymous letters, written in a strange rhyming style which led to the writer of these being termed 'the poet'. Ruth also felt she was being followed. On one terrifying occasion she was attacked and stabbed while getting into her car in a multi-storey car park; she struggled to break free and managed to drive to a phone box and call for help. An extensive police investigation was undertaken over a three year period. Eventually it was discovered that 'the poet' was a dissociated part of Ruth; she had been writing letters to herself. The recognition of this led to a severe depression and she began analytically oriented psychotherapy. Eventually she remembered what had actually happened in the car park. A dissociated part of her had insisted that she stab herself. By the time she had got to the phone box she had altered her memory narrative to produce the account of having been attacked by 'the poet'. Stone reports that Ruth was helped considerably by her therapy. There were indications of severe abuse in her childhood.

The possibility of confabulation in DID has led some commentators, especially those associated with the false memory societies, to argue that most dissociative narratives of childhood abuse are probably objectively false (see Brandon, Boakes and Green 1998; Merskey 1995). Some of these, drawing particularly upon the analysis by Pope and Hudson (1995) argue that there is no objective evidence that either repression or dissociation of traumatic memory is possible; they further emphasise that it is too much remembering of painful experiences that is often the problem for those who have been traumatised or abused. This position simply does not hold up to scrutiny. It rests upon an acknowledgement of one pole of the biphasic response to trauma – the intrusion of unwanted painful memory – while ignoring the other pole – the state of numbing, not thinking and not remembering. Moreover, there are in fact over 30 studies suggesting motivated forgetting of childhood trauma (Brown, Scheflin and Hammond 1998); although each may have their methodological limitations, this robust finding across many different samples and methods cannot legitimately be dismissed in the extraordinary way that some attempt to do.

Sometimes it is argued that the unusual or incomprehensible nature of abuse that is occasionally reported is itself grounds for assuming that such accounts are a product of 'false memories'. Thus Brandon et al. (1998) comment, 'There are of course some memories so bizarre or impossible that they are not credible. If something could not happen, it did not happen.' (p.304). The problem with this dogmatic position is that it rests upon a subjective and arbitrary view of what is deemed 'credible'; what may appear credible to one person may seem incredible to another. Recent prosecutions, such as those of Fred and Rosemary West, and the West Country intergenerational abuse case, indicate that extremely bizarre and 'unbelievable' abuse of children can indeed take place; in the latter case a defence of 'false memory' was unsuccessfully attempted. While we must not assume that all the memory narratives of DID patients are necessarily true in a literal or objective sense, we should surely not confuse our subjective evaluation of their credibility with an objective assessment of their truth. (More extensive discussion of contemporary disputes about memory can be found in Mollon 1998.)

Origins and functions of dissociative states

One view is that multiple personality disorder or dissociative identity disorder is essentially an iatrogenic illness, reflecting a current fad among fringe practitioners. It is argued that the characteristic phenomena of DID are the result of a combination of suggestible patients and suggestive therapists who are obsessed with a particular theory (see Aldridge-Morris 1989; Fahy 1988; Merskey 1992; Piper 1995; Spanos 1996). I believe there is some merit in this argument, in that patients with DID often are quite suggestible and endeavour to comply with whatever they discern the therapist appears to expect or want. Moreover, I have no doubt that some approaches to the treatment of DID that are excessively active, directive or suggestive may well leave the patient in a worse state. Those who emphasise this position tend also to draw attention to the dangers of the iatrogenic creation of false memories of childhood sexual abuse.

However, few who have actually encountered, spontaneously, phenomena of severe dissociation would consider this explanation to be anything more than partial and superficial. Most clinicians who have written about their work with DID (see Chu 1998; Kluft 1994; Mollon 1996; Putnam 1989; Ross 1997) regard it as a kind of long-term, complex post-traumatic stress disorder resulting usually from severe childhood abuse. This abuse would typically be in a context such that no external escape was possible, and no source of help or support was available. This concept of an origin in child-hood trauma must be distinguished from the more usual concept of simple post-traumatic stress where there is a constellation of symptoms which can be traced back to a known experience of severe trauma; often there is no ob-jective evidence for the childhood trauma when an adult presents with DID.

While severe interpersonal trauma in childhood seems a plausible basis for the development of DID, we should not assume that this necessarily is the essential cause. There might, for example, be patients with DID whose childhood was not pervaded by abuse. Extreme loneliness could conceivably play a part. Another contributor could be constitutional factors (a probable instance of this is described by Williams 1992, discussed in Mollon 1996).

One further requirement for the creation of a state of DID may be a sufficient capacity for pretence and fantasy and also for spontaneous self-hypnosis. Some (see Mollon 1996; Putnam 1989; Ross 1997) regard DID as a mental state and structure which makes use of pretence as a means of coping with the unbearable. Kluft (1994) states:

> On a clinical and descriptive level, MPD [multiple personality disorder] is, intrinsically, no more than a brutalised child's whimpering in the night and wishing with desperate earnestness that he or she were someone else, somewhere else, and that what had befallen him or her had befallen someone else. Most parsimoniously put, MPD appears to be a dissociative condition of childhood onset. (p.16)

Dissociation itself is a natural capacity – the ability to become absorbed in a particular activity or focus of thought so that other information or activity is left without conscious attention – which is exploited for defensive purposes when a child is subjected to severe and repeated abuse. This 'switching off' or 'numbing' out may then develop further, through the vehicle of imagination, to develop an elaborate world of alter personalities. The controversy sometimes raised as to whether alter personalities are really full personalities or not, is from my perspective an obsessional distraction; obviously there is one personality which is structured dissociatively – but we have to call the dissociative parts something!

Alters come in all shapes and sizes. They may be child or adult, male or female, human or non-human. Child parts typically reflect the experiences of abuse at different ages. Fierce 'protectors' are usually in place, whose function is to protect the children – and especially to guard against dangerous intrusions by a therapist. Other parts are based upon identification with the abuser, or may stand for staunch loyalty to the abuser. Some may operate like internal lobbyists, aiming to invalidate or 'shout down' the reports of interpersonal trauma presented by others within the system. Various adult alters may have developed to cope with particular life tasks, such as work or marriage.

The apparent benefit of the dissociative structure is that the person can at times be in states of mind which are not displaying the residues of severe trauma. However, such stability as can often be achieved by the dissociative system is inclined to break down as the years go by, especially when the person has her or his own children, or when the children reach the age the person was when the original abuse began. It is often then that psychotherapeutic help is sought.

In practice, for those who make use of psychiatric diagnostic systems, DID would often not be seen as existing entirely alone. People who have suffered sustained abuse and neglect as children are likely to have problems which might include borderline personality disorder, anti-social personality disorder, disorders of mood, and somatisation disorder, among others (North *et al.* 1993). Often authors writing about DID are at pains to distinguish this state from schizophrenia, pointing out that not uncommonly dissociative patients are misdiagnosed as schizophrenic. In particular, it is argued that hallucinatory voices experientially located internally (sometimes called pseudo-hallucinations) are characteristic of DID, being expressions of the alter personalities, while voices experienced as external are characteristic of schizophrenia. Personally, I have become less certain of this absolute distinction. Both DID and schizophrenia involve a retreat to a relatively private world of fantasy. In DID the defensive aspect of this is obvious insofar as it appears to have evolved as an escape from an unbearably abusive reality. However, schizophrenic states can also give the impression, if one spends long enough listening to the patient, that reality has proved too difficult, confusing or humiliating to bear for one reason or another. Moreover, some DID patients I have worked with have at times given the impression of a schizophrenic state, while at other times this would not be the case at all.

Some basic principles of therapy with DID

How should the clinician proceed when confronted with a patient presenting dissociatively, bearing in mind that it is not always possible to discern this potential in advance? Since I am in background a psychoanalytic psycho-therapist, I tend to favour a psychoanalytically oriented approach to therapy with those traumatised in childhood – that is, a stance which takes account of transference and psychodynamic conflict. Some modifications to the standard approach are necessary, however, particularly in relation to the need to reduce anxiety. I also believe that an approach based upon cognitive therapy can be helpful.

In my view, the most important principle in working with people with DID, or related states, is the need to proceed with extreme caution. People with DID are often extremely vulnerable. They may present as deceptively well-functioning, but their potential for destabilisation in response to par-ticular kinds of stress may be considerable; this may result in self-harm and other damaging behaviours, as well as a general loss of the capacity to cope with the tasks of everyday life. One of the potentially most destabilising stresses is that of entering psychotherapy. Almost always the prospect of therapy will stir up intense internal conflict and 'civil war'. Some parts of the patient may be eager to communicate and to trust the therapist, while other parts may be adamantly, even violently, opposed to this. It is by no means certain that psychotherapy of a kind that explores the inner world will be helpful or appropriate. In some cases it may make matters worse.

The appropriate stance, it seems to me, is one of responding thoughtfully, cautiously and respectfully to the cues and initiatives presented by the patient. On this basis there can be a careful negotiation of whether and how to proceed. If there are indications of conflict and severe anxiety in relation to the venture of psychotherapy, then these should be acknowledged explicitly. I tend to emphasise two points in particular: first, that I have no wish and no power to impose a 'solution' from outside – that I can only try to facilitate internal communication and negotiation; second, that it is important for the patient to seek internal consensus about whether and how to proceed. There will almost certainly be parts of the patient which feel that entering psychotherapy is an utterly mad and dangerous venture; it is important to understand and acknowledge this point of view – that on the basis of the patient's experience it is not safe to trust anyone, and if a therapist appears trustworthy, that just indicates how clever he or she is in their preparation to abuse and victimise the patient. A particular crisis of trust usually develops when child parts of the patient attempt to reach out and communicate with the therapist; this movement may be violently opposed by the internal 'minders' and 'bouncers'.

It is unwise at any point to attempt to override anxiety or resistance. Often it is necessary to allow the patient to withdraw, or to suspend or abandon therapy in order to reduce anxiety. The patient's safety, from his or her own self-destructive impulses or overwhelming affect, should be the paramount concern; any exploration which may potentially cause anxiety must take second place to this. People who have been traumatised in childhood frequently are left deficient in capacities to calm themselves down when aroused or agitated; at these times the danger of self-harm is increased. It is often helpful to encourage the patient to think about less damaging ways of reducing unbearable tension – ideally, through finding appropriate social support.

Great care should be taken to avoid imposing a view, either of the nature of the patient's mental state or of its historical origins. Many patients will have suffered early family environments in which they learned to adapt and comply with whatever they perceived the abuser to require; this may be repeated and re-enacted in the transference to the therapist, such that a false presentation and developmental history is created on the basis of compliance with a dominant therapist. On the other hand, it is important to respond thoughtfully to the cues and hints provided by the patient. Gradually the patient may come to experience the therapy as providing a calm, receptive and thoughtful ambience, a setting in which boundaries are respected, and may be able to use this as a basis for a review of his or her life and its history.

Not all the literature on work with dissociative states gives adequate emphasis to clinical dangers. Some of the American writings from the late 1980s now seem, in retrospect, to have been overly optimistic. Further discussion and guidelines for cautious treatment of DID and related states is given in Chu (1998) and Mollon (1996; 1998).

Hazards to the therapist

While it is appropriate to give emphasis to the need for caution with regard to the well-being of the patient with DID, the hazards to the therapist should also be noted. Work with DID and other patients who have been inter-personally traumatised in childhood can be disturbing, disorienting and traumatising to the therapist. An empathic indwelling in the strange yet compelling subjective world of DID may insidiously undermine the thera-pist's normal sense of reality. His or her usual framework and boundaries of therapy may gradually slip. Losing the reassuring bearings of familiar theory, and finding the technical ground increasingly fluid, the therapist new to this work may stumble into a chasm – or perhaps a vortex – of confusion and terror.

The exposure to narratives of severe childhood abuse can be traumatising to the therapist. This vicarious traumatisation may be combined with the anguish of uncertainty regarding the veracity of the narratives, to produce an effect which is distinctly toxic. Therapists immersed in work with abuse victims may find that they come to inhabit a psychological world that is alien to their friends, family or colleagues. This alienation from those who have not encountered trauma may at times be combined with the experience of being hated by the patient. A person who has suffered persistent abuse in childhood may have the potential not only to identify with the role of victim, but also to take up the position of abuser in relation to the therapist as victim. A therapist drawn to the role of rescuer may at a certain point be viewed by the patient (or by part of the patient) as abuser in some respect – and as a result may become the victim of the patient in the role of seeker of vengeance. The patient may claim that the therapist has made him or her worse, or that the therapist has created the state of DID, or has implanted false memories. In some instances a patient may realign with someone whom he or she has identified as an abuser – and the therapist becomes their prey.

The therapist considering taking on for long-term psychotherapy a patient abused in childhood would be wise to reflect on the following stark point and its implications. The nature and severity of the abuse will be reflected in the transference; that is how the therapist will be viewed at certain periods (or by certain parts of the patient). Will this be bearable, containable – will it be safe? How will the patient treat a therapist whom he or she regards as an abuser?

To venture into the world of DID is to encounter a condensed and seething microcosm of society's conflicting attitudes towards knowledge of childhood sexual abuse. Within the one patient can be found victims, perpetrators, those seeking revenge, those wishing to deny or minimise abuse, those who would blame the child for the abuse, those who would confabulate and falsely allege abuse as well as those who would falsely deny abuse. The therapist who responds to pleas for help may face intense hostility both from within the patient and from the wider society.

References

Aldridge-Morris, R. (1989) *Multiple Personality: An Exercise in Deception.* Hove: Erlbaum Associates.

Bleuler, G. (1950) *Dementia Praecox or The Group of Schizophrenics.* New York: International Universities Press.

Brandon, S., Boakes, J. and Green, R. (1998) 'Recovered memories of childhood abuse. Implications for clinical practice'. *British Journal of Psychiatry 172*, 296–307.

Brown, D., Scheflin, A.W. and Hammond, D.C. (1998) *Memory, Trauma Treatment and the Law.* London: W.W. Norton and Co.

Chu, J.A. (1998) *Rebuilding Shattered Lives: The Responsible Treatment of Complex Post-Traumatic and Dissociative Disorders.* New York: John Wiley and Sons.

Fahy, T.A. (1988) 'The diagnosis of multiple personality disorder: A critical review'. *British Journal of Psychiatry 153*, 597–606.

Fairbairn, R. (1952) *Psychoanalytic Studies of the Personality.* London: Routledge.

Freud, S. and Breuer, J. (1893–5) 'Studies on hysteria'. In *Standard Edition of the Complete Psychological Works of Sigmund Freud, Vol II.* London: The Hogarth Press.

Freud, S. (1940) 'Splitting of the ego in the service of defence'. *Standard Edition of the Complete Psychological Works of Sigmund Freud, Vol. XXII.* London: The Hogarth Press.

Herman, J.L. (1992) *Trauma and Recovery.* New York: Basic Books.

Herman, J.L. and Van der Kolk, B.A. (1987) 'Traumatic antecedants of borderline personality disorder'. In B.A. Van der Kolk (ed) *Psychological Trauma.* Washington, DC: American Psychiatric Press.

Kluft, R.P. (1994) 'Multiple personality disorder: Observations on the etiology, natural history, recognition, and resolution of a long-neglected condition'. In R.M. Klein and D.K. Doane (eds) *Psychological Concepts and Dissociative Disorders.* Hillsdale, NJ: Erlbaum Associates.

Merskey, H. (1992) 'The manufacture of personalities: The production of multiple personality disorder'. *British Journal of Psychiatry 160*, 327–340.

Merskey, H. (1995) 'Multiple personality disorder and false memory'. *British Journal of Psychiatry 166*, 281–283.

Mollon, P. (1996) *Multiple Selves, Multiple Voices: Working with Trauma, Violation and Dissociation.* Chichester: John Wiley and Sons.

Mollon, P. (1998) *Remembering Trauma. A Psychotherapist's Guide to Memory and Illusion.* Chichester: John Wiley and Sons.

North, C.S., Ryall, J.E.M., Ricci, D.A. and Wetzel, R.D. (1993) *Multiple Personalities, Multiple Disorders, Psychiatric Classification and Media Influence.* New York: Oxford University Press.

Piper, A. (1994) 'Multiple personality disorder'. *British Journal of Psychiatry 164*, 600–612.

Pope, H.G. and Hudson, J.L. (1995) 'Can memories of childhood sexual abuse be repressed?' *Psychological Medicine 25*, 121–126.

Putnam, F. (1989) *Diagnosis and Treatment of Multiple Personality Disorder*. New York: Guilford Press.

Rosenfeld, H. (1971) 'A clinical approach to the psychoanalytic theory of the life and death instincts: An investigation into the aggressive aspects of narcissism'. *International Journal of Psycho-Analysis 52*, 169–178.

Rosenfeld, H. (1987) *Impasse and Interpretation*. London: Tavistock Publications.

Ross, C. (1997) *Multiple Personality Disorder* (2nd edn). New York: John Wiley and Sons.

Schreiber, F.R. (1973) *Sybil*. Chicago: Henry Regnery.

Spanos, N.P. (1996) *Multiple Identities and False Memories. A Sociocognitive Perspective*. Washington DC: American Psychological Association.

Stone, G. (1994) *Little Girl Fly Away*. New York: Simon and Schuster.

Van der Hart, O. and Horst, R. (1989) 'The dissociation theory of Pierre Janet'. *Journal of Traumatic Stress 2*, 4, 399–414.

Williams, D. (1992) *Nobody Nowhere*. London: Doubleday.

Working with Individuals and Groups in Organisational Settings

CHAPTER 14

Containment, Supervision and Abuse

Dick Agass

A skilled and experienced social worker was counselling a female client with an extremely violent family history, which included having been sexually abused by her father. After one particularly harrowing session with her client, the worker was returning to her office when she was alarmed to find herself driving through a red light. On another occasion, again after a very gruelling session, she went back to her office, wrote up the session and then went home for the weekend. Over the weekend, however, she became convinced that she had inadvertently put the casenotes in the waste-bin, or perhaps posted them to someone, instead of putting them in the filing cabinet, and she had a strong urge to go back to the office to make sure the notes were safe.

I begin with these incidents because they illustrate a key aspect of the phenomenon I want to discuss in this chapter – namely the impact on any professional worker of severe disturbance within an individual or a family, and the extent to which this disturbance can be contained, thought about and dealt with by the worker in a way which not only preserves their own sanity but also offers some alleviation of the client's distress. As this worker's supervisor, it was clear to me that the appalling events of her client's life and the acutely painful feelings stirred up in the counselling sessions were steadily getting under her skin, affecting her sleep and her personal relationships and making her feel, in her own word, 'contaminated'. She had come to feel so invaded and poisoned by what her client was communicating to her, both verbally and in less easily identifiable ways, that she had developed a strong and largely unconscious urge to rid herself of the case altogether (bin the notes), which troubled her greatly because it conflicted with her professional responsibilities, as well as with her view of herself as a conscientious and caring person. Hence, I think, her guilt-laden urge to go back and rescue the casenotes from her own unacknowledged desire to dispose of them. The incident of going through the red light, which she herself put down to over-load, could perhaps be understood at a less conscious level as a warning to herself that in working with this client she was having to override her own internal danger signals, thus putting her own mental and physical well-being increasingly at risk.

Such experiences are not uncommon in any area of work closely involved with human suffering, and there are some classic studies of the impact of physical illness or mental disturbance on professionals and professional systems (see Main 1957; Menzies 1959). One very experienced mental health social worker on a recent training course I was conducting said she found it remarkable how one or two of her clients seemed to 'discharge a whole load of disturbance' into her, so that her normal ability to leave her work behind her when she went home was completely undermined. She added, 'I've no idea how they do it'.

It is this whole question of 'how they do it' that I want to examine first: how workers can come to feel disturbed by their clients without necessarily understanding what this disturbance is or how it got in. This means looking beyond the consciously distressing aspects of a particular case to a deeper level of interpersonal process which is largely unconscious. Unless we have a way of understanding and thinking about such processes they are likely to have an adverse effect on our own psychic balance as well as on our work, leading either to some kind of retaliatory acting out towards the client, or to illness and burn-out.

My discussion will focus on the psychoanalytic concepts of projective identification (Klein) and containment (Bion), and the particular concern of this chapter is the vital importance of supervision in helping the worker to contain and understand the client's experience as a necessary step towards rendering that experience more understandable and manageable for the client. It is also argued that cases involving any combination of physical, emotional or sexual abuse present special difficulties for the worker, who is likely to feel abusive or abused, and in some degree contaminated (as the first worker above put it) by exposure to the client's experience (Agass and Simes 1992).

Having been a consumer, as well as a provider, of supervision for many years and in many different settings – including 'live' supervision in a family therapy team, and both group and individual supervision in psychotherapy – I am more than ever convinced that trying to work in any depth without it is like shooting the rapids without a lifejacket. What one hears most often from social workers and related professionals working in the public sector is that they hardly ever have the opportunity or the help to examine their work in any depth, still less its effect on themselves, beyond the purview of administrative and statutory requirements. In writing this chapter I have therefore tried to keep in mind the practitioners referred to above, and others like them, who spend their working lives exposed to their clients' disturbance and cope largely on their own with its impact.

Projective identification and containment

The concept of projective identification originates with Melanie Klein (1946), and describes an unconscious defence mechanism of very early development in which the infant deals with intense primitive anxieties by segregating its good and bad objects (the psychoanalytic term for the *person* towards whom an impulse or feeling is directed (external object), or the intrapsychic version of that person (internal object)) together with the 'good' and 'bad' parts of the self linked to these objects, and then doing its best, in phantasy to ensure that these good and bad aspects of its experience remain separate. In this way everything unconsciously perceived as bad and harmful is split off internally and may then be projected into the outside world. As Feldman (1992) helpfully summarises:

> Klein came to use the term 'projective identification' to describe this process whereby the infant projects (primarily) harmful contents into his object (for example, into his mother), and by the same token projects those parts of his mental apparatus with which they are linked. In so far as the mother then comes to contain the bad parts of the self, she is not only felt to be bad, as a separate individual, but is *identified* with the bad, unwanted parts of the self. (p.75)

The parts of the ego projected in this way become identified with the object, and are no longer experienced as belonging to the self. For example, aggressive impulses, once projected, may then be perceived as originating in the object and directed at the self (Klein's paranoid-schizoid position). 'Good' parts of the self may also be projected into an object as a means of keeping them separate, and therefore safe, from the 'bad'. Through a constant cycle of projection and introjection, the projected parts of the self, both good and bad, are taken back in, together with parts of the object, and in favourable circumstances the ego gradually becomes stronger and more integrated, more able to tolerate the co-existence of good and bad impulses towards whole, separate objects (Klein's depressive position).

It is stressed that projecting parts of ourselves in this way is a normal aspect of human relating which continues throughout life and which forms the basis of our capacity to empathise or identify with other people. Normally this means that we can identify with someone else but then pull ourselves out again into our own skin, so to speak, without any real danger of being lost inside the other person or getting our own identity confused with theirs. If, however, there are problems in an individual's early development, he or she may fail to develop any cohesive sense of self or any clear ego boundaries, with the consequence that splitting and projective processes become established as the primary mode of relating to others, perhaps operating in an increasingly rigid and irreversible way.

Some severely disturbed individuals – referred to as 'borderline' precisely because of this problem with their own internal and external boundaries – live in a more or less permanent state of narcissistic identification with other people so that they no longer have any clear sense of 'who's who'. Through projective identification the painful reality of separateness can be avoided by the illusion of being part of another person, being inside them, and so on. Projective identification may also be used as a means of taking over and controlling an object or acquiring its attributes, turning it into a possession or an extension of the self.

If Klein's original emphasis was on the *defensive* nature of projective identification – especially ridding the self of its unwanted parts – then Bion developed the notion of projective identification as the infant's earliest means of *communication* with the mother. According to Bion (1962a, b) the infant projects its frightening and unbearable feeling-states into the mother, who, in favourable circumstances, 'contains' them, and then, in her emotionally attuned handling of the infant (holding, comforting, feeding) gives them back to him in a more manageable form – a function which, over time, the infant introjects and becomes more able to manage for himself. Again it is stressed that this is a normal part of human development, and that it continues to be refined throughout life as an essential component of human relating. If something goes wrong with this process in infancy, if there is no 'container' for the unmanageable feelings, or one which cannot contain them but only push them back at the infant in an unmodified state, then these feelings are rendered even more frightening and may give rise to states of overwhelming anxiety and disintegration.

It is this concept of projective identification as a communicative process which now underlies any psychodynamic approach to interpersonal process, especially in relation to the intensely powerful feelings that can be stirred up in therapists or other helping professionals by their clients or patients – the countertransference. By analogy with the containing mother, professionals need to develop a capacity for what Bion calls 'reverie', a state of mind in which painful, confusing and sometimes unbearable feelings and impulses can be contained and reflected upon so that the client may be able to reintroject these raw states of feeling, together with an increased capacity to cope with them internally rather than by projecting them into, or repeatedly acting them out with, other people. Perhaps I can illustrate some of this with an example from my own social work experience.

I was once involved in a home visit to one of my clients, whom I now think of as borderline, though at the time he was considered schizophrenic, as part of a combined operation with other mental health professionals to admit his acutely depressed girlfriend to psychiatric hospital. My client was very opposed to this plan, and from the moment I arrived he was unusually hostile towards me, apparently holding me responsible for the whole situation. As I waited with him in one room while his girlfriend was being seen in another, he became more and more agitated, pacing around the room and generally sounding off in a rather menacing way. I remember at one point being quite clear in my mind that if he assaulted me I would hit him back, regardless of any personal or professional consequences. The tension mounted until eventually his girlfriend was taken away, at which point he made some superficial cuts on his wrist with a razor blade.

As his day-centre worker and I were leaving, he followed us down the stairs, jostling me and complaining angrily about what had happened. In the car park he draped himself across the bonnet of my car in a somewhat histrionic attempt to prevent us from driving away. He then clung on to the side of the car, and for a moment I felt so agitated myself that I nearly drove off at speed with him still attached. My colleague asked me to stop the car and then got out and gently put his arm round the client, took him to one side and spoke to him reassuringly for a few minutes. This completely calmed him down and he was able to let us leave.

The whole incident left me feeling ashamed and puzzled that I had been so affected by the client's distress. I knew I had been in more frightening situations without feeling half so agitated, and my relationship with the client, both before and after this incident, never carried the same emotional charge. However, when I think of my response in terms of *the client's own internal state projected into me*, the incident makes much more sense. In other words, I think the fear I experienced was his own desperate inner panic at losing someone whose identity had become (through projective identification) a vital part of his own, her removal thus threatening him with the depletion and emptiness so characteristic of schizoid dependency. As well as reacting in this way out of self-preservation, I think he was also struggling at some level with a painful sense of his own responsibility for his girlfriend's condition, the majority view among the professionals certainly being that her deterioration had been caused by him.

We can thus see two distinct kinds of projective identification at work here. First, the *communicative*, involving an intense inner panic at having his partner (together with the parts of himself projected into her) taken away from him, and a desperate need to defend himself against this 'assault' – all of which was communicated very directly to me through a kind of primitive distress signal, arousing in me the same panic and fear of attack. Second, the *evacuative*, involving his own internal struggle with blame and shame, and his need to rid himself of any sense that he might have contributed to his girlfriend's mental collapse. This too was projected onto me, so that, although I felt I could see through his crude attempts to blame me for what was happening, I still had the disturbing sense that I had let him down in some way – perhaps by not taking enough care of his mental state during our relationship. This feeling intensified after the visit when I blamed myself for mishandling the whole situation.

What the client needed, and what my colleague intuitively provided, was an empathic, containing response – while all I could think about was driving off as quickly as possible. Indeed, if I had been able to think at all about what was happening I might have realised that the client's internal state was being expressed in his behaviour (desperately clinging on to a departing object), while my own response reflected the plight of his partner (having to get away in order to survive).

There are two further points to draw from this example. The first is that, although it may be quite obvious, on a conscious level, that the client is trying to pressurise you into feeling something – in the above case by being openly belligerent and blaming – it is often impossible to know at the time exactly *how* you are being affected because the underlying process is an unconscious one. All you know, in the words of the worker quoted earlier, is that some kind of disturbance is being discharged into you. In fact, it may not even be clear *whose* disturbance it is, and the worker may initially experience it as his or her own. It may only be at a much later stage, if at all, that the nature and origin of this disturbance can be discovered, and then perhaps only after considerable self-examination, or with the help of skilled supervision. The second and closely related point is that once this underlying dynamic is understood, it becomes all too easy to project all the disturbance back into the client, effectively blaming him or her for the uncomfortable internal states that have been transferred to us. Although these internal states originate in the client, they have to find a fertile foothold in the worker's own personality in order to take root, and we are each susceptible to different kinds of projections. It is an uncomfortable experience to have clients homing in like this on our own areas of disturbance. In the above example, an understanding of unconscious process would certainly have helped me to make sense of my reactions, but it would not have removed the need to look at my inability, in those circumstances, to contain the client's distress.

I suggest that what is projected is not only a set of feelings or impulses but an object relation, which may then be acted out unknowingly between the client and professional workers or between different professionals or their agencies. Britton (1981) gives a lucid account of this phenomenon, together with a sound theoretical basis for understanding it.

The following example was presented by a mental health social worker in a supervision workshop I was facilitating. The client she presented was described as a 'borderline personality disorder', an immediate clue to the likelihood of splitting and projective processes as a prominent feature. The client was said to be unable to care for her children, who were both up for adoption, or herself. She had a history of sexual abuse, both in her family and at residential school, but had only recently disclosed that the original abuser had been a family member. Her dealings with her siblings were described as 'very confused and dishonest', and she had a consistently hostile relationship with her mother. The worker described her struggles with this client, particularly during a period of inpatient psychiatric care, when the client would constantly complain about the worker not visiting enough, but then, when she did visit, would either refuse to talk to her at all or else simply ask her to carry out routine tasks. The worker said she was constantly aware of the client's hostility, and felt she could never give her what she needed. She also felt denigrated by the ward staff, who knew 'their' patient very well from her frequent admissions, and who made it obvious in various ways that they shared her feelings about the worker's lack of experience and commitment.

Listening to the worker it was obvious that the pressure of her client's behaviour towards her was taking its toll. She had been obliged to take some sick leave (quite possibly, though not consciously, related to this client), and had contemplated getting the case transferred to another worker. Above all she felt used by the client, who seemed intent on devaluing her by keeping the relationship on a menial level while constantly complaining about the lack of any real help. Clearly the worker had been on the receiving end of some forceful projections, and there are strong indications of an abusive dynamic at work here, with its familiar noxious blend of favouritism and degradation. The worker's sense of being trapped in something confusing and demeaning that could hardly be called a relationship but was the only thing on offer, and her desperate desire to escape – by going off sick or transferring the case – could certainly be viewed as projected elements of the client's own early experience of abuse. In subjecting the worker to this experience the client seems to have been unconsciously replaying her internal drama with the roles reversed, recruiting the nurses to join in the abuse of the worker.

This is a clear example of the way in which a key aspect of a client's inner experience not only transmits itself to an individual worker but may also be enacted between her and the other professionals. In fact the situation here is reminiscent of Main's (1957) classic description of a group of psychiatric patients who were remarkable not only for the intractable nature of their problems but also for the special status they acquired in the course of their treatment careers. Main found that these patients somehow managed to stimulate superhuman efforts and intense rivalries among the hospital staff for the honour of being admitted to a loyal 'in-group' of carers. Within this inner circle the patient would bestow confidences in such a way that each nurse thought she alone enjoyed this privileged intimacy. Although Main does not go into specific case histories, the dynamic he describes is wholly consistent with an abusive family system in which the abuser deploys a divisive strategy of favouritism and secret alliances, deluding his victims into feeling 'special' for being thus exploited. Main also points to the rifts and the blurring of professional roles and boundaries which always occur with such patients, and this again mirrors the breaching of personal and generational boundaries in sexual abuse. It is interesting to note with Main that these rifts tend to occur along fault-lines already existing in the professional system, for example, as here, between hospital- and community-based workers (cf Agass and Preston-Shoot 1991).

To return to our example, the social worker's intense experience of being left out (something she shared, no doubt, with the client's children) may be understood as a projection by the client of her own unbearable early experience of a relationship with a cold, uncaring maternal object – a situation she had managed to reverse in the hospital setting, so that dedicated professionals were now caring for *her* while *someone else* was being left out in the cold.

Containment, supervision and the capacity to think

One consistent feature in these examples is that the workers became so caught up in their clients' experience that they found it virtually impossible to *think*. The development of an infant's capacity for thought is a key aspect of Bion's theory of the container and the contained, and though the details of this theory are beyond the scope of the present chapter, it will be helpful to summarise its essential elements.

Following Freud (1911), Bion (1962a, 1962b) viewed thinking as a developmental achievement in which the illusion of omnipotent control of one's object world is gradually abandoned in the face of reality. At the risk of drastic over-simplification, projective identification, if it is adhered to as the primary mode of relating to objects, becomes a way of *not thinking* about, or learning from, experience. Thinking involves difficult psychic work, and the toleration and working through of painful and conflicting emotional states. Through projective identification these unwelcome states can be evacuated into other people as raw, unprocessed matter (Bion's 'beta elements') the psychic equivalent of eliminating unwanted substances from the body. In this way painful experience can be avoided by repeatedly getting other people to enact it so that they, and not the subject, are obliged to suffer its effects. The result may be that very little in the subject's internal world is ever really engaged with or worked through before it gets discharged in some kind of activity, or acted out, as it is usually termed. For thinking to become possible there has to be an experience of a containing object which can detoxify the projected elements and render them (by a process Bion calls 'alpha function') more susceptible to symbolisation, thought and mental work.

My thesis here is that, even with some of our most damaged and disturbed clients, it may be possible to bring this function into play, to contain and process elements of their experience so that they can begin to reintroject them and work on them internally, instead of constantly getting rid of them, and in the process depleting themselves, by projective identification. I want to show in a very simple way how supervision can sometimes fulfil this containing role for the worker or therapist while they themselves are struggling to contain the client's material. If successful, this process can result in emotional growth for both client and worker.

The first of two examples I will present concerns a 19-year-old female client who referred herself to a social work team specialising in drug and alcohol abuse. Her presenting problem was her drinking, but the focus of the work quickly settled on the fact that she had been sexually abused by her paternal grandfather as far back as she could remember, often while her mother was in the house. Up to the age of seven she knew she did not like what her grandfather did to her, but did not realise it was wrong. When she was nine he moved away, but she continued to live in fear that he would come back and get her. It was not until she was 13 that she told her mother about the abuse, and then only because she thought the grandfather was going to move back in with them. To their credit her parents believed her straight away (it seems likely he had abused others in the family too) and banned him from the house. Despite her relief she could not deal with the abuse and its effects on her, and as she got into her teens her behaviour went more and more off the rails. She drank excessively and was recklessly promiscuous. Sometimes she stepped off the curb with her eyes closed to see if she was 'meant' to die. She was aware that intensely violent feelings built up inside her, but the only way she could deal with them was by some sort of blood-letting, either cutting herself or getting herself injured in fights, which felt to her like getting the abuser out of her system. By the time of her self-referral she had at least found some stability and support, sharing a house with a number of other women whom she seemed to regard as a surrogate family.

The reason the worker asked for help with this case was that she felt she lacked the mental health experience to deal with some of her client's rather strange ideas and experiences. For example, the client said she had 'presences' who were with her in varying combinations and with varying intensity: one was described as a short and hostile male presence, while another was a benevolent female presence. She also believed that she had seven parts to her, and that the presences could take these parts away. She could feel reasonably well with five, but knew that if she went down to three she would be in dire trouble. Once the pieces were lost she had to find them again. She was apparently convinced that she would die at 25, and had a vision of someone driving past in a car and shooting her in the head. She also suffered from sleep disturbance and perceptual distortions, for example doors appearing to be the wrong size when she looked at them. All these things, together with the fact that she still talked to her cuddly toys, made her afraid that she was mad. Several years previously she had been sent for an EEG and remembered being told that it showed 'something wrong with her brain'.

I could see that the worker had made a good relationship with her client, who seemed very committed to their weekly sessions. The main business of supervision was to contain the intense anxiety stirred up in the worker, who was quite sure she had no means of understanding, let alone alleviating, her client's disturbed mental state.

It is a familiar feature of abuse victims that their mental capacities are shut down by their experience because it is quite simply too traumatic to take in. The only way they can survive is often to split themselves internally in an attempt to safeguard an inner sanctum of the ego in which they can hope to take refuge. The resulting loss of parts of themselves and their mental functions can be catastrophic. I think a similar internal situation is evident here in the client's description of 'parts' of herself which are constantly under threat from malevolent internal objects (presences), with the presence of good objects apparently maintaining a precarious balance. It was notable that the worker, a very skilled practitioner, was quite sure she lacked the mental capacity to deal with this case, as though in phantasy she too, like her client, had 'something wrong with her brain' or had metaphorically been shot in the head. Becoming stupid, sometimes to the point of severe intellectual impairment, is a well-documented intrapsychic defence among victims of abuse (Sinason 1992). This made it all the more vital for supervision to provide a space in which the worker could recover her own intuitive and intellectual skills so that the horror of her client's experience could be thought about and assimilated.

The client's behaviour was alarmingly self-destructive, representing a perverse attempted solution to the original abuse (Milton 1994). In supervision we considered her dissociative response to the trauma, which had split up her internal world, played havoc with her development and left her in a state of disintegration. The malevolent male presence almost certainly represented the abuser, while the perceptual disturbances might be understood as involuntary flashbacks to a child's-eye view of a (bedroom?) doorway. As for the seven 'parts' of her that regularly went missing, I suppose there is an obvious association with seven days of the week, and seven was also the age at which she realised the abuse was wrong. What more poignant lament for the time stolen from her by her abuser?

It emerged that the worker herself had continued a relationship with her own cuddly toys well into adulthood, and this helped her to identify with the child within her client who longed for contact but who at the same time was frightened and mistrustful of the grown-up world. The worker was aware of an unspoken appeal from her client to care for her, and at times to make physical contact. She felt uneasy about this and used supervision to strengthen her own personal boundaries. This undoubtedly led to a strengthening of the client's boundaries as well, and to a deepening of the relationship. As for fears about brain damage, a simple check with the appropriate medical team revealed that the client's EEG had been within the normal range, which came as a great relief to the client as well as opening up new pathways in the worker's own thinking. As the worker grew in confidence, the client too began to change. In psychodynamic terms, the worker was being taken in as a good object, which led to a strengthening of the ego. Her relationship with her mother, whom she had always blamed for letting the abuse happen, improved considerably, and she managed to bring her drinking more under control. Follow-up contact a year after the end of the sessions found the client in employment, in a stable, non-abusive relationship and generally feeling much better about herself and more in control of her life.

My second example brings us back to our starting point: the worker who got in a panic about what she might have done with her client's casenotes. I cannot give a full account of this case, but I want to discuss certain aspects of it which have a bearing on our theme. As in the previous example, the client's experience was so traumatic that it had been expelled from awareness, together with vital parts of her mental apparatus, leaving her in a severely dissociated and under-functioning state.

The client's family history was dominated by her father's violence, and there had been changes of continent and even changes of name, evidently to avoid detection. The biggest uprooting occurred after the death of her mother while they were living abroad. The client was not told directly about this but remembered her father dropping her off at school and saying to her, 'Tell your teacher your mother's dead'. Three days later they were back in

England with a different family name. Like the previous client, but this time in an almost literal sense, her life had been broken up in pieces, and then any connection between the pieces destroyed, so that her internal world had become a totally dark and terrifying place. As well as witnessing her father's assaults on her mother, she had herself been beaten and sexually abused by him, and it soon became clear that the acute anxiety symptoms which had prompted her referral were part of an internal crisis caused by fragments of this early experience breaking back through into her awareness.

Looking back, I think that from the outset the worker was under intense unconscious pressure from the client *to have this awareness for her*, to contain the knowledge of what had happened in her life, together with all the unbearable feelings associated with it. This seemed to be confirmed at one point by the client dreaming that she was being abused by her father while the worker was in the room watching and being disgusted. Disgust, however, was only part of what was being projected. As the client recalled witnessing her mother being beaten up and raped by her father, the worker felt completely overwhelmed, out of her depth and unable to help. What emerged here was the client's unbearable sense of helplessness and guilt that as a child she had not done anything to protect her mother. This internal state was also being projected into the worker, reinforced by the comment that, in telling her about these events, she was trusting the worker with her life, as she still feared her father would kill her if he found out. An atmosphere of extreme danger was thus recreated in the sessions, with the worker in the role of a helpless onlooker, paralysed by fear and disgust, and feeling totally responsible for a life poised on a knife-edge.

There were times when the worker felt so overwhelmed by what she was being required to contain – for example, the chilling intimation that the client may well have witnessed her mother being killed by her father – that she longed for the whole experience to go away. She felt abused by what was being projected into her, which had something of the force and impact of a rape, invading and contaminating her and making her feel barely able to inhabit her own internal space.

But then, as frequently happens in working with trauma, the roles were reversed. In the build-up to describing the details of her abuse, the client began to feel that the worker could 'make' her do anything, whether she wanted to or not. For her part, the worker felt it was vital in this phase of the work to push the responsibility back to the client as to when and how she should talk about her experience. Having attempted to deal with the original trauma by shutting it out of her mind, the client found that she had no words with which to describe it, and only the vaguest idea of body parts and functions. The worker duly helped her with the terminology, but reported in supervision that it felt a bit like forcing something down the client's throat. A situation then developed in which the client felt more and more 'made' to do something against her will, and had moments of seeing her father's mocking, triumphant face super-imposed on the worker's. At this point the worker felt she had 'become' the abuser for her client and that the therapy was lost. However, the situation was contained, and the client was eventually able to put into words her father's abusive acts, which included putting his penis in her mouth.

What I want to emphasise here is that the client could only deal with her unbearable internal states, once they had started to make a comeback from her original attempts to get rid of them, by projecting them into the worker and by engaging her in various re-enactments of the original trauma. The worker experienced an inrush of this unprocessed, 'beta-element' experience, and was very nearly overwhelmed by it. Abuse cases of this kind are known to stir up hostility, repugnance and hate in the worker, often leading to burn-out (MacCarthy 1988). Supervision provided the 'alpha function', the container in which this horrific raw material could begin to be processed. I suppose one could describe the supervisor in these circumstances as a kind of 'auxiliary ego', to adopt a term of Strachey (Strachey 1934), getting alongside the worker and expanding her capacity to deal with the impact of the client's experience, to reflect on it and to put it into words. This was especially difficult here because the original trauma had left the client with no internal container for her own experience, and hence no capacity to deal with it symbolically in language and thought.

In such cases the words themselves, when offered by the worker, may be experienced as re-inflicting the original trauma in a very direct and concrete way (Garland 1997). It was thus with great difficulty that the worker managed to communicate her own processing of this material back to the client, not just through verbal comments and interpretations but through her whole way of relating, as well as through the containing structure of the sessions themselves. Most importantly, the worker needed to survive the experience and to communicate to the client that it was both survivable and susceptible to understanding and working through. The outcome in this case, as in the previous one, was very satisfactory. Several years later, the client was found to be much happier and more stable, coping better with all aspects of her life and catching up on her lost education by studying for a degree.

Conclusion

In case I seem to be suggesting with these (necessarily simplified and summarised) examples that a containing experience of supervision is all that is needed for successful work with such clients, let me conclude with the obvious point that the most important factors here are still the personal attributes and professional skills of the worker. However, these attributes and skills are unlikely to be effective without the availability of a good-enough experience of supervision as a space for containment and psychic processing. I would add that a specialised training in counselling or psycho-therapy is highly advisable for professionals involved in these areas of work, and that having a personal experience of therapy is an invaluable aid to utilising what is, after all, our most potent and yet most fragile resource – ourselves.

Acknowledgements

I am indebted to the practitioners referred to in this chapter and to the clients in the last two case examples for their permission to use this material.

References

Agass, D. and Preston-Shoot, M. (1991) 'A psychodynamic and systems approach to practice'. *Human Systems: The Journal of Systemic Consultation and Management 2*, 121–137.

Agass, D. and Simes, M. (1992) 'The adult legacy of childhood sexual abuse: Individual therapy with adult mental health referrals where CSA is the key factor'. *Practice 6*, 1, 41–59.

Bion, W.R. (1962a) 'A theory of thinking'. *International Journal of Psycho-Analysis 43*, 306–310. Also in *Second Thoughts*. London: Heinemann (1967).

Bion, W.R. (1962b) *Learning from Experience*. London: Heinemann.

Britton, R. (1981) 'Re-enactment as an unwitting professional response to family dynamics'. In S. Box (ed) *Crisis at Adolescence: Object Relations Therapy with the Family*. New Jersey: Jason Aronson, Inc. (1994).

Feldman, M. (1992) 'Splitting and projective identification'. In R. Anderson (ed) *Clinical Lectures on Klein and Bion*. London: Routledge.

Freud, S. (1911) 'Formulations on the two principles of mental functioning'. *Standard Edition of the Complete Psychological Works of Sigmund Freud, Vol. XII*, 215–226.

Garland, C. (1997) 'Issues in treatment: A case of rape'. In C. Garland (ed) *Understanding Trauma: A Psychoanalytical Approach*. London: Duckworth Tavistock Clinic Series.

Klein, M. (1946) 'Notes on some schizoid mechanisms'. In *The Writings of Melanie Klein. Vol 3: Envy and Gratitude and Other Works 1946–1963*. London: The Hogarth Press (1975).

MacCarthy, B. (1988) 'Are incest victims hated?' *Psychoanalytic Psychotherapy 3*, 2, 113–120.

Main, T.F. (1957) 'The ailment'. *British Journal of Medical Psychology 30*, 3, 129–145. Reprinted in *The Ailment and Other Psychoanalytic Essays*. London: Free Association Books (1989).

Menzies, I.E.P. (1959) 'The functioning of social systems as a defence against anxiety: A report on a study of the nursing service of a general hospital'. *Human Relations 13*, 95–121. Republished as 'The functioning of social systems as a defence against anxiety.' In *Containing Anxiety in Institutions: Selected Essays. Vol.1*. London: Free Association Books (1988).

Milton, J. (1994) 'Abuser and abused: Perverse solutions following childhood abuse'. *Psychoanalytic Psychotherapy 8*, 3, 243–255.

Sinason, V. (1992) *Mental Handicap and the Human Condition*. London: Free Association Books.

Strachey, J. (1934) 'The nature of the therapeutic action of psycho-analysis'. *International Journal of Psycho-Analysis 15*, 275–293. Reprinted 1969, *50*, 275–292.

CHAPTER 15

Working as an Organisational Consultant with Abuse Encountered in the Workplace

Judith Brearley

That a damaged person may well be a damaging person has always been a recognised concept in psychotherapy; the relevance of this in organisational life is now beginning to be acknowledged. The aim of this chapter is two-fold: first, to explore some of the processes whereby anxiety, pain, trauma and stress – whether experienced by individuals, groups or entire institutions – may become contagious and reverberate at different levels in potentially destructive ways; and second, to look at the challenges of working creatively with those involved, to identify the problem and to gain understanding of cause-and-effect links, in order to achieve both a measure of damage limitation and healthier ways of interacting in the future.

Awareness that women and men may be abused at work by the 'system' or by colleagues has taken time to develop; people tend to deny the fact in much the same way as various forms of child abuse were disavowed until recently. As with child abuse, the use of euphemisms, the existence of myths and misconceptions, of clashes of perspective on what is 'normal', and sub-cultures where violence or oppression is commonplace all conspire in creating resistance to attempts to raise consciousness of the phenomenon.

Locating the problem

In his comprehensive study of adult bullying, Randall (1997) draws attention to 'what is really a hidden epidemic of intentional aggression.' (p.viii) in both the workplace and the community. He defines bullying as 'the aggressive behaviour arising from the deliberate intent to cause physical or psycho-logical distress to others' (p.4). The sorts of behaviours which fit this definition include the following:

- *Overt aggression,* threats of violence, physical attacks.

- *Covert aggression* which 'produces effects that are cumulative, long-term, corrosive and completely unacceptable, [such as] manipulating holiday schedules, making excessive demands for output, influencing promotion prospects, spreading rumours, gossiping, etc.'. (Randall 1997, p.54)

- *Disparagement,* repeated unjustified criticism, humiliation, public berating, screaming abuse, character assassination, smear campaigns.

- *Oppression and discrimination* based on race, gender, sexual orientation, age, disability, physical size or appearance.

- *Scapegoating,* for example, blaming an individual or group for incompetence when the problem resulted from the organisation's failure to provide proper conditions for good work to be done.

- *Sexual harassment:* innuendoes, sexist ridicule, unwanted touching, indecent exposure, molestation, all coupled with attitudes of denial such as, 'Boys will be boys! It was just a bit of fun! Anyway, they ask for it!' (Herbert 1994)

- *Victimisation of 'whistle-blowers',* as in the geriatric nurse ashamed that he was 'forced to witness, nay inflict, such outrageous neglect on a dying man' (Pink 1994, p.170–171), and of the social worker, first ignored then dismissed when she tried repeatedly to share her well-founded concerns about the high incidence of child abuse in residential care in North Wales.

- *Exploitation of the workforce* by compelling them to accept persecutory shift patterns and/or a relentless workload; junior hospital doctors have long known of the risk of this to patients, as well as its damaging impact on their own health.

- *Failure to provide adequate support* to front-line workers in the aftermath of major disasters, and denial of responsibility for work-induced trauma.

All the above cause untold harm, but it is evident that classification and definition are problematic. The various categories have unclear or over-lapping boundaries. The degree of intentionality varies; some perpetrators may be partially unaware of their actions, or an abusive outcome may result from a series of neglectful or incompetent decisions made by a number of people. There is little consensus about what is unlawful, unethical, unacceptable, and what is merely trivial and irritating. Perceptions of the seriousness of certain behaviours are contradictory. Only a proportion of the overall problem is subject to Health and Safety at Work or Sex Discrimination legislation. The Dignity at Work Bill ran out of parliamentary time in 1997. Disciplinary matters may be dealt with by grievance procedures and industrial tribunals, or regarded as coming within equal opportunities policies. Trade unions provide help in making personal injury claims for many workers who cannot afford their own lawyer or rely on legal aid, as in the following examples.

John Walker, a social services manager in Northumberland, was paid compensation for stress-induced illness caused by unreasonable workload, possibly the first case of its kind (Randall 1997). A man was driven to suicide having allegedly been subject to a vindictive, oppressive and 'macho' style of management. His widow received damages from North East Essex Mental Health NHS Trust (Gibb 1998). Anthony Ratcliffe, a deputy head teacher in Pembrokeshire, who had retired on health grounds because of alleged bullying by the head teacher, made a successful claim for damages (Clarke 1998). These cases involved out-of-court settlements of £200,000, £25,000 and £100,000 respectively.

However, cases where any formal action is taken, successfully or not, remain the tip of the iceberg. A national opinion poll (NOP) survey conducted for the Trades Union Congress (TUC) in 1998 found that 11 per cent of workers had been bullied, and 27 per cent said their colleagues had been. The National Workplace Bullying Advice Line, set up in 1996, received 3000 calls in its first two and a half years. Increasing numbers of victims are sharing their experiences with Employee Assistance Programme counsellors (Carroll 1996; Reddy 1993). Stress claims are notoriously difficult to prove; who is to decide what is 'unreasonable' or 'unbearable'? Even in some cases where settlements were reached, employers did not accept the allegations made or that they were in breach of their obligations.

A fundamental feature of much workplace abuse is an imbalance of power between victim and perpetrator, which compounds the immense difficulty of producing evidence, overcoming the loss of confidence, sense of vulnerability and fear that the intimidation has already produced, and risking further damage. We do not yet have an established terminology for all the varieties of potentially abusive experience in the workplace, which makes it even harder to ascertain its extent or have it taken seriously.

The complex interplay of individual, group, organisation, legislation and environment

> One of the services the law performs is to transform complex messy situations involving intricate human relationships and a multiplicity of possible causes and effects into a simple story which makes sense and holds a moral for everyone. The children were abused. The stepfather did it. (King and Trowell 1992, p.1)

So far, the discussion has tended to imply that abuse in the workplace can similarly be understood in simplistic terms, and blame allocated. This is of course far from the truth. A combination of interacting factors is always involved. In the rest of this chapter, an attempt will be made to explore in more depth the intricacy of the processes involved.

A poignant object lesson is provided by Martin Ruddock, the social work team manager at the centre of the Kimberley Carlile child abuse inquiry (London Borough of Greenwich 1987). Reflecting on his experience, he points out that effective job performance results from the interaction of the competence of the individual, the organisational environment and the job demands. At the time the child died, he was relatively new in the post, the demands of the work were extreme and the organisation felt unsafe. Both the inquiry and the media tended to emphasise stress and individual pathology, while failing to give weight to the work environment and system, and the ways in which the system can fail the individual (Ruddock 1998).

Individual behaviour does not happen in a vacuum, but in the context of roles and structure, inter- and intra-group relationships, policy and resources, and the specific culture and history of the institution within the wider, increasingly turbulent, political and economic climate, as the following case example also shows.

A residential community for disturbed and troublesome young adults was at point of breakdown, at risk of tragedy or scandal because of serious under-resourcing – a state of affairs denied by senior management. Middle managers bearing the brunt of this were suffering severe anxiety and resentment, over-working to the point of burn-out, feeling guilty about exploitation of junior colleagues and terrified that residents were being harmed. They were harshly criticised whenever they tried to share their concerns with their boss. He had established the agency on a shoestring many years previously out of a sense of vocation, self-sacrifice and deep commitment to a marginalised group. Not only were service-users now arriving with extra difficulties, such as HIV or drug abuse, but also expectations and standards had changed over the years, in terms of the staffing levels, supervision arrangements, salaries and facilities now seen as appropriate. The director was having great difficulty in making the necessary, but to him alien, adjustments in culture, attitude, fund-raising and management.

Understanding the problem in the light of psychodynamic theory

The concept of unconscious anxiety and its associated defences is particularly helpful as we try to make sense of damaging relationships and behaviour. Although some anxiety is useful in alerting us to a problem and motivating us to take action, beyond a certain point it becomes paralysing and destructive. A person then often needs to resort to defence mechanisms, which might also be thought of as coping mechanisms, in order to survive emotionally. Denial is one of the most familiar defences, commonly in operation when we hear bad news: 'No, it's not true! I can't take it in!' Defences such as this also operate at the group or even societal level, as Mattinson (1988) shows. She and her colleagues, experienced marital therapists, wished to study the psychological impact of unemployment, and sought referrals of couples affected by redundancy, but few were forthcoming, even from GPs in areas of high unemployment. They gradually realised that 'people do not want to know about the reality of adverse effects of unemployment on others' (p.4), so they collectively used unconscious denial as a defence against an unpalatable truth.

Two other defence mechanisms particularly relevant to organisational life are splitting and projection. Ambivalence – simultaneously holding two opposed and conflicting feelings – is very difficult to sustain, and when the anxiety involved becomes too great, it often happens that an individual or group will express only one set of emotions, leaving others to express the now split-off and projected other set.

Referring to the miners' strike of 1984–5, and the printers' union violent picketing in 1986, Mattinson (1988) describes how:

> ...[in] a change from old to new patterns of work, the split between changers and resisters of change at a group or social level is often enacted in long-fought-out struggles, ...each side becomes more entrenched... and less able to hear the point of view of the other as it fights to maintain its own power and, therefore, the means to dominate and manipulate the other side. The ill-treatment of the resisters of change becomes more flagrant, as the frustration in the face of the inevitable becomes more violent in its expression. (p.183)

'It is the propensity of unconscious anxiety and its associated defences to distort perceptions of the self, of others, and of events, leading to inappropriate and ineffective response to reality...' (Woodhouse and Pengelly

1991, p.11). This is just as true in the workplace as it is in personal relationships. One manifestation of these distorted perceptions is the strong tendency for difficulties originating at the societal or organisational level to become personalised, and to find expression in conflict between individuals. For example, a community mental health project in an area of severe deprivation had local residents strongly represented on the management committee. From the early days of the project, potentially valuable differences between professional staff and local managers seemed to become personified in destructive conflict between the chairperson and the project leader.

Obholzer (1994) identified 'three layers of anxiety that need to be understood before they are addressed: primitive anxieties, anxieties arising out of the nature of the work, and personal anxieties' (p.206). It is the subtle interplay of these forces seeping into various aspects of organisation life which impact powerfully on well-being and efficiency at work. Primitive anxieties, which beset any human being from time to time, that have the quality of a nightmare – terror, dread, feelings of being abandoned or in extreme danger – put us in touch with the absolute vulnerability and dependency of a tiny infant. Personal anxieties are those triggered when current challenges to our security and well-being cause us to re-experience specific earlier fears or unresolved issues, by no means all of which are in conscious awareness. For example, the advent of a new, strict and critical boss may cause a worker to relive hitherto buried experiences as a child of never feeling valued and accepted by a harshly punitive parent, or the threat of redundancy may arouse afresh the panic and shame of debt or homelessness in the worker's family of origin. Over and above these, and resonating with them, are those anxieties specific to a particular work setting, such as the demand on the probation and prison services to manage on behalf of society the conflict between care and control enacted by their clients.

The classic example of the resonance of work-related anxieties with primitive and personal ones is provided by Menzies (1959) in her study of hospital nursing. Being confronted with suffering and death, risk and uncertainty, having to carry out distasteful or frightening tasks, and being in close physical contact with patients not only cause high levels of stress in individual nurses, but also provoke collectively enacted unconscious defensive behaviour. This then becomes a significant and pervasive ingredient in the functioning of the entire institution, powerfully influencing nurse-patient and hierarchical relationships in a negative way. Helpful communication is reduced, tasks are performed less effectively, anxiety is heightened, and more defences are resorted to; a classic vicious circle. The defensive techniques identified by Menzies include splitting the nurse–patient relationship, depersonalisation (referring to patients as 'the liver in bed 10'), detachment and denial of feelings, purposeful obscurity in the formal distribution of responsibility and avoidance of change. Such socially structured defences, because they are embedded in the culture and transmitted to new generations of workers by means of largely unexamined practices and attitudes, are notoriously resistant to change. Woodhouse and Pengelly (1991) effectively show how, by means of the self-same processes, the characteristic anxieties, dilemmas and defences of specific professions, such as general practice or marriage counselling, seriously impede transactions between them and limit the extent of useful interprofessional collaboration.

Especially for staff in the caring professions, the distress, disturbance and tragedy of the clients is likely so to compound and amplify primitive and personal anxieties that workers lacking adequate support will increasingly resort to a variety of unconscious strategies in order to survive what would otherwise be experienced as an intolerable degree of anxiety.

How early experiences find shared expression in organisational life

Most people share a tendency from time to time of casting colleagues in the role of, say, bad father, idealised mother, or favoured child, and then responding as if the attribution were valid, to the detriment of more reality-based perceptions and functioning. In psychodynamic psychotherapy such transference phenomena can be studied and worked with because the setting is designed precisely for that purpose. By contrast, in organisational life, transference, although ever-present in disguised form, is much harder to address. The priority is usually to get on with the job rather than to understand workers' feelings and relationships. Transference is only intermittently perceived, less often acknowledged, and very seldom accurately made sense of. We experience the distress of our own and others' distorted perceptions and behaviour, but opportunities to reflect on these in a way that achieves beneficial change are rare.

Staff who suffered abuse in their own childhood are likely to be particularly sensitised to any workplace behaviour reminiscent in specific ways of their early trauma. The impact varies; the new edition of the problem triggers regression or breakdown in some, resorting to phobic avoidance in others, and over-identification and over-involvement in yet others.

> The manager of a centre for troubled families with very young children had suffered abandonment, broken attachments and chronic insecurity throughout her own childhood. Later she had two unhappy marriages. Academically able, she qualified in residential child care and gravitated

towards work with exactly those situations only too familiar to her in her personal life. Such unmet needs, coupled with a strong wish to do good and to be liked, gave her an inflated view about her capacity to solve the families' problems. Because she was unable to tune into them as they really were, this clouded her assessment of their needs. She had favourites among them, was over-familiar, somewhat intrusive and free with inappropriate advice. Her anxiety was such that she could not get through a session without a cigarette. Her real kindness, coupled with extreme personal vulnerability, was disarming to the extent that although these shortcomings were known about by experienced colleagues and her line manager, it was very difficult indeed to confront her with them. This, together with the exceptional stress facing the whole community at the time, meant that an unacceptable state of affairs persisted.

This example also highlights the significance of motivation of staff in terms of unconscious choice of a particular profession, clientele or institutional setting: 'Professional "helpers", be they social workers, psychiatrists, or any other, may be the only people willing to perform a difficult and thankless task. Their willingness may arise precisely because they are also getting something from the process psychologically' (Skynner 1989, p.158). The worker with a specific sort of difficult childhood experience may be attracted to work with people who share their own difficulties, believing that it offers hope of working through the problem and moving on. As Mattinson (1999) says: 'By…settling in one type of job which both highlights and affords containment for what can be a problem internally, a person is giving himself the chance of maturing and healing old psychological wounds' (p.34).

Again, the process has a group dimension as well as an individual one, in that staff who are drawn to a particular profession or setting are likely to have similar internal needs as their colleagues. There are healthy and potentially developmental aspects of these phenomena: workers' destructive impulses may be sublimated and contained, and their empathy with clients and job satisfaction may be enhanced. Here, however, we are concerned with the ways in which such processes can contribute to abusive behaviour at work, and to what extent such damage can be prevented. Skynner addresses precisely this issue in his thought-provoking paper 'Make sure to feed the goose that lays the golden eggs', quoted above. In his opinion, those who exploit vulnerable people as a means of meeting their own needs are the ones who have to deny and split off the painful feelings about their own deprivation, projecting them into others; giving the children what they did not have themselves. Because they cannot face directly the pain of their neglect, neither can they allow themselves to be fed emotionally, thus perpetuating a vicious cycle of deprivation. By contrast, those who can acknowledge their loss are in a position to receive support and take in new learning, especially if their agencies provide space for reflection on the work, supervision and in-service training. This brings growth, maturity and the capacity to 'feed' others, leading to a virtuous circle of mutual nurture.

The contribution of attachment theory to organisational understanding

The formulations of Bowlby and his colleagues on attachment theory are now regarded as among the most significant theoretical contributions in psychoanalysis since Freud. Their findings are testable, validated by empirical research, and clinically relevant. Furthermore, parallels are being established between intrafamilial and societal experiences of security and insecurity (Bowlby 1988; Holmes 1993; Marris 1991).

Marris (1991, 1996) suggests that in a turbulent world we have a strong need to find 'structure of meaning' in our circumstances in order to make sense of what is happening and to preserve a thread of continuity in our lives. If our purposes are imbued with meaning, then we can go forward creatively; otherwise we react destructively. Building on this idea, he says:

> ...the more likely our environment is to engender unintelligible, un-expected and disruptive events, the less support we have...a society that best protected its members from grief and depression would organise its relationships so they were as stable, predictable, understandable and careful of attachments as humanly possible. (Marris 1991, p.83)

Loss and change, including uncertainty, reorganisation, closure

It is common to find in organisational life that people are expected to adjust to enormous changes immediately, with no time and space allowed for the necessary transitional processes to be worked through. The sudden dis-banding of a closely-knit group of colleagues, a spate of redundancies, the closure of a factory all have massive repercussions on people's ability to pay the mortgage, their sense of identity and self-esteem, their marriage and family life and hope for the future. As in personal bereavement, the way in which the bad news reaches the workers affects the outcome. To read about the loss of one's job in the local paper, or to be made redundant and told to clear one's desk and leave instantly, adds insult to injury and seriously disables the adjustment process.

However, although closure is a familiar and very topical way of exper-iencing change in organisational life, other types of loss are equally if not more painful, for example, the realisation that a significant person has seriously betrayed the trust placed in him or her. This is especially true in enterprises in which, as in a family, values of loyalty, commitment, mutual respect, non-exploitation and co-operation are held particularly dear.

A clergyman had engaged in various forms of sexual impropriety and abuse of power over years. Why should the disavowal of the problem, the maintenance of the 'secret' and the inability to confront it have persisted for so long? Certainly those affected knew little or nothing of other victims. Also, he had striking gifts in some areas of his work. Above all it seemed that people's ethical, moral, fiduciary and spiritual assumptions about ministry powerfully buttressed their wish not to have to think the unthinkable about someone upon whom they had depended.

The likelihood is that shock, panic, outrage and blame about such losses will resonate and be amplified through the system, causing bad feeling between people who more than ever need each others' goodwill and understanding. Exactly when what is needed is the chance to express feelings, to engage in mutual reflection and review, the time and opportunity for these precious processes is almost completely eroded. This has both an individual and a collective impact. Low morale, high sickness rate and burn-out affect staff members personally. Furthermore, colleague, team and agency relationships, and the work itself, all suffer, and the overall impact on families, communities and society at large is immeasurable.

The nature of psychodynamically oriented organisational consultancy

Motivation to use consultancy

Issues of abuse rarely come to the consultant neatly labelled as such, even by the victims themselves. There will have been many barriers to speaking about it openly: fear of reprisal, loss of job prospects. Requesting external help is never an easy matter; it may be viewed as admitting failure, there is often fear of exposing personal weaknesses or being attacked, and some will have vested interests in holding on to the status quo. The complex issues which motivate a group to take this step are likely to be ill-understood and perceived differently by the various parties. The consultant may be engaged to work with a key individual or a particular project group, and thus may not have easy access to other relevant people or levels in the hierarchy. The training officer or middle manager who authorises the work may have no power and limited influence with decision-makers at board or directorate level. If the consultancy is a major project and the organisation is highly motivated to engage with it, then it is possible to elicit further co-operation from higher managers, but these conditions do not often pertain.

Consultancy is essentially a voluntary activity requiring a basic willingness on the part of a majority of consultees to at least give it a try; without this it is bound to fail.

> A small voluntary agency was almost falling apart because of a serious conflict among its paid staff, and between them and the project leader. They agreed to explore problems with an outsider, who was then subjected by a powerful and vocal sub-group to the same fierce hostility and total lack of co-operation as the leader had experienced. It was as if the profound lack of trust in this resistant group made any change in the *status quo* utterly threatening for them.

'Outsiderness'

This is a crucial factor. Objectivity, even-handedness and lack of vested interests play an important part in creating a secure base for staff to explore difficult experiences. They may well be feeling mistrustful, caught up in warring factions, possibly traumatised, and will require containment and a facilitating environment if any progress is to be made. The consultant's peripheral situation offers the potential to be a valuable catalyst. Despite the need to absorb a lot of data about the context, it is helpful if the consultant can also tolerate being in Keats' (1818) state of 'negative capacity', that is, 'when man is capable of being in uncertainties, mysteries, doubts, without any irritable reaching after fact and reason'. This enables the consultant to be more fully receptive, able to hear the music behind the words, and to consider the significance of these.

Assessment of the complicated web of influences and awareness of boundary issues

Considerations of purpose, focus, time, place and way of working present themselves from the moment of referral for consultancy, as do the sometimes complex issues of confidentiality. How much of the work should be carried out directly with the group presenting the problem, and how much with other parts of the hierarchy or structure impinging on them? Could intervention with individuals of subgroups achieve progress, or would it exacerbate splits and tensions? Should the work be episodic, longterm or simply a one-off session? What sort of feedback, verbal or written, might be offered? When does consultancy shade inappropriately into management, or supervision, or therapy? Answers to questions of this sort are by no means self-evident, and there is always a degree of risk in deciding one way or another. The consultant's well-developed self-awareness, ability to hear 'the music behind the words' of the transactions, and readiness to share responsibility for such choices with the group are some of the qualities which ensure ethical practice.

Understanding of projective identification, countertransference and the reflection process

Thorough grasp of these unconscious processes serves as an essential tool for the psychodynamically-oriented consultant, in much the same way as for the psychotherapist. The term 'projective identification' refers to the way an individual may unconsciously disown feelings which seem unmanageable by 'dumping' them onto someone else so powerfully that the other person actually begins to experience those feelings or attributions as their own. The unconscious aim is not only to get rid of the feelings, but also to convey their significance to another person, who may be better able to survive them and make sense of them. These irrational transactions have long been recognised in couple and family relationships, and their existence and relevance in organisational life is now becoming better understood.

In the case of the clergyman described earlier, when the facts of his abuse finally emerged and were acknowledged, he began to blame and criticise members of the congregation with such vehemence that they were made to feel as if they were now abusing him. The sense of guilt and responsibility they already felt from not having been able to confront the problem much earlier was greatly compounded. Their struggles to recover from the trauma became even more complicated and painful. Hopkins and Lister (1995) offer valuable and comprehensive insights into the management of such a situation.

The closely related process of countertransference usually refers to those intense feelings and responses stirred up in the therapist by the client's story, behaviour and reactions. Monitored carefully to screen out what is personal to the worker, these provide a valuable clue to what the person most wants to communicate and yet cannot at that point put into words (Brearley 1991). The reflection process, or mirroring, is a very complex phenomenon arising from the above processes. It was identified by Mattinson (1975) who experienced it in social work supervision, although it has application also to therapy and consultancy. A particular transaction may leave the worker unusually burdened with anxiety, distress, confusion or anger, making it likely that those feelings have been dumped on him or her by the client. In an attempt to convey what is hard at that stage to express or explain verbally, the worker may unconsciously mimic aspects of the encounter, acting in uncharacteristic ways in supervision or with colleagues. The value of understanding this process, through positive use of the consultant's countertransference, is that it helps the strength and nature of the problem to be seen with greater clarity.

Expression of feelings

Fully acknowledging the distress and anger in a situation and allowing it to be expressed can sometimes transform the atmosphere and mood of the group. At first, resentment and blame are often prominent, but if the validity of people's experience is respected, then there develops a greater willingness to listen to each other and to reflect on what is happening. This in turn makes negotiation with related grounds more likely to be effective, reversing a vicious spiral.

The members of one profession in an NHS trust were suffering chronic low morale, high sickness rates and internal conflict. Collectively they had also become the object of scorn for other groups, including administration staff, colleagues in closely related professions and managers. It quickly emerged that over a period of years the successive heads of the department had been seriously inadequate for the job. The current boss, who was on sick leave, had been very disturbed and intimidating. All this was known to the administration, but no action had been taken. This was in effect a leaderless group which had been starved of resources, and given no appropriate supervision or in-service training. Botched decisions about deployment had provoked antagonism between them. Individuals had been personally undermined by their boss. To add insult to injury, they were being blamed and scapegoated for problems caused predominantly by others. Yet they were committed to their vulnerable client group, and struggling against the odds to offer a service.

After an initial assessment phase, the organisational consultant fed back to management this different formulation of the problem. Work with the staff group was designed, first, to enable them to recover from their chronic malaise both by acknowledging the unreasonableness of their position and by exploring ways they might have contributed to the problem; and second, to become a more cohesive group in touch with their individual and collective strengths. With help they wrote a discussion paper proposing better ways of functioning and detailing their needs. Management were helped to respond more respectfully to staff, to find an appropriate way of dealing with the departmental head (early retirement on health grounds), to agree an improved staffing structure and to ensure more adequate resourcing in terms of accommodation and equipment.

Containment

Garland (1988, p.188) convincingly suggests that 'the effective carrying out of the primary task is the group's powerful container'. She worked with the entire staff group of a general practice shortly after one of the doctors had been killed by a psychotic patient. Using Bion's (1961) definition of the primary task as that which is essential to the group's survival, she saw the aim for the four meetings with this traumatised work group as being to re-establish its capacity to continue with its *raison d'etre*. This did not mean simply getting on with the job; as the workers discovered, that was impossible. Instead, a temporary shift in the primary task became necessary, which could be expressed as, 'What do we have to do before we get back to work?' The therapist/consultant enabled them to create some space in which they could begin to bear thinking about it, to express a whole gamut of feelings of anger and distress, to mourn their losses, to find ways of protecting themselves from being overwhelmed by the media and the workload, to share tasks effectively again and to plan a memorial.

A transitional approach to the management of change

This was developed by Harold Bridger on the basis of Winnicott's concept of transitional phenomena (Ambrose 1989; Bridger 1990; Winnicott 1971). It includes a number of key ideas which taken together help the consultant to steer a way through the complicated material being encountered. An *open-systems perspective* involves balancing and optimising the interplay of forces both from within the organisation and from an increasingly turbulent environment, accepting the inevitable uncertainty and complexity, and acknowledging the interdependence of all parts of the system. *Development potential* refers to those people who show creativity, welcome innovation, and perceive external changes as chances for new developments rather than threats; they are most likely to respond by helping to find solutions and trying out new ways of working. The notion of the *double task* means paying attention to not only getting the job done, but also periodically reviewing and monitoring how it is done, ensuring the objectives are still relevant and well understood. Linked with this is the idea of transitional space, ensuring that time and space is made for the second task of reviewing and learning from experience, for thinking creatively about a range of possibilities. Such activity can be especially valuable when a new team comes together or a new way of working is being established; it means having sanction from the wider organisation and willingness on the part of group leaders to put at least a short moratorium on the everyday work in order to find ways of functioning more effectively in the longer term.

Experiences of consultancy in two contrasting instances of school closure serve to highlight the impact of various interacting factors on outcome. The first involved a residential school for youngsters, who had already suffered neglect, abuse and family breakdown. Local government reorganisation, political changes and indecisiveness led to rumour and lengthy debilitating uncertainty, and the entire process took two years, during which planning blight became increasingly evident. To make matters much worse, higher management behaved in a seriously persecutory, incompetent and neglectful fashion, which amounted to abuse. They failed to listen, withheld vital information, gave contradictory messages, delayed necessary decisions, by-passed agreed procedures and bungled the redeployment and redundancy processes. They totally ignored the head teacher's sensible and wise proposals about managing the closure process. Not only did they fail to acknowledge and value the work done by the school in such stressful circumstances; they even publicly disparaged the skills of those to whom they were not offering jobs. Despite the undoubted competence and commitment of senior staff, and the consultant's best efforts, staff members' health and family relationships suffered, and they fought a losing battle against becoming fragmented, mutually hostile and cynical. They were deprived of the chance to make satisfactory endings, and they moved on with lessened confidence, a sense of failure and many unresolved issues.

In the second situation, involving a secondary school in a deprived area, there was only limited input from higher management and advisory staff, but by comparison it was far less undermining. As in the previous example, the head possessed wisdom and foresight, and consultancy was available to him, his colleagues and the principal teachers. All these factors together enabled senior staff to offer leadership and respond sensitively. They supported and valued other staff members, who in turn found they had the capacity to support the students both educationally and emotionally (a positive example of the reflection process discussed earlier). Despite extreme stress, and not without some casualties, they succeeded in effecting a satisfactory transfer process, found ways to mourn their loss, planned good ending rituals and held on to a sense of pride in their achievements. Significantly, sickness rates and absenteeism remained below the regional average throughout the nine month process.

Ways forward

The need for a culture shift away from a narrowly defined occupational health towards the fostering of organisational health is just beginning to be more widely recognised. We can no longer be content with mere troubleshooting. In addition, a range of preventative strategies need to be identified and implemented. These might include the following:

- Provision of adequate human relations learning and support for managers.

- Effective and empathic management of transition.

- Stress awareness input at all levels.

- Understanding of the interfaces between line management, supervision and in-service training, and recognition of the dangers of offering inadequate supervision.

- Human resources policy documents stating values, rules and clear guidance on procedures, made credible by firm implementation when required.

- Information about a wide range of resources, and encouragement to access these.

- Readiness to use external consultancy where relevant.

Issues for further debate

- Is there a contradiction between regarding bullying as intentional while focusing so much on unconscious processes? How far does the degree of consciousness and intentionality have a bearing on the capacity of the person to change?

- Is it possible to draw a distinction between some individuals who are the sources of a process of abuse, and others who may be acting out an institutional process as though they were channels?

- How wide a scope, therefore, does unconscious anxiety have in assessing and dealing with workplace abuse?

As Scott (1998) has suggested, it seems that unconscious anxiety is an 'extra' bit (maybe an enormous bit) that the psychodynamic perspective brings. It is not the explanation for all abuse, and helping the organisation and its members address it will not deal with all problems. However, by including this often missing element in the analysis the consultant can help remove some of the fog, so that the projections can be reowned, projective identifications handed back and behaviours seen for what they are. Tragedy, accident and crime can be labelled as such. Disturbing experiences can be better understood and therefore more successfully managed. Effective work, morale and creativity can to some extent be safeguarded and encouraged.

References

Ambrose, A. (1989) 'Key concepts of the transitional approach to managing change'. In L. Klein (ed) *Working with Organisations: Papers to Celebrate the 80th Birthday of Harold Bridger*. London: Tavistock Publications.

Bion, W. (1961) *Experiences in Groups*. London: Tavistock Publications.

Bowlby, J. (1988) *A Secure Base: Clinical Applications of Attachment Theory*. London: Routledge.

Brearley, J. (1991) 'A psychodynamic approach to social work'. In J. Lishman (ed) *A Handbook of Theory for Practice Teachers in Social Work*. London: Jessica Kingsley Publishers.

Bridger, H. (1990) 'Courses and working conferences as transitional learning institutions'. In E. Trist and H. Murray (eds) *The Social Engagement of Social Science*. Vol 1. *The Socio-Psychological Perspective*. Philadelphia: The University of Pennsylvania Press.

Carroll, M. (1996) *Workplace Counselling*. London: Sage.

Clarke, A. 'Stressing the need for dignity at work'. *The Times*, 25 August 1998.

Garland, C. (1988) *Understanding Trauma: A Psychoanalytical Approach*. London: Duckworth.

Gibb, F. 'Employers pay out £300m over stress at work'. *The Times*, 10 September 1998.

Herbert, C. (1994) *Eliminating Sexual Harassment at Work*. London: David Fulton Publishers.

Holmes, J. (1993) *John Bowlby and Attachment Theory*. London: Routledge.

Hopkins, N. and Laaser, N. (eds) (1995) *Restoring the Soul of a Church: Healing Congregations Wounded by Clergy's Sexual Misconduct*. Minnesota: The Liturgical Press.

Keats, J. (1818) Letter to G. and T. Keats. 13 January 1818.

King, M. and Trowell, J. (1992) *Children's Welfare and the Law: The Limits of Legal Intervention*. London: Sage.

London Borough of Greenwich (1987) *A Child in Mind: Protection of Children in a Responsible Society*.

Marris, P. (1991) 'The social construction of uncertainty'. In C.M. Parkes *et al.* (eds) *Attachment Across the Life Cycle*. London: Routledge.

Marris, P. (1996) *The Politics of Uncertainty: Attachment in Private and Public Life*. London: Routledge.

Mattison, J. (1975) *The Reflection Process in Casework Supervision*. London: Institute of Marital Studies.

Mattison, J. (1988) *Work, Love and Marriage*. London: Duckworth.

Menzies, I.E.P. (1959) 'The functioning of social systems as a defence against anxiety: A report on a study of the nursing service of a general hospital'. *Human Relations 13*, 95–121 Also in Menzies Lyth, I. (1988) *Containing Anxiety in Institutions*. London: Free Association Books.

Obholzer, A. and Roberts, V.Z. (eds) (1994) *The Unconscious at Work: Individual and Organisational Stress in the Human Services*. London: Routledge.

Pink, G. (1994) 'The price of truth'. In *British Medical Journal 309*, 1700–1705.

Randall, P. (1997) *Adult Bullying: Perpetrators and Victims*. London: Routledge.

Reddy, M. (1993) *EAPs and Counselling Provision in UK Organisations: An ICAS Report and Policy Guide*. Milton Keynes: Independent Counselling and Advisory Service.

Ruddock, M. (1988) 'Yes, and but, and then again, maybe'. In R. Davies (ed) *Stress in Social Work*. London: Jessica Kingsley Publishers.

Scott, D. (1988) Personal communication with the author.

Skynner, R. (1989) 'Make sure to feed the geese that lay the golden eggs'. In J. Schlapobersky (ed) *Institutes and How to Survive Them*. London: Routledge.

Winnicott, D.W. (1971) *Playing and Reality*. London: Tavistock Publications.

Woodhouse, F. and Pengelly, P. (1991) *Anxiety and the Dynamics of Collaboration*. Aberdeen: Aberdeen University Press.

Psychodynamic Reflections on Social Policy

CHAPTER 16

Desire and the Law

Andrew Cooper

The tendency on the part of civilisation to restrict sexual life is no less clear than its other tendency to expand the cultural unit. Its first, totemic phase already brings with it the prohibition against an incestuous choice of object, and this is perhaps the most drastic mutilation which man's erotic life has in all time experienced. (Freud 1930)

Frontier creatures

In 'The Ego and the Id' (1923), Freud describes the ego as a 'frontier-creature'. This idea occurs in the famous passage in which he describes the ego as a 'poor creature owing service to three masters and consequently menaced by three dangers: from the external world, from the libido of the id, and from the severity of the super-ego' (p.56). As a frontier-creature, he says

> ...the ego tries to mediate between the world and the id...tries to remain on good terms with the id, [but]...in its position midway between the id and reality, it only too often yields to the temptation to become sycophantic, opportunist and lying, like a politician who sees the truth but wants to keep his place in popular favour. (p.56)

In this passage Freud indicates that the ego and its relationship to inner and outer reality is essentially unstable, a precarious equilibrium sustained in the face of the temptations of the pleasure principle and the excessive prohibitions of the superego. In the discussion which follows I propose that in child abuse practice we are always working at the frontier; working, in fact, to reinstate the reality principle, which *is* the frontier between the enactment of perverse or deluded states of mind and psychosocial order. Because child abuse is a transgression by one person (usually an adult) against another recognised in the society as a child, 'the frontier' is inscribed (or not) equally in the intrapsychic, interpersonal and social domains. Thus the principles governing the operation of the social and legal institutions charged with responding to child abuse, and the personnel who constitute them, can be understood as continuous with, even if different from, those which pertain to our therapeutic dealings with individuals and families. One way I explore the connection between legal and therapeutic functions in child abuse is through the notion of someone being available to 'bear witness' to the damage inflicted by abuse, and to examine how this function in therapy is different from but related to similar functions in the public realm. At one extreme this includes the function of being a witness in court; but also how the private and public may become conflated and confused, leading in turn to damaging confusions about the relationship of the public and private realms in our social and therapeutic responses to child abuse.

The playwright Arthur Miller once wrote that only several years after the first production of *A View from the Bridge* did he realise the quasi-incestous nature of the relationship between the characters of Eddie Carbone and Catherine (uncle and niece) portrayed in the play. Hitherto he had understood his play to centre on the moral and political tragedy of Eddie's betrayal of his community and the illegal immigrants he is harbouring in his home. Of course, the play is about both these themes, or more importantly, their indivisible link with one another. One mark of Miller's and other dramatist's greatness is their ability to disclose the symbolic unities which order different, but connected, domains of human experience and activity, and *A View from the Bridge* does this in its exploration of the complex relationship between intrapsychic, family and social expressions of law and its transgression.

Child abuse, and our professional and social responses to it, require that we engage with precisely this same spectrum of complexity. But – as in other domains of social and medical welfare which cross the boundary between private troubles and public issues, or internal and external worlds – we are notoriously bad at developing frameworks of thought or action which help us manage the tensions between different paradigms, perspectives or vertices through which a single situation can be understood and influenced.

At their best, artists, particularly perhaps novelists and playwrights, appear to have something which no variety of traditional theory has: the ability to condense multiple perspectives into a single, circumscribed and unified field of experience without loss of the specificity attaching to the different dimensions comprising the totality. This is not a question of 'resolving' tension or conflict, or dispersing them in some kind of mystical unity, but of the capacity to keep alternatives in play without sacrificing meaning or significance in any domain. This, I propose, is in sharp contrast to the tendency, at least in the social work profession, towards either polarisation and destructive competition between theories and practices, bland eclecticism, unthinking managerialism, or any of the other ways we have found to absent ourselves from full engagement with the predicaments of the children and adults with whom we work. Consistent with this approach, in this chapter my use of the term 'desire' is intended to connote the ambiguity or bi-valence of human relationships which are governed by many con-figurations, elisions and reversals of destructive and loving impulses.

I suggest that a distinctively aesthetic stance towards therapeutic or welfare practice in child abuse and protection is not just illuminating but positively emancipatory. This stance is justified by a recognition of the extreme complexity of this field of work, which I argue only an aesthetically informed response is *capable* of dealing with. The thesis is illustrated by reference to some clinical and practice examples, as well as a range of modern artistic explorations of the dynamics of abuse. The territory of this enquiry is bounded by the absurdities of legal positivism and the exclusive pursuit of forensic truth in child abuse cases on the one hand, and the madness and delusion of false and/or recovered-memory disputes on the other. These are the polar extremes of a distinctively modern epistemological crisis, in which, as is well known, the latter has sometimes found itself a bewildered defendant in the court of the former. Notwithstanding the confusion entailed by the incursion of institutional law into the realm of deep subjectivity, child abuse, and especially sexual abuse, does always ask that we address ourselves to both the social significance of intrapsychic disturbance, and the psychic origin and meaning of the social transgression. Thus, if we are not to have automatic recourse to institutional law to respond to such transgressions, we are compelled to take up a position (as practitioners, citizens and clients) with reference to other forms of law which define and circumscribe the domains of the acceptable and the forbidden.

This terrain, however, is inherently also one of uncertainty and instability. The peculiar irony of contemporary cultural anxiety about sexual abuse and the status of fantasy and memory, is that in an era when Freud and the doctrines of classical psychoanalysis are under incessant public attack, never was there more evidence within the public domain itself of their validity. Public disclosure of widespread child sexual abuse, paedophilia and incest in our societies reveals how precarious and uneven are the achievements of psychosexual 'maturity', both for large numbers of individuals and, it would seem, for the civilisation as a whole. The costs of civilisation and social order, which Freud so clearly articulated, do not take the form of a once-only down-payment, but a perpetual struggle to balance the psychic economy in which there is no guarantee that the achievements of one generation will be inherited by the next.

Faced with this knowledge in its raw manifestations, practitioners in the field of child abuse can only find themselves confronted with the fluctuating stability and certainty of their own developmental achievements; the temptation, or more accurately the internal and external pressure, to adopt defensive solutions to aggressive and sexual countertransference responses at the clinical and social levels, follows after. Thus if we are to avoid resorting to either authoritarian or perverse strategies, I suggest that we must be prepared not simply to uphold, but to constantly *rediscover and recreate*, the meaning of law and its relation to desire. This is, after all, the task which confronts the children and adults with whom we work, and who, for want of a more elegant formulation, suffer, or have been made to suffer, from damage to this relation in the broadest sense; I find it hard to think of this as anything but a *cultural* intervention, encompassing a simultaneous relation to subjective, inter-personal and social being. I will try to specify this claim by reference to Bion's theory of 'Transformations' (1965), after first exploring the 'terrain of uncertainty' from a number of different clinical and cultural perspectives.

Who did what to whom? The indeterminacy of memory

A patient who had been quite severely and repeatedly physically abused by his father up until his early adolescence came to a session one day and recounted a memory in which at the age of about four, during a family visit to some relatives, he had lost control of his bladder and bowels, causing his father to beat him. Among other interpretations, I linked this memory to the fact that the patient used the toilet before every session (this was quite early in the treatment), something that to date had been left outside the sessions, but known to both of us. The patient returned the next day and said that he had gone away and felt able to think more clearly about the memory, and it now seemed to him that events had been the other way round: his father had beaten him, perhaps because he had been pestering to go home, and he had lost control of himself as a result of the beating.

Soon, it began to emerge that in the present this man suffered occasional near-psychotic lapses, in which he experienced catastrophic anxiety arising from a belief that he had made some kind of a mistake, which he had not in fact made. For example, he turned up on time at a supervisor's room for an appointment, and not finding him in, collapsed into a state of anxiety believing that today was tomorrow and that the appointment had therefore been the previous day, that the supervisor would be furious and his career would be in ruins. He returned to 'reality' only when the supervisor phoned him in his room enquiring if he was coming to the appointment. However, rather characteristically, and hopefully, the patient was able to re-group himself and bring these states of mind to therapy where we could look at them together. As it became possible to work with these states of mind more directly within the transference, a whole area of rather paranoid borderline psychic functioning opened up for work.

Writing in 1925, about trauma and memory, Pierre Janet says:

> Memory, like belief, like all psychological phenomena, is an action; essentially it is the action of telling a story. Almost always we are concerned here with a linguistic operation, quite independent of our attitude towards the happening… A situation has not been…fully assimilated, until we have achieved, not merely an outward reaction through our movements, but also an inward reaction through the words we address to ourselves, through the organisation of the recital of the event to others and to ourselves, and through the putting of this recital in its place as one of the chapters in our personal history. (pp.662–663)

The patient's recitals in psychotherapy are of a special kind in a special situation. I do not think that the events brought by the patient I have described were 'recovered' in therapy; rather, in the presence of someone whom I presume he experienced as sufficiently able to hold in mind the anxieties associated with it, the uncertainties about the veracity of the ordering of events and so on, it became possible for him to reconstruct and develop a new narrative for this episode, in which he takes up a different position in the constellation of events from the one inscribed in the original. What is 'recovered' here is something more like a spontaneous capacity to 'see things differently'. That something happened is not in doubt in the patient's mind, but who exactly did what to whom, in what order, is in doubt, and in his contemporary experience frequently remains so. I believe that the patient's new narrative probably accords better with events 'as they actually happened', although I also think it is right to suspend absolute judgement about this.

Via his concept of *Nachtraglichkeit* (rather unsatisfactorily translated for us as 'deferred action', or *après coup*), Freud held that '…the material present in the form of memory-traces [is] subjected from time to time to a *rearrangement* in accordance with fresh circumstances – to a *retranscription*' (Freud 1896). Laplanche and Pontalis (1988) suggest in their discussion of this concept that, 'It is not lived experience in general that undergoes a deferred revision but, specifically, whatever it has been impossible in the first instance to incorporate fully into a meaningful context. The traumatic event is the epitome of such unassimilated experience' (p.112).

It may be rather stretching a point, but in the case of my patient I think of the fresh circumstances to which Freud refers as providing the occasion for retranscription as the therapeutic context itself. Despite his experiences at the hands of his father, this man has developed a more clearly ambivalent attitude towards his father than he is able presently to achieve towards his mother. From the beginning his complaint about his mother has been that she was hopelessly passive and did not manage to protect him, or his siblings, or indeed herself, from father's violence. Early in the transference relationship this was expressed in terms of the patient's anxiety that I would not be sufficiently potent to act or know what to do should he become very disturbed or need to enter hospital. It seems then, that mother was a witness to, and fully cognisant of, the traumatic events of this patient's childhood. But over time I have come to understand his complaint about her rather less in terms of her incapacity to act and more in terms of the absence of her, or *somebody's*, ability to help him process and make some sense of his internal response to trauma.

Somewhere inside himself, this patient does have a sufficiently good and reliable parental couple to allow him to have established and make quite good use of a cooperative therapeutic alliance. His recall of abuse is available to him, and to us, but arguably has only been transformed into true *memory*, by virtue of the presence of another mind able to help process and think about psychic experience in a new way. Yet how tenuous this possibility was, even for this patient, was revealed much later in the therapy when he told me he had been afraid to let me know of his revised version of events in childhood, in case I would be angry because he had lied the previous day. Once again as Janet (1925) remarks:

> Strictly speaking, then, one who retains a fixed idea of a happening cannot be said to have a 'memory' of the happening. It is only for convenience that we speak of it as a 'traumatic memory'. The subject is often incapable of making with regard to the event the recital which we speak of as a memory: and yet he remains confronted by a difficult situation in which he has not been able to play a satisfactory part... (p.663)

We arrive then, at an initial formulation which suggests why psychoanalysis is so uneasily and ambiguously positioned with respect to child abuse. True memory, on the view I am advancing, is *indeterminate* with respect to the question of the 'real event' or 'what actually happened'; *Nachtraglichkeit*, or re-transcription, is not about recovering a determinate or mimetic relation-ship between memory and historical events, but a meaningful and essentially creative one. And yet where trauma has occurred by virtue of external im-pingement or assault, events clearly are, or were, *determinate*. In some sense it happened this way, or that; it happened, or it did not. As therapists we are concerned with meaning, but in cases involving trauma, necessarily at times find ourselves preoccupied with questions of historical accuracy. In the public domain, where child abuse is concerned, the focus or direction of concern may often be the reverse.

In a remarkable but little remarked passage, Bion (1967) elucidates exactly the psychic situation presented above:

> There needs to be a recognised formulation which is understood by all psychoanalysts to display the invariants in an event which is unconscious because obscured by memory, *although* it has happened, and an event which is manifest because disclosed by desire though it has *not* happened. Memory and desire may be regarded as past and future 'senses' ... of the same 'thing'. Making use of sense in this way, a formulation desire would have the same value as memory, the former referring to an event that had happened and the latter to an event that had not happened and therefore not usually described as being 'remembered'. A patient who could be described in terms of conversational English as 'remembering' something that had not happened would resemble a patient who was described as hallucinated. Conversely the patient who did *not* remember what *had* happened through the operation of desire, or *remembered* what had *not* happened, through the operation of the same agency, should likewise be recognised as belonging to the same psychic group of 'hallucinosis'. (pp.143–144)

Because I have little doubt that some version of the childhood events recounted by the patient involving an assault by his father did 'happen', and even less doubt with respect to the contemporary muddle he reports, I prefer to think of his state of mind as deluded – involving systematically distorted beliefs about causality and sequence held, even if temporarily, with complete conviction. But the more general lesson we may draw from this episode, and from the theorisations of both Janet and Bion, is that there is no form of memory which provides a privileged, certain, or mimetic relation to 'the facts'. The facts are in principle and forever beyond recovery or even access, mediated or partly constituted as they are by imagination, hallucination, delusion – by the desire which all actors bring, but differentially, to the same 'event'.

In which case, what status can we possible assign to the effort to establish the facts, as we frequently must, and for the sake of psychic health, need to be able to? My patient is in possession of a fact which can be represented as something like 'On a particular day, my father beat me'. But by itself what meaning does this have? At the trial of Jon Venables and Robert Thompson for the killing of Jamie Bulger, the writer Blake Morrison (1998) noted:

> The trouble with murder trials, I realised after a week or so, is that they concern themselves with circumstances not motives – with Who and How

and Where and When, but never Why. The circumstantial and scientific evidence pointed overwhelmingly to the boys' guilt. I, and I think others there, began to feel a bit wearied by it – something else to feel guilty about, being bored in the middle of an appalling murder trial. (p.422)

And this is the point: the facts are empty, dumb, as Christopher Bollas (1995) has written, and 'boring'. They are woven through the fabric of reality like the continuous thread which binds the material of a rug: invisible, entirely subordinated to design, colour, texture, the desire which went into its making, but without which all this unravels; in themselves meaningless but also the ground of all meaning. Thus the double-category error perpetrated by the law when it seeks to privilege the facts is, first, to pretend as positivism always does that this is a value neutral search for 'truth' rather than an epistemologically fated privileging of one modality of it above all others; and, second, to discard all other modalities as bothersome 'noise' or interference, rather than the actual substance of human concern, dependent upon, but not reducible to, the facts.

The missing chorus – David Mamet's *Oleanna*

The logic of this enquiry leads inexorably towards questions of false and recovered memory. But I want to broach this difficult, not to say dangerous, area from what I hope is a fresh and illuminating angle. David Mamet's (1992) play *Oleanna* rapidly became subject to numerous competing readings after it was first performed in the UK. I think *Oleanna* lends itself to interpretation as a play about the problem of memory and the status of events, including childhood abuse and adult re-enactments of this.

Indeed, even those who have not seen the play will probably remember it because of the events which surrounded its performances which are, I propose, directly connected to the way it problematised for audiences questions about the status of events themselves. Towards the end of the play, the college lecturer John becomes so enraged with the student, Carol, who has alleged improper conduct, sexual advances and, finally, attempted rape against him, threatening his career and family security, that he does assault her, throwing her to the ground and beating her. On several nights, sections of the London theatre audiences watching the play reportedly erupted in spontaneous shows of approval for his action and vilification of Carol. These events were widely reported in the newspapers, and the play acquired a rather overdetermined reputation, which I fear detracted from its complexity and subtlety as a drama. Before returning to think about the meaning of these events, I want to sketch in some of the psychological forces at work in the dramatic narrative of the play.

Carol is a young student who, in the action of the play, we see in John's office struggling to express her anxiety and humiliation that she may be failing, that she does not understand John's lectures, his book, or many of the words he uses. She says: 'I don't *understand. I* don't *understand.* I don't understand what anything means...and I walk around. From morning 'til night: with this one thought in my head. I'm *stupid'* (p.12). In a succession of clumsy and futile gestures, John tries to reassure her, let her off the hook, indicate he identifies with her – and mostly succeeds only in continuing to patronise her. Near the end of the first act, Carol is about to disclose something to John: 'I always...all of my life...I have never told anyone this...' (p.38). But she never makes the disclosure because the phone rings. He answers it, and at the end of the call does not pick up the thread of their dialogue: we never discover what Carol was on the point of revealing. However, at another level, the dramatic structure of the first act is highly suggestive of what the quality of Carol's experience might be. Throughout her halting, stumbling, frustrated efforts to communicate with him, and his ill-attuned attempts to respond, their dialogue is constantly interrupted by phone calls from John's wife. They are in the closing stages of buying a new house, and there are complications. The telephone conversations are charged with tension, anxiety, confusion, the implication is that John is under pressure to leave and attend to matters elsewhere. In these interruptions, it is as though Carol is cruelly and repeatedly exposed to the primal scene, an urgent and distracted parental intercourse which occupies John's mind completely while it lasts, obliterating Carol. Much later in the action of the play Carol screams, 'You think I want "revenge". I don't want revenge. I WANT UNDER-STANDING' (p.71). As an attempt to provide conditions in which she might have found understanding, what John offers her in Act One falls about as far short of the ideal as it is possible to imagine. And her revenge on him for this failure is indeed terrible.

Not only does Carol succeed in attacking and destroying the symbolic roots of psychic security by ruining John's attempt to make a secure home for himself and his family; in her allegations she distorts, perverts, corrupts the truth of what happened between them, which culminates in her redefining his paternalistic gestures towards her as attempted rape. She and her group of supporters are pressing charges. 'The "court" officers...? The "court" officers...?' John repeats, baffled to the point of exhaustion (pp.60–61). How has this affair become a matter for the courts, he might be asking himself. And how may I defend myself, for there are no witnesses to events other than myself and my accuser?

I speculate that theatre audiences found John's predicament intolerable for a number of reasons. Certainly the accumulating force of projected, introjected and reprojected rage in the transactions between the two characters heightens the tension in our identifications with them to a near-intolerable degree. But more than this, in Carol's retreat to a fixed, utterly inflexible and distorted version, or memory, of the meaning of what took place, it is as though John also finds himself entirely at the mercy of a sadistic and omnipotent agency which threatens to engulf him. His violent outburst is a last desperate attempt to hold on to sanity. Within the dramatic setup on stage, it is the absence of a third figure (or perhaps in the crucial phases as John is engulfed, it is really a *second* figure), functioning in some way to represent or mediate with an alternative version of events, that is intolerable. In its identifications, the audience is hurtled into isolated despair in the same way we may speculate Carol herself was at the end of the first act, when John turns away from her as she stood at the brink of her disclosure. So also I think the audience is compelled then to become this other figure, rising up to bear witness that, 'No, it wasn't like that.' But it is already too late, and the audience can only, as I understand they actually were, be drawn into a sadistic and hating identification for or against one or other protagonist.

Oleanna is a play whose dramatic structure is in search of a chorus. Lacking the function which the chorus of classical Greek tragedy performs, the audience is simply exposed full blast to the impact of events too painful to be assimilable. In a sense then, *Oleanna's* early audiences were compelled to become the chorus the play lacks, but found themselves in no position to master and process the psychic pain they confronted, in the manner which a true chorus does. On the night I saw the play, there was no audience outburst, and I wondered in retrospect if by then sufficient of those present had, like me, heard of what had occasioned these eruptions, and thus the dramatic trauma was to some degree already assimilated in the mind of the audience. Fred Alford (1992), in his psychoanalytic study of Greek tragedy writes that:

> Often pain sharing is the task of the chorus, and we see this no more clearly than in Sophocles's *Electra*, where the chorus of women of Mycenae seeks to become one with the protagonist's suffering... Why is sharing pain so important? Why does it help? Pain and suffering isolate us... This is the reason that (Sophocles') Philoctetes says that 'the sickness in me seeks to have you beside me'... It is no accident that Philoctetes terrible suffering results in his isolation on a deserted island. (p.157)

If trauma cannot be processed in the mind, if omnipotence rules in the inner world, if there is no benign witness, in the different senses I have hinted at, available to forge a connection between inner isolation and outer reality, then there can be no hope of justice. Cases in the American courts centring on false or recovered memories of abuse seem to me to exemplify this. Just as the terror implied in the two-person antagonism of *Oleanna* derives from the possibility that only one version of reality will ever escape the sealed world which the characters inhabit, so these real cases appear to come down to a straight contest about which of two diametrically opposed 'remembered' accounts will be believed and publicly endorsed. It may be that under these conditions the 'right' verdict is nevertheless achieved to the extent that 'something happened' or it did not, but since what is absent is any independent means of knowing or strongly suggesting whether or not it has, justice has become a game of chance. Thus, loss of 'reality sense', of any independent access to, or capacity to agree on, 'the facts' defeats the possibility of justice; facts, or the capacity to discover them in principle, turn out to be the precondition for justice rather than its aim or object.

Revenge, tragedy and the inner courtroom

One could say that the patient I described earlier has in his more disturbed areas a kind of courtroom in his mind. But it is a topsy-turvy courtroom, in which the innocent are on trial, the guilty are making false allegations, and the judges lack all compassion or capacity for balanced judgement. More often than not he is in the dock, but may also take up the position of prosecutor or sadistic judge. This emerges most clearly at points when he seems in danger of repeating his history of abuse with his own child. I think we could say that present in this scene, there is no equivalent of a jury, of 12 'good men (or women) and true', to weigh the evidence, interpret the concept of 'reasonable doubt' or the 'balance of probabilities', and link the function of the courtroom to the wider social reality of ordinary citizenship. Juries, of course, are corruptible too, but it occurs to me that their function is to represent the capacity for thinking in circumstances where most other parties may have powerful investments in not doing so. This is why we appropriately become concerned when judges deliver tendentious summings-up and 'misdirect' the jury.

Not a great deal has been specifically written, at least from a psycho-analytic perspective, about the development of an internal sense of, or capacity for, justice, but it can be clearly related to what Freud said about the momentous step taken at the point the reality principle is instituted, which ushers in the ability to discriminate between what is good and what is true. In his paper 'Psychic reality and unconscious belief', Britton (1995) elaborates the relationship between the capacity for belief, doubt and knowledge. The capacity for belief is clearly associated with the capacity for doubt; belief is not knowledge, and the person who is capable of belief must be capable of relinquishing a belief. I may profoundly wish that someone is innocent of a charge, but if I am to demonstrate a capacity for the exercise of justice, I must be able to entertain the possibility that they are not. Omnipotent thinking cannot be the basis for the exercise of a sense of justice.

A good deal has been written about the potential for re-enactment of the dynamics of abusing situations inside the social institutions – case conferences, courts, the media and wider society – which engage with it; less about damage to the most basic capacities to think, believe, distinguish true from false, fantasy from reality, memory from desire and how this may in turn distort the capacity of institutional functioning in the public sphere. It is the pressure which the tyranny of such states of mind may exert on the public domain which leads me to discuss briefly a second modern drama, which I feel encapsulates the central predicaments which I have been trying to explore.

Law and the reality principle – Arthur Miller's *A View from the Bridge*

Arthur Miller's (1961) play *A View from the Bridge* turns on the incestuous desire of the central character Eddie Carbone, for his niece. Catherine's parents died when she was young, and she has been raised by Eddie and Beatrice. In the action of the play, she is now an adolescent, and falling in love for the first time. This is the development that gradually exposes Eddie's desire to everyone but himself. Eddie displaces his jealousy on to the boy who Catherine loves, and becomes fixated with the belief that he is homosexual. In the course of the play he repeatedly consults a lawyer, Alfieri, and insists over and again that there must be some way to stop this marriage, some law against what is about to happen. Alfieri is also the play's chorus, and here he speaks with the audience:

> It was at this time that he first came to me…I remember him now as he walked through my doorway – His eyes were like tunnels; my first thought was that he had committed a crime, but soon I saw that it was only a passion that had moved into his body like a stranger. (p.45)

In fact, it is Eddie Carbone who wants to insist that a crime is about to be committed – the marriage of his niece to a boy he believes 'ain't right', is homosexual – and that Alfieri should take steps to prevent it. Slowly we come to understand, with Alfieri, that the only crime is in Eddie's mind, the oedipal crime of his desire for Catherine. Eddie's deluded state of mind places Alfieri, Beatrice and Catherine – and in fact the whole society represented in the play – under terrible pressure to join him in his delusion, which would, of course, result in the enactment of an injustice. Alfieri, from his position as the chorus figure, moving between engagement in the action of the play and communication with the audience, also represents the reality principle. As Eddie hectors him, Alfieri first holds the line which must be held, but also understands what is before him:

> *Alfieri:* Eddie, look – I have my own children. I understand you. But the law is very specific. The law does not... You have no recourse in the law Eddie...
>
> Eddie I want you to listen to me. (*Pause.*) You know, sometimes God mixes up the people. We all love somebody, the wife, the kids... But sometimes there's too much. You know? There's too much, and it goes where it mustn't... The child has to grow up and go away, and the man has to learn to forget... Let her go. That's my advice...because there's no law, Eddie...
>
> [And a little later]:
>
> *Alfieri:* She wants to get married Eddie. She can't marry you, can she?
>
> *Eddie (furiously)*: What're you talkin' about, marry me! I don't know what the hell you're talkin' about!
>
> *Alfieri:* ...Put it out of your mind. Can you do that?

Foregoing legal intervention, it is as though Alfieri tries to instigate psychic repression instead. But Eddie, of course, cannot forget, and Alfieri must stand by helpless as he hurtles towards his end. Eddie's death at the end of the play does represent the victory of the reality principle, but at a great cost which the whole society of the play has borne. Alfieri's final soliloquy to the audience is, I feel, a sad and genuinely depressive reflection upon this, of a sort which by comparison *Oleanna* does not provide for us.

Eddie Carbone's baffled insistence that the law intervene in and resolve his internal predicament, seems to me to encapsulate the paradox which has afflicted English child-protection work for the last decade or more. Child abuse is a crime, but also much more than just a crime. I am in no doubt that one dimension of our social response to child abuse must be the provision of a capacity for some form of public affirmation, on behalf of victims, of the wrongness of what they have suffered. The prosecution of abusers can represent one way in which this is achieved.

But if the arrangements which our society puts in place to respond to abuse, or allegations of it, must succeed in discriminating between the enactment of a delusion and the occurrence of a real harm, then this is what English legal culture is singularly ill-equipped to manage. The problem, as I hope to have made clear, is that delusional states of mind may be present at the core of situations both where actual abuse has occurred and where it has not. Thus the kind of truth which forensic responses to these situations demand, is *in principle* unobtainable, because of the damaged states of mind which inhere in them. Yet this is no reason why society should abandon the effort to find a response which continues to affirm what, to put it at its crudest, it holds to be right and wrong. If the law represents the social enactment of the reality principle, equally the reality principle need not, and invariably does not, find expression in society only through institutional law.

The lie – Russell Banks' *The Sweet Hereafter*

This proposition, that institutional law is the particular and limited expression of a deeper, developmentally prior, and more fundamentally constitutive relation between human experience and an idea of 'law' as the ground of all psychosocial ordering, is the theme of Russell Banks' novel, *The Sweet Hereafter* (1997). Something 'caused the crash' to the school bus which kills 14 children in the small town of Sam Dent. But the opening words of the book, an interior monologue by the driver of the ill-fated bus, tell us that whatever it was is lost forever in the swirling snowstorm of the morning of the crash, or may never have actually been there: 'A dog – it was a dog I saw for certain. Or thought I saw. It was snowing pretty hard by then, and you can see things in the snow that aren't there, or aren't exactly there, but you can also see some of the things that are there, so that by God when you do see something, you react anyhow…' (p.1).

A lawyer, Mitchell Stephens, comes to the town seeking to encourage the bereaved parents to litigate. He doesn't know against whom, but he knows he will find somebody, or some institution, to prosecute. As he asserts to one of the bereaved mothers, 'There is no such thing as an accident', so there must be a cause, and there must be a locus of blame. 'My task is to represent them only in their anger, not their grief', Stephens says, but we are also shown that he is himself in flight from his own grief and guilt concerning his drug-addicted, parasitic daughter.

The plotting of this complex story eventually turns on the actions of Nichole, a teenage survivor of the crash, also a victim (survivor) of sexual abuse by her father, who is now a party to Stephens' negligence suit. Nichole defeats both Stephens and her father through the testimony she gives about the circumstances of the accident, as she apparently 'recovers' a memory of noticing the speedometer of the bus registering well over the limit. The driver is thus blamed, but the legal case and the possibility of corporate compensation collapses. In so doing she recovers her own power to discriminate clearly between right and wrong, and between truth and lies, implicitly restoring order to the corrupted moral universe of her family and township, to which the perverse motives of those pursuing 'justice' was in her view contributing. She uses the public proceedings to reassert her capacity to know the truth, to reclaim the psychological autonomy which her father has stolen from her. She does this by telling a lie, but the ability to tell a lie depends in its turn upon the ability to know truth from lies, which as the novel makes clear, the abuse had compromised in her. Thus moral and psychological 'order' is reasserted in the same gesture through which corrupt or perverse deployment of the law is rejected. Law must represent not just anger but also grief. 'But Daddy knew why I had lied. He knew who was normal and who wasn't. Mr Stephens couldn't ever know the truth, but Daddy always would' (p.216).

It appears that there is an immanent relation between grief and law. What is this? A man whose father was a solicitor came for psychotherapy. Some years before, he and his wife had awoken one day to find the bailiffs about to repossess their house. Their small business, which he ran, had degenerated into financial chaos with no proper accounts, taxes and bills unpaid, rent overdue. He had successfully covered up this situation not only to his wife but also to himself. As the therapy unfolded, it emerged that his mind, like his attic, garage, and filing cabinets was full to bursting with hoarded, secreted, unclassified contents. He felt his memory to be near the point of breakdown with the effort of single-handedly controlling and managing this immense disorder.

Just as he failed to order and classify his worldly goods, so he had established within himself no clear distinctions between people – parents and children, men and women, old and young, therapists and friends. A close friend had died some years earlier but he had been unable to bring himself to attend the funeral, and had never attended one in his life. In his internal world, nothing was ever relinquished or mourned. This radical repudiation of the laws of nature, 'the order of things', inscribed in the necessity of sexual and generational difference, depends upon a refusal to grieve and let go. It is a refusal to relinquish an exclusive attachment to mother, and acknowledge the 'law of the father', the reality of three-person relationships which ushers in the reality principle itself.

In Freud's words, the capacity to distinguish what is good from what is true, what we wish to be the case from what is the case, is the foundation of the possibility of justice. Yet, viewed this way, law or 'legality' appears paradoxical – doubt rather than absolute certainty, narrative construction rather than mimetic memory, multiplicity rather than simplicity, desire *and* law rather than desire *or* law – this is the order of things.[1] The extremities of the states of mind which so often underlie child abuse, Eddie Carbone's tragic delusion, are on a continuum with the normal, not a radical break with it. Positivist law, the impossible search for certain facts, is at the end of the opposite continuum, as much a delusion, but as capable as Eddie of seducing us with its convictions. As practitioners, how are we to proceed in a world of inherent uncertainty, wherein different and contested interpretations of the same events are often the norm, truth is in principle beyond recall, but moral and practical commitments must be made and decisions reached and implemented? In fact, there is every reason to suppose that much of the time good practitioners working in institutional conditions which support the containment of primitive anxieties and allow space for doubt and uncertainty to be processed, manage well enough in the service of the children in their care. Yet the questions posed in this chapter seem to me to be forever lying in wait to subvert our precarious hold on a good-enough practice. If one can tolerate the difficulty of trying to understand him – and it is quite possible that I have not, I believe that Bion's theory of transformations provides a basis, a support in fact, for the nearly impossible tightrope walk we are asked to make.

Transformations

Bion begins his enquiry into the nature of experience and the origins of mind from a position which exposes him to the very problems he is trying to solve – the two-person world of the psychoanalytic session in which a single reality may be apprehended in apparently quite unrelated ways by the two persons present, problematising all truth claims. I take Bion to make just one assumption in his method of philosophical enquiry, namely that there subsists within this two-person domain an unknowable, but certainly existing, shared property or invariant, which he calls 'O'. As Bion says, 'What the absolute facts are can never be known, and these I denote by the sign "O"' (1965 p.17). Invariance may be a detectable common property of related inner and outer world occurrences, or of the shared phenomenology of analyst and patient, or of any actual or potential intersubjectively known situation. Speaking of processes of catastrophic change, Bion says,

> [The analyst]…must see that certain apparently external emotionally charged events are in fact the same events as those which appeared in the precatastrophic stage under the names bestowed by the patient, of pains in the knee, legs, abdomen, ears, etc., and by the analyst, of internal objects. In brief what present themselves to the outward sense of analyst and patient as anxious relatives, impending lawsuits, mental hospitals, certification, and other contingencies apparently appropriate to the change in circumstances, are really hypochondriachal pains and other evidences of internal objects in a guise appropriate to their new status as external objects. (p.9)

Social workers, who understand only too well the immanent relationship between the outer and inner world manifestations of case dynamics, are unlikely to be taken aback by this passage. Likewise, we can see that the events and relationships which unfold in *A View from the Bridge*, reveal Eddie

Carbone's internal-object world – the whole play is a study in enacted transference and countertransference dynamics, and the capacity of the threatened immigrant community to contain and withstand the pressure of his assault on their precarious psychological and social reality. This is saying something more than that a single event or drama admits a variety of readings, for such a formulation gives us no clue as to how or why a particular reading can be evaluated as meaningful, that is, as bearing within it a *connection* with its object, or as Bion would have it, 'O'.

For Bion, and for the aesthetic stance towards psychosocial phenomena in the professional field which I am deriving from his theory of transformations, all occurrences in the human field are necessarily laden with desire – whether it be love, hate, curiosity and the search for knowledge, or their antitheses, which he denoted by a minus sign: '-L', '-H', and '-K'. Two occurrences or more may be conjoined so that we take there to be a relationship of influence or significance between them, but 'L, H, and K must be regarded as an essential element among all the elements seen to be constantly conjoined' (p.71).

A hypothesis, theory or reading of a situation which concerns us, equally and unavoidably becomes an aspect of the situation itself and capable of effecting a transformation within it; the play I saw is not the play you saw, or the one which I saw an hour afterwards, when I have worked over its meaning for myself and developed a narrative for my experience of it. In Bion's metaphor, the reflection in the lake, disturbed by atmospheric change, could be said to affect the atmospheric conditions, as much as the other way round – only a theory of cause and effect precludes this, and Bion is not overly concerned to privilege such a theory over any other (p.71).

If this seems gratuitous or bizarre, consider the situation presented by the first psychotherapy patient discussed in this chapter: one could say that in both his present understanding of his past, and the influence of his present experience of the past upon his present, he *suffers* from a mistaken theory of causes. Our job in child abuse or protection work is not to pursue a correct theory of causes as a prelude to decision or action, but to sustain sufficient courage in the face of all the emotional forces acting to prevent it, to believe and bear witness to the belief that something happened; and that through the effort of maintaining emotional contact with the child's experience of this something, we may be able to think our way towards what, if anything, to do so that the attendant suffering can be alleviated.

Something happened

I want to indicate what I mean by reference to my own first encounter with child sexual abuse as a practising social worker. It occurred in about 1985, towards the very end of what seems in retrospect like an age of innocence.

This is what happened: a woman came to the social services office one day and I was the social worker on duty. In the course of an hour she managed to convey to me that she suspected her husband might be sexually interfering with their five-year-old daughter in some way. She thought her husband was depressed, and it seemed their own marital and sexual relationship had deteriorated recently. She had no 'evidence', although I think she had come home one day and found him asleep on the sofa with the girl, and something had troubled her about this. She was full of fear, uncertainty, distressing suspicion that something was wrong. My sense was that she felt that if she were right, it was beyond her belief, but certain signs had led her to entertain the unthinkable. When we interviewed the father, he was full of theatrical denial, and at one point proclaimed, with accompanying gestures, 'I would rather put a gun to my head and shoot myself than even think such a thing'.

My colleague and I did some rather clumsy play-work with the child, but drawings of the house, and who slept where, left us none the wiser. At a subsequent session I had with the mother, she seemed to have lost any grip on the emotional certainty which had informed her suspicions. I recall emerging from this interview feeling I, too, had lost all purchase on the truth. Was the mother taking a distorted revenge on her husband because of the current sexual difficulties between them? Or should I continue to trust in the tentative conviction of her original communication? Was the father a terrified abuser, or a terrified innocent? The stark message from my own countertransference was that somebody was losing their grip on reality, but who and about what?

A child-abuse conference (as it was called at that time) was convened and the child's name placed on the register. My colleague and I did some joint work with the couple on their relationship, with, as I recall, a definite idea in mind that if nothing else, clear parent-child boundaries needed to be re-established. Something happened, because at the third session we were met by a hand-holding couple, and a smiling, still anxious, but apparently relieved mother. It was made quietly clear that we were not needed or wanted any longer.

Neither I nor my colleague knew what had happened. My best guess is that the father was turning away from his wife in anger, and starting to confer a childlike sexual attention on his own daughter, and that when the mother presented herself to us it had been an act of considerable emotional courage. In those days we were not taught much about sexual abuse, but I do recall that early on in my involvement in the case, various aspects of what I was experiencing suddenly clicked very definitely with what I did know. Quite simply, it was as though the triangular structure of this small family unit had started to revolve in front of the mother's eyes, so that she found her husband replacing her own affections with those of her daughter, as though for him there was a simple equivalence. I think it was this sense of the world turning upside down that she first brought to me.

Today, the conduct of this case would be quite different. Whether the finely honed forensic skills which social workers and others must bring into play right at the outset would bring anybody any closer to either the truth of what was happening, or any better understanding of it, is, I believe, doubtful. It is perfectly possible, given public awareness of the handling of sexual abuse investigations, that today this mother would never approach us for help in the way she did. However, despite the impenetrable core of uncertainty in this case, my recollection is that I and my colleague did feel sure of what our job was under the circumstances. Something was very wrong in this family, and the mother's suspicions needed to be taken seriously. Whether or not the father was being unjustly accused was really beside the point; our job was to convey a clear message to him, in fact to both parents, about where we stood in the matter of differentiating between adult sexual relationships and adult–child ones. As Britton (1989) succinctly summarises it while discussing infant development, 'the parents' relationship is genital and pro-creative; the parent-child relationship is not' (p.85). My colleague and I quite consciously modelled ourselves as an adult pairing who were prepared to speak openly between ourselves, and to this couple, about these distinctions, and to let our socially given authority sit comfortably in the room as we did this. Perhaps it is not really the point, and I am happy to debate the matter, but I felt then and still do, that under the circumstances we did a good enough job in this case.

In memory, I can still see myself and my colleague sitting with this couple in the lounge of their flat. We were not in any ordinary sense of the term 'doing therapy', nor were we simply enacting a role as social police; in so far as we were doing something of both, each was inflected by the other. I think that the reason why *A View from the Bridge*, and especially the lawyer Alfieri's role in proceedings, struck me so forcibly when I saw it is because it showed that somebody has to do this job. That is, carry the responsibility for reaffirming the boundary between inner psychic reality and outer material and social reality, and for the resolution of the oedipus complex in favour of reality, which is what installs this boundary.

This is what to be a 'frontier-creature' in child-protection work means. Our understanding of the forces which may attack, subvert, damage and corrupt the ego has deepened considerably since Freud wrote this passage. When these forces take hold in the shape of child abuse, then the con-sequences ripple outwards as well as inwards, threatening the social unit of the family, the public institutions and personnel which are called upon to respond, and eventually, maybe, a society's whole relationship to itself. The task of responding at the frontier is about containing this effect, without colluding; it is about holding the line through the use of authority, but with minimum necessary resort to accusatory, punitive, adversarial and revengeful modes of conduct; otherwise we simply re-enact the states of mind which are seeking dominance within the original situation. In turn, this speaks to the need for institutional arrangements at the frontier, which are capable of continuing to think in the face of intense pressure to obliterate this capacity. How the law accommodates to, and respects, desire, and vice versa, is the continuing question for our times which child sexual abuse has posed.

Notes

1   'Legality' is not to be confused with 'that which is lawful'. Rather I believe it is intended to equate to the general ontological necessity of lawlike principles, or categories which order experience, as the ground of thought, sanity and reason. Without 'legality' there would only be primary and not secondary process thinking (Freud), symmetrical and not asymmetrical thinking (Matte Blanco) or noumena and not phenomena (Kant), and thus nothing approximating to human experience of the world. Some clue as to how the world might seem were this to be the case is provided by the experiences of the first patient described above. The distinctions embedded in ordinary experiences of causality, sequencing, attributions of responsibility, fantasy and reality, are all subject to the possibility of reversal, inversion and equation.

References

Alford, F. (1992) *The Psychoanalytic Theory of Greek Tragedy*. New Haven: Yale University Press.

Bion, W. (1965) *Transformations*. London: Karnac Books.

Bion, W. (1967) *Second Thoughts*. London: Karnac Books.

Banks, R. (1997) *The Sweet Hereafter*. London: Vintage.

Bollas, C. (1995) *Cracking Up*. London: Routledge.

Britton, R. (1995) 'Psychic reality and unconscious belief'. *International Journal of Psychoanalysis 76*, 19–23.

Freud, S. (1923) 'The Ego and the Id'. *The Standard Edition of the Complete Psychological Works of Sigmund Freud*, Vol. *XIX*, 3–66. London: The Hogarth Press.

Freud, S. (1930) 'Civilisation and its Discontents'. *The Standard Edition of the Complete Works of Sigmund Freud*, Vol. *XXI*. London: The Hogarth Press.

Janet, P. (1925) *Psychological Healing*, Vol. *1*. London: Allen and Unwin.

Laplanche, J. and Pontalis, J. (1973) *The Language of Psychoanalysis*. London: The Hogarth Press.

Mamet, D. (1993) *Oleanna*. London: Methuen.

Miller, A. (1961) *A View from the Bridge/All My Sons*. Harmondsworth: Penguin.

Morrison, B. (1998) 'On childhood and violence'. *British Journal of Psychotherapy 14*, 4, 420–428.

CHAPTER 17

Social Work Responses to Domestic Violence in the Context of Child Protection

Margaret Bell

Whatever theoretical perspective one takes, violent behaviour in families – especially where there are children – is disturbing and dangerous. Physical violence is the most frequently reported, although research, as well as accounts by women and children, have demonstrated that the violence takes many forms, ranging from murder, to rape and mental cruelty (Mooney 1995). The extent and nature of the damage caused in families by domestic violence, including the links with child abuse, are now generally recognised. Gibbons *et al.* (1995) found domestic violence present in 27 per cent of their sample of approximately 2,000 child protection referrals. Farmer and Owen (1995) report higher rates. Research has demonstrated that children may be seriously affected by witnessing the violence directed at their mothers, and may be attacked themselves in the incident (Casey 1987). Although the majority of incidents of domestic violence are against women, the number of identified males who experience violence is increasing, along with elderly people, people in gay and lesbian relationships and between siblings.

While this decade has witnessed greater understanding of the impact of domestic violence on the women and children involved, and statutory and voluntary agencies are developing structures and services in response, less is known about the impact of this work on the professionals. Experience and research is suggesting that the personal and professional dynamics of helping in these cases can mirror the family interactions in front of them. For social workers in particular, they also reflect society's profound ambivalence about state intervention with regard to rights to privacy on the one hand, and the need to protect vulnerable people on the other. These reflective and inter-active processes influence social policy and social work practice on a number of different levels, including inter- and intra-agency as well as between client and practitioner. They also influence and are influenced by the agency and organisational structures set up to address the problem of domestic violence. Finally, they find expression in the sometimes acrimonious disputes between researchers and academics about the nature of domestic violence, explanations for its occurrence and the resultant interventions.

My intention in this chapter is to explore the transactions between practitioners and families, and within and between organisations working with families in which domestic violence is occurring from a psychodynamic perspective. The discussion will draw on two research studies by Bell. One was undertaken in 1996 to identify the needs of, and service provision for, children and young people in Leeds who had witnessed and/or experienced violence against their mothers (Bell 1996). The other was a large-scale study of the involvement of parents in child protection investigations in a northern city in 1992 (Bell 1999). These studies provide us with important information about the ways in which professionals perceive and respond to violent behaviour in families, as well as the shape of the organisational response. Clearly, professionals have very different levels of awareness of the existence of domestic violence, different ways of understanding it and different ways of responding to it, as do the families with whom they are in close contact. The reasons for this are complex, but the focus in this chapter is on psychodynamic understanding.

Secrecy and denial

Families go to extreme lengths to hide the existence of violence. Professionals in the Leeds domestic violence study described a number of ways in which family members successfully concealed it. Mothers did not disclose violence against themselves for a number of reasons: some feared retribution; others were afraid they would be judged incompetent as parents. In many cases, their male partners avoided discussing the issue by absenting themselves or excused their violent behaviour with reference to alcohol. Children adopted various strategies to avoid telling, although the impacts – emotional, physical and sexual abuse – were harder to hide. Mullender and Morley (1994) found that in many of the cases they researched the parents believed – mistakenly – that the violence had not been seen by the children. However, accounts by children suggest that they quickly learn that to talk about what they have witnessed is either unacceptable or dangerous – a silence that is compounded by cultural or familial beliefs that it is better not to discuss upsetting events with children, and that violence is acceptable.

Turning to the behaviour of the professionals, the study suggested that they, also, were often reluctant to see domestic violence. Social services staff reported that the process of identification was 'almost incidental – very sort of pot-luck'. GPs were seen as being key to early identification and referral, but were generally unaware: 'I have been in general practice for 24 years, and can hardly recall any cases in this category'.

Professionals only became aware of the existence of violence some time after the child presented with symptoms of distress; the child or other family member trusted the professional enough to tell; or another professional involved passed on the information. Even in cases where it was known domestic violence did exist it was not, in itself, defined as a child protection issue. So while the symptoms of distress were identified and acted on in child protection terms – the professionals suggested that 42 per cent of the child protection referrals turned out to also involve domestic violence – in other cases where it was known violence existed child protection issues were not identified. The potentially disastrous consequence of professional blindness is vividly illustrated by the death of Sukina Hammond at the hands of her father (O'Hara 1994). Although social services were aware of violence against Sukina's mother, her name was removed from the at risk register shortly after a vicious attack on her mother and just before her death.

The Bridge Child Care Consultancy Service (1991) suggested two linked reasons why the existence of domestic violence in the Hammond household was overlooked – that the investigating social worker perceived it to be acceptable, and that the details of the assaults were not pulled together. In analysing other inquiry reports, Munro (1998) reports a pattern of social workers 'losing' key bits of information and of being 'ignorant' in assessing the relationship between abuse of the mother and risk to the child. Other strategies of avoidance in child protection work have been noted. In Bell's child protection research the social workers, in according priority to collecting evidence of abuse, did not explore the family background and did not draw on theories which would help them to understand the significance of what they were seeing. At the same time, the focus on information gathering meant there was little time left to engage with the traumatic feelings experienced by families undergoing the investigation. The question clearly arises as to why behaviour so violent it can result in a child's death is not recognised by those best placed to respond to it. Some explanations may be found by exploring the emotional content of the transactions.

Personal responses

Accounts by women and children of their experiences of family violence have in common feelings of uncertainty, fear, confusion, guilt and helplessness. The following account of a ten-year-old boy reliving in court the night he witnessed his mother's murder provides a good example:

I had been in bed for five minutes waiting for my Mum. She was doing her teeth in the bathroom. Dad went into the bathroom. He was really cross – very, very cross. The door was closed. I heard a wallop and went in. His hands were on her neck; he was squeezing and I pulled him off. He pushed me out of the room, slammed the door shut and bolted it.

This little boy intervened in an attempt to protect his mother. Other children may be immobilised and silenced by terror. As we have seen, the responses of professionals may similarly be driven by fear and anxiety. In situations of domestic violence there is danger. In working with families in which violence is occurring, practitioners – predominantly women in the case of social work – expose themselves to physical violence, intimidation and harassment, sometimes of a sexual nature, and are advised to take such threats seriously. The presence of a Dobermann pinscher and a boa constrictor in Sukina Hammond's household understandably aroused terror. More subtle, covert ways of intimidating social workers and arousing fear, such as sexual innuendo, have been described by Milner (1996). Such intimidation is most successful in controlling client-worker interactions, in preventing workers from accessing and engaging with the family's weaker members, and in deflecting attention from violent men.

Less transparent and more difficult to quantify, but often more powerful, are situations where the resonance between clients' and practitioners' emotional lives makes external events 'seek out and speak to raw sense data from the past' (Woodhouse and Pengelly 1991). Families in which there is violence, we know arouse anxiety and feelings of helplessness in those who seek to help them (see Dale *et al.* 1986; Morrison 1992). Overwhelming in themselves, such feelings will be intensified when they resonate with personal experience. Recent research suggests that many of us will have personal experience of violence at home. Caroll (1994) reports that one in ten women suffer violence at the hands of their partner in a given year, and this is likely to be an underestimate because of under-reporting. It is possible, furthermore, that social workers may have increased vulnerability. There is evidence that motivation to do social work often derives from some tragic life event. Rochford (1991) found that experience of loss, both normal and exceptional, was a driving force for a number of social work students. So social workers – and their supervisors and their managers – are very likely to be carrying feelings associated with their own early experiences, as well as their present family relationships, into their daily work. Where the situations they face resonate with and mirror situations from their own past and present, the feelings re-experienced will be intense, overwhelming and difficult to contain. They will then be imported into the work situation through processes of identification, projection, transference and countertransference, as is known to happen when therapists intervene in dysfunctional families.

Many of the empirical studies of work with abusive families describe a pattern which can be better understood with reference to these concepts (see Mattinson and Sinclair 1975). There is, in much family work where children are at risk, a belief that the mother is the protector of the child and responsible for the emotional climate of the family and running of the household. At the same time, there may be underlying assumptions that the interests of mother and child necessarily coincide and that fathers are unavailable. Intervention is therefore focused on the mother. Social workers who are predominantly female, and whose primary responsibility is to protect the child, may – especially when the family feels unsafe – find themselves inclined to identify with the mother and to project negative feelings on to the father. While such an identification may serve some professional and personal needs, it is likely to be dysfunctional for the family. In assigning the mother the role of protector, unreasonable expectations can add to her burden and her needs may be overlooked.

In so far as the children are concerned, their needs might be different. The benefits of leaving a violent partner/parent, for example, have to be weighed against the raft of losses which, for the children, may also involve change of school and the loss of paternal attachment. In similar ways the role of the extended family can be overlooked. In interviewing 23 of the social workers in the child-protection research, Bell found that only three had spoken to grandparents or aunts or uncles before the conference, even when they were known to be important attachment figures for the child. In most cases the social workers said they 'had not thought of it', while others said they did not want to be responsible for 'seeping' damaging information into the extended family network: 'I think the maternal grandmother should have been involved, but she is unaware of the marital violence so this would have caused problems in the conference and after it'.

So, there is evidence that social workers work primarily with the mother. There are a number of reasons for this, including practical ones, but the explanation offered here, with reference to unconscious processes, is supported by looking in detail at the social work practice. There is a clear danger that identification with one family member means that the needs of the others, men as well as children, will be overlooked and the worker may lose sight of the whole picture.

The invisibility of men

The absence of men from social work interventions in situations of domestic violence has already been noted. The Leeds domestic violence study provided evidence of a dearth of services for men, and this finding is supported by other research (Humphreys 1999; Milner 1996). Again, there are parallels with statutory work with children and families. Bell (1999) found that men were commonly absent from child protection assessments and from initial child protection conferences where key decisions are made. In the child protection study, 94 per cent of the mothers were invited to the conferences as against 44 per cent of the fathers – despite the fact that only 21 per cent of the children involved lived with their mother alone. Fathers who had left the marital home were not pursued at all, even where they had maintained contact.

One explanation for the absence of men from professional interventions, as already suggested, is that social workers quite properly fear being attacked themselves. The exercise of power in violent families is generally associated with men, and is intimidating. So one way of managing issues of gender and power is for the man not to be seen at all, or for his violent behaviour to be 'understood and excused' – often with reference to alcohol. Featherstone and Trinder (1998) have suggested that the feminist movement contributed to the absence of men from therapeutic interventions by constructing a discourse in which power is portrayed in an over-simplified, one-dimensional way. In this way men can become stereotyped as dominant villains acquiring all negative attributes, while women acquire only positive (nurturing) ones. Such a discourse could support defensive strategies in workers, such as splitting along gender lines.

Interventions

The processes of splitting and the resultant stereotyping are also reflected in the way services are organised for families in which there is domestic violence. As Stanley (1997) has pointed out, the culture of separateness has been fed by the way services to women, children and violent men have been split. The needs of women experiencing domestic violence have predominantly been met within the voluntary sector, mainly by Women's Aid, whose refuges preserve physical safety by excluding men and maintaining secrecy. The needs of children have been defined in child protection terms and are addressed largely by social service departments. Work with men has traditionally been located within the criminal justice framework and is thus not associated with local authority family support systems. Such a tripartite split in conceptions of the problem and service provision both reflects and is reflected in choices of intervention.

Uncertainty surrounds whether or not couple or family work should be undertaken. On the one hand working with couples where there is violence may be both unsafe and be perceived as blurring issues of criminal responsibility. On the other, since over half of the women who seek refuge do continue their relationship (see Frude 1993) there is a strong argument for working with the couple in an attempt to effect change. The existence of violence in couple relationships does compound the difficulties of couple work. In couple partnerships it is common for clear messages to be given to the worker that it is unsafe to intervene – especially where there are powerful family secrets and dysfunctional relationships. Ambivalence about seeking help to change may also be communicated. Double messages about changing established patterns of behaviour may be communicated within the couple relationship and to those outside it, so it is very unclear what is being said or asked.

This ambivalence and lack of clarity has a particular resonance for social workers in the 1990s. Social work as a profession is not clear where it stands in relation to couple work. The competency-based approach to training is in many ways antithetical to the psychodynamic approaches that underpin couple work. Further, the under-developed legal framework for supporting women and children at home contributes to social workers' sense of insecurity. The lack of clarity about women's rights, for example, to a shared home or compensation for injury, and the alarming variation in the courts' response to violent crimes, add to a fear of being unsupported and out of control of the direction a case may take within the criminal justice system. There are, thus, a number of factors contributing to the reluctance to work with couples. Containment is therefore important – important for the family and, for personal and professional reasons, for the social worker.

There are a number of similarities between the dilemmas faced by social workers addressing issues of domestic violence and those faced in Cleveland. In situations of domestic violence, the best course of action is rarely straightforward, resources are limited, and legal intervention may result in family breakdown. For social workers operating The Children Act (1989) there is the added difficulty of managing the joint injunction to protect the child from harm in a situation known to be abusive, while at the same time supporting parental responsibility. There are, therefore, a number of ambiguities in the tasks facing social workers. These ambiguities are deskilling and disempowering, and they reflect the situation of the entrapped partner. In these situations collusions can emerge which, as we have seen, lead to unhelpful splitting mechanisms and to other strategies of avoidance.

Other strategies of avoidance

So far we have identified some of the strategies employed by professionals which enable them to avoid or to engage in only limited involvement in situations of domestic violence, and offered some psychodynamic explanations. Not seeing and not naming the violence and its effects, compartmentalizing the evidence and avoiding couple interventions provide important protective functions for social workers involved in unsafe domestic situations. Milner and Humphreys have located others. Both noted that violence was often referred to in notes or meetings in gender-neutral terms, where it was reframed as marital conflict or fighting. They also found that social workers often failed to record the existence of violence in case-notes or to report it in conferences. Bell found that when parents were present in child-protection conferences there was a shared fear that disclosure of known violence could rebound catastrophically on the women and children. It was not uncommon for professionals to collude with one partner in keeping secret facts which were highly relevant to the risk assessment. As a health visitor said: 'Father's violent behaviour has meant that social services no longer visit the home, and his threats inhibited workers from fully discussing the facts in mother's presence. People were clearly scared of father finding out what they had said, so wouldn't speak in front of his wife'.

Naming other issues as the problem is another strategy of avoidance. The respondents in the Leeds domestic-violence study reported that the adverse effects on children were often attributed to other causes – even where it was known there had been violent attacks in the household. Treating a symptom, for example, of a child's aggressive behaviour, as the problem served to avoid turning the spotlight on the violent parent. There are thus a number of ways in which the professionals, like the families they work with, may avoid making public or intervening in situations of domestic violence.

Power in organisations

Lack of awareness, denial and avoidance also operate at agency and institutional levels. Most of the agencies involved in responding to violent-family situations also use force – either legitimately, for example, compulsory detention – or illegitimately, as in pin-down. Hearne (1996) has suggested that agencies working with violent people reflect this violence in managerial and work cultures which are oppressive and patriarchal. In social service departments few women occupy managerial positions. In 1990, 82 per cent of the senior managers were men, although 86.5 per cent of the workforce comprised women. Howe (1986) has suggested that there is horizontal as well as vertical gender segregation in that women's attributes are seen as fitting them for fieldwork tasks associated with domesticity. The distribution of labour within social service departments and the hierarchical structuring along gender lines can thus be said to reproduce the inequality and discrimination experienced by women in society. Feminists would argue that such institutionalised patriarchal structures are at the root of men's violence towards women. Such inequality in social service departments may contribute to social workers' identification with less powerful members in the family noted earlier. Gender, therefore, operates at different levels in the caring professions, and this impacts in a number of ways.

Policy and procedures

One of the ways in which managerial processes are structured to allay practitioners' anxiety is by the development of policies and guidelines which can reduce complex personal and professional responses to material tasks. That institutional processes are commonly used as strategies for managing anxiety and for promoting personal and professional distance, especially where children are at risk, is well documented. Menzies Lyth (1988) has described how nurses use hierarchical procedures as a way of managing unbearable anxiety in a hospital ward. Other writers, such as Hallett (1995) and Bell, have described similar processes operating in child protection work, where the managerial emphasis is on procedural regularity, rather than empathic and sensitive engagement with families. The interviews with social workers in Bell's child protection research revealed a preoccupation with procedures for interagency collaboration which left little capacity for the social workers to work with the families distress at the same time. In this way it can be seen that procedures may be used as a socially organised agency defence for managing professional anxiety, and may promote defensive practice. Institutional defences can thus constellate in ways which are mutually reinforcing and detrimental to client-worker and professional transactions.

Interagency work

The processes operating within agencies to structure emotional and professional distancing can also be seen to operate between agencies. Situations of domestic violence, like child abuse, require a multi-agency response within a zone of uncertainty. It is not unusual for social services, police, education, health, housing, probation, the Crown prosecution service and voluntary agencies to be involved in one case. In each agency, violence is defined in a characteristic way by managers and their staff and in ways which reflect the agency's functions and structure and their particular professional and occupational ideologies. So, for example, in housing, violence may be highly relevant to housing need, but it is not necessarily the dominant operative definition for clients. In the police force, as the recent Killingbeck initiative (Hanmer and Griffiths 1998) is demonstrating, the task of prosecution may run counter to what all family members want or to what other agencies, such as social services, judge will avoid family breakdown. The potential for dissonance and conflict between agencies, as between agencies and families, is thus ripe. As we have seen, the pervasive way of managing the anxiety provoked by these transactions – in family and in professional systems – is by avoidance. Where avoidance operates, professionals split defensively into factions. Agencies then construct policies and procedures which support their own culture and provide their workers with a means of fending off unbearable anxiety. Procedures can thus be seen to function defensively across professional boundaries by preventing the working through of anxiety at a personal level and so hindering collaboration which would have made their tasks easier.

Conclusion

Violence is very much a part of social work. However, as the processes which have served to render domestic violence invisible are being peeled away, social workers who have traditionally approached their profession with enthusiasm find themselves in a job which is increasingly nasty and frightening. Having long been uneasy about the authoritative aspects of their role, they fear they have become defined as people who control rather than as people who are there to help. At the same time, they are bombarded with multifaceted explanations for the causes and maintenance of family violence and with multifactorial models of theory and intervention with no clear direction as to where social work is going, or where to pitch their intervention. Underlying these uncertainties and conflicting ideologies is a quite natural and appropriate anxiety where people are being damaged and hurt. The challenge for them is to make this anxiety work for them and their clients, not against them.

Twenty-five years ago, in exploring the potential for working with couples from a social services base, Mattinson and Sinclair (1975) noted that the way the workers behaved towards one another was a modified, and more sophisticated version of what the families did to each other. The workers used words rather than fists, but the marital war, they said, was imported into the workers, who in turn exported it into the organisational hierarchy. We could add that the institution in turn exports the war back into the workers, and so on. Although unsurprising, it is nevertheless depressing to find evidence of the same circular conscious and unconscious transactions so many years on.

So what can help? Self-awareness and the capacity to critically reflect upon what belongs to the self and what to the other are essential so that the strategies of avoidance we have identified do not continue to be used defensively to prohibit involvement. Reflection in particular is necessary to prevent being sucked into the fights and predicaments of these unhappy families, to stand apart and to offer help confidently that is appropriate to the needs of all the members of the family. Developing the capacity to contain and manage complexity and uncertainty is also necessary. Social workers need to draw on knowledge and theories which will help them to make sense of the fragmentation and complexity they have in front of them, and to clarify the social-work task so that it is not primarily defensive. There is a need to explore power in a more nuanced way. This may enable more effective engagement with the violence in the adult couple relationship, as well as more confident and constructive engagement with professionals in other agencies. An exploration of the way in which power operates in and between organisations is also indicated. As we have seen, organisations support defensive practice in a number of ways. Employers need to counter this by providing quality supervision, supportive management and effective interagency training. Supervision provides valuable clues to clients' underlying dilemmas. To enable workers to manage anxiety and to combat emotional distancing, supervision needs to focus on personal issues in a way that provides containment and promotes reflection (Agass, chapter 15, above). Professionals, like the families they work with, need to feel safe if they are to engage effectively with the helplessness and despair of families in which violence is occurring.

References

Bell, M. (1996) 'A survey of the needs of and service provision for children and young people in Leeds who have witnessed/experienced domestic violence'. York: University of York.

Bell, M. (1999) *Child Protection: Families and the Conference Process*. Aldershot: Ashgate.

Bridge Child Care Consultancy Service (1991) 'Sukina: An evaluation report of the circumstances leading to her death'. London: Bridge Child Care Consultancy Service.

Carroll, J. (1994) 'The protection of children exposed to marital violence'. *Child Abuse Review* 3, 6–14.

Casey, M. (1987) *Domestic Violence Against Women*. Dublin: Dublin Federation of Refuges.

Dale, P., Davies, M., Morrison. T. and Waters, J. (1986) *Dangerous Families: Assessment and Treatment of Child Abuse*. London: Tavistock Publications.

Cleveland (1988) *Report of the Enquiry into Child Abuse in Cleveland*. London: HMSO.

Farmer, E. and Owen, M. (1995) *Child Protection Practice: Private Risks and Public Remedies*. London: HMSO.

Frude, N. (1993) *Understanding Family Problems: A Psychological Approach*. Chichester: Wiley.

Gibbons, J., Conroy, S. and Bell, C. (1995) *Operating the Child Protection System*. London: HMSO.

Hallett, C. (1995) *Inter-Agency Co-operation in Child Protection*. London: HMSO.

Hanmer, J. (1995) Domestic violence and social care: A report on two conferences held by the social services inspectorate. March 1995. London: Department of Health.

Hanmer, J. and Griffith, S. (1998) Domestic violence and repeat victimisation. London Policy Research Briefing Group. Note 1/98.

Hearn, J. (1996) 'The organisation of violence: men, gender relations, organisations and violence'. In B. Fawcett, B. Featherstone, J. Hearn and C. Toft (eds) *Violence and Gender Relations,: Theories and Interventions.* London: Sage.

Howe, D. (1986) 'The segregation of women and their work in the personal social service'. *Critical Social Policy 15,* 21–35.

Humphreys, C. (1999) 'Avoidance and confrontation: Social work practice in relation to domestic violence and child abuse'. *Child and Family Social Work 4,* 1, 77–87.

Mattinson, J. and Sinclair, I. (1975) *Mate and Stalemate.* Oxford: Blackwells.

Maynard, M. (1985) 'The response of social workers to domestic violence'. In J. Pahl (ed) *Private Violence and Public Policy.* London: Routledge and Kegan Paul.

Menzies Lyth, I. (1988) *Containing Anxiety in Institutions.* London: Free Association Books.

Milner, J. (1996) 'Men's resistance to social workers'. In B. Fawcett, B. Featherstone, J. Hearn and C. Toft (eds) *Violence and Gender Relations: Theories and Interventions.* London: Sage.

Mooney, J. (1994) *The Hidden Figure: Domestic Violence in North London.* London: Islington Crime and Police Prevention Unit.

Morrison, T. (1992) 'The emotional effects of child protection work on the worker'. *Practice 4,* 4, 253–270.

Mullender, A. and Morley, R. (1994) *Children Living with Domestic Violence.* London: Whiting and Birch.

Munro, E. (1998) 'Improving social workers knowledge base in child protection work'. *British Journal of Social Work 28,* 89–105.

NCH Action for Children (1994) *The Hidden Victims: Children and Domestic Violence.* London: NCH.

O'Hara, M. (1994) 'Child deaths in context of domestic violence: Implications for professional practice'. In A. Mullender and R. Morley (eds) *Children Living with Domestic Violence.* London: Whiting and Birch.

Pahl, J. (1985) *Private Violence and Public Policy: The Needs of Battered Women and the Responses of the Public Services.* London: Routledge and Kegan Paul.

Rochford, G. (1991) 'Theory, concepts, feelings and practice: The contemplation of bereavement within a social work course'. In J. Lishman (ed) *Handbook of Theory to Practice in Social Work.* London: Jessica Kingsley Publishers.

Stanley, N. (1997) 'Domestic violence and child abuse: Developing feminist social work practice'. *Child and Family Social Work 2,* 135–145.

Woodhouse, D. and Pengelly, P. (1991) *Anxiety and the Dynamics of Collaboration.* London: AUP.

CHAPTER 18

Reparative Experience or Repeated Trauma?

Child Sexual Abuse and Adult Mental Health Services

Carol-Ann Hooper and Juliet Koprowska

There is now increasing recognition of the impacts of childhood sexual abuse on adult mental health. While many factors mediate its effects and the majority of those who have been sexually abused in childhood do not suffer long-term psychopathology (Finkelhor 1996), it is clear that such experiences increase vulnerability to a wide range of mental health problems. High prevalence rates of childhood sexual abuse have been found in psychiatric outpatient and inpatient populations (see Muenzenmaier *et al.* 1993), and among those described as 'severely mentally ill' (Goodman *et al.* 1997; Rosenberg, Drake, and Mueser 1996) on whom health and social services are now enjoined to concentrate their efforts and their limited resources (DoH 1995a). Moreover, research in the US suggests that the experience of the systems of care for adults with serious mental illness of people with a history of childhood sexual abuse is significantly different from those without such a history. Newmann *et al.* (1998) found that people with histories of childhood sexual abuse used significantly higher numbers both of days in inpatient, nursing home and residential treatment setting care and of hours in out-patient care, and hence had significantly higher costs of care. Whether this is the result of the impact of their childhood trauma on their needs, or the failure of services to address them effectively, or both, it is clearly important to look carefully at the interaction between this group and the services they use, both in the community and in hospital/residential settings.

Mental health services have long been dominated by a medical model, which locates the origins of mental illness in biology and accords the medical profession authority over both problem and 'cure', despite the limited success of the medical profession in developing 'cures' and the high risk of iatrogenic effects. In addition, there is an inherent contradiction in according doctors authority over the patient's life in order to restore their mental health, while mental health requires the 'patient' to develop authority over their own life (Morgan 1998). While Morgan (1998) found in a consultation with users of mental health services that 'the strikingly consistent theme was the wish for relationship' (p.179), the medical model maintains professional distance and difference from the client – the doctor is assumed to carry all knowledge/ expertise and health, the patient no knowledge and all illness – and the treatment is expected to work regardless of the relationship between them. By contrast, a psychodynamic perspective places the relationship between worker (of whatever profession) and client at the core of the process by which clients' distress may be relieved and their well-being enhanced.

Recognition of the role of childhood sexual abuse – and other forms of childhood abuse – in mental illness has added an increased urgency to crit-iques of the medical model. Ignoring the experience of abuse may mean not only that treatment fails to address an important source of distress, but that it may replicate the person's experience in childhood where invalidation from others from whom help is sought or might be expected may add significantly to the original trauma of abuse (Bowlby 1988). This potential to replicate abuse within the mental health system, in a variety of ways (Lubotsky Levin *et al.* 1998), may well contribute to the higher use of services by adults sexually abused in childhood via a repeated cycle of ineffective intervention exacer-bating abuse-related mental health problems. Jennings (1998) has argued therefore that a shift is required from a medical- to a trauma-oriented paradigm if mental health services are to meet the needs of adults sexually abused in childhood. While it does not seem to us necessary to reject the medical model altogether, it is equally clear that taking into consideration the role of childhood sexual abuse in mental health problems, its impact on the person, their social networks and other aspects of adult functioning requires a radical rethink of service provision (see Bills and Bloom 1998; Harris 1998; Kalinowski and Penney 1998). This chapter aims to contribute to the development of a trauma-oriented paradigm informed by psychodynamic perspectives, drawing on research with adults who were sexually abused in childhood, which explored their experience of services, both in the com-munity and in hospital.[1]

We use the term 'survivors' rather than 'people who have been sexually abused in childhood' despite a preference for the latter description. Both we and some of our interviewees have reservations about the term 'survivor' because it defines a person's identity through only one aspect of their experience, can carry its own stereotypes and stigma, and perhaps obscures the pain of abuse. We use it for economy and because it captures a significant aspect of adult autonomy and potential for recovery.

We sought to make sense of survivors' experience of services in relation to their experience of abuse and its influence on their life, taking into account the interaction of past and present, of internal and external worlds in interpreting their accounts. Below we discuss first the nature of their abuse, some impacts particularly relevant to the use of services, and what we mean by repeated trauma and reparative experience. We then identify ways in which both during the process of accessing services and the ongoing experience of services, service providers can retraumatise on the one hand, or offer a reparative experience on the other. The distinction between accessing and experience of services is somewhat schematic since the two are clearly interwoven.

Abuse and recovery – trauma, repeated trauma and reparative experience

While the research was explicitly focused on adult survivors of childhood sexual abuse, for most of the interviewees child sexual abuse was only a part of the story of their abuse. Many had experienced other forms of abuse in childhood, including physical, emotional and psychological abuse, physical and emotional neglect. For some, abuse from the same abusers (sometimes sexual, more often emotional) had continued into their adult lives. Many had also been revictimised as an adult by others, including boyfriends, husbands and strangers. Consideration of the impacts of abuse on adult mental health clearly needs to place child sexual abuse within the context of broader life experience, both past and present. In addition, attachment theory draws attention to the role of primary relationships in childhood development, and we have suggested elsewhere that the impacts of sexual abuse are likely to depend on the combination of abusive and caring relationships people have had as children, their age at the onset of abuse and its duration, and on the place the abusive relationship occupied in their attachment networks (Hooper, Koprowksa and McCluskey 1997). Some of our interviewees had always remembered their abuse. Others had blocked the memories and/or the emotions associated with them from consciousness (Bowlby 1988) and found them re-emerging later in an abuse-related crisis in adulthood, triggered by direct reminders of the abuse, events involving loss and change and/or the therapeutic process.

Childhood abuse can have a profound impact on every aspect of a person's life, including their ability to seek help when they need it and hence their use of services. Attachment theory recognises that human infants come equipped with instinctive careseeking behaviour, designed to stimulate complementary instinctive caregiving responses from older people. Care-seeking behaviour 'is elicited by pain, fatigue, or anything frightening, and also by the caregiver being, or appearing to be, inaccessible.' (Bowlby 1988, p.82). A child whose caregiver(s) are reliable and responsive will develop a secure attachment to that caregiver, and will normally seek the proximity of his or her 'secure base' (the caregiver) when under threat, thus facilitating protection and survival. The interaction between them will also be internal-ised to form an 'internal working model' of the relationship, which operates as a kind of template for the child's image of her or himself and expectations of the caregiver in future. While children develop different internal working models for different relationships – and may be securely attached to one caregiver but not another – the combination of their experiences in different relationships, especially but not only their ongoing primary relationships, construct the generalised expectations of others which influence the care-seeking which normally continues throughout life in circumstances of pain, illness, fatigue or loss.

Some of the people in our study had had reliable and responsive non-abusive caregivers for part of their lives, before, after or concurrently with their experiences of abuse. Others had had what appeared to be unremittingly terrifying childhoods, and many had experienced the long-term 'low warmth, high criticism' environments now thought to be most damaging to children (DoH 1995b). The conflict for children who are abused by the adults who are their primary attachment figures is that the threat which prompts careseeking arises from the person or people to whom they would expect to turn for comfort and protection. Crittenden (1995) describes the strategies which small children develop to placate these dangerous care-givers, for example becoming avoidant and ashamed, inhibiting their own feelings, being compulsively compliant and blaming themselves for parental rejection and anger. Seligman (1975) also shows how continued assaults which cannot be escaped – where the abused person's attempts to avoid pain make no impact on their circumstances – can lead to depression and despair. Defensive exclusion of traumatic material (Bowlby 1988) can take a number of forms, including amnesia and idealisation of the abuser (de Zulueta 1993). In such circumstances the careseeking system of the attachment dynamic (Heard and Lake 1997) may be inhibited, distorted or suppressed.

While the impacts of childhood abuse are likely to relate to the specific combination of experiences of the individual and the context in which they occurred, there are common traumagenic dynamics which it is important that professionals understand if they are to avoid repeating them. In relation to child sexual abuse, these include: sexual intrusion or developmentally inappropriate demands; betrayal of trust by a caregiver; the imposition of secrecy and denial of the child's reality; stigmatisation which leaves the child feeling bad and different from others; and powerlessness as the child's needs are repeatedly subordinated to those of the abuser and access to alternative relationships and/or escape cut off (Bowlby 1988; Finkelhor 1986; Herman 1994). Emotional abuse in addition commonly involves rejection, shaming and degrading criticism, objectification, deprivation, overburdening of responsibility and distortion of the child's reality (DoH 1991 and 1995b; Kirkwood 1993). Some of the ways in which service providers can, often unwittingly, replicate such dynamics are illustrated below.

It is equally clear from our study that professionals in a variety of different contexts can contribute to a reparative experience for survivors. Some of our interviewees were engaged in therapeutic relationships which were providing such a reparative experience, i.e., enabling them to remember and mourn their childhood experiences (or at least process the emotions associated with them), reappraise their internal working models of relationship and regain trust, safety and connection with others (cf Hooper *et al.* 1997 for fuller discussion). It may well be easiest for such reparative experience to be provided in the context of psychotherapy, and psychotherapists were indeed the most highly rated professional group in our study. However, other individuals in the public and voluntary sectors from a variety of professional backgrounds were equally highly valued, as were some experiences of groups (self-help and led), and it is therefore worth addressing not only the need for more resources for psychotherapy, important though that is, but also what contributes to reparative experiences in other contexts.

A core theme in distinguishing experiences which were retraumatising from those which were reparative was the quality of relationship between survivor and service provider, or in terms of the attachment dynamic between careseeker and caregiver. Heard and Lake (1997) consider that human relating can be either 'supportive and companionable' or 'dominant vs. submissive'. Supportive and companionable relating is secure, unthreatened and unthreatening; it is mutually respectful, 'protective, explanatory and exploratory' (p.34). Dominant vs. submissive relating, by contrast, is defensive, involving coercion and control on the one part, and submission on the other. Those who do not submit are likely to be 'shamed and humiliated' (p.35). Both patterns of relating are grounded in our biological inheritance, although supportive and companionable relating is a more recently evolved pattern, and the capacity to adopt this mode is influenced by the individual's experience and environment. We suggest that experiences of services which are retraumatising often reflect a dominant vs. submissive mode of relating on the part of the 'caregiver' (as does abuse) while supportive and companionable relating is more likely to contribute to a reparative experience.

The capacity of workers for supportive and companionable relating is affected by their personal lives (past and present), their professional training and supervision, and the organisational and policy context:

> Caregivers who are most likely to show D/S [dominant vs. submissive] patterns are those whose internal supportive systems undermine their attempts to be competent, whose personal supportive environment cannot be maintained and who have no effective external support available. When faced with too many careseekers, or ones that are uncooperative, such caregivers feel incompetent and powerless. To regain a sense of control and competence, there is a marked tendency for them to fall back on coercive controlling or avoidant patterns of relating. (Heard and Lake 1997, p.92)

While the personal, professional and policy environments are important, so too is the cultural environment. Recourse to dominant vs. submissive patterns may be supported by constructions both of the doctor-patient relationship and of masculinity, although such patterns are not exclusive either to the medical profession or to men.

For staff to provide the supportive and companionable relating which we believe survivors require, they too need a supportive environment. In practice, despite the best conscious intentions of managers and practitioners, services are too often unconsciously organised defensively to shield staff from the anxiety generated by proximity to patients' pain and distress, as Menzies Lyth (1988) found in her study of general nursing. In such an environment, dominant vs. submissive relating is more likely to emerge, as professionals unable to respond to survivors' needs, whether expressed directly or indirectly, instead expect the survivor to fit in with (submit to) their own personal or professional styles, routines or preconceptions. Such dominant vs. submissive relating can emerge in many forms, all of which have the potential to retraumatise survivors and some of which are illustrated below.

Accessing services

Access to services is affected by numerous factors, including the existence, extent and temporal organisation of appropriate service provision, access to information about services and the availability and costs of transport and childcare. However, the complex and often protracted nature of the process of accessing services is also influenced both by the ability of survivors to seek care, and by the responses of others to their efforts. It is this relational dimension to the process, involving the careseeking and caregiving systems of the attachment dynamic (Heard and Lake 1997), that we wish primarily to discuss.

The careseeking behaviour of people in our study had clearly been affected by the impacts of abuse on their internal working models of relationship in a variety of enduring ways, as well as by the bribes and threats with which abusers commonly attempt to maintain the secrecy surrounding sexual abuse. Some had been so persistently undermined and criticised as children that they had little trust in anyone, did not expect to be believed, or anticipated rejection and blame even if they were believed. Others had little, if any, sense of entitlement to their needs being met, and worried about being a nuisance to service providers or taking up services that others might need more. Some had particular fears of authority figures. It is likely that those who have experienced the most severe abuse may often be those least able to seek help. As one interviewee put it, when she was in most pain it simply did not occur to her to seek help because in her 'internal place…there is no one', that is, she had no access to an internal representation of a potential caregiver. This woman had been emotionally abused from a very early age by her mother, and sexually abused from three or four by her father, and had no memory of anyone she had been able to trust as a child.

Despite these internal inhibitors to careseeking, our interviewees had sought help. As children, several had tried to tell their teachers at school. Others who had not told anyone directly nevertheless felt they had given clear signals that they were in trouble – by running away from home, attempting suicide, performing poorly or behaving aggressively at school, or complaining of unexplained physical symptoms, for example. Children's indirect cries for help almost invariably fell on the stony ground of indifference to the meaning of their behaviour, and direct disclosure was met with disbelief, and sometimes punishment (mostly from parents).

As adults, some had told professionals with whom they were in contact either for matters unconnected with abuse or for a variety of abuse-related problems. Such professionals included health visitors, GPs and social workers, psychiatric and general hospital staff, counsellors and groups run by voluntary organisations. Those who told were sometimes met with good caregiving, responsive to their needs. Many, however, were met with disbelief and dismissiveness. In cases where professional responses repeated the inadequate experiences of caregiving to which survivors were accustomed, their internalised expectations of the dangers or the pointlessness of careseeking were powerfully reinforced. One woman who was referred to a psychologist by her GP during her 20s when suffering from depression, told him a small part of her abuse and was told it was normal for brothers to experiment with their younger sisters (as her brother had of course also claimed). It took her ten years to tell anyone again.

A number of our interviewees had, as adults, been asked about childhood experiences, and sometimes specifically about abuse, by professionals. For some this enabled them to talk about their abuse, for others it did not. Where mental health assessments have been required to include such inquiries (for example, in some parts of the US) the identification of traumatic experiences has increased (Eilenberg et al. 1996). The relational context in which such inquiries are made and their timing is important however; people in our study had made some clear choices about who to tell and when, influenced partly by their own life circumstances but also by their perceptions of the potential caregiver. The offer of a continuous, supportive relationship to facilitate trust, implicit or explicit permission to talk about abuse, and encouragement to take up help all contributed to overcoming the internalised inhibitions against telling and asking for/accepting help. The introduction of such inquiries without the development of appropriate services may, however, be of dubious value to survivors. Eilenberg et al. (1996) found that only in a minority of cases where a trauma history had been identified was it used to develop a suitable treatment plan. In our study, too, even where the person's abuse became known, appropriate service provision was not always made. Telling of abuse only to fail to receive effective help may repeat the experience many survivors had in childhood.

Experience of service provision

There is a wide range of ways in which service provision may retraumatise survivors. We will first identify briefly some fairly obvious ways in which this may occur, then discuss in more depth particular policy or professional issues which illustrate the potential for either repeated trauma or reparative experience.

Three of our thirty interviewees had been sexually abused by people with a professional duty of care towards them. Professional misconduct of this kind is of a different order from the other service issues explored below, in that it is deliberately exploitative. Previous research has also uncovered the extent of sexual harassment and abuse experienced by adult patients in psychiatric wards, especially women in mixed-sex wards, from other patients (Bartlett and Mezey 1995; Copperman 1991). Clearly, managers of health and social care services have a responsibility to protect their users from further violence, whether from staff or other users.

Leavings, endings and referrals can all evoke painful feelings of rejection or abandonment, and can betray the survivor's trust in the caregiver if not carefully handled. Continuity was very highly valued, and several survivors mentioned a reluctance to start again the slow, painful process of building trust with someone new if a worker left. Necessary discontinuities could be tolerated, however, if due care and respect for the survivor's interests were shown. Breaches of confidentiality were perhaps the most intensely felt betrayal of trust, and workers who passed on information about the survivor's abuse – no doubt with good intentions of protecting others' interests but without discussing them first with or considering the implications for the survivor – could do considerable damage to the survivor's recovery.

Unsurprisingly, given societal attitudes to mental illness, having to use mental health services at all and being labelled with psychiatric diagnoses were often experienced as stigmatising, reinforcing the sense of difference and badness some survivors already felt and creating a sense of injustice, especially when their abusers had received no such 'punishment'. Survivors were also frequently given the message that they should subordinate their own needs to those of others – other users (competing for scarce resources), professionals (with whose routines they were expected to fit in), and sometimes their relatives. While there are, of course, constraints and conflicting needs and imperatives, which differ in different professional contexts, how these are handled plays a large part in whether they result in a retraumatising or a reparative experience.

The medical model

The ways in which intrusive and controlling medical treatments such as ECT, excessive use of drugs (especially when given without explanation) and restraint may retraumatise survivors of abuse have been vividly described by Jennings (1998). In our study, professionals who adhered to an exclusively medical model of mental illness, focusing on symptoms without understanding of, or interest in, their roots and relying on medication alone as a solution, could cause considerable distress, leaving survivors feeling unheard, invalidated and objectified. Such an approach reflects not only the mutually reinforcing interests of the medical profession and the pharmaceutical industry in the use of drugs, but also a dominant vs. submissive mode of relating: the patient is told that if they comply with instructions, they will improve. We suggest that supportive and companionable relating may both reduce distress and increase compliance in those circumstances where medication is of value as *part* of a treatment approach, as it clearly was to some of our interviewees. One woman who had been prescribed lithium for years had never been given a diagnosis or had the medication explained. Only when a new psychiatrist spent time with her discussing these matters did she begin to persist with medication and become stable. Another woman had an arrangement with her psychiatrist to self-medicate when she recognised the early signs of depression or hypomania, again according her the opportunity to participate in her own treatment from a position of knowledge and choice.

Therapeutic approach, style or context

Dominant vs. submissive relating also manifested itself when survivors were expected to submit to the preferred approach or style of the worker at the expense of their own needs, or to work in a context against their preference. Several people complained of psychologists who insisted on focusing only on the present and not the past. For some people, at some times, a focus on the here-and-now was valued; but for others the dismissal of the past's relevance recalled years of being silenced and of subordinating their needs to those of others. On the other hand, an over-deterministic emphasis on the past – one woman had been told she was 'preconditioned for depression' by her childhood – could reinforce both stigma and powerlessness, suggesting the negative impacts of abuse were as inescapable as the abuse had once been. Similarly, some people wished to focus on issues other than abuse, such as the break up of a relationship, and were frustrated by workers who insisted that abuse was the key issue.

Several people also complained of silence from their therapists, which left them anxious and bewildered about how to make use of the therapeutic encounter. One man described sitting in silence with his psychologist for long periods, wondering what to say. When he suggested the psychologist ask him questions, the reply was, 'What would you like me to ask you?' Such a frustrating response reinforced his powerlessness to influence his situation. The psychologist's ultimate aim might have been for the survivor to take responsibility for his own recovery, but by not explaining his approach he was taking a dominant stance, likely to elicit submission. True empowerment requires sufficient supportive and companionable attention to the person's unmet needs for care to enable them to use such responsibility in their own interests (see Kalinowski and Penney [1998] for a good discussion of empowerment in mental health services).

Choice about whether to be seen at home or at an office was important, and people made different choices at different times, for a variety of different reasons, for example, fears of encountering colleagues at a clinic. The physical environment had a sometimes unpredictable impact, although Spartan, formal settings and workers who sat behind desks tended to be disliked, and bright, cheerful rooms and workers who sat companionably with them to be appreciated. Similarly, people often have strong feelings about the gender of the worker, and while most of the women preferred a female worker, these too are not always predictable. Harris (1998) suggests that all aspects of personal work – including seating arrangements and the like – should be negotiated with survivors so as to avoid imposing unwanted arrangements.

Managing constraints

The current context for health and social care is one where efficiency, expressed as increased throughput, is at a premium, and short-term contracts with frequent reviews are increasingly the norm. In a culture of audit, the quality of human relationship and care can easily be lost sight of. To some extent, constraints are unavoidable – service providers can never concentrate all their time and resources on one person, so competing needs and demands have to be managed. For many survivors, though, constraints such as these may replicate the experience of having one's needs subordinated to those of others. The CPN who told her client, 'I can't see you more than once a fortnight as I've too much paperwork', could perhaps have made the point in less memorably dismissive fashion.

Many survivors felt that short-term contracts did not provide sufficient time or safety for them to embark on the work they needed to do, while several who had been given an open-ended or long-term commitment felt that at last they had the chance to begin the work of recovery. Service providers may favour short-term work not only for cost reasons but to minimise dependency, yet safe dependency is the precondition for recovery from experiences of childhood sexual abuse. Heard and Lake (1997) also argue that the careseeking system is 'goal-corrected', suggesting that people will leave of their own accord once their needs are met.

The meaning of time boundaries, in terms of length and frequency as well as number of sessions, varied over time and between people. Time boundaries inscribe the limits of the caregiver's availability, and are likely to evoke painful emotions associated with loss, deprivation and absence of care. For some people, knowing the boundaries contributed to safety; for others the limits to availability remained a constant source of pain and distress. The degree to which clients were involved in negotiating time boundaries also seemed to influence their feelings about them. Many placed a high value on flexibility and a great sense of privilege was attached to boundaries being extended on occasion.

Responses to self-harm

Some survivors had experienced punitive attitudes to self-harm, which appears to be regarded by some staff, especially in Accident and Emergency (A&E) departments, as wasteful of scarce resources, though there are signs that the culture may be changing (Anderson 1997). Self-harm – including cutting, burning and overdosing – constitutes an attempt to manage psychic pain and sometimes to seek care. Although the release of endorphins sometimes brings physical relief, and the behaviour can become addictive (Bills and Bloom 1998), this 'reward' is clearly not an adequate explanation for the behaviour. As Sinason (1992) argues, 'the patient who hurts [themselves] is not the same person as the one who is hurt' (p.154). Object relations theory provides an account of the process of internalisation of intolerable experience which is managed through the process of splitting. Both the aggression and the experience of aggression are internalised, separated and repressed. These split off parts of the self continue to attack and be attacked (Fairbairn 1952). Self-harm can therefore be understood as a physical enactment of psychological processes where one part of the self is the assailant, and the other the assailed.

When people seek care after self-harming, staff showing punitive attitudes (and sometimes frank cruelty) ally themselves with the abuser from the past and the internalised attacker, rather than complementing care-seeking with caregiving. They relate in dominant vs. submissive mode, shaming the careseeker. One interviewee reported being kept waiting in an A&E department for hours, being stitched without anaesthetic, and having injuries to her arms stapled rather than sutured. Another described, by contrast, a psychiatric nurse who tended her wounds in a non-judgemental way, and a counsellor from a voluntary organisation who clearly empathised with the part being hurt. A 'repair kit' service set up between consultant psychiatrists and A&E was also described which was highly valued by the woman who had experienced it. Named individuals were given a first aid box containing sterile dressings so that, unless their cuts needed stitches, they could dress themselves, returning to A&E for new supplies when they ran out. This seems to us quite literally a reparative service: it enabled the survivor to care for herself in response to hurting herself, thereby making an alliance with and strengthening her internalised caregiver. (We hypothesise that she had internal working models of caregiving relationships stemming from adolescent experience and a long and secure marriage.) The 'repair kit' service also exemplified supportive and companionable relating.

Hospital wards

Psychiatric hospital wards had provided respite from the demands of everyday life and asylum in times of emotional crisis for some of the people in our study. Such wards had often felt unsafe to survivors however, for a variety of reasons, including their lack of control over the environment, the mix and behaviour of other residents, their treatment by staff, and fears generated by past experiences of the medical profession. Nurses were potentially important caregivers, and people prized those who responded to them with empathy and kindness. A number of people, however, said that nursing staff on psychiatric wards made little or no effort to communicate with them, and while claiming to be 'busy', could be seen chatting with staff and other patients or shut in the nursing office.

Staff on admission wards in particular are expected to spend long shifts in the company of highly distressed people, many of whom have terrible stories to tell. It is perhaps not surprising that they do not always solicit confidences with which they may feel ill-equipped to cope. Such avoidance of contact, however, which may serve a defensive purpose for staff, can easily replicate the neglect many survivors have experienced in childhood. Another woman found very different behaviour by staff – in this case the constant presence of staff who supervised her continuously, even while on the toilet, on a weight-gaining programme for anorexia – similarly distressing. Although the staff were no doubt unaware of the impact of their behaviour, since she had not felt able to tell about her abuse, they were unwittingly repeating the situation she had experienced as a child where she had no refuge from her abusive brother. It may be that taking action such as discharge against medical advice is sometimes an attempt to restore a sense of self-efficacy, as well as an attempt to escape a situation which feels abusive.

Hospital experiences can be of enormous value, and there is clearly potential for supportive and companionable relating within such an environment, both between patients and between patients and staff. One woman had spent a long period in a ward established as a therapeutic community, much of it on a treatment section because of her high level of violence and self-harm. She described an emphasis on people rather than patients, with everyone on first name terms. Diagnoses were not important; 'life problems too difficult to manage out there', was the reason for admission. Community meetings addressed difficult behaviour and issues such as whether people were making use of the unit; violence was presumed to have a meaningful cause and its impact on others was openly discussed. Stimulating and interesting activities were available, individually tailored therapy was provided. For this woman, a primarily trauma-oriented rather than medical model appears to have been employed. She was well aware that it had been an expensive ward to run, and that it was no longer organised along the same lines. However, it is clear that the therapeutic community model can be used to transform even the most challenging of ward environments, and lead to the discharge of long-term patients with difficulties previously thought to be intractable (Bills and Bloom 1998).

Conclusions

We have shown a number of ways in which service providers may (often un-wittingly) repeat aspects of the traumatic experiences which have contributed to people's mental health problems. Some of these experiences occurred many years ago when awareness of child sexual abuse was considerably less. Much has changed – children who told of abuse in school would receive a very different response today, although the risk of invalidation remains, especially from the hopelessly ineffective criminal justice system. Despite increased, though by no means universal, awareness of the role of child sexual abuse in adult mental health problems however, its significance remains contested. Moreover, the extent of relevant training and supervision received by workers in contact with survivors of abuse is highly variable both between and within professions. The risk of repeated trauma in many of the ways described in this chapter therefore remains high. Nevertheless many positive experiences were reported, and good caregiving, characterised as much by the personal responsiveness and genuine interest of the worker as by their knowledge and experience, could occur in a variety of contexts, despite a variety of different constraints.

If services are to reduce the risk of retraumatising survivors, professionals in a wide range of settings, including primary and secondary health care, social work and the voluntary sector, need relevant training. Organisations need to ensure that staff are selected carefully, that caseloads are reasonable and that adequate support and supervision are available to enable workers to adopt a supportive and companionable mode of relating. This is likely to be in the interests of all users, not only those who are survivors. Appropriate services, including long-term psychotherapy, groups and 24-hour crisis care to support people in the community, and safe and supportive residential care, not necessarily in a medical environment, need to be provided. Information about specialist services and mainstream sources of help, statutory and voluntary, needs to be widely available and should actively encourage careseeking.

Such changes carry costs, but so too do the failures of the present system, and there may well be an economic case for change although the data to support it is patchy as yet.[2] Equally important, however, is the humanitarian case for change. The inadequacies of current mental health services reflect both the dominance of the medical model of mental illness and, on a broader level, what Hochschild (1995) refers to as a postmodern response to the 'care deficit' in society, which legitimates lack of care by minimising the need for it. To offer only a three month contract to a person who received minimal care throughout their childhood exemplifies such an approach. It is shortsighted to imagine that the impact of childhood abuse can be undone without a much greater commitment to and valuing of care.

Notes

1 The research involved questionnaires completed by 81 survivors, and semi-structured interviews conducted with 30 of them to explore their use and experience of services in greater depth. In each sample, 90 per cent of respondents/interviewees were women, 10 per cent men. Further details of the research are given in the full report, available from the authors at Department of Social Policy and Social Work, University of York, Heslington, York, YO10 5DD. The research was funded by North Yorkshire Health Authority and supported by North Yorkshire Social Services Directorate and a project group comprised of representatives of local statutory and voluntary organisations and including organisations run by and for survivors. The views expressed are those of the authors.

2 Jennings (1998) has calculated that the cost of intensive trauma-oriented psychotherapy for two sessions a week over seventeen years would have been far less than the cost of the days spent in hospital by her daughter whose experience of abuse was consistently ignored by the mental health system. For those survivors whose capacity to care for their children effectively is impeded by their own unmet needs, the costs of the present system's failures are borne also by their children whose unmet needs for care may in their turn create further demands on services.

References

Anderson, M. (1997) 'Nurses attitudes towards suicidal behaviour. A comparative study of community mental health nurses and nurses working in an accidents and emergency department'. *Journal of Advanced Nursing 25*, 1283–1291.

Bartlett, T.C. and Mezey, G. (1995) 'The extent of violence among psychiatric inpatients'. *Psychiatric Bulletin 19*, 600–604.

Bills, L.J. and Bloom, S.J. (1998) 'From chaos to sanctuary: Trauma-based treatment for women in a state hospital system'. In B. Lubotsky Levin *et al.* (eds) *Women's Mental Health Services: A Public Health Perspective.* London: Sage.

Bowlby, J. (1988) *A Secure Base: Clinical Applications of Attachment Theory.* London: Routledge.

Copperman, J. (1991) 'No refuge from rape?' *OPENMIND 51*, 4.

Crittenden, P.M. (1995) 'Attachment and psychopathology'. In S. Goldberg, R. Muir and J. Kerr (eds) *Attachment Theory: Social, Developmental and Clinical Perspectives.* New Jersey: The Analytic Press.

Department of Health (1991) *Working together under the Children Act 1989.* London: HMSO.

Department of Health (1995a) *Building Bridges: A Guide to Arrangements for Inter-agency Working for the Care and Protection of Severely Mentally Ill People.* London: DOH.

Department of Health (1995b) *Child Protection: Messages from Research.* London: HMSO.

de Zulueta, F. (1993) 'The unspeakable: Child sexual abuse'. In F. de Zulueta (ed) *From Pain to Violence: The Traumatic Roots of Destructiveness.* London: Whurr Publishers.

Eilenberg, J., Fullilove, M.T., Goldman, R.G. and Mellman, L. (1996) 'Quality and use of trauma histories obtained from psychiatric outpatients through mandated inquiry'. *Psychiatric Services 47*, 2, 165–169.

Fairbairn, W.R. (1952) *Psychoanalytic Studies of the Personality.* London: Tavistock Publications.

Finkelhor, D., Arayi, S., Baron, L., Browne, A., Peters, S.D. and Wyatt, G.E. (1986) *A Sourcebook on Child Sexual Abuse.* London: Sage.

Finkelhor, D. (1996) 'Long-term effects of sexual abuse'. Paper presented at 'Child Abuse and Neglect Conference.' Dublin: August 1996.

Goodman, L.A., Rosenberg, S.D., Mueser, K.T. and Drake, R.E. (1997) 'Physical and sexual assault history in women with serious mental illness: Prevalence, correlates, treatment and future research directions'. *Schizophrenia Bulletin 23,* 4, 685–696.

Harris, M. (1998) 'Modifications in services delivery and clinical treatment for women diagnosed with severe mental illness who are also survivors of sexual abuse trauma'. In B. Lubotsky Levin *et al. Women's Mental Health Services: A Public Health Perspective.* London: Sage.

Heard, D. and Lake, B. (1997) *The Challenge of Attachment for Care-Giving.* London: Routledge.

Herman, J. (1994) *Trauma and Recovery.* London: Pandora.

Hochschild, A.R. (1995) 'The culture of politics: Traditional, postmodern, cold-modern, and warm-modern ideals of care'. *Social Politics 2,* 2, 331–346.

Hooper, C.A., Koprowska, J. and McCluskey, U. (1997) 'Groups for women survivors of childhood sexual abuse: The implications of attachment theory'. *Journal of Social Work Practice 11,* 1, 27–40.

Jennings, A. (1998) 'On being invisible in the mental health system'. In B. Lubotsky Levin *et al.* (eds) *Women's Mental Health Services: A Public Health Perspective.* London: Sage.

Kalinowski, C. and Penney, D. (1998) 'Empowerment and women's mental health services'. In B. Lubotsky Levin *et al.* (eds) *Women's Mental Health Services: A Public Health Perspective.* London: Sage.

Kirkwood, C. (1993) *Leaving Abusive Partners.* London: Sage.

Lubotsky Levin, B., Blanch, A. and Jennings, A. (eds) (1998) *Women's Mental Health Services: A Public Health Perspective.* London: Sage.

Menzies Lyth, I. (1988) 'The functioning of social systems as a defence against anxiety'. In *Containing Anxiety in Institutions.* London: Free Association Books.

Morgan, H. (1998) 'Looking for the crevices: Consulting with users of mental health services'. *Soundings 8,* 171–183.

Muenzenmaier, K., Meyer, I., Struering, E. and Ferber, J. (1993) 'Childhood abuse and neglect among women outpatients with chronic mental illness'. *Hospital and Community Psychiatry 44,* 7, 666–670.

Newmann, J.P., Greenley, D., Sweeney, J.K. and Van Dien, G. (1998) 'Abuse histories, severe mental illness and the cost of care'. In B. Lubotsky Levin *et al. Women's Mental Health Services: A Public Health Perspective.* London: Sage.

Rosenberg, S.D., Drake, R.E. and Mueser, K. (1996) 'New directions for treatment research on sequelae of sexual abuse in persons with severe mental illness'. *Community Mental Health Journal 32,* 4, 387–400.

Seligman, M.E.P. (1975) *Helplessness: On Depression, Development and Death.* San Francisco: Freeman.

Sinason, V. (1992) *Mental Handicap and the Human Condition: New Approaches from the Tavistock.* London: Free Association Books.

CHAPTER 19

The Repudiated Self

The Failure of Social Welfare Policy for Older People

Joan Harbison

This chapter discusses social policies relating to the mistreatment of older people. First it contextualises the issue by commenting on constructions of ageing in Western societies within the last 50 years. It is argued that in their assumptions about the nature and value of older people, recent Western constructions of ageing have consistently reflected or incorporated notions of social and political-economic utility, as well as shifting views of biological determinism. The extent to which these constructions are implicit in many of the policies and practices which relate to ageing, older people and their mistreatment is also considered. A psychodynamic lens is then used to explore how the internalisation of various societal views of older people may have affected the behaviours of groups and individuals, including older people themselves. The lens used here is one which acknowledges an unconscious whose contents may or may not be accessible to an individual at any point in time, as well as the relationship of past experiences to present behaviours. It allows consideration of how these 'internal and intrapsychic forces' (Newton *et al.* 1986, p.207) may affect how older people view themselves, and how they are viewed by others. An integrating theme of the discussion is the failure of society to allow for the construction of positive social identities for older people. In this context, older people and others may repudiate aspects of themselves and others associated with 'old age'. The distancing from and/or denial of ageing may contribute both to the mistreatment of older people and to ineffective societal responses to it.

Finally, conclusions are drawn about the ways in which new and critical understandings of ageing in its social and political-economic context may support the development of social policies which promote the reintegration of older people into a more compassionate world.

Constructions of ageing in Western society

The idea that 'the elderly' as a group are economically, and inevitably physically and mentally, dependent on younger members of society has been an overt and predominant belief in Western cultures within the last 50 years (Byetheway 1995; Vincent 1995). This view became established during the 1950s and 1960s when gerontological theorists introduced (and debated) the notion of older people's gradual disengagement from life as they exited from the labour market and other social roles and moved towards death (Cumming and Henry 1961; Green 1993). Townsend (1981) discussed how from a social policy perspective: '...the dependency of the elderly in the 20th century is being manufactured socially...there is the imposition, and acceptance, of earlier retirement; the legitimation of low income; the denial of rights to self-determination in institutions; and the construction of community services for recipients assumed to be predominantly passive' (p.5).

Concepts of the dependency of older people are now under revision, for a variety of reasons, by various interest groups including government policy-makers and some older people themselves (Encel 1995; Friedan 1993; Harbison and Morrow 1998).The term 'successful ageing' can be found in the title of popular and scholarly texts from the mid-1980s onward (see Novak 1985). Further, this latest perspective on ageing, which celebrates the opportunities and freedoms it can bring, is increasingly backed not just by theory but by a growing body of research evidence (Rowe and Kahn 1998). Hence gerontologists are now putting forward a revisionist view of ageing which identifies it as a '...period of development' (Prosen 1996).

The implications of constructions of ageing for older people's lives: Revisiting dependency

Critics of the social disengagement theory of ageing have suggested that this theory was initially closely connected with the needs of the labour market. In fact, retirement became '...in a real sense a euphemism for unemployment' (Townsend 1981, p.10; see also Phillipson 1982). As well, the creation of these dependencies is seen as intentionally removing the autonomy of older people in order to manipulate them as a group. It required them:

> ...to depend on the state through pensions and welfare payments and on welfare professionals who control and determine the 'needs of the elderly'. The government action to expand privatised welfare, including residential care, created markets for the entrepreneurs in care, and state 'welfare' created a set of dependent client groups who could be used in the political and economic interests of capital, groups of professional and bourgeois political parties. (Vincent 1995, p.167)

Changing socio-economic and demographic conditions, in particular ageing populations, now appear to be a major factor in attempts to shift the 'dependency' of the increasing numbers of older people away from the state and on to families or older individuals themselves (Biggs 1996). The validation of public perceptions of older people as requiring more than their fair share of goods and services, especially health services, and at the expense of the young, can be viewed as strategies which '…allow governments to shift potential blame from their own economic management [failure] to particular segments (or victims) within the society' (Gibson 1995, p.22; see also Gee and McDaniel 1994; Minkler 1991; Vincent 1995). Indeed, there is increasing potential for a positive view of a 'third age' (Laslett 1994) which is attached to the 'young old' to become coercive in its implications that this age group can be fully responsible for their own 'successful' ageing. Higgs notes that, in any case, many older people want to avoid entering a 'fourth age' when '…the medical gaze which becomes almost statutory at the age of 75 observes, investigates and regulates older people' (1995, p.548). In Canada, long-term demographic trends suggest a reversal in the labour market that will result in older workers being '…called upon to remain in the labour force, or attempts made to entice the early retired to return to the labour force' (McDonald and Chen 1994, p.113).

Once, relatively healthy older people were encouraged to seek institutional care; now only very frail older people are eligible for government support. This group requires considerable, costly assistance. The relatively lower profit margins or limited funding supplied by governments, associated with the operation of such facilities, mean that the minimal level of care allowable by regulation, if not lower, is prevalent. At the same time the promise of government policies that community care will offer '…a humanitarian way of supporting older people with care needs' through individualised plans and resources is rarely implemented (Tester 1996, p.188). Hence, both in institutional and community care, responsibility for the quality of care, as opposed to 'basic services' often falls on 'informal' care-givers such as family members, most often women, who themselves are frequently limited in capacities and resources.

In summary, it can be said that within the last 50 years the construction of ageing and of older people in Western society has undergone a fundamental change. Beginning with a position where the legitimised expectations of being older included dependencies both on individuals and the state, ageing is now being reconstructed to remove the legitimisation of dependency for most older people. The extent to which this reconstruction is the consequence of political-economic manipulation, social evolution, or the advancement of scientific knowledge about the ageing process, is a matter for speculation and debate. The relationship between the evolution of constructions of ageing, and their impact both on the self-perception and self-identity of individuals as they age, and on the understanding of, and responses to, the mistreatment of older people (elder abuse) is discussed in the following section.

Constructing ageing – constructing 'elder abuse': Responses to the mistreatment of older people

From an historical perspective there are indications that in Western societies there never has been a 'golden age' in which older people in general, as opposed to elites, were highly respected and well treated (Biggs, Phillipson and Kingston 1995; Byetheway 1995; Glendenning 1993; Hareven 1978; Phillipson 1993). However, public recognition of the mistreatment of older people and its emergence as a social problem have occurred within the last 25 years (Baumann 1986; Biggs 1996; Leroux and Petrunik 1990; McCallum 1993; Ogg and Munn-Giddings 1993).[1] There is limited discussion in the literature of the reasons why elder abuse has so relatively recently emerged as a social problem. However, Leroux and Petrunik (1990) suggest that:

> ...[it] can be viewed as part of several social trends: the construction of old age as a social problem and the rise of experts on the elderly, such as gerontologists; the emergence of the family violence rubric and the inclusion of violence against the elderly as one form of violence under this rubric; and the increased criminological interest in the victimisation of the elderly accompanying the 'greying' of the population. (p.654)

Of note is the fact that Leroux and Petrunik's reasoning does not include the agency of older people themselves. Rather, it reflects the interpretations of professionals and policy-makers (see discussion in Hugman 1995). There is no doubt about the commitment of professionals and academics to the cause of elder abuse, as the recent proliferation of articles, texts and journals on the subject suggests. These expert discourses about needs (Fraser 1986) focus on: definition (including definitions that are termed connotative [conceptual], structural [criteria-based – physical, mental, material and so on], and denotative [exemplars]). They also reflect a traditional medical model approach in their references to prevention, detection, assessment, intervention and treatment (Beaulieu and Belanger 1995; McCallum 1994).[2]

This individualising and pathologising approach to the mistreatment of older people has been criticised on the grounds that it removes elder abuse from its social, cultural and historical context (Baumann 1986). As well, Manning (1985) refers to '...technical depoliticised responses...where the professional expert becomes the judge of the solutions available' (p.161).

Researchers generally call for greater efforts to define and understand elder abuse in both quantitative and qualitative terms in order that service providers may improve their programmes and interventions (Spencer 1995). While older people may be used as informants or assistants they are rarely central to the generation of new knowledge about elder abuse. In other words, just as older people's agency is missing in the identification of elder abuse as a social problem, their voices are rarely heard in describing their experiences of mistreatment outside of the context of professional help.

In explaining the failure of older people to take ownership of 'elder abuse and neglect' much of the literature focuses on older people's emotional and physical vulnerabilities. It connects these vulnerabilities to the negative impact of betraying abusive family members and others, guilt and embarrassment at exposing their oppressors, and fears of abandonment and retaliation (see, for instance, Tomita 1990). However, others suggest that the ageism inherent in professionals, legislation and institutions, an ageism that presumably reflects that of society in general, inhibits older people from acting. This perception is confirmed by the findings of studies such as those of Harbison *et al.* (1995) which concluded that older people wanted to avoid a 'negative identity by association' with elder abuse, and Podnieks (1992) who found that her informants' positive identities depended on seeing themselves as independent 'copers'. Empirical studies of older people in general consistently find that they rate their physical and mental health higher than professionals do (Heidrich and Ryff 1996).

Allowing older people to remain in circumstances of abuse does not sit well with most of those who have knowledge of these situations, whether professional providers of services, policy-makers, politicians or the general public. At the very least there is a wish to avoid the horror stories about horribly abused and neglected people which appear in the media from time to time. Knowledge of abuse comes with the corollary that 'something must be done' and the assumption that interventions will result in benefit to the older person (McDonald, Pittaway and Nahmiash 1995). In some jurisdictions this view is expressed through mandatory reporting legislation which provides a legal requirement of action on the authorities. But, since most abused older people, and the perpetrators of abuse, refuse to acknowledge that it is happening, 'doing something about it' rarely brings successful outcomes. For instance, not infrequently the 'rescued' abused person initiates a return to the abusive situation. So there is a risk that rescue-style interventions may result in the older person being further isolated and alienated from potential sources of support and help (McDonald, Pittaway and Nahmaish 1995; Spencer 1995).

The discussion above juxtaposes the commitment of most service providers to intervention in the mistreatment of older people with the reluctance of most older people to acknowledge that mistreatment, even of themselves. It also suggests that service-provider commitment is linked to positive professional self-identity, while older people's reluctance is connected to the need to maintain a positive personal self-identity. Below is a further exploration of psychodynamic issues in relation to the mistreatment of older people.

The place of a psychodynamic framework in understanding and addressing the mistreatment of older people

Psychodynamic interpretations and society

A number of reasons have been suggested above to explain responses to the mistreatment of older people at the societal level. These are readily associated with a psychodynamic framework, which generally accepts that behaviour includes '…thoughts and feelings as well as actions', that 'unconscious processes [based on an accumulation of previous experiences] exist so that the determinants [of behaviour] are multiple and often out of the immediate awareness of the individual' and that 'a key element in the process of change is understanding' (Stricker 1995, p.xiii). Hence, the internalisation over time, through unconscious processes, of pervasive and negative stereotypes of ageing can be seen as leading to the inequitable and harsh treatment of older people (Tomita 1990).

The tendency to deny the existence of mistreatment may be associated with the desire for modern Western democracies to construct themselves as good societies which take responsibility for the general well-being of their members. This collective understanding of the state as good can be seen as essential to the psychological well-being of the society as a whole, as well as to its individual members. Psychological well-being in its turn is connected to the maintenance of the stability of the state and the success of its political economy. It is important, therefore, that the behaviour of the state and its institutions should not become too dissonant from the image internalised by its members of what a good state should be. In general terms, the outcome is that responses to emerging social problems are geared to minimise the demands on the state, while at the same time dealing with social and psychological aspects of the problem which might lead to destabilisation (Epstein 1994). For, despite the negative assumptions about older people, one can imagine the repercussions today of a situation in which there was no response to the public and private visibility of their mistreatment.[3]

The abuse of older people, within the context of institutions, has only recently been recognised and has received relatively little attention. Power relations have been identified above as an important aspect of institutional life affecting mistreatment. Other elements of the nature of institutions which contribute to the potential for abuse are discussed in detail elsewhere in this volume. With regard to institutionalised older people, it is important to note that they are frequently physically and mentally frail, and lack positive social identities and valuation by others. Even where they have potential advocates in friends or family, they may not want to be seen as complainers or may fear that their complaints may not be accepted or believed; or their families may be hesitant to complain on their behalf for fear of repercussions (Harbison and Melanson 1987). The people charged with institutionalised older people's direct care are often poorly educated and trained, underpaid and themselves oppressed. Taken in the context of an ageist society which is at best ambivalent about its older members, the mistreatment that is from time to time exposed to public view in institutions is unfortunately unsurprising (Glendenning 1993; Phillipson 1993).

The intervention plans and protocols which are seen as the legitimate way to 'deal with elder abuse', whether in institutional or community settings, reflect the reduction of social problems to professional/technical ones discussed above. The expressed hope of professional experts is that, given sufficient knowledge and behavioural guidance, providers will know objectively what they should do in particular situations of mistreatment of older people (Manthorpe 1993). At the level of the individual provider, other dimensions in the search for solutions come into play. The provider's beliefs about what is right are associated with their own cultural and social norms and their experiences within their family context. This personal level in relationships (Phillipson 1993) between professional service providers and mistreated older people is addressed by Tomita (1990), who comments on the work of Dorpat, a psychoanalyst, and Matza, a sociologist. Both warn practitioners against supporting directly, subtly or indirectly, by attitudes and by actions, the condoning of inappropriate behaviour. The authors present denial in two different contexts. Dorpat, the psychoanalyst, treats denial in the context of intra-individual characteristics, while Matza, the sociologist, interprets denial in relationship to norms within the social system (p.182).

These two levels of context may interact in mutually reinforcing ways. Professionals' personal concerns and issues, conscious or unconscious, and their impact on behaviour towards older people are rarely discussed in the literature on service provision, however. As Baltes (1996) argues, 'to obtain a full picture we need to be guided not only by what people think but also what they do without knowing (awareness) why they behave the way they do' (p.163).

Psychodynamic interpretations and the individual

Responses to elder abuse are most commonly predicated on the notion that the mistreatment stems from dysfunctional family interactions. These are frequently seen as a consequence of: negative aspects of the family situation, most often 'caregiver stress' (the situational model); as an imbalance of power in familial relationships (exchange theory); and as an intrafamilial cycle of violence (symbolic interactionism) (McDonald *et al.* 1991; Tomita 1990). Interpretations focus on the interpersonal but also refer to the individual pathology of the victims and perpetrators. They have been found to be lacking in explanatory power as they fail to explain why individuals in similar circumstances and/or with similar personal and psychological histories behave differently (Tomita 1990). As well, in addressing domestic violence, feminists and others have taken issue with these frameworks, urging instead more sociologically based interventions with greater attention to gender, power and social context (Harbison and Morrow 1998; Neysmith 1995; Ogg and Munn-Giddings 1993; Phillipson 1993; Tomita 1990).

Psychodynamic interpretations may, however, have a valuable role to play in understanding mistreatment of older people. An important theme is their struggle to retain a positive self-identity. It has been suggested earlier that older people in Western societies will most likely have internalised negative and ambivalent messages about their value at the societal level. These messages refer to all aspects of their self-identity. Not only does ageing produce limitations in physical and mental functions for the older individual, there is active fear and repugnance in society associated with the physical manifestations of the ageing body (Phillipson 1993). Despite protestations about the high valuation of volunteerism, positive value for the individual is mostly associated with present capacity to produce in the market economy. In combination, these societal views, whether consciously acknowledged or not, cast ageing and dependency in a negative light. This may explain why many older people want to avoid the master status of old age (Leroux and Petrunik 1990, p.653), or dependency on state services (Baltes 1996). Where income is concerned, however, perhaps because it makes an essential contribution to their independence, a majority of older people tend to accept, or even demand, their entitlements especially where these reflect social reciprocity (Harbison and Morrow 1998).

From an ideological point of view, most Western democracies have retained a strong belief in the family as the appropriate source of aid and support for its members. Indeed, despite objections from feminists that the family can be a source of oppression for many women (Harbison and Morrow 1998) this position is strengthening in the present era of neo-conservatism and global economy. While research in the area is limited, it appears that among older people the range of responses to dependence on their families is as diverse as older people themselves. For instance, recent research has suggested that some older people do not wish to be dependent even on their families (Baltes 1996; Phillipson 1993). This has sometimes been interpreted as wanting to avoid being a burden, especially where the child and the child's partner are raising children of their own. A more positive interpretation is that older people prefer to retain a separate identity from their families if they have the means to do so. However, given society's negativity about older people and the implications for other choices, it is not surprising to find that some older people cling to their families, including spousal relationships – especially if this reflects a strong cultural tradition – even if they are abusive, and despite offers of help.

Further explanation is required when older people not only remain in an abusive situation but also protect and justify the behaviour of their abusers ('He is really a good boy; he only hurts me when he is drunk'). Tomita (1990), basing her argument on 'neutralisation theory', suggests that elder abuse victims may come under the influence of the perceptions of the dominant perpetrator. This may be reinforced by the fact that despite some discrepancies in the research findings (see Harbison *et al.* 1995; Neysmith 1995; Pillemer and Finkelhor 1988a; Pittaway *et al.* 1995), it seems that most abusers are men, and the recipients of abuse women. The relatively large numbers of older women abusers, as compared with those in younger age groups, may in part be accounted for by the fact that demographically speaking there are more older women than men. Research also suggests that more than 50 per cent of elder abuse may occur in spousal relationships (Neysmith 1995; Podnieks *et al.* 1990). The dominant perpetrator may reflect the unconscious values and wishes of society, and the recipient may see little option but to stay ('We've been together for over 40 years – who else would have me?').

Also associated with this protection of the abuser by the abused may be the wish to maintain a positive self-identity as a coper (Podnieks 1992), as opposed to the more usually understood response to fear and coercion. This need for positive self-identity can also be extended to those who do not live with their abusers or even have frequent contact with them but who continue to allow themselves to be exploited ('She's having a hard time these days, she wouldn't take my money if she didn't really need it'). Reactions are sometimes expressed in terms of guilt ('I didn't have enough time to spend with him when he was a child because I had to go out to work to support us both; if I had, perhaps he would have turned out differently'). Here the notion that earlier childhood experiences have made a major contribution to the abuser's behaviour is included.

In considering why individuals become abusers it is important to note the many social roles that they occupy as male and female spouses, sons and daughters, family members, friends, neighbours, and formal and informal caregivers and acquaintances (Neysmith 1995). The nature and degree of what is defined as elder abuse is also diverse, including physical, psycho-logical and material abuse (Kozma and Stones 1995). Holding or seizing power provides the opportunity for abuse whether it involves physical battery, financial exploitation, refusing access to grandchildren, or leaving a food tray out of reach. However, the question of why some people use these opportunities in abusive ways and others do not is poorly understood. Research intended to extend this understanding is frequently weak in conceptualisation, design and methodology (Kozak, Elmsie and Verdon 1995; Pillemer and Finklehor 1988b). A central feature of this conceptual weakness is that most researchers disregard feminist analyses of power relations within society in general, and intimate male–female relationships in particular (Biggs, Phillipson and Kingston 1995; Dobash and Dobash 1990). Hence, researchers have generally not asked questions that would allow these dimensions to be explored.

Dependency is one example where this lack of exploration leads to inadequacy in findings and their interpretation. Strong research evidence indicates that abusive caregivers are more likely to be dependent on the abused older person for money and housing than the reverse. The lack of attention to this evidence has been taken by some as a failure to address ageist assumptions that older people's dependency on others and caregiver stress are the most important variables associated with abuse. For instance, Pillemer and Finkelhor conclude that '…instead of well-meaning caregivers who are driven to abuse by the demands of an older person, elder abusers appear to be severely troubled individuals with histories of antisocial behaviour or instability' (1988b). The question arises of how this interpretation can include those spousal abusers who are women, many of whom are dependent on husbands for money and housing. One explanation offered is that older women, schooled in the oppression of patriarchy, are taking revenge on impaired husbands for abuse or oppression that occurred earlier in their relationships (Biggs, Phillipson and Kingston 1995; Pittaway et al. 1995). As well, women may be more likely to reveal themselves as abusers than men, and men to consider themselves as abused when women act physically to defend themselves.

Factors which have been consistently found to be associated with abuse are mental illness and alcoholism (McDonald et al. 1991; Pillemer and Finkelhor 1988b). Both of these may remove inhibitions preventing abuse rather than being independently causal, and may in turn also be, in part at least, responses to childhood abuse or to stress in the caregiver. It seems likely that in any one instance of abuse a complex constellation of factors is involved (Biggs 1996), and that '...various types of abuse require different explanations' (Pittaway *et al.* 1995, p.42).

Fundamental to elder abuse may be an internalised ageism on the part of the perpetrator. Negative societal valuation of older people may 'give permission' to the abuser to express their anger and frustration at what they perceive as deficits in their own lives, by acting negatively towards them. In particular, within familial relationships they may base their actions on notions that they have not received what they should have from the victim. As well, family members and formal or informal caregivers may perceive the victim as taking more than their due. Ageist constructions of older people's social status, personalities and bodies may mean that forced proximity with the older person and/or the intimacy of physical caregiving may induce revulsion and panic in the observer based on a need to deny the inevitability of their own ageing, that is the repudiation of a future self. A person without employment or future earning power has low social status. Deterioration of the body is associated not only with loss of the aesthetic ideal of youthfulness, but eventually with loss of control of mind and bodily functions (Phillipson 1993). Deterioration of the mind disrupts rational/cognitive interaction with others. These conditions bring with them vulnerability to exploitation through dependencies. Ultimately, frail older people become seen as less than human, and therefore deserving of treatment as subhuman. They may be imbued by their abuser with motivations of the abusers' choosing. For instance, Baltes (1996) reviews a study by Wahl (1991) which found that social partners (nurses) in both institutional and community settings '...thought that dependent behaviour was caused by the residents [for example] they claimed that the residents refused to act, were lazy, did not listen to instructions, etc.'. In other words, they viewed these older people as having the ability to behave differently when they could not. Is this another dimension which may contribute to the mistreatment of an older person? Does experiencing the older person in this way return the abuser to a state of childhood, where the old person becomes at times the reincarnation of the 'bad or inadequate parent' who did not then, and cannot now, respond to felt needs and wants?

Conclusion

An important theme in the foregoing discussion has been society's negative view of ageing, the consequent devaluing of older people, and how these views reflect conflicts between conscious and unconscious processes in individuals and in society. These conditions have a powerful impact on older people's experiences, politically, institutionally, interpersonally and intra-psychically. For change to occur for older people, each of these dimensions of their experience must change. The present tendency for older people, with token participation, to defer to professional experts to mediate their relations with government cannot lead to fundamental change in their position in society – in how they are perceived or in how they perceive themselves. Their experiences will remain determined by experts. Foucault, for instance, suggests that in effect people can become the psychic 'property of "experts"' (Strinati 1995, p.253). However, older people's relationships with experts are beginning to change. Senior activists are now engaging in educational efforts aimed at defining and explaining elder abuse to older people and others, and at offering advice on how they, as individuals, can take steps to prevent or address mistreatment (Podnieks and Baillie 1995; Weiner 1991). Gerontologists are beginning to acknowledge the need for ageing to become viewed in more positive ways. Psychologically, ageing can now be under-stood as a developmental process (Prosen 1996). Physiologically, it can be seen as a period of increasing limitations, but ones which for most of a person's life can be addressed or managed to maximise independence. If the prediction of a need for older people to return to the labour market is fulfilled – providing they are not ghettoised into low status, low paying jobs – this will also hasten a new era for ageing. The ageing of populations underpins these changes.

In most Western societies by the end of the first decade of the new millennium, 'dramatic changes in the age structure' associated with the post-war baby boom, will result in a relatively larger proportion of people aged 65 and over than ever before (Sax 1993). And the larger proportion of these who are women will consist of many who will have been influenced by the women's movement to have greater potential for political action than previous generations. In combination with the 'expanding consumer move-ment' (Sax 1993), with its assertion of rights, it may yet be that more groups of older people, particularly those most privileged by education and income, will transcend their intragroup diversity and assert themselves in the political arena with regard to their rights and interests (Harbison and Morrow 1998; Prosen 1996). This would be the behavioural prerequisite for changes in intergroup relations whereby older people would both demand and receive respect as equal citizens (Biggs, Phillipson and Kingston 1995). For the present generations of older people, modest changes in how they are treated may be achieved by educating society in general, and older people and professionals responsible for intervention in particular, about ageing in ways that avoid negative stereotypes (Grant 1996; Wiener 1991). This would include knowledge and understanding of: social and political-economic issues as they relate to ageing; research-based information about physical and mental aspects of ageing; and the conscious and unconscious processes associated with ageing, at the societal, institutional and individual levels (Baltes 1996). Programmes should be provided for perpetrators who wish to end their abusive behaviour (Kingsley and Johnson 1995), and for older people who choose to remain in abusive situations (Podnieks 1992; Wolf and Pillemer 1994). In the final analysis, how older people's relationship to the abuse of themselves and others is understood as a basis for intervention, must acknowledge and respect what older people want.

Notes

1   The term 'elder abuse' has become generic in its use, but at the same time, because of the narrowness of its construction, it can be distinguished from the more broadly based 'mistreatment of older people'.

2   In other words, just as ageing itself has been medicalised and pathologised, so too have responses to perceived mistreatment of older people. In Canada: '...four major competing constructions of 'elder abuse and neglect' referring to four differing needs discourses can be discerned in legislation, programmes and services, and in the actions of individuals' (Harbison and Morrow 1998). These include the construction of mistreated older people as: 'adults in need of protection'; 'victims of domestic violence'; 'persons subject to illegal acts'; and 'agents for their own lives'. These constructions have resulted, respectively, in efforts to help older people: through legislation, programmes and services specifically targeted at abuse; through offers of services aimed at resolving situations of domestic violence; through publicising their rights under the criminal code and encouraging them to charge perpetrators; and through encouraging their participation in educational offerings and self-help programmes. It is notable that so far none of these constructions has engaged more than a small minority of older people in action, whether on their own behalf or on that of their peers.

3   The state also of course, through its hegemonic processes and its social policies, influences how various groups are valued, and therefore how they are treated and expect to be treated.

References

Baltes, M.M. (1996) *The Many Faces of Dependency in Old Age.* Cambridge: Cambridge University Press.

Baumann, G. (1989) 'Research rhetoric and the social construction of elder abuse'. In J. Best (ed) *Images of Issues: Typifying Contemporary Social Problems.* New York: Aldine de Gruyter.

Beaulieu, M. and Belanger, L. (1995) 'Intervention in long-term care institutions with respect to elder mistreatment'. In M.J. MacLean (1995) (ed) *Abuse and Neglect Of Older Canadians: Strategies For Change.* Toronto: Thompson Educational Publishers, Inc..

Biggs, S. (1996) 'A family concern: Elder abuse in British social policy'. *Critical Social Policy 16,* 2, 63–87.

Biggs, S., Phillipson, C. and Kingston, P. (1995) *Elder Abuse in Perspective.* Buckingham and Philadelphia: Open University Press.

Bytheway, B. (1995) *Ageism*. Buckingham and Philadelphia: Open University Press.

Callahan, J.J., Jr. (1988) 'Elder abuse: Some questions for policymakers'. *The Gerontologist 28*, 4, 453–458.

Cumming, E. and Henry, W.E. (1961) *Growing Old: The Process of Disengagement*. New York: Basic Books.

Dobash, R.E. and Dobash, R.P. (1990) 'How theoretical definitions and perspectives affect research and policy'. In D.J. Basharov *Family Violence*. Washington, DC: AEI Press.

Encel, S. (1995) 'Age dependency: Myths and realities'. In S. Graham (ed) *Dependency, The Life Course and Social Policy*. University of New South Wales, Australia; SPRC Reports and Proceedings No. 118.

Epstein, L. (1994) 'The therapeutic idea in contemporary society'. In A.S. Chambon and A. Irving (eds) *Essays on Postmodernism and Social Work*. Toronto: Canadian Scholars' Press.

Fraser, N. (1986) *Unruly Practices: Power, Discourse and Gender in Contemporary Social Theory*. Oxford: Polity Press/ Blackwell Pubs.

Friedan, B. (1993) *The Fountain of Age*. New York: Simon and Schuster.

Gee, E. and MacDaniel, S. (1994) 'Social policy for an aging society'. In V. Marshall and B. McPherson (eds) *Aging: Canadian Perspectives*. Ontario: Broadview Press/Journal of Canadian Studies.

Glendenning, F. (1993) 'What is elder abuse and neglect?' In P. Decalmer and F. Glendenning (eds) *The Mistreatment of Elderly People*. London: Sage.

Globe and Mail (1998) 'Here's the good news about growing old'. Canada, 27 June, D17.

Green, B.S. (1993) *Gerontology and the Construction of Old Age: A Study and Discourse Analysis*. New York: Aldine de Gruyter.

Grant, L.D. (1996) 'Effects of ageism on individual and health care providers' responses to health aging'. *Health and Social Work 21*, 1, 9–15.

Harbison, J., Couglan, S., Downe-Wamboldt, B., Elgie, R., Melanson, P. and Morrow, M. (1995) *Mistreating Elderly People: Questioning the Response to Elder Abuse and Neglect*. Vol.1. Halifax, Canada: Dalhousie University, Health Law Institute.

Harbison, J. and Melanson, P. (1987) 'Collaboration between nursing and social work in long-term-care institutions'. *Canadian Journal on Aging 6*, 159–173.

Harbison, J. and Morrow, M. (1998) 'Re-examining of the social construction of elder abuse and neglect: A Canadian perspective'. *Ageing and Society 18*, 691–711.

Harevan, T.K. (1978) (ed) *Transitions: The Family and Life Course in Historical Perspective*. New York: Academic Press.

Heidrich, S.M. and Ryff, C.D. (1996) 'The self in later years of life: Changing perspectives on psychological well-being'. In L. Sperry and H. Rosen (eds) *Aging in The Twenty-first Century: A Developmental Perspective*. New York and London: Garland.

Higgs, P. (1995) 'Citzenship and old age: The end of the road?' *Ageing and Society 15*, 535–550.

Hugman, R. (1995) 'The implications of the term "elder abuse" for problem definition and response in health and social welfare'. *Journal of Social Policy 24*, 4, 493–507.

Kosma, A. and Stones, M.J. (1995) 'Issues in the measurement of elder abuse'. In M.J. MacLean (ed) *Abuse and Neglect of Older Canadians: Strategies for Change*. Toronto: Thompson Educational Publishers, Inc.

Kozak, J.F., Elmslie, T. and Verdon, J. (1995) 'Epidemiology of the abuse and neglect of seniors: a review of the national and international literature'. In M.J. MacLean (ed) *Abuse and Neglect of Older Canadians: Strategies for Change*. Toronto: Thompson Educational Publishers, Inc.

Laslett, P. (1994) 'The Third Age, the Fourth Age and the Future'. Review of 'Carnegie Inquiry into the Third Age', *Life Work and Livelihood in the Third Age*, 'Final Report of the Inquiry'. Carnegie United Kingdom Trust, 1993, Dunfermline, Fife.

Leroux, T.G. and Petrunik, M. (1990) 'The construction of elder abuse and neglect as a social problem: A Canadian perspective'. *International Journal of Health Services 20*, 4, 651–663.

MacLean, M.J. (1995) (ed) *Abuse and Neglect of Older Canadians: Strategies for Change.* Toronto: Thompson Educational Publishers, Inc.

Manning, N. (1985) *Social Problems and Welfare Ideology.* Aldershot: Gower Publishing.

Manthorpe, J. (1993) 'Elder abuse and key areas in social work'. In P. Decalmer and F. Glendenning (eds) *The Mistreatment of Elderly People.* London: Sage.

McCallum, J. (1993) 'Elder abuse the new social problem'. *Modern Medicine of Australia 9*, 74–83.

McCallum, J. (1994) *Elder Abuse Australianised.* Paper prepared for the NSW Conference on Abuse of Older People, 29 October, 1994. Australia.

McDonald, L. and Chen, M.Y.T. (1994) 'The youth freeze and the retirement bulge: Older workers and the impending labour shortage'. In V. Marshall and B. McPherson (eds) *Aging: Canadian Perspectives.* Peterborough, Ontario: Broadview Press/Journal of Canadian Studies.

McDonald, L.P., Hornick, J.P., Robertson, G.B. and Wallace, J.E. (1991) *Elder Abuse and Neglect in Canada.* Toronto: Butterworths.

McDonald, L., Pittaway, E. and Nahmiash, D. (1995) 'Issues in practice with respect to mistreatment of older people'. In M.J. MacLean (ed) *Abuse and Neglect of Older Canadians: Strategies for Change.* Toronto: Thompson Educational Publishers, Inc.

Minkler, M. (1991) '"Generational equity" and the new victim blaming'. In M. Minkler and C. Estes (eds) *Critical Perspectives on Aging: The Political and Moral Economy of Growing Old.* New York: Baywood.

Newton, N.A., Brauer, D., Gutmann, D. and Grunes, J. (1986) 'Psychodynamic therapy with the aged: A review'. *Clinical Gerontologist 5*, 3/4, 205–243.

Neysmith, S.M. (1995) 'Power in relationships of trust: A feminist analysis of elder abuse'. In M.J. MacLean (ed) *Abuse and Neglect of Older Canadians: Strategies for Change.* Toronto: Thompson Educational Publishers, Inc.

Novak, M. (1985) *Successful Aging: The Myths Realities and Future of Aging in Canada.* Ontario: Penguin Books.

Ogg, J. and Munn-Giddings, C. (1993) 'Researching elder abuse'. *Ageing and Society 13*, 389–413.

Pittaway, E.D., Westheus, A. and Peressini, T. (1995) 'Risk factors for abuse and neglect among older adults'. *Canadian Journal on Aging 14*, 2, 20–44.

Phillipson, C. (1982) *Capitalism and the Construction of Old Age.* London: MacMillan.

Phillipson, C. (1993) 'Abuse of older people: sociological perspectives'. In P. Decalmer and F. Glendenning (eds) *The Mistreatment of Elderly People.* London: Sage.

Pillemer, K. and Finkelhor, D. (1988a) 'The prevalence of elder abuse: A random sample survey'. *The Gerontologist 28*, 1, 51–57.

Pillemer, K. and Finkelhor, D. (1988b) 'Causes of elder abuse: Caregiver stress versus problem relatives'. *American Journal of Orthopsychiatry 59*, 179–187.

Podnieks, E. (1992) 'Emerging themes from a follow-up study of Canadian victims of elder abuse'. *Journal of Elder Abuse and Neglect 4*, 1/2, 59–111.

Podnieks, E. and Baillie, E. (1995) 'Education as the key to the prevention of elder abuse and neglect'. In M.J. MacLean (ed) *Abuse and Neglect of Older Canadians: Strategies for Change.* Toronto: Thompson Educational Publishers, Inc.

Podnieks, E., Pillemer, K., Nicholson, J.P., Shillington, T. and Frizzell, A.F. (1990) *National Survey on Abuse of the Elderly in Canada.* Toronto: Ryerson Polytechnical Institute.

Prosen, H. (1996) 'Aging in the twenty-first century: Postscript'. In L. Sperry and H. Rosen (eds) *Aging in the Twenty-First Century: A Developmental Perspective.* New York and London: Garland.

Rowe, J.W. and Kahn, R.L. (1998) *Successful Aging.* New York: Pantheon Books.

Sax, S. (1993) *Ageing and Public Policy in Australia.* Sydney, Australia: Allen and Unwin.

Sellers, C.S., Folts, W.E. and Logan K.M. (1992) 'Elder mistreatment: A multidimensional problem'. *Journal of Elder Abuse and Neglect 4,* 4, 5–23.

Spencer, C. (1995) 'New directions for research on interventions with abused older adults'. In M.J. MacLean (ed) *Abuse and Neglect of Older Canadians: Strategies for Change.* Toronto: Thompson Educational Publishers, Inc.

Stones, M.J. (1995) 'Scope and definition of elder abuse and neglect in Canada'. In M.J. MacLean (ed) *Abuse and Neglect of Older Canadians: Strategies for Change.* Toronto: Thompson Educational Publishers, Inc.

Stricker, G. (1995) Foreword. In M. Nichols. and T. Paolino Jr. (eds) *Basic Techniques of Psychodynamic Psychotherapy.* New Jersey: Jason Aronson Inc.

Strinati, D. (1995) *An Introduction to Theories of Popular Culture.* London and New York: Routledge.

Tester, S. (1996) *Community Care for Older People: A Comparative Perspective.* Basingstoke and London: Macmillan Press.

Tomita, S.K. (1990) 'The denial of elder mistreatment by victims and abusers: The application of neutralization theory'. *Violence and Victims 5,* 3, 171–184.

Townsend, P. (1981) 'The structured dependency of the elderly: The creation of social policy in the twentieth century'. *Ageing and Society 1,* 1, 5–28.

Townsend, P. (1986) 'Ageism and social policy'. In C. Phillipson and A. Walker (eds) *Ageing and Social Policy: A Critical Assessment.* Aldershot: Gower Publishing Co. Ltd.

Vincent, J.A. (1995) *Inequality and Old Age.* London: University College London.

Wahl, H.-W. (1991) 'Dependence in the elderly from an interactional point of view: Verbal and observational data'. *Psychology and Aging 6,* 238–246.

Weiner, A. (1991) 'A community-based education model of identification and prevention of elder abuse'. *Journal of Gerontological Social Work 16,* 3/4, 107–119.

Wolf, R.S. and Pillemer, K. (1994) 'What's new in elder abuse programming: Four bright ideas'. *The Gerontologist 34,* 1, 126–129.

The Contributors

Dick Agass is a UKCP registered psychotherapist in private practice in West Yorkshire and a consultant psychotherapist in the Bradford Community Health NHS Trust, based at Lynfield Mount Hospital, Bradford. He was a mental health social worker for nearly twenty years, and has published work on psychodynamic and systemic approaches to practice and on the long-term effects of childhood sexual abuse, as well as having been a guest editor and acting editor of the *Journal of Social Work Practice*. For twelve years he was a member of the clinical team at the Leeds Family Therapy and Research Centre at Leeds University. He is currently completing further clinical training as a psychoanalytic psychotherapist at the Lincoln Centre, London.

Margaret Bell is a lecturer in Social Work at the University of York. Her teaching and research interests are largely in the field of child care and protection, with a particular focus on interagency issues, service user involvement and working in partnership. Recent funded research projects have included a large scale empirical study of the involvement of families in child protection investigations, the use of the Department of Health Looking after Children materials in social work training and in practice, and the impact on children of witnessing domestic violence. Her practice experience includes working as a guardian ad litem, and wide experience of social work in the health field. Professional affiliations include membership of the York Family Court Forum, the Social Work Research Group and BASPCAN.

Judith Brearley trained in medical social work. Her psychoanalytic psychotherapy training was undertaken at the Scottish Institute of Human Relations. She was Senior Lecturer in Social Work at Edinburgh University until 1991. She now works in private practice as a psychotherapist and organisational consultant. The latter entails helping managers and staff teams in health, education and social work, the churches and the voluntary sector with conflict, trauma, closure or new developments. She also offers supervision to people in the caring professions, and teaches art therapists, counsellors, child psychotherapists, theological students and others. She is President of Couple Counselling Scotland, and is author of a number of academic papers and of *Counselling and Social Work* (Open University Press, 1995).

Frances B. Carter is a licensed Systems-Centered® practitioner, social worker and artist who works in private practice in Philadelphia, Pennsylvania seeing individuals, couples and groups. Currently, she is a trainer, supervisor and consultant in the practice of SCT® in the United States and Europe. She has trained with Yvonne Agazarian, the developer of Systems Centered Therapy, and is a founding member of the Systems-Centered® Training Institute, a member of the American Group Psychotherapy Association, the International Association of Group Psychotherapy, the University of York Attachment Research Group and a Consulting Affiliate to Friends Hospital in Philadelphia.

Andrew Cooper is Professor of Social Work at the Tavistock Clinic and University of East London, and an associate member of the British Association of Psychotherapists (BAP). In recent years he has contributed to a series of European research programmes comparing child protection systems and practices. This work has informed his thinking about the relationship between child abuse, psychotherapy and the law.

Stephen Frosh is Professor of Psychology at Birkbeck College, University of London, and Consultant Clinical Psychologist and Vice Dean in the Child and Family Department at the Tavistock Clinic, London. He is the author of numerous academic papers and several books, including *For and Against Psychoanalysis* (Routledge, 1997*), Sexual Difference: Masculinity and Psychoanalysis* (Routledge, 1994), *Identity Crisis: Modernity, and the Self* (Macmillan, 1991) and *The Politics of Psychoanalysis* (Macmillan, 1987; second edition 1999). He is joint author, with Danya Glaser, of *Child Sexual Abuse* (Macmillan, second edition 1993) and co-editor with Anthony Elliott of *Psychoanalysis in Contexts* (Routledge, 1995). He is currently, with Ann Phoenix, involved in a research project on 'Emergent Identities: Masculinities and 11–14-Year-Old Boys'.

Joan Harbison is Associate Professor and full-time faculty member at the Maritime School of Social Work, Dalhousie University, Nova Scotia. She practised social work in the health field in the United Kingdom and Canada. She was educated at Trinity College Dublin, the University of Edinburgh, and the University of Toronto where she took her Ph.D. Her interests in the areas of health and ageing have led to a current focus of her research and publication on responses to the mistreatment of older people.

Jeremy Hazell is a psychoanalytic psychotherapist and a full member of the British Association of Psychotherapists (BAP). He is a founder member of Severnside Institute of Psychotherapy (Bristol), Author of *Personal Relations Therapy: The Collected Papers of H.J.S. Guntrip.* (Jason Aronson, 1994) and *H.J.S. Guntrip, a Psychoanalytical Biography.* (Free Association Books, 1996) and many papers. He is also a member of the Advisory Board of the Stockholm Academy for Psychotherapy.

Nancy Caro Hollander is Professor of Latin American and Women's History at California State University, Dominguez Hills. She is also a research psychoanalyst, and associate member of the Psychoanalytic Center of California. She has published many articles on a variety of topics related to political repression, liberation struggles, gender and institutional oppression, the psychology of political authoritarianism, and the impact of social trauma due to military dictatorships in Latin America. Her most recent book is *Love in a Time of Hate: Liberation Psychology in Latin America* (Rutgers University Press, 1997)

Jeremy Holmes is Consultant Psychotherapist at the Department of Psychiatry, North Devon District Hospital, Barnstaple, Devon.

Carol-Ann Hooper is Lecturer in Social Policy at the University of York. She has worked in the fields of violence against women and child abuse since the early 1980s, both as a counsellor and researcher, and in voluntary sector and academic contexts. She is the author of *Mothers Surviving Child Sexual Abuse* (Routledge, 1992) and of many articles on violence, abuse and social policy. Her recent research includes the evaluation of a project offering family support in a housing association context and, with Juliet Koprowska, a study of the experiences of service provision of adults who were sexually abused as children.

Juliet Koprowska is a lecturer in Social Work at the University of York. She was a practising social worker in the field of adult mental health for many years. She is interested in incorporating knowledge from a variety of perspectives, including the user perspective, to enhance the quality of professional training and practice.

Una McCluskey is a lecturer in social work at the University of York. She is a professional member of the Yorkshire Association for Psychotherapy and registered with the UKCP. She is a member of the Scottish Institute of Human Relations and the Systems-Centered Training Institute in Philadelphia. She has published in *Psychotherapy, Human Relations, The Journal of Family Therapy* and the *Journal of Social Work Practice* on assessing and working with individuals, couples and families from psychodynamic and systemic perspectives. She is presently conducting research into affect attunement in adult psychotherapy and exploring the place of affect attunement and empathy within the 'attachment dynamic'.

Phil Mollon is a psychoanalyst (British Psycho-Analytical Society), psychotherapist (Tavistock Society) and a clinical psychologist (British Psychological Society). His Ph.D. was concerned with shame and other disturbances in the experience of self and gave rise to his first book, *The Fragile Self. The Structure of Narcissistic Disturbance* (Whurr, 1993). He has also written extensively about dissociative states of mind and about the controversies over recovered memory. Currently he is writing about the psychoanalytic legacy of the 'self psychology' contribution of Heinz Kohut. He works full time at the Lister Hospital in North Hertfordshire.

Francis M. Mondimore is a psychiatrist at the Johns Hopkins Hospital and a member of the faculty in psychiatry and behavioural sciences of the Johns Hopkins University School of Medicine, both in Baltimore, Maryland. He is the author of several books on mental health issues, including *A Natural History of Homosexuality* (Johns Hopkins University Press, 1996).

Shirley Truckle is a consultant child and adolescent psychotherapist, trained at the Tavistock. She is also an adult psychotherapist and professional member of the West Midlands Institute of Psychotherapy. She is director of the Birmingham Trust for psychoanalytical psychotherapy, organising tutor for their child psychotherapy trainings and surviving mother of four.

Valerie Sinason is a psychoanalyst, child psychotherapist, poet and writer. She is a consultant research psychotherapist at St Georges Hospital Psychiatry of Disability Department and Director of the Clinic for Dissociative Studies. She has published over 60 chapters and papers and nine books on abuse and disability. *Mental Handicap and the Human Condition* (Free Association, 1993) is her key text on learning disability. Her last collection of poems, *Night-Shift*, was published by Karnac Books in 1996.

Lennox K. Thomas has a background in clinical social work and probation before training in family therapy and psychoanalytical psychotherapy. He is joint Course Director of the University College, London, MSc in Intercultural Psycho-therapy and was Clinical Director of Nafsiyat Intercultural Therapy Centre in London. He is a staff member on the Tavistock Clinic MA Programme in Child Protection and serves as an external examiner to university based training in social work. He has long-term teaching posts in Germany, Denmark and the Caribbean and is in private practice.

Susan Vas Dias is an Attachment-based psychoanalytic psychotherapist. She was trained by Anna Freud at the Anna Freud Centre and has worked in the NHS for 22 years. Currently she holds the post of Consultant Paediatric Psychotherapist at Queen Elizabeth Children's Services, Royal London Hospital, London. She is Clinical Consultant to and Chair of the Training at the Centre for Attach-ment-based Psychoanalytic Psychotherapy (CAPP). She is a Training Therapist and Supervisor. Her publications include papers in the *Journal of Child Psychotherapy, The Archives of Disease in Childhood, and Clinical Child Psychology and Psychiatry*.

Subject Index

311

Author Index